BOOK LOAN

Please RETURN or RENEW it no later
than the last date shown below

ANALYZING
QUALITATIVE DATA

ANALYZING QUALITATIVE DATA

Log-Linear Analysis for Behavioral Research
Second Edition

JOHN J. KENNEDY

New York
Westport, Connecticut
London

Copyright Acknowledgments

The author and publisher gratefully acknowledge permission to use the following copyrighted materials.

Goldsmid, C. A., Gruber, J. E., and Wilson, E. K. "Perceived Attributes of Superior Teachers (PAST): An Inquiry into the Giving of Teacher Awards." *American Educational Research Journal, 14* (1977), 423-440. Copyright © 1977 by the American Educational Research Association, Washington, D.C. Reprinted by permission.

O'Connor, G., and Sitkei, E. G. "Study of a New Frontier in Community Services: Residential Facilities for the Developmentally Disabled." *Mental Retardation, 13*, 4 (1975), 35-39. Copyright © 1975 by the American Association on Mental Deficiency. Reprinted by permission.

Library of Congress Cataloging-in-Publication Data

Kennedy, John J.
   Analyzing qualitative data : log-linear analysis for behavioral
research / John J. Kennedy. — 2nd ed.
      p.   cm.
   Includes bibliographical references and indexes.
   ISBN 0–275–93446–2 (alk. paper)
   1. Log-linear models. 2. Psychometrics. 3. Psychology—Research.
4. Education—Research.   I. Title.
BF39.K457   1992
519.5'02415—dc20   91–4936

British Library Cataloguing in Publication Data is available.

Copyright © 1992 by John J. Kennedy

Library of Congress Catalog Card Number: 91–4936
ISBN: 0–275–93446–2

First published in 1992

Praeger Publishers, One Madison Avenue, New York, NY 10010
An imprint of Greenwood Publishing Group, Inc.

Printed in the United States of America

The paper used in this book complies with the
Permanent Paper Standard issued by the National
Information Standards Organization (Z39.48–1984).

10 9 8 7 6 5 4 3 2 1

To the memory of
Jum C. Nunnally
a fine teacher and an excellent author

Contents

Figures and Tables

Preface

The first edition of this book was published in 1983 under the title *Analyzing Qualitative Data: Introductory Log-Linear Analysis for Behavioral Research*. Its purpose was to illuminate the basic features of log-linear analysis. At that time, the majority of researchers in behavioral fields knew very little about this relatively new generalized approach to the analysis of contingency table data. The use and acceptance of the 1983 edition demonstrated that a book-length introductory treatment of log-linear modeling was both needed and appreciated.

During the 1980s, the use of log-linear statistical models in behavioral and life-science inquiry has increased markedly. Concurrently, log-linear theory, which was developed largely during the previous decade, has been streamlined and refined. An aim of this second edition is to acquaint old and new readers with these refinements.

The biggest change that occurred during the 1980s, however, has been the increased availability of user-oriented computer programs for the performance of log-linear analyses. During this period, all major statistical packages (i.e., BMDP, SAS, and SPSS) introduced either new or improved computer programs designed specifically for the specification and fitting of log-linear models. As a consequent, the enhanced ability of practicing researchers to perform log-linear analyses has been accompanied by an enhanced need for didactic explanations of this system of analysis—for explanations of log-linear theory and method that can be readily understood by practitioners and graduate students who do not possess recondite backgrounds in mathematical statistics yet desire to obtain a level of understanding beyond that which is typically offered by cookbook approaches to statistical topics. Another aim of this second edition is to fulfill this need.

As before, this book has been prepared for readers who have had at least one intermediate-level course in applied statistics in which the basic principles of factorial analysis of variance and multiple regression were discussed. Also as before, to assist readers with modest preparation in the analysis of quantitative/ categorical data, this edition will review topics in such relevant areas as basic probability theory, traditional chi-square goodness-of-fit procedures, and the method of maximum-likelihood estimation. Readers with strong backgrounds in statistics can skim over these preparatory discussions, which are contained largely in Chapters 2 and 3, without prejudice.

Because the origins of log-linear methodology are diverse, several approaches can be taken to its formulation and application. The general approach of the 1983 edition, maintained in this second edition, is associated with Professor Leo A. Goodman of the University of Chicago. Readers who have been exposed to the Goodman approach, however, will occasionally find treatments of topics in this book that are somewhat at variance with Goodman's writings and the writings of his associates. Aside from the modest mathematical requisites, experimental and ex post facto research rather than the survey are emphasized. Expect, therefore, to see relatively greater emphasis given here to research situations in which the intent is to determine whether groups of subjects differ with respect to a categorical response (or dependent) variable. In fact, beginning with Chapter 6, attention will be directed almost exclusively to the study of group differences with respect to one or more response variables. As will be shown, special log-linear models, known as asymmetrical or logit models, will be used to estimate group and interaction effects in a manner that resembles the estimation and testing of effects in the analysis of variance. Moreover, interpretation of group effects is more apt to be couched in terms of differences between geometric means (on a log scale) as opposed to odds ratios. In sum, the approach taken to log-linear modeling in this book is essentially that advanced by Goodman, but I have modified it to exploit, whenever possible, the synonymity between log-linear analysis and the analysis of variance. As suggested by the success of the first edition, this modification has been appreciated especially among researchers in fields with strong experimental traditions, such as psychology and medicine.

Finally, readers familiar with the 1983 edition will find that in addition to expanded treatments of numerous topics, two entirely new topics are introduced in the present edition. There is a new chapter (Chapter 6) devoted to a discussion of follow-up procedures, termed *focused comparisons*, that resemble in a number of respects *t* test contrasts that are often computed to clarify the results following an analysis of variance. Also new is a chapter (Chapter 9) devoted to an introductory discussion of *configural frequency analysis*, a taxonomical technique rooted in log-linear methodology that may be used to identify discernable groups of subjects who share a common profile of response to multiple categorical variables. I trust that both old and new readers of this book will find these new topics to be of immense value.

Finally, I am deeply grateful to a number of people who, directly or indirectly, helped me with this edition. To Dr. Andrew J. Bush of Baptist Memorial Hospital in Memphis and Dr. Janet C. Rice in the Department of Biostatistics and Epidemiology at Tulane University, two valued colleagues with whom I have had the opportunity to offer a number of short professional courses on log-linear methods, go my special thanks for their friendship, encouragement, and intellectual guidance. I am similarly indebted to one of my current and best students, Hak Ping Tam, and to one of my former students, Debora Ann Grale of North Coast Behavioral Research in Cleveland, for their long hours, insights, and special help with the preparation of this manuscript. In addition, for her help with the manuscript, my thanks go to my secretary, Barbara E. Heinlein.

1

Qualitative Data and Statistical Techniques

Qualitative data, also known as categorical data, are cross-tabulations within the context of contingency tables. Until recently, the analysis of qualitative data was limited, for the most part, to data within two-dimensional contingency tables. For such tables, the use of chi-square goodness-of-fit procedures, which were developed early in the history of statistics by Karl Pearson, have proven to be of immense value. Often, however, researchers possess information that is sufficient to structure contingency tables of more than two dimensions. Further, they often desire to subject tables of higher dimensionality to a comprehensive, simultaneous analysis. Unfortunately, prior to the 1970s, the methodology that would permit the desired analysis was not refined sufficiently to be of assistance to practicing researchers.

Then, due to the pioneering efforts of Grizzle, Starmer, and Koch (1969), Goodman (1970, 1971a, 1971b), Bishop, Fienberg, and Holland (1975), Bock (1975, ch. 8), and Krauth and Lienert (1973), among others, a revolution transpired in the analysis of multidimensional cross-tabular data. Major advances developed along at least three distinct lines.

The first line of development can be traced directly to Grizzle, Starmer, and Koch (1969). Their approach, sometimes called the GSK approach, employs the method of *weighted least-squares* (WLS) regression to estimate parameters in models that are formulated to explain categorical response variables. WLS regression, as used in the GSK approach, is particularly flexible with respect to analyzing response variables that consist of more than two categories.

A second line of development has been the application of log-linear models to qualitative data. Log-linear analysis has had numerous contributors. The most prominent contributions, however, emanate from a text authored by Bishop, Fienberg, and Holland (1975) and from the extensive writings of Goodman (e.g.,

1978). The Goodman approach in particular has been cited frequently in the behavioral research literature, especially in the sociological literature. Moreover, this approach has been explicated for practitioners in a variety of fields via a number of didactic papers (Shaffer, 1973; Marks, 1975; Knoke & Burke, 1980; Kennedy, 1982, 1988; Green, 1988).

In addition to more frequent usage, log-linear models differ from the WLS models of the GSK approach in two important respects. First, parameters that appear in log-linear models are estimated by the method of *maximum likelihood* (ML), not ordinary least-squares (OLS) or WLS. Second, log-linear models can be used either to investigate *relationships* between or among variables (i.e., a symmetrical analysis) or to determine the *effects* of selected categorical variables on a designated response variable (an asymmetrical analysis). WLS modeling, in contrast, is limited, for the most part, to the latter type of determination.

The third development occurred in West Germany where, during the 1970s, methodologists were exploring the use of regression and log-linear models (specifically the analysis of residuals from these models) as a means of identifying personality types and clinical syndromes (Krauth & Lienert, 1973). Their work has produced a methodology known as *configural frequency analysis* (CFA). Briefly, CFA is a classification technique that attempts to identify discernable clusters or groups of subjects that manifest similar profiles of response on two or more categorical variables.

As before, the principal intent of this second edition is to introduce behavioral and life-science researchers to the theory, operations, and typical applications of log-linear contingency table analysis, and to do so, whenever possible, within a conceptual framework that is compatible with the analysis of variance (ANOVA). The contents of the initial edition have been updated and, in a number of areas, expanded, consonant with advancements that have appeared during the 1980s. Entirely new to this second edition, however, is a chapter on focused comparisons (Chapter 6), a methodology designed to assist analysts when they have a need to follow up the results of a log-linear analysis, and a chapter on configural frequency analysis (Chapter 9). It is hoped that the exposition of log-linear methodology, augmented with discussions of follow-up procedures and CFA, will increase still further the number of practitioners who will use these relatively new techniques in their research and appreciate their use in the work of others.

QUALITATIVE VARIABLES AND DATA

Ironically, terms most basic to an area of study often prove to be most difficult to define. Definitions are required, nevertheless, and because this volume deals with the study of categorical variables and resultant qualitative data, an attempt will be made to clarify these terms. We will attend first to a discussion of the general nature of data, returning subsequently to a brief discussion of categorical variables.

The Nature of Data

In most instances, data gathered during the course of a behavioral investigation consists of *measurements*, numbers assigned to objects or events according to a set of rules. Implied by this definition of measurements is that there are a number of rules used in the process of assigning numbers. Due largely to the scholarship of Stevens (1946), at present there is substantial agreement that the process of number assignment (i.e., measurement) is governed by four fundamental sets of rules. These four sets of rules give rise to four *scales of measurement*, or, more simply, four types of data: nominal, ordinal, interval, and ratio data. Since these four types of data are discussed extensively in most introductory textbooks in statistics and measurement, only the principal features of each are reviewed below.

Nominal Data. Nominal scaling connotes classification. Briefly, the objects or events of concern are examined for underlying similarities (or differences) and subsequently grouped on the basis of observed *qualitative* distinctions. Examples of nominal scaling abound. For instance, nominal scaling is implemented when research subjects are classified according to their gender, sexual orientation, ethnic background, type of learning disability, or similar characteristics. Now, if the numbers of subjects falling into respective categories of a variable such as gender or ethnic background are tallied, the resultant counts or frequencies constitute nominal data. Simply put, nominal data consists of frequencies observed within categories of a nominal or categorical variable.

Notice that nominal scaling barely conforms to the definition of measurement presented earlier since in most instances the act of assigning numbers is optional; moreover, when numbers are assigned to groups or categories, they serve merely as labels to facilitate coding or identification. Because qualitative categorization is so rudimentary and the act of assigning numbers is so arbitrary, many theorists do not seriously regard nominal scaling as a formal measurement process. Nominal scaling merits serious consideration, however, for not only is this manner of measurement frequently used in behavioral research, but the analysis of nominal data also constitutes the subject matter of this text.

Ordinal Data. A unidimensional *quantitative* continuum underlies ordinal scaling operations. Unlike in nominal scaling, the assignment of numbers reflects degree rather than kind. With the knowledge that some subjects (or units of interest) have more or less of a particular trait than others, subjects can be ordered from highest to lowest on the trait in question and numbers can be assigned consecutively to reflect this ordering. The assigned numbers, called *rank values*, are no longer just labels of convenience but instead denote a relative position in an ordered array. Collectively, rank values are data, specifically ordinal data.

It should be understood that the analytical techniques presented in this book are not generally applicable to ordinal data—at least not to ordinal data in their pristine form. There is, however, an exception: If subjects are first categorized largely on the basis of qualitative attributes (i.e., nominal scaling), and then the various categories are rank ordered on the basis of a quantitative dimension (i.e., ordinal scaling), the variable and associated frequencies within categories (i.e., data) may well be amenable to the techniques described herein. For example, subjects answering a questionnaire were asked to indicate their approximate income on an ordered scale by checking one of several presented categories (e.g., less than $10,000; $10,000 to $19,999; $20,000 to $29,999; etc.), the resultant data associated with this *ordered categorical variable* can be treated by several of the methods I shall describe.

Interval Data and Ratio Data. A unidimensional *quantitative* continuum also underlies interval scaling and ratio scaling. In both cases, one has knowledge that some subjects possess more or less of a particular trait than others. Unlike ordinal measurement, for these kinds of data one is able to specify how much more or less of the trait is possessed by various subjects.

Turning first to interval scaling, subjects can be placed on a continuum that is characterized by equal-interval numerical values. Consequently, meaningful differences between and among subjects can be inferred by the simple subtraction of respective scale values. Examples of attributes that often lend themselves to interval scaling, and hence produce interval data, are (1) achievement, when based on classroom examination performance, provided that the examination contains a sufficient number of objective test items; (2) typing proficiency as reflected by the number of errors made on a typing test; and (3) short-term memory as indicated by the number of trials required to reproduce a list of words.

Turning next to ratio scaling, in addition to units of equal size, a natural or inherent *zero point* can be specified. Since the absence of the measured trait can be identified, a ratio comparison can be made between two measures. That is, it can be said that one value is so many *times* larger or smaller than another. Instances of ratio data are encountered frequently in everyday life: height, weight, and measures of volume are but a few examples. Unfortunately, this most mathematically tractable form of data is not encountered frequently in behavioral research.

A recognized advantage of dealing with either ratio- or interval-appearing data, sometimes referred to simply as *metric* data, is that they are often amenable to *parametric* statistical analyses. For example, if one or more explanatory (independent) variables are being examined in relation to a metric response (dependent) variable, then, depending on the specific situation, a technique such as the analysis of variance (ANOVA), analysis of covariance (ANCOVA), or bivariate or multiple regression may be appropriate. Should there be two or more metric response measures, the analyst will likely search out a multivariate technique such as linear discriminant analysis, multivariate analysis of variance (MANOVA), or canonical variate analysis. In either case, being able to treat response measure data as interval (or ratio) generally permits the adoption of a parametric statistical procedure (as opposed to a nonparametric procedure), and, through such an adoption, the realization of greater relative efficiency (i.e., the increased probability of achieving statistical significance) and informational yield.

Rarely is it ever justified to try to circumvent the use of parametric procedures by "scaling down" reliably gathered metric data in order to give them the appearance of ordinal or nominal data. There are, of course, exceptions to this rule. If responses to a ten-point equal-interval-appearing scale did not distribute themselves in a manner consistent with the distributional assumptions of a parametric technique, and instead, responses clustered about the low and high ends of the scale, consideration should be given to structuring response into two categories (e.g., low vs. high). The restructured dichotomous variable may be amenable to one of the analyses discussed in this book.

Perhaps a better illustration of an exception to the rule is a variable such as Educational Attainment as measured in terms of the highest grade level successfully completed (e.g., 11th grade, 12th grade). Granted, this variable has the appearance of being interval, and thus might be treated legitimately as either a metric explanatory (independent) or response (dependent) variable in a parametric analysis. But if certain social and economic dimensions of this variable are considered, its interval nature becomes questionable. There is, for example, far greater "social" distance between the 11th grade and the completion of the 12th grade (i.e., high school graduation) than, say, between the 10th grade and the completion of the 11th grade. Though there are statistical advantages associated with treating Educational Attainment as a metric variable, consideration should instead be given to structuring the variable as an ordered categorical variable, for in many instances such a construction will more accurately reflect the variable's essential nature and will lend itself more readily to substantive interpretation.

In any event, in social inquiry, often *all* variables of concern, both explanatory and response variables, are distinctively categorical. Consequently, the parametric procedures cited above are either not appropriate or not as desirable as the procedures to be discussed in this book.

To this point I have established that the discussions to follow will be devoted exclusively to the statistical analysis of qualitative data; in other words, nominal data in either inherent or scaled-down form. Incidentally, a number of alternative terms are used to denote qualitative data. Common synonyms are attribute data, discrete data, classification data, categorical data, and enumeration data. In multidimensional contexts, synonyms for qualitative data that will be used on occasion in this book are cross-tabs, cross-tabular data, cross-classifications, and contingency table data.

Categorical Variables

Categorical variables give issue to qualitative data. As we now know, categorical variables may be *ordered* (e.g., grade level or income level) or they may be *unordered* (e.g., ethnic background or religious affiliation). In most instances, we will be dealing with the latter type of variable. A distinction must also be made between a variable that is composed of only two categories and a variable that is defined by more than two categories. We know that the former is termed a *dichotomous* variable (or, sometimes, a binomial variable). The unordered variable of Gender, consisting of a male and female category, is a dichotomy. A variable that is structured so that it presents more than two categories will be called a *polytomous* variable, though sometimes the adjectives *polychotomous* or *multinomial* are used. Political Affiliation, when defined by the categories of Republican, Democrat, and Independent, is an unordered polytomy. An example of an ordered polytomy is Class Standing as defined by freshman → sophomore → junior → senior.

The subject matter of this text consists of statistical methods (primarily methods associated with log-linear models) that are appropriate for use when research subjects are cross-classified on the basis of two or more categorical variables, and a simultaneous assessment of effects, or relationships among these variables, is desired. In addition to satisfying a number of conditions that will be discussed, all variables to be subjected to a log-linear analysis, as well as to a configural frequency analysis (CFA), will be categorical—ordered or unordered, dichotomies or polytomies.

BASIC CONSIDERATIONS

The intent of this section is twofold. The first is to enhance the reader's appreciation of the fact that the fundamental nature of a research problem (i.e., the types of research questions asked or the hypotheses advanced) carries with it important implications for how subjects should be sampled and how the data obtained from subjects should be analyzed. The second intent is to review conditions that, within reason, should be satisfied prior to performing either the classical chi-square test developed by Pearson (1900) or the newer procedures associated with the generation and evaluation of log-linear models.

To provide a context for the ensuing discussion of these points, consider, somewhat in isolation, the following two qualitative variables: Gender of Subject, and Subject's Attitude toward a U.S. constitutional amendment that would prohibit abortions. Let us symbolically refer to the first variable (Gender) as the A variable. Further, let i be a subscript to denote the various categories subsumed by Variable A where i varies from 1 through a (i.e., $i = 1, 2, 3, \ldots, a$). Note that since A is a dichotomous variable here, $a = 2$. Our second variable (Attitude toward the Amendment) will be symbolized by B and subscripted by j, where $j = 1, 2, 3, \ldots, b$. Assume for the moment that B is also a dichotomy (hence, $b = 2$); hence, we have:

A: *Gender of Subject*

A_1 = females

A_2 = males

B: *Attitude toward the Amendment*

B_1 = oppose

B_2 = support

Now, in a typical research setting, one of two *modes of inquiry* will likely be adopted. That is, there are two general types of research questions that can be asked or, if justified, two general types of hypotheses that can be subjected to test: symmetrical and asymmetrical.

Symmetrical vs. Asymmetrical Inquiry

One can ask, for example, whether Variables A and B are independent—as opposed to being associated, related, or correlated. Independence, or lack of association between A and B, implies that males and females respond in approximately the same manner when expressing their views on the abortion amendment; or, alternatively, subjects who have expressed either a positive or negative view are equally represented, in a proportional sense, by both males and females. Because a question (or hypothesis) dealing only with the presence or absence of an association between variables can be approached bilaterally, the mode of inquiry may be said to be *symmetrical*.

When inquiry is symmetrical, one would not designate one of the variables as the explanatory variable (or independent variable) and the other as the response variable (or dependent variable), for should an association be manifested between A and B, it may be that Variable A is the agent that accounts for the observed outcome in B, or that B may be responsible for the observed outcome in A. Still, however, as often is the case, some variable or set of variables other than A or B may be influencing both A and B such that they vary systematically together. In any event, if the intent of the research is to determine whether there is an association between variables or whether there is support for an a priori hypothesis that posits an association between two variables, then the mode of inquiry and subsequent analysis is symmetrical.

In marked contrast is inquiry that seeks to determine whether subjects who fall into respective categories of one variable differ appreciably in their response to the other variable. A researcher might ask whether the attitude of males and females is different with respect to the abortion-amendment issue. Here, Variable A assumes the status of an *explanatory* variable, while Variable B constitutes, in effect, a *response* variable. This perspective is distinctly unidirectional or asymmetrical, and not bilateral, as was the case previously. Hence, the analysis to be applied can be termed *asymmetrical*. As we shall see, symmetrical and asymmetrical inquiry are related. If, for instance, Variables A and B are determined to be independent, it will then follow that there will be no material differences in the way in which males and females respond to the abortion issue.

Should *A* and *B* prove to be associated, however, effects due to Gender will be seen; that is, the pattern of female response to the abortion question will be different from that observed for males.

In latter stages of the research process, it is likely that inferential statistical techniques will be used to pursue one of the two modes of inquiry just mentioned. Some inferential techniques—techniques such as simple correlation, multiple correlation, and canonical correlation—are used primarily to identify and test relations between or among variables. Still others—techniques such as ANOVA and MANOVA—serve to document statistically significant effects or differences between and among group means, or, in the case of MANOVA, group centroids. Unfortunately, all too often a sufficient distinction is not made between these two modes of inquiry in discussions of qualitative data analysis. I shall attempt to overcome this shortcoming, for, as has been mentioned, the adopted mode of inquiry carries with it major implications for sampling and data interpretation.

Sampling Strategies

Recall that the function of inference in statistics is the generation of reasonable statements about *parameters* (population values) based on a careful examination and analysis of *statistics* (sample values). Requisites to valid statistical inference are a definition of one's target population and access to a sample that is representative of this population. Recall further that a random selection of subjects from the target population for inclusion in samples not only constitutes the ideal method to achieve representation but also is fundamental to the proper operation of the machinery of statistical inference. The manner by which randomization is used to build samples depends in large measure on the investigator's intended mode of inquiry.

When inquiry is symmetrical, *all* variables are viewed as response variables. Consequently, cross-classified subjects comprise a single sample; collectively, subjects constitute a sample of size *n*. Moreover, since the intent here is to investigate the nature of variable relations as they exist in a targeted population, it follows that the best method for obtaining a representative sample is to draw a sample of size *n* from the target population—or to draw it from a population that is accessible yet still similar to the target population. With such a sample, statistical inferences concerning the number, nature, and intensity of discovered relationships can be made with little or no prejudice. In sum, the sampling method of choice for symmetrical inquiry is to determine in advance the desired tabular *n* and then draw for study a simple random sample from the population of interest.

Greater flexibility is afforded the investigator when the intent is to explore the effects of one or more explanatory variables on a designated response variable. Of course, simple random sampling procedures, as were just recommended for the symmetrical case, is acceptable when the inquiry is asymmetrical. However, drawing stratified random samples is often preferred. Recall for a moment the example in which female and male students are to be compared relative to how they respond to the Abortion Amendment Variable. Rather than obtaining a simple random sample drawn from the college roster, which at some colleges would result in markedly unbalanced main-marginal frequencies for Gender (e.g., the U.S. Military Academy), it would be more advantageous to stratify the college population by gender and subsequently draw from each strata a random sample of equal size. All things being equal, fixing the size of the main marginals for levels of an explanatory variable (e.g., Gender) so that females and males are equally represented will, for this example, enhance the efficiency of the analysis. That is, balanced or approximately balanced main marginals for Gender will enhance the probability of being able to document a statistically significant difference in response between females and males.

As a further example, consider an investigation involving two explanatory variables, say Gender (1 = female, 2 = male) and Religion (1 = Catholic, 2 = Jewish, 3 = Protestant, 4 = other), and an attitudinal response variable (1 = favor, 2 = oppose). Here, in advance of obtaining representative samples, the investigator could fix frequencies of the main marginals for Gender so that they are equal, fix the marginals for Religion so that they are balanced, or better yet, fix the sizes of the eight Gender–Religion subsamples so that they will be equivalent. In short, in the asymmetrical case, respective frequencies of explanatory variables may be fixed, and fixed to advantage, as long as frequencies associated with the response are free to vary.[1]

But let us acknowledge that it is not always possible in practice to select samples at random to the extent that might be desired. When samples cannot be drawn at random, two options are available. The researcher may elect to define the desired population to which inference will be made and then proceed intelligently to use all relevant available information in an attempt to structure a sample that appears to be representative of the target population. (Structuring a judgment sample, however, is more easily said than done.) A second option, and the only option available when the sample has been predetermined, is to study the sample at hand and then attempt to describe a population from which the sample in question could have been drawn. Neither option is a satisfactory substitute for random sampling; however, research is an enterprise broader than the exact application of statistical methodology. Even if requisite conditions are not completely satisfied, statistical methods can still be of value.

Cross-Classification of Subjects

Assume for our working example that (1) the variables Gender and Attitude (for short) have been adequately defined so that, with respect to each, subjects can be unequivocally classified; (2) the essential nature of inquiry (symmetrical versus asymmetrical) has been determined; (3) a sampling scheme appropriate to the nature of inquiry has been adopted (completely random vs. stratified random); and (4) information pertaining to Gender and Attitude has been obtained

Table 1.1
Cross-Tabulations (Frequencies) by Gender and Attitude Toward a Constitutional Amendment: An Example of a 2 × 2 Contingency Table

| | Attitude toward the Amendment | | |
Gender of Student	Opposed	Support	Marginal Totals
Female	40	10	50
Male	20	30	50
Marginal Totals	60	40	100

from each member of the sample. The next step is to marshal the sample information in preparation for descriptive and inferential analysis. The device used to organize and display qualitative/categorical data is a *contingency table*.

To construct a contingency table, the researcher first places subjects into the category belonging to Variable *A*, classifies them again on Variable *B*, and then crosses *A* and *B* in a manner similar to factorial design arrangements common to the analysis of variance (ANOVA). The result of this joint classification is a two-dimensional contingency table, which is alternatively called a two-dimensional table of cross-tabulations.

Before we examine the table, we should keep the following in mind. First, a sample member is associated with only one cell in the table; hence, for now, repeated measurements, as are seen in certain ANOVA designs, are precluded. Second, frequencies or counts, not proportions or percents, are displayed in a contingency table. (It is often helpful, however, to convert observed frequencies into proportions that, when done, will give a *table of cell proportions*.) Finally, realize that contingency tables and corresponding tables of cell proportions are not limited to two dimensions. For example, if information is available on three categorical variables, subjects can be cross-classified on all three variables, producing a three-dimensional contingency table. Eventually, we will be working with three-, four-, and five-dimensional tables.

But first consider the simple table that is appropriate for our working example, a 2 × 2 contingency table, so labeled because the row variable (Variable *A*) consists of two categories, and the column variable (Variable *B*) also consists of two categories. Contingency tables of this type are frequently called *fourfold tables*, a description that specifically informs us that the table contains four *elementary* cells. Fourfold tables have been of great interest to statisticians because, like classical experimental designs in which all factors consist of two levels, these tabular configurations have a number of interesting properties and applications. A fourfold table containing hypothetical data obtained from a sample of 100 undergraduate students is presented in Table 1.1.

From Table 1.1 several inferences can be cautiously advanced. For example, if the 100 subjects ($n = 100$) in fact constitute a representative sample of the background population (i.e., all undergraduates in a college), and if the data are being examined from a symmetrical perspective, then it appears that there is an association between Gender and Attitude because, in a proportional sense, males tend to favor the amendment more than do females. Approached from the other direction, subjects who do not support the amendment tend to be overly represented by members of the female group. From an asymmetrical perspective, assuming Gender to be the explanatory variable, a differential response by gender to the abortion issue is suggested by these data. Males appear to favor the amendment in greater proportion than do females. Regardless of perspective, however, strong inferences concerning the state of affairs in the background population cannot be made at this point since we know that the apparent association, or male-female difference, could be the result of sampling error. To determine whether the data in Table 1.1 represent an outcome that is over and above that which could have occurred by chance, a test of statistical significance needs to be performed.

Tests of Significance

Inference in statistical work is used to (1) generate point estimates of and confidence intervals about population parameters (estimation) or (2) assess the credibility of hypotheses pertaining to population parameters or conditions (hypothesis testing). The latter function will receive the greater attention in this book. Recall that three general steps are involved in the process of testing a hypothesis:

Step 1. A hypothesis is advanced in null form that either claims that a population parameter is equal to a specified value or that a prescribed condition exists in the population of interest. In either case, it is the null hypothesis, and not an alternative version of the null hypothesis, that is subjected to test.

Step 2. A sample (or samples) assumed to be representative of the population is drawn. Then, an observed sample value or sample statistic (a value or statistic that corresponds to the parameter offered by the null hypothesis) is first computed and then assessed. In most instances, the comparison between the observed sample value and the parameter stated in the null hypothesis is implemented within the context of a formula that yields a *test statistic* (e.g., an F statistic or a χ^2 statistic).

Step 3. The computed test statistic is related to the appropriate *sampling distribution*, a distribution of all possible test statistics that theoretically would result from repeated sampling under the null hypothesis. Almost always, sampling distributions are tabled (e.g., an F table, a χ^2 table, etc.). If the computed test statistic falls on an extreme tail of the sampling distribution (i.e., the region of rejection), we conclude that it is not likely that the sample in hand could have been drawn from the population posited under the null hypothesis. That is, grounds appear sufficient for rejection of the null in favor of acceptance of a logical alternative to the null. On the other hand, should the test statistic not fall in the region of rejection, evidence is insufficient for rejection of the null.

The steps outlined above are executed extensively in the analysis of qualitative data, and hence there will be ample opportunities to become reacquainted with them in this book. Be prepared, however, to adopt a more flexible posture with respect to these inferential procedures as we approach discussions of log-linear analysis, especially when log-linear models are assessed in a symmetrical analysis. As will be seen, a major feature of log-linear analysis is the fitting of statistical models, with each model representing a different hypothesis, where the most appropriate model will be selected for subsequent interpretation and use. The process of model fitting and selection in symmetrical inquiry is not as prescribed as are the aforementioned decisions regarding the rejection of a null hypothesis. However, therein lies the challenge of working with log-linear models.

A number of additional understandings merit brief mention in this introductory chapter. Most basic is knowledge of statistical procedures that are appropriate for various types of contingency tables. Consider again the 2×2 contingency table shown in Table 1.1. For this type of table, if certain assumptions can be made and certain underlying conditions are met, the data analyst can select from among three analytical techniques: (1) a normal deviate test (z test) between two sample populations, (2) Pearson's classic chi-square test, or (3) a log-linear analysis. The choice of specific technique depends on the nature of inquiry (symmetrical or asymmetrical) and the amount and the nature of information desired. For a two-dimensional contingency table of a size larger than 2×2, either Pearson's chi-square or a log-linear analysis is appropriate. Finally, should the contingency table be a dimensionality greater than two, say a $2 \times 2 \times 2$ table, then the log-linear approach is clearly preferable.

Irrespective of table dimensionality, or irrespective of whether a z test, a Pearsonian chi-square test, or log-linear analysis is being performed, associated with all these tests is a common family of sampling distributions. Under null hypotheses, outcome probabilities are described by the *multinomial law*, or an extension of this law known as the *product-multinomial law*. Technically, the multinomial law produces the appropriate *sampling distribution* for analyses that are symmetrical, while the product-multinomial law applies to analyses that are asymmetrical. These laws are discussed in the next chapter.

Having established, at least initially, that *exact* sampling distributions of observed sample frequencies are provided by either the multinomial or product-multinomial laws, it must be pointed out that in most of our work we will not be directly consulting these exact sampling distributions. We will work instead with sampling distributions resulting from the distribution of chi-square statistics, distributions that *approximate* the exact sampling distributions given by the multinomial and product-multinomial laws. In other words, in the presence of reasonably large samples, the computed test statistic will be a goodness-of-fit chi-square statistic, which in turn will be related to a chi-square sampling distribution, with the latter serving as an approximation to the exact multinomial or product multinomial. Again, considerable explication of these relations is needed, and this will be provided in the next chapter.

Finally, although much has been made of the distinction between symmetrical and asymmetrical analyses and the differential consequences thereof, both analytic orientations produce the same estimates of population cell frequencies and the same goodness-of-fit test statistics. This distinction, therefore, has major consequences for sampling and the interpretation of results but not for the mechanics of the analysis.

THE FOREST BEFORE THE TREES

Now that we have a general understanding of the nature of data and of symmetrical and asymmetrical approaches to the analysis of data, we can better appreciate the developments of the last two decades that have revolutionized the field of qualitative data analysis. At the outset, reference was made to the appearance during this period of log-linear models, weighted least-squares (WLS) regression models, and configural frequency analysis (CFA). Earlier reference was not made, however, to the parallel development of still another technique, *logistic regression* (Cox, 1970). Logistic regression was introduced for the purpose of analyzing dichotomous response. It is a regression-based technique, but maximum likelihood, not least-squares, is the method used to estimate model parameters. The taxonomy displayed in Table 1.2 attempts to place logistic regression and the three aforementioned systems in perspective relative to their respective roles in the arena of qualitative data.

Investigating Relationships

For use in symmetrical inquiry, notice in Table 1.2 that WLS and logistic regression are not cited as candidates for consideration. This, of course, is because one variable must be designated as a response or criterion variable when either of these regression-based techniques are performed. Only log-linear models are cited in the table as being appropriate for use in the symmetrical mode, and their use in this mode is only appropriate when all variables are categorical.

From a historical perspective, realize that log-linear models were developed initially primarily for sociological and survey researchers in academe, researchers who frequently work with variables measured at discrete levels and who frequently desire to uncover variable linkages or test social theory. Symmetrical inquiry, therefore, has been most strongly emphasized in the log-linear literature

Table 1.2
Taxonomy of Statistical Techniques for Qualitative Data by Mode of Inquiry and Nature of Defining Variables

STATISTICAL TECHNIQUES	Response Variable	Explanatory Variables
	NATURE of DEFINING VARIABLES	
	Symmetrical Inquiry	
General Log-Linear Models	two or more categorical variables	not applicable
	Asymmetrical Inquiry	
Logistic Regression	a dichotomous outcome variable	all metric, or all categorical, or a mixture of both
WLS Regression (GSK Approach)	a dichotomous or polytomous outcome variable	all categorical
Logit-Model Log-linear Analysis	a dichotomous or polytomous outcome variable	all categorical
	Description/Classification	
Configural Frequency Analysis	three or more categorical variables	not applicable

(see Bishop, Fienberg & Holland, 1975; Fienberg, 1977; Upton, 1978). The application of log-linear models in pursuit of symmetrical inquiry will receive considerable attention, though it must be said that in this book somewhat greater attention will be given to the specialized use of log-linear models in the asymmetrical mode.

Documenting Group Effects

Table 1.2 presents three techniques for consideration when there is a response variable: logistic regression, WLS regression, and log-linear modeling.

Logistic Regression. As mentioned, this technique is designed for use with a dichotomous response variable. The response variable is reexpressed as a quantity termed a *logit* (see Hosmer & Lemeshow, 1989, p. 6), and the more flexible logit transformation is regressed on two or more explanatory variables as is done in multiple regression. In the regression, however, maximum-likelihood estimation procedures, not least-squares procedures, are employed to estimate the coefficients in the regression equation. Not only is logistic regression different from WLS regression in terms of the method used to estimate parameters, but unlike WLS methodology of the GSK approach (and, for that matter, log-linear methodology), the explanatory variables on which response measures are regressed do not have to be exclusively categorical. Even though conventional applications of logistic regression are limited to dichotomous outcomes, maximum flexibility is afforded the analyst with respect to the selection of explanatory variables. All explanatory variables may be metric, all may be categorical, or, as is most commonly observed, a mixture of metric and categorical variables. Strictly speaking, therefore, logistic regression is not confined to the analysis of cross-tabulations in contingency tables.

When logistic regression is used to analyze contingency table data (that is, a dichotomous response is regressed on two or more categorical explanatory variables), the results are comparable to those produced by the asymmetrical application of log-linear models. In fact, if effect coding (sometimes called deviation coding) is used to describe the categorical explanatory variables in the regression equation, logistic regression and log-linear analysis will give results that, for all intents and purposes, are identical. The feature common to both techniques is the method of maximum likelihood, and it is this shared method of parameter estimation that equates these techniques when used in the context just described. To date, logistic regression has been used primarily by investigators in the fields of biology and medicine. Despite acceptance in these and related fields, and the current availability of software to perform logistic regressions (e.g., BMDP/LR and SAS LOGISTIC), until recently, logistic regression has not been described at a level so that it is comprehensible to most practicing researchers. Since space is not available in this book to adequately treat logistic regression, interested readers are referred to a recently published introductory text on this topic by Hosmer and Lemeshow (1989), and a didactic paper by Rice (in press).

WLS Regression. The use of WLS as proposed by Grizzle, Starmer, and Koch (1969) permits a regression analysis of both dichotomous and polytomous response.[2] In this approach, a dichotomous or polytomous outcome is expressed as a function (often a logarithmic function of the probability associated with one state of affairs as opposed to the probability associated with another state of affairs), and this function is regressed on two or more categorical variables. The regression departs from logistic regression and the more familiar ordinary least-squares (OLS) linear regression in that WLS procedures are used to estimate regression coefficients.

Incidently, there are a number of compelling factors that militate against the use of OLS procedures (e.g., OLS regression, ANOVA, discriminant analysis, etc.) when the response is categorical, but I will postpone a discussion of them until Chapter 8. For now I simply point out the most obvious limitation of OLS: Variances for categories of outcome are directly related to respective proportional response; hence, inviting violations of the assumption of equal variances. To minimize the deleterious consequences of violating this assumption, in GSK methodology, the variances estimated for each regression coefficient are not assumed to be homogeneous but instead are intentionally weighted by the inverse of variances computed for each estimate.[3] By so doing, parameter estimates associated with categories of explanatory variables are "adjusted" for unequal variances, thus removing a major objection to the use of least-squares regression for the analysis of categorical response. It is WLS regression as used in the GSK approach that is currently the default analysis in CATMOD, the Statistical Analysis System (SAS) subprogram for use when data are qualitative.

Because analysts are afforded a great deal of flexibility relative to creating response functions, WLS as used in the GSK approach has been promoted as a most desirable methodology for analyzing polytomous response (Forthofer & Lehnen, 1981, p. 4). For example, if an analyst wants to compare groups of subjects in terms of proportional response on an outcome variable, the flexibility of WLS regression will permit the analyst to make and test desired comparisons on a metric of proportional difference. The log-linear analyst, in contrast, technically is restricted to interpreting group comparisons in terms of differences in average logged odds, a metric that is not always optimal in behavioral application.

Notwithstanding its ability to formulate and analyze complex response, WLS has come under criticism when used to assess proportional response. Often cited as problematic is the fact that proportions estimated by the regression equation are unbounded; that is, in theory, estimated proportions may be negative or greater than unity. Moreover, reasonably large samples are needed to assure that resultant p (probability) values associated with test statistics (e.g., chi-squares) are valid (Bock, 1975, 506). Most telling, however, is the fact that WLS yields estimated proportions that have larger variances than their log-linear counterparts when models other than what I shall term the saturated model are assessed (Goodman, 1972b; Haber, 1985).

Log-Linear Models. Log-linear models are presented as an alternative to WLS regression in Table 1.2 when inquiry is asymmetrical. Log-linear models in this context possess a number of desirable qualities. Foremost among the advantages is the fact that model parameters, called *lambda parameters*, are estimated using maximum likelihood. We will reserve our discussion of the method of maximum likelihood (ML) until the next chapter except to note here that ML is not only the most statistically efficient method for the estimation of proportional response (hence, frequency of response), it is also the method that is most compatible with sampling distributions that govern dichotomous (binomial) and polytomous (multinomial) outcomes.

When inquiry is asymmetrical, we will learn that only a subset of potential log-linear models are deemed relevant for analysis. Relevant models are often termed *logit models* when the outcome variable is dichotomous. When the response variable is polytomous, relevant models will be referred to as *generalized logit models*. In either case, we are going to observe that logit or generalized logit-model analyses exhibit many features that are common to traditional multifactor ANOVAs.

In an effort to be objective, it should be acknowledged that the use of log-linear models, particularly generalized logit models, has been plagued in the past by problems occurring during the follow-up phase of the analysis. Out of necessity, log-linear analysts have had to rely heavily on model parameter estimates (namely, estimates of lambda coefficients) to both locate and interpret effects. The interpretation of lambda parameters can be troublesome not only because often there are too many lambdas to consider (Clogg & Eliason, 1987), but also because they are difficult to interpret. To repeat, in a prescribed sense, lambda parameters indicate the differences in average logged odds ratios. Attempting to communicate the nature of group difference in terms of odds ratios on a logarithmic scale has not always been an effortless task for the data analyst, as the majority of research consumers are not comfortable with this metric.

Fortunately, many of the problems associated with the explication of generalized logit-model results can be minimized. Regression-based methods that have been illustrated briefly by Bock (1975, pp. 531–35), and the more recent tabular-reformulation methodology advanced by Kennedy and Bush (1988), currently permit log-linear analysts to test specific single degree-of-freedom contrasts on polytomous variables in much the same way as *t*-test contrasts are performed following an ANOVA. The latter methodology, in particular, yields comparisons that are (1) highly focused and hence easily interpretable, (2) independent of order of performance, (3) capable of affecting an exact partitioning of the composite component chi-square, and most important, (4) may be interpreted, if desired, in terms of differences in proportional response. Indeed, the ability to implement focused comparisons on the response variable (the salutary feature of the GSK approach) can now be achieved in large measure following an asymmetrical log-linear analysis. Chapter 6 is devoted to a discussion of the methodology of focused comparisons.

Identifying Discernable Groups

In the realm of parametric statistics, a variant of common factor analysis called the Q technique or one of several "cut-and-try" methods of profile analysis are used when one wants to determine if subjects fall into different groups or clusters on the basis of similarity of response to multiple metric variables (Nunnally, 1978, ch. 12). If multiple variables are all categorical, similar determinations may be made. That is, when subjects are cross-classified on three or more categorical variables, formalized extensions of residual analysis (Haberman, 1973) can be used to identify elementary cells in a contingency table, or other variable combinations, where membership is discernably high or low. These formalized procedures are subsumed by the term *configural frequency analysis*

(CFA). Although CFA makes extensive use of log-linear models, CFA is presented in a separate category in the taxonomy (Table 1.2) because it is used primarily as a descriptive technique.

Knowledge of CFA has not been widely disseminated in the English-speaking world (but see Lienert & Krauth, 1975, and von Eye, 1990). Moreover, so far, substantive applications have been limited for the most part to clinical investigations. Still, I believe that CFA possesses a great potential for creative use in a variety of fields, especially epidemiology, marketing research, and related pursuits. For these reasons, the final chapter of this book will introduce readers to CFA.

It is hoped that this chapter has helped the reader develop a clearer understanding of the nature of qualitative data and the topics and techniques to be addressed in this book. Looking ahead, readers who presently have a good grasp of multinomial probability theory and classical chi-square goodness-of-fit procedures may elect to proceed immediately to Chapter 4, where they will be introduced to log-linear analysis. However, readers who could profit from a review of traditional chi-square and related procedures prior to their study of log-linear methodology are encouraged to continue with the next two chapters.

NOTES

1. An exception is found in the design of case-control studies, which are often conducted in epidemiological research. Here, categories of ''response'' are fixed—subjects with a particular disease are matched with similar subjects sans the disease—and frequencies associated with ''explanatory'' variables are free to vary so that correlates (i.e., risk factors) with response can be identified.

2. In the GSK approach, regression coefficients are weighted by the variances of their corresponding variates. In the computational process this is accomplished by introducing a diagonal matrix that contains the reciprocals of corresponding variances on the principal diagonal. This particular approach, therefore, is sometimes called *diagonal weighted least-squares*, a label that serves to distinguish it from a related weighted least-squares approach where, in addition to the reciprocals of variances on the principal diagonal, the introduced computational matrix also contains the reciprocals of respective covariances in off-diagonal cells.

3. There are two strategies that are used currently to weight regression coefficients. The strategy used most frequently, and used in the GSK approach, is to weight variable coefficients by the reciprocals of their respective variances. The reciprocals are contained on the principal diagonal of a diagonal matrix that is incorporated into the matrix formulation that is solved to produce estimates of regression coefficients. Technically speaking, this strategy is termed diagonal weighted least-squares, though this description is rarely made in practice, to differentiate it from an alternative strategy, which is used in certain applications of covariance structure analysis (e.g., LISREL), where a more comprehensive process of weighting is affected through the use of a variable matrix that contains the reciprocals of variances on the principal diagonal and the reciprocals of covariances in off-diagonal cells.

2

Statistical Foundations

Populations, samples, and sampling (probability) distributions—each of these plays a special role in statistical inference.

Enhanced knowledge of *populations*, of course, constitutes our prime objective. Recall that it is the intent of inference in statistics to either (1) generate estimates of unknown population values, called *parameters*, and, if desired, to place confidence intervals about these estimates, or (2) subject to test statements concerning the value or equivalence of parameters. Generating point estimates (of parameters) and determining the accuracy of those estimates is known as estimation. The latter type of inference—inference in which a null hypothesis is subjected to test—is called hypothesis testing.

In either case, parameter estimates or decisions about the viability of null hypotheses are based on a careful study of a *sample* that is assumed to be representative of the population of interest. From sample observations, *test statistics* are computed. The computation of a t statistic or a χ^2 (chi-square) statistic constitute only two of many specific examples that could be offered.

Last, but far from least, is the distribution that provides the crucial linkage between populations and samples that enables us to posit either estimates or conditional conclusions about the status of null hypotheses. These mathematical probability distributions are called *sampling distributions*. The sampling distribution of a particular statistic, such as a t or χ^2, may be viewed as a *relative frequency distribution* made up of an infinitely large number of statistics independently computed from samples (of size n) which have been drawn from the population (or populations) specified by the null hypothesis. In short, sampling distributions are relative frequency distributions of all possible test statistics resulting from repeated sampling under the null.

As a consequence, sampling distributions are used to assess the probability that a test statistic, computed on a particular sample, could have emanated from the population specified by the null hypothesis. If it happens that a test statistic fits snugly in the middle of its sampling distribution, then there is no basis for rejecting the null hypothesis. On the other hand, if the sample test statistic falls well into the tail of the sampling distribution, then current evidence suggests that it is not likely that the sample in question was drawn from the null population. And to the extent to which the computed test statistic represents an unlikely occurrence under the null, grounds are sufficient to reject the null hypothesis.

This chapter presents an overview of selected sampling distributions that describe qualitative response. Presented first is the distribution of dichotomies (binomial variables) and the *binomial law* which specifies the nature of sampling distributions associated with these variables. Extensions of the binomial law, namely the *multinomial law* and the *product-multinomial law*, will be considered subsequently, for these extensions describe the sampling distributions of polytomous variables. This review chapter closes with a brief discussion of *maximum-likelihood estimation*—the method of estimation used to estimate parameters in log-linear models.

The contents of this chapter may appear at first to be far removed from direct, practical application, since the emphasis here is on background theory rather than "nuts-and-bolts" application. In fact, readers most anxious to begin applying log-linear methods in their work can skim through this chapter without incurring deficiencies that would make the reading of subsequent chapters more difficult. At some point in the process of learning about and applying log-linear methods, however, even the most application-oriented researcher will want to become more comfortable with the mathematical-statistical underpinnings of qualitative data analysis. Aside from satisfying the intellect, obtaining at least an elementary appreciation for the statistical bases of qualitative analysis can only lead to its application with greater confidence, authority, and, possibly, creativity. At some point, therefore, the reader is encouraged to tackle the contents of the following sections so that some of the nagging mysteries often associated with the analysis of qualitative data can be dispelled.

DICHOTOMIES AND THE BINOMIAL LAW

The probability theory associated with dichotomies was established in the early part of the eighteenth century largely in an attempt to predict the outcomes of games of chance. James Bernoulli (1654–1705), in particular, is credited with the development of the majority of basic principles and mathematical proofs pertaining to dichotomous events. Before we attempt to apply Bernoulli's work to the dichotomous outcomes of behavioral studies, a review of several basic principles may prove helpful.

Bernoulli Trials and Resultant Sequences of Events

A Bernoulli trial yields an outcome, or event, that is unequivocally dichotomous. The toss of a coin which can only result in a "head" or a "tail" constitutes such an event. The roll of a six-sided die, whereby a successful roll is considered to be the appearance of a six—all other outcomes are deemed a failure—is a Bernoulli trial. Inquiring of a research subject whether he or she is either in favor of, or opposed to, a constitutional amendment that would prohibit abortion is also a Bernoulli trial if the response is structured so that it is dichotomous.

In both gambling and research, however, our interest usually extends beyond the outcome of a single trial. Indeed, multiple trials leading to multiple outcomes generally are of interest. To accommodate this, let n stand for the number of trials of interest and, unless otherwise stated, assume that the n ensuing events are not only mutually exclusive (in a single trial, only one specified event can occur) but also independent (the occurrence of a specified event from one trial is not influenced by the occurrence of any other). We will have occasion later to discuss mutual exclusivity and independence at greater length.

For now, we seek answers to the following three questions: (1) How many distinct sequences (permutations) are possible within n independent Bernoulli trials? (2) What is the probability of observing a sequence that contains a specified (desired) number of outcomes? (3) How many distinct sequences contain a specified number of desired outcomes? The answers to these questions will facilitate our understanding of the binomial law.

We begin with an example based on the roll of a fair six-sided die. Assume that the desired outcome is the roll of a six: the five remaining outcomes are not desired. Now, the probability of observing a six in one roll of a die is .1667 (rounded to the fourth decimal place), and under normal circumstances this probability will not change over successive rolls. This establishes a most important a priori condition for our work—namely, prior knowledge of the probability of the desired outcome for a single trial and hence for successive trials. Further, for Bernoulli trials, knowledge of the probability of the desired outcome determines the probability of the undesired outcome. Therefore, if we let the numeral 1 denote the desired outcome and let the numeral 0 denote an undesired outcome, the respective probabilities for a single roll or trial are

P_1 = probability of observing a 1 = .1667

P_2 = probability of observing a 0 = .8333

However, since our concern is with multiple trials, consider four trials ($n = 4$) and a sequence or ordering of outcomes whereby a six results from the first roll of the die, a non-six results from the second roll, then another non-six appears, and the last roll produces a six. In our notation, this distinct sequence, or *permutation*, is

Seq: 1, 0, 0, 1

This permutation is, of course, only one of a number of distinct sequences that could result from four rolls of the die, which brings us to the first of our three questions: How many distinct sequences are theoretically possible from executing n independent trials?

To answer this first question, let k stand for the number of mutually exclusive outcomes that are possible for a single trial. In general, k is an integer greater than 1 but for a Bernoulli trial, k by definition is equal to 2. Now recall that the number of distinct sequences or permutations in n independent trials can be determined by

No. of Seq. $= k^n$ (2.1)

For Bernoulli trials, Equation 2.1 may be written

No. of Seq. $= 2^n$ (2.2)

And since 2 raised to a power of 4 equals 16, there are 16 distinct sequences that could come about in four rolls of the die. (These 16 distinct sequences are given in the middle column of Table 2.1.)

The second of our three questions involves determining the probability of a distinct sequence being observed. To calculate this value, prior knowledge of the probability of a desired outcome in a single trial must be known. For our example, this is known—that is, $P_1 = .1667$. Calculations will be facilitated if we let the symbol f_1 stand for the number of desired outcomes (i.e., sixes) in the sequence and let f_2 represent the number of undesired outcomes (i.e., non-sixes) in the sequence. Thus, for the sequence in question (number 8 in Table 2.1), $f_1 = 2$, and $f_2 = n - f_1 = 2$. Now for Bernoulli trials in general, the probability of observing a distinct sequence is given by

$P(\text{Seq.}:\ldots\ldots) = (P_1)^{f_1}(P_2)^{f_2}$ (2.3)

Substituting into Equation 2.3 the parameters of our working and performing the indicated algebra gives

$$P(\text{Seq.: } 1, 0, 0, 1) = (.1667)^2(.8333)^3$$
$$= (0.278)(.6944)$$
$$= .0193$$

Table 2.1
Distinct Sequences and Their Probability of Occurrence for Four Bernoulli Trials

Sequence No.	Sequence	Probability
1	1 1 1 1	.0008
2	1 1 1 0	.0039
3	1 1 0 1	.0039
4	1 0 1 1	.0039
5	0 1 1 1	.0039
6	1 1 0 0	.0193
7	1 0 1 0	.0193
8	1 0 0 1	.0193
9	0 1 1 0	.0193
10	0 1 0 1	.0193
11	0 0 1 1	.0193
12	1 0 0 0	.0965
13	0 1 0 0	.0965
14	0 0 1 0	.0965
15	0 0 0 1	.0965
16	0 0 0 0	.4822

Note: The a priori probability of observing a 1 has been established as .1667.

Thus, if we were to roll four dice a large number of times, in the long run we would expect that the prescribed sequence (i.e., $1 \rightarrow 0 \rightarrow 0 \rightarrow 1$) would result about 2 percent of the time. This computed probability value is presented in Table 2.1 along with the outcome probabilities of the remaining 15 distinct sequences.

Examination of Equation 2.3 and Table 2.1 reveals that not only does the distinct sequence in question have an outcome probability of .0193, but all sequences in which $f_1 = 2$ and $f_2 = 2$ also share this outcome probability. Therefore, for a specified number of desired outcomes (i.e., for a given value of n), Equation 2.3 provides the outcome probability irrespective of the temporal or linear arrangement of the sequence. That is, Equation 2.3 gives the probability of any *combination* of n dichotomous outcomes containing f_1 outcomes, a fact that the reader is encouraged to verify.[1]

We will now attempt to answer the third question, which concerns the number of possible sequences or combinations that will exhibit a specified number of desired results. The number of ways (combinations) of choosing f_1 things (observing f_1 outcomes) in a series of n Bernoulli trials is given by

$$\binom{n}{f_1} = \frac{n!}{(f_1!)(f_2!)} \tag{2.4}$$

Let us use this equation to determine how many sequences or combinations of four Bernoulli trials ($n = 4$) will contain two sixes ($f_1 = 2$). Remembering that 4! (read, four factorial) is $4 \times 3 \times 2 \times 1$, substituting into Equation 2.4 and solving gives

$$\binom{4}{2} = \frac{4 \times 3 \times 2 \times 1}{(2 \times 1)(2 \times 1)} = \frac{4 \times 3}{2 \times 1} = \frac{12}{2} = 6$$

Incidently, the above result is supported by the information shown in Table 2.1. As an exercise, it is suggested that Equation 2.4 be used to verify that

$$\binom{4}{1} = \binom{4}{3} = 4$$

and that

$$\binom{4}{0} = \binom{4}{4} = 1$$

The Binomial Law

To this point, it has been established that if we know the probability of a desired outcome for a Bernoulli trial (e.g., $P_1 = .1667$), then for a series of independent trials (i.e., $n > 1$):

1. Equation 2.2 will give the number of permutations or distinct sequences.
2. Equation 2.3 will generate the mathematical probability that a sequence containing f_1 desired outcomes will occur.
3. Equation 2.4 will reveal the number of sequences containing f_1 desired outcomes.

We are now in a position to use the formulations above to write an equation to give the probability of obtaining a given outcome irrespective of distinct sequence.

Recall that we have established that 2^n distinct outcome sequences are possible. Moreover, some of these sequences will contain precisely f_1 desired outcomes. (Only if $f_1 = n$ or if $f_2 = 0$ will there be only one distinct sequence containing precisely f_1 desired outcomes.) If we were to select just one of these desired-outcome sequences and then determine its probability of occurrence, it would be $P_1^{f_1} P_2^{f_2}$. However, with the exceptions noted above, there will be more than one sequence or combination of events containing f_1 outcomes. Hence, if the probability of observing a single desired sequence is $P_1^{f_1} P_2^{f_2}$, but there are

$$\binom{n}{f_1}$$

such sequences to be observed, it follows that the probability of observing a sequence containing f_1 is

$$(P_1^{f_1} P_2^{f_2}) \binom{n}{f_1}$$

More formally, the probability of observing f_1 desired outcomes, given n trials, is

$$P(f_1, f_2 | n) = \frac{N!}{(f_1!)(f_2!)} P_1^{f_1} P_2^{f_2} \tag{2.5}$$

Equation 2.5 represents the sought-after binomial law, the law that governs the sampling distributions of independent dichotomous responses.

Let us use the binomial law to calculate the probability of observing two sixes in four rolls of a fair die. We substitute the appropriate values into Equation 2.5 and solve:

$$
\begin{aligned}
P(2,2|4) &= \frac{4!}{(2!)(2!)} (.1667)^2 (.8333)^2 \\
&= (6)(.0193) \\
&= .1158
\end{aligned}
$$

Probabilities for the remaining combinations, calculated by similar means, are summarized below:

$$
\begin{aligned}
P(0,4|4) &= (1)(.4822) = .4822 \\
P(1,3|4) &= (4)(.0965) = .3860 \\
P(2,2|4) &= (6)(.0193) = .1158 \\
P(3,1|4) &= (4)(.0039) = .0156 \\
P(4,0|4) &= (1)(.0008) = .0008
\end{aligned}
$$

With knowledge of the probabilities associated with all possible outcomes (all values of f_1) for the working example, it is possible to construct a relative frequency distribution of respective outcome probabilities. A histogram, depicted

Figure 2.1
Expected Relative Frequency of Observing a Six in Four Rolls of a Die

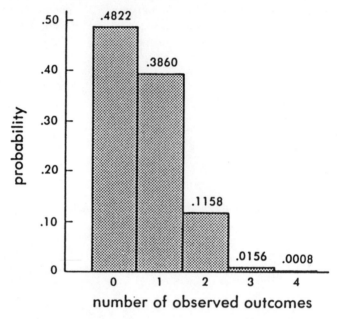

number of observed outcomes

in Figure 2.1, is most appropriate here because the distribution is discrete, not continuous. Realize that the distribution depicted is a sampling distribution: the sampling distribution for any dichotomous response variable with parameters $P_1 = .1667$ and $n = 4$. Notice that this particular sampling distribution is not symmetric about .1667, the *expected value* or mean of the distribution. Only if P_1 is set at .5000 will the distribution of binomial events turn out to be symmetric about .5000, its expected value.

Concrete Illustrations

To apply our work so far, imagine that we suspect that at a crucial moment in a game of chance the croupier has surreptitiously substituted a "loaded" die for a fair die. Moreover, we suspect that at critical points involving four consecutive rolls of a single die, the croupier's chances of winning the game are being enhanced by the biased die which, in the long run, will produce a disordinate number of sixes. Assume that we have but one opportunity—one critical series of four rolls—to test our hypothesis that achieving a six on the roll of this die is greater than .1667. (Note that this is analogous to being able to obtain only a sample of size four in a behavioral study.) Further, since absolute certainty is beyond our grasp, we will be willing to assume a 5 percent risk of concluding that the die is biased when in fact it might not be. (In short, we establish the level of significance at .05.)

To conduct the test, the following steps are executed implicitly.

1. We state the null hypothesis. The hypothesis to be subjected to test is: $H_0: P_1 = .1667$.

2. We establish a reasonable level of significance, say $\alpha = .05$.

3. We draw from the population of critical throws a representative sample of events. For the case at hand, this constitutes the observance of four critical rolls of the suspected biased die (i.e., $n = 4$).

4. We calculate the appropriate sample statistic or statistics. Here, assume that the four critical rolls produced a six, a two, a six, and then another six. Thus, in our notation,

Seq.: 1, 0, 1, 1

indicating that $f_1 = 3$.

5. We relate the observed sample statistic to an appropriate sampling distribution to determine the probability associated with the observed sample outcome. That is, the observed outcome ($f_1 = 3$) will be compared to the probability distribution displayed in Figure 2.1.

6. We posit a conditional conclusion relative to the tenability of the stated null. Here, the probability of observing *three or more* sixes in four rolls of a fair die is $.0156 + .008 = .0164$, an unlikely, albeit possible, result. However, since earlier we decided that any sample outcome that could be expected less than 5 percent of the time would lead us to reject the null, we do reject it in favor of a logical alternative. We conclude, therefore, that $P_1 > .1667$. The die was loaded during the four critical rolls.

Consider a more realistic example, one in which a civil service examination was given to police officers for the purpose of selecting candidates who are eligible for promotion. In this example, exam results for individuals were scored dichotomously: they either passed or failed the examination. Of those who took the exam, 30 percent were members of a minority group. However, only 1 minority group member was present on a list of 10 individuals who passed the exam, which prompted the concern that the examining procedure had an "adverse impact" on minority applicants. It might be argued, for example, that if a population of officers who took the exam consisted of 30 percent minorities, and if there is absolutely no basis for even suspecting an adverse impact, then in the long run, 30 percent of those who pass the exam would be members of the minority. However, the present sample of size 10 contained only 1 successful minority member. Let us, therefore, undertake to assess the likelihood of observing only a 10 percent minority success rate, assuming that the examination does not impact adversely on minorities. The analysis proceeds as follows:

1. A statement of the null. In the population it is assumed that the probability of minority success is at least .30; that is, $H_0: P_1 \geq .30$.

2. An a priori determination of alpha. Set $\alpha = .05$.

Figure 2.2
Lower-Tail Probabilities for a Binomial Sampling Distribution Where $n = 10$ and $P = .30$

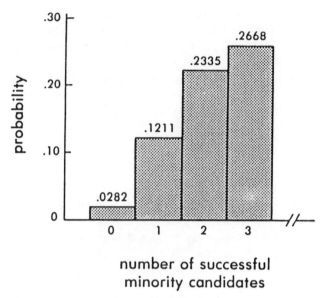

number of successful
minority candidates

3. An examination of relevant sample statistics. Here $n = 10$ and the outcome of interest (minority success) was $f_1 = 1$.

4. A comparison of the observed sample results (i.e., $f_1 = 1$) with results to be expected given that the null hypothesis is true. To generate the sampling distribution, the distribution that describes expected results under the null, Equation 2.5, is used. Specifically, Equation 2.5 can be used repeatedly to generate at least the lower tail of the exact discrete sampling distribution for $n = 10$ and dichotomous outcomes. For example, the most extreme lower-tail outcome is one whereby no members of the minority group and 10 members of the majority group pass the exam. The probability of this extreme outcome is

$$P(0, 10|10) = \frac{10!}{(0!)(10!)}(.30)^0(.70)^{10}$$
$$= (1)(1)(0.282)$$
$$= .0282$$

Admittedly, on an examination where $P_1 = .30$, it is possible to have no successful minority candidates on a list of 10, but in the long run this outcome will occur less than 3 percent of the time. Equation 2.5 is used again to determine the next most extreme outcome (i.e., $P(1, 9|10)$), and, subsequently, all other lower-tail outcome probabilities needed to perform the test. The results of this work, which the student should at least partially verify, are summarized in Figure 2.2.

5. Finally, a conditional conclusion is advanced with respect to the viability of the null hypothesis. A comparison of the observed sample outcome ($f_1 = 1$) with the sampling distribution of Figure 2.2 indicates that the probability of observing 1 or fewer minorities in 10 is $.0282 + .1211 = .1493$. However, since the probability of observing 1 or fewer minorities is greater than .05—the level of significance established for this research—present evidence is not sufficient to reject the null.

Large Sample Approximations to the Binomial

Consider again the results of a promotional examination, but instead of 10 officers on the list of successful candidates, assume that the list contained 30 candidates ($n = 30$) and that the same percentage of minority group members was represented on the list. That is, 3 of the successful candidates, or 10 percent, were minorities. An exact binomial test of the null hypothesis that $P_1 = .30$ could be conducted as before. Now, however, greater computational effort would be required to generate the lower tail of the sampling distribution. Specifically, it would be necessary to employ Equation 2.5 to calculate $P(0, 30|30)$, then $P(1, 29|30)$, then $P(2, 28|30)$—and such additional probabilities as will be required to generate at least the region of rejection of the sampling distribution. In fact, six probability calculations are needed to construct the 5 percent lower-tail region of rejection for this problem. All things being equal, the larger the sample, the greater the labor required to generate the region of rejection. For a sample of 300, the computational labor required to perform an exact binomial test would be, for all practical purposes, prohibitive.

Fortunately, if sample sizes are sufficiently large, the use of the binomial theorem to generate sampling distributions can be circumvented through the use of the *central limit theorem*. In part, this theorem holds that as n becomes infinitely large, the normal distribution becomes the limiting form of a binomial distribution for a fixed P_1. Under most conditions, therefore, the standard normal probability distribution constitutes a good approximation to the discrete binomial distribution when samples are sufficiently large.

A question that is often asked is how large a sample must be to justify the use of the normal distribution in place of the exact binomial. A specific sample size cannot be given because an adequate response depends on the relationship between the parameter contained in the null (i.e., P_1) and the size of the sample (n). Briefly, as the null parameter approaches .50 (hence, P_2 approaches .50), a sample size as small as 10 will produce a discrete binomial distribution that, for practical work, is reasonably approximated by the continuous normal distribution. However, as the null parameter deviates from .50, a larger n is required for reasonable approximation to the binomial. For example, with respect to our initial example where $P_1 = .30$ and $n = 10$, the symmetric unit normal is not an acceptable substitute for the exact asymmetrical binomial. (If sketched, a visual comparison of these two distributions would reveal unacceptable discrepancies particularly in the tails of the distribution.) However, for our later example, where $P_1 = .30$ but $n = 30$, the normal does sufficiently approximate the binomial for most applications.

As a practical guide, the *rule of five* is offered as a means to judge whether a normal distribution, and hence a z test, can be used in place of the more cumbrous binomial calculations. This loosely defined rule holds that the normal distribution is a reasonable approximation to the binomial when the product of the null parameter and sample size exceeds 5. Applying the rule to our initial example ($n = 10$) produces a product whose value is

$$nP_1 = (10)(.30) = 3.0$$

and, since 3 is less than 5, the use of a "large-sample approximation" is discouraged. In contrast, when applied to our second example ($n = 30$),

$$nP_1 = (30)(.30) = 9.0$$

an outcome that justifies the use of an approximate z test.

Since the unit normal can be used to approximate the binomial for the working example involving 30 successful testees, let us conduct a z test on the null $P_1 = .30$, a test that will require far fewer computations than its corresponding binomial test. The major steps follow.

1. Statement of the null, $H_0: P_1 \geq .30$.
2. Establishment of the level of significance, say $\alpha = .05$ for a lower-tail test.
3. Calculation of relevant statistics on the representative sample. On the list of successful candidates ($n = 30$), recall that 3 were minorities. Therefore, $f_1 = 3$, and the corresponding observed sample proportion, denoted by lower-case p with subscript "1" is

$$p_1 = \frac{f_1}{n} = \frac{3}{30} = .10$$

4. Computation of the test statistic, an approximate z statistic in this instance, that may be variously expressed as

$$z = \frac{f_1 - nP_1}{\sqrt{nP_1P_2}} = \frac{f_1 - nP_1}{(nP_1P_2)^{1/2}} = \frac{p_1 - P_1}{(P_1P_2/n)^{1/2}} \tag{2.6}$$

Be sure to notice that the radical sign indicating the degree of the required root (the square root in this case) has been replaced by the equivalent operation of raising quantities enclosed within parentheses to corresponding fractional exponents. Henceforth, there will be frequent use of this versatile mathematical convention in this book. Returning to the test, substitution of numerical values associated with the current working example into the right-most version of Equation 2.6 results in

$$z = \frac{.10 - .30}{[(.30)(.70)/30]^{1/2}} = \frac{-.20}{.0837} = -2.39$$

5. Comparison of the computed test statistic to the *critical z* value ($z_\alpha = -1.65$) that defines the lower-tail region of rejection on the unit normal sampling distribution. In this case, the comparison indicates that a significant result has been achieved.

6. The conclusion: Reject the null in favor of the alternative hypothesis that the proportion of minorities passing the examination is less than .30. Evidence supports the suspicion that the examination has had an adverse impact on minorities.

Before considering an extension of the binomial theorem, two brief but important points should be made. The first is that there is a direct link between the unit normal probability distribution and the single-*df* chi-square probability distribution. Specifically, $z^2 = \chi^2$ when the χ^2 is distributed on a single degree of freedom. Thus, for dichotomous responses in the presence of large samples, the chi-square distribution defined by one degree of freedom also serves as an approximation to the binomial. This point will be developed in greater detail in the next chapter.

The second point is that even in the presence of large samples, neither the unit normal nor the single-*df* chi-square are good approximations to the binomial when the P_1 parameter (or, conversely, the P_2 parameter) is so small that the rule of five cannot be satisfied. A case in point would be a test on the null hypothesis that $P_1 = .05$ using a large sample of, say, 60. For this and similar cases, there exists another probability distribution—the Poisson distribution—which is a better approximation of the binomial distribution.

POLYTOMIES AND THE MULTINOMIAL LAW

The rationale and the formula for binomial distributions can be generalized to trials that have more than two outcomes. For example, suppose that instead of classifying subjects who passed a promotional examination in a dichotomous manner (i.e., minority or majority), subjects were classified in a polytomous manner such as black, Caucasian, or Hispanic. The generalization that describes the distribution of a polytomous outcome is known as the multinomial rule or law.

The Multinomial Rule for a Polytomous Variable

If we again let k stand for the number of outcomes per trial (hence, $k = 3$ in the example above), then the multinomial equation can be written:

$$P(f_1, \ldots, f_i, \ldots, f_k | n) = \frac{n!}{\prod\limits_{i=1}^{k} f_i!} \prod_{i=1}^{k} P_i^{f_i} \tag{2.7}$$

Equation 2.7 is a straightforward extension of Equation 2.5. The notation $\prod\limits_{i}^{k}$ denotes the *product operator*, which functions much like $\sum$, the summation operator, except that constituent factors (frequencies of proportions) are multiplied—in this case multiplication begins with subscript $i = 1$ and terminates with $i = k$.

We will exercise the multinomial equation for a situation in which the population of test-takers is 70 percent Caucasian, 20 percent black, and 10 percent Hispanic. Assume that 10 test-takers passed the exam ($n = 10$), of which 8 were Caucasian and 2 were black. Given the population parameters cited above, what is the probability that a sample of 10 successful candidates will contain 8 Caucasians, 2 blacks, and no Hispanics, assuming, as we have done before, that the examination does not impact adversely on members of these respective groups? Substituting into Equation 2.7 the numerical values peculiar to this example, and remembering that $0!$ and $(.10)^0$ are both equal to unity, we obtain

$$
\begin{aligned}
P(8,2,0|10) &= \frac{10!}{(8!)(2!)(0!)}(.70)^8(.20)^2(.10)^6 \\
&= (45)(0.576)(.0400)(1) \\
&= .1038
\end{aligned}
$$

Since the probability of the outcome specifically observed is in excess of .10, and since by traditional criteria this outcome probability is too large to reject the null hypothesis below

H_0: $P_1 = .70$ and $P_2 = .20$ (hence, $P_3 = .10$)

attempts to generate additional lower-tail probabilities for outcomes more indicative of adverse impact are not needed.

As we have just seen, it is relatively easy to calculate the probability of a *specific* polytomous outcome. This cannot be said, however, for the generation and subsequent graphing of multiple outcomes associated with a sampling distribution. Just generating the relevant tails of the sampling distribution, for determining the respective probabilities of sample outcomes more deviant from a null than the observed outcome, can be a more arduous task, especially for higher values of n and k. As we shall learn in Chapter 3, however, the more convenient chi-square distribution provides a good approximation of the exact multinomial when samples are reasonably large. We simply point out for now that had our sample been larger, say $n = 50$, a chi-square distribution could have been used in place of the exact multinomial to test the null hypothesis cited above.

The Multinomial Law and Contingency Tables

My focus to this point has been on single qualitative/categorical variables. My work in this book, however, will focus on two or more qualitative variables that will be crossed to form contingency tables. We need, therefore, to consider the relevancy of the multinomial theorem in these environments.

Consider again a two-dimensional table where, as in Chapter 1, we let A be the generic symbol for the row variable. Further, we denote the constituent categories or levels of Variable A by the subscript i, where $i = 1, 2, \ldots, a$. Let B stand for the second variable, the column variable, a variable that is subscripted by j, where $j = 1, 2, \ldots, b$. Generally, the uppercase letters P and F will be used to denote population proportions and frequencies, respectively. Thus, P_{ij} represents a parameter, specifically the proportion associated with the ith level of A and jth level of B. Corresponding sample proportions and frequencies will be indicated by lowercase letters; hence, p_{ij} and f_{ij} stand, respectively, for the observed proportion and frequency in the cell located in the ith row and jth column of the table. Additional notation will be introduced as needed.

When variables are crossed and contingency tables are formed, exact sampling distributions are usually described by either the multinomial law or a variation of this law known as the *product-multinomial law*. The sampling model determines, in large measure, whether the multinomial or product-multinomial law is appropriate. Two sampling models, random and fixed, were mentioned in Chapter 1. Briefly, the multinomial rule governs the exact distribution of sample statistics when *simple* random sampling is appropriate, while the product-multinomial law is the basis for sampling distributions when *stratified* random sampling is employed. These points merit greater elaboration.

If a sample of size n is drawn at random from a population and sample members are cross-classified on the basis of two (or more) qualitative variables, then, as noted, the straightforward version of the multinomial law is the basis for the sampling distribution. Said differently, if all we do is to arbitrarily fix (establish) the overall size of the sample (n), thus permitting selected subjects the opportunity to be placed in any one of the table's ab cells, then Equation 2.7 can be used either to (1) determine the outcome probability of a given set of cross-classified data or (2) generate a complete sampling distribution.

Of course, to use Equation 2.7 to perform the work indicated above, either the elementary cell parameters must be known or they must be assumed under a null hypothesis. For example, using the data of Table 1.1, if we desire to test the null hypothesis that the variables Gender and Attitude toward the abortion amendment are *independent* (not correlated), we shall learn from the next chapter that the population proportions that reflect this independent state for these data are $P_{11} = .28$, $P_{12} = .12$, $P_{21} = .42$, and $P_{22} = .18$. Referring back to Table 1.1., we are reminded that the four elementary cell frequencies observed for the sample of size 100 were $f_{11} = 33$ ($p_{11} = .33$), $f_{12} = 7$ ($p_{12} = .07$), $f_{21} = 37$ ($p_{21} = .37$), and $f_{22} = 23$ ($p_{22} = .23$). To determine the exact probability of achieving these observed elementary cell frequencies, given that the two variables are independent, Equation 2.7 can be implemented as suggested below.

$$P(33,7,37,23|100) = \frac{100!}{33! \cdot \ldots \cdot 23!}(.28^{33} \cdot \ldots \cdot .18^{23})$$

However, the solution to the above only yields the probability of observing the precise frequencies, in the expression, under the null. Of greater practical interest would be the specification of probabilities of *all* possible outcomes that are deviant from the null. To assess the likelihood of deviance from the null, the tail (or tails) of the multinomial sampling distribution must be constructed. To accomplish this, Equation 2.7 would need to be executed repeatedly, a most tedious task to say the least. However, Equation 2.7 need not be used to construct sampling distributions when and if the size of the sample is reasonably large. Instead, we can use the chi-square, for, as we have learned, this distribution approximates the multinomial well to the extent to which the rule of five is satisfied.

THE PRODUCT-MULTINOMIAL RULE

An alternative to fixing the overall sample size (i.e., *n*) is to fix the size of respective levels of one (or more) of the variables. Recall that when inquiry is asymmetrical, it is often desirable to stratify the population and to randomly draw a desired number of subjects from each population stratum. If, for example, the study dealing with attitude toward an antiabortion amendment were to be implemented at a military college where female students were decidedly in the minority, and if the investigator's intent were to compare male and female response to the abortion issue, then intentionally fixing the numbers of males and females in the sample so that both sexes will be well represented would be justifiable. In fact, if the total size of the sample is to be 100, then the greatest statistical efficiency (power) for comparisons between females and males will result by drawing at random 50 females from the short roster and 50 males from the longer roster.

However, one must realize that arbitrarily fixing the sample sizes of the levels of the sex variables consequently limits one's ability to conduct a symmetrical analysis. Relationships apparently discovered in such an analysis would lack validity for the population of interest because the student sample would not be representative of the student population in the college. On the other hand, the fixed sampling scheme suggested above is valid for asymmetrical inquiry, which seeks to document differences between the proportional response of females and males with respect to the attitudinal response variable.

Now, when the n's of respective levels of an explanatory variable are fixed, the exact sampling distribution of observed frequencies is given by a variant of Equation 2.7 called the product-multinomial rule. To apply the product-multinomial rule to our working example, the following three operations will be put into effect.

1. The multinomial law (i.e., Equation 2.7) will be used at the first level of the explanatory variable (i.e., A_1 = females) to calculate the probability of observing f_{11} and f_{12} under the hypothesis that the respective population parameters are P_{11} and P_{12}.

2. The multinomial law will be used at the second level of the A variable (i.e., A_2 = males) to assess the probability of realizing f_{21} and f_{22} under the hypothesized parameters P_{21} and P_{22}.

3. The product of probabilities calculated within levels of the explanatory variable will be taken as the probability of obtaining the four observed elementary cell frequencies in the fourfold table, under the known or assumed parameters. It should be emphasized, here, that the product of respective multinomials will result in a known probability distribution *only if respective multinomials are independent*—an important requisite condition that we will encounter again and that is generally tenable when different, unrelated subjects are assigned or classified to the different levels of Variable A.

Perhaps the product-multinomial is best appreciated through a careful study of its algebraic formulation. Stipulating that the sample size associated with the ith level of explanatory variable A will be symbolized by n_1^a (where in this instance n_1^a equals the number of females and n_2^a equals the number of males), the product-multinomial equation for a fourfold situation would be

$$P(f_{11}, f_{12}, f_{21}, f_{22} | n_1^a, n_2^a) = \prod_{i=1}^{2} \frac{n_i!}{(f_{i1}!) (f_{i2}!)} P_{i1}^{f_{i1}} P_{i2}^{f_{i2}} \tag{2.8}$$

As a careful examination of Equation 2.8 reveals, differences in the number of subjects in levels of the sex variable (Variable A) do not systematically affect the product-multinomial probability. Incidently, this is not true for Equation 2.7. For the product-multinomial, however, differences in the numbers of male and female participants are, in effect, "adjusted" so that only their respective profiles of proportional response to the attitudinal variable will affect the product solution. Thus, it follows that the reference distribution for asymmetrical inquiry is the product-multinomial. But again, in practice, exact sampling distributions prescribed by this law are rarely calculated. Instead, exact distributions are approximated by the chi-square when samples are deemed sufficiently large.

So far in this chapter we have learned that the multinomial and product-multinomial laws describe the exact sampling distributions of contingency tables. The multinomial is assumed for cross-classifications resulting from a fixed sample size of n; the product-multinomial is assumed when the respective categories of at least one qualitative variable are determined or fixed by the investigator. The sampling model not only determines what manner of sampling distribution is appropriate but can also influence the *directionality* of an analysis. Simply put, random sampling from the population of interest is the desired requisite for a symmetrical analysis where exact probabilities under a specified null hypothesis may be generated by the multinomial law. Either a random or fixed sampling scheme, however, can be used for an asymmetrical analysis; but if the latter sampling scheme is selected, then it is the product-multinomial law that yields exact probabilities under the null. In the following chapters, both sampling distributions will be approximated by the chi-square in our work with larger samples. Moreover, it will be seen that the mechanics of analysis will not be affected by the choice of sampling model, but the directionality of the analysis (symmetric vs. asymmetric)—and hence, the interpretation of results—will be very much tied to the manner in which the sample is drawn.

MAXIMUM-LIKELIHOOD ESTIMATION

The general method of maximum likelihood (ML) was developed by R. A. Fisher. ML is used to estimate parameters (i.e., lambdas) in log-linear models and concurrently to generate elementary cell frequencies that are expected under hypotheses embodied by log-linear models. Recall that a principal feature that distinguished log-linear analysis (and logistic regression) from the other statistical techniques discussed in connection with Table 1.2 was the use of maximum-likelihood methods, as opposed to least-squares, as the basis for parameter estimation. Moreover, whereas most behavioral researchers are familiar with the principles associated with ordinary least-squares (OLS) estimation as implemented in conventional regression and the ANOVA, the same cannot be said for ML estimation. Hence, the most basic features of ML estimation will be surveyed in this section.

Desirable Properties of Estimators

We start by considering a *point estimator*, a statistic that provides us with a specific numerical *estimate* of a parameter of interest. An arithmetic mean ($\overline{X}$), when computed on a sample so as to serve as an estimate of a population mean (μ), is a point estimator. A sample proportion observed in the ijth cell of a contingency table (e.g., p_{ij}^{ab}) is a point estimator when used to estimate the population proportion P_{ij}^{ab}.

There are a number of methods that can be used to obtain a point estimate—

OLS and ML are but two such methods. To enhance our ability to generalize, let $\hat{\theta}$ stand for an unspecified estimator of parameter θ. Often two or three estimates, each emanating from a different method, stand in competition for the part of being chosen as the "best" estimator of θ. The mean, median, and mode, for example, are estimators of μ. Selecting the so-called best estimator is not as difficult as it might at first appear because a number of desirable characteristics for estimators have been identified that serve as criteria to aid in choosing between and among alternative statistics. These desirable characteristics are briefly described below.

Unbiasedness. A point estimator is unbiased if its *expected value* (the mean of its sampling distribution) is equal to the population value to be estimated. In general, lack of bias means

$$E(\hat{\theta}) = \theta$$

which, in turn, means that the sampling distribution of $\hat{\theta}$ centers about θ in the long run.

Consistency. To the extent to which an estimator approaches the value of the estimated parameter as the size of the sample becomes large, the estimator is said to be consistent. That is,

$$P(\hat{\theta} \to \theta) \to 1 \text{ as } n \to \infty$$

which is read: The probability that $\hat{\theta}$ approaches θ as n becomes larger in size is unity. This means that as n becomes larger, the sampling distribution of the $\hat{\theta}$'s becomes more concentrated and less variable.

Efficiency. To the extent to which the sampling distribution of an estimator becomes concentrated and less variable, the estimator is efficient. Efficient estimators have relatively small standard errors. That is,

$$S.E.(\hat{\theta}) \to \text{small}$$

Comparatively speaking, the estimator whose sampling distribution has the smallest standard deviation (i.e., standard error) is sometimes called a *minimum variance estimator*.

Sufficiency. The property of sufficiency, attributed to R. A. Fisher, refers to the amount of sample information needed to estimate a parameter. An estimator is said to be sufficient if it utilizes all available sample information that potentially can enhance the estimation of θ. Thus, $\hat{\theta}$ would be a sufficient estimator of θ if no other estimator can add to or improve on the estimation of θ.

Having reviewed four properties that make for a good estimator, as the reader may have hypothesized, different methods of estimation tend to promote the attainment of different properties. Indeed they do. Moreover, although estimators produced by the method of least-squares have much to commend them—least-squares still has no rival when it comes to fitting curves to data when certain assumptions about the data are tenable—ML estimators, when obtainable, are extremely attractive. ML estimators are both consistent and efficient (at *least* as consistent and efficient as any other estimator), and ML estimators can be said to be sufficient if a sufficient estimator, in fact, exists. It is only with respect to the unbiased property that ML estimators fall a bit short of the mark. Though it will not effect our work with log-linear models, for the record I must point out that ML estimators often tend to possess some degree of bias.

The Method of Maximum Likelihood (ML)

Unlike the more familiar method of least-squares, the mathematical derivation of ML estimators necessitates a priori knowledge of how the sample event (statistic) of interest is distributed in the population. Thus, if we desire to determine $\hat{\theta}_{ML}$, the maximum-likelihood estimator of θ, we must first be able to specify the *density function* (a mathematical equation describing a distribution) for the observed sample event. The function, of course, describes sample outcomes in terms of a parameter or parameters. The parameter (or parameters) in the density function that makes the sample event most likely is termed the ML estimator.

To illustrate, consider a sampling event whose density function is known to us—the number of designated dichotomous events (say, "successes" as opposed to "failures") observed over n trials or occasions, a statistic described by a density function known as the binomial law. The binomial law was described earlier by Equation 2.5. Recall that if we know (or are willing to assume) the numerical value of the population parameter P_1 (hence, $P_2 = 1 - P_1$), it can be inserted in the function, and the probabilities of sample outcomes (f_1's) can then be determined. However, solving for the probability associated with an observed sample event (f_1), given parameter P_1, such as we did earlier in this chapter, is *not* our immediate intent. Rather our intent here is to determine the value of P_1 that, in the long run, will make the observed outcome f_1 most likely. Hence, we reverse our line of reasoning and work by starting with a sample outcome (say $f_1 = 3$ in a sample where $n = 10$), then ask: What value of P_1 would make $f_1 = 3$ most likely? The central idea is to search among the many possible values that can be taken on by P_1 in an effort to find the value of P_1 that will cause f_1 to be the modal outcome.

If we reverse the process implicit in Equation 2.5 by replacing parameters with as yet unspecified estimates of these parameters, we are able to ostensively define the concept of *likelihood*, a concept that is not synonymous with probability. That is, for a dichotomous outcome, the numeric value that represents the likelihood of occurrence (denoted L) for estimates of P given n and f is

$$L = \frac{n!}{(f_1!)(f_2!)}(\hat{P}_1)^{f_1} (\hat{P}_2)^{f_2} \tag{2.9}$$

which, when applied to the recent example, is

$$L = \frac{10!}{3! \ 7!}(\hat{P}_1)^3(\hat{P}_2)^7 \tag{2.10}$$

Since our goal is to identify $\hat{P}_{ML}$—the $\hat{P}_1$ (or $\hat{P}_2$) that makes observed outcomes most likely—the task becomes one of considering all possible estimates of the population proportions in the *kernal* of Equation 2.10, that portion of the equations that contains the parameters, so that eventually the $\hat{P}_1$ that maximizes L, the value of the likelihood function, can be found.

It will be apparent to many readers that this task is most directly accomplished through the use of differential calculus. However, in the present instance, eventually we should also be able to identify a parameter estimate that will produce the largest L by substituting various trial values for $\hat{P}_1$ (e.g., .25, .29, .30, .31, etc.) in the function and determining which trial value produces the largest L. As an example, let us assess the likelihood of observing $p_1 = 3/10 = .30$, assuming that our first trial estimate of P_1 is .25. We do this by inserting .25 for $\hat{P}_1$ in the likelihood function and solving for L. Since we plan to conduct multiple trials where $n = 10$ and $p_1 = .30$, the factorial factor appearing in Equation 2.9 will be a constant quantity for all trials; hence, its elimination will serve to simplify trial calculations without affecting trial results. The simplified likelihood (L^*) that results from our first trial is

$$\begin{aligned} L^* &= (\hat{P}_1)^3(\hat{P}_2)^7 \\ &= (.25)^3(.75)^7 = (.015625)(.133484) \\ &= .002086 \end{aligned}$$

An alternative computational strategy that we would surely adopt if our sample n were larger would be to exponentiate both sides of the simplified likelihood equation and thereby solving for the natural log of L^*. This computation, which yields what is termed a *log likelihood*, is performed below:

$$\begin{aligned} \ln L^* &= (3) \ln .25 + (7) \ln .75 \\ &= (3) (-1.386294) + (7)(-0.287682) \\ &= (-4.158883) + (-2.013775) \\ &= -6.172658 \end{aligned}$$

If the antilog of -6.172658 is obtained, it will be found to be .002086. Parenthetically, aside from computational convenience, the log likelihood will play an important role in our subsequent discussion of the likelihood-ratio chi-square.

We can conduct another trial by substituting $\hat{P}_1 = .29$ into the function, where it will be found that $L^* = .002218$ (ln $L^* = -6.111149$). Substituting $\hat{P}_1 = .30$ will yield $L^* = .002224$ (ln $L^* = -6.108448$). Substituting $\hat{P}_1 = .31$ gives $L^* = .002218$ (ln $L^* = -6.111149$). If we continued in this manner, we would find that the likelihood function achieves its maximum value when $\hat{P}^1 = .30$. In sum, eventually we would verify empirically what we likely had known intuitively, namely, that observed p is the "best" estimate of corresponding population P in the sense of maximum likelihood.

Readers who are familiar with differential calculus realize that a general solution can be obtained by (1) differentiating the density function with respect to P, the unknown estimator, (2) setting the resultant derivative to zero, and (3) finding the maxima.[2] If we use the suggested calculus on the density function for the binomial distribution, the most likely value of P, given the observed outcome f, will turn out to be f/n. Simply put, the calculus will show that the ML estimator of a population proportion conveniently turns out to be the corresponding proportion computed on a representative sample.

Though our cursory discussion of the method of maximum likelihood has been limited to the dichotomous case, the same logic can be extended to polytomous cases described by either the multinomial or product-multinomial laws. In the chapters to follow, we will be concerned with estimating the proportion (and hence, frequency) of subjects belonging to certain variable combinations and using these estimates either to identify relations in symmetrical analyses or to document group differences in asymmetrical analyses. And since we know that sample proportions and frequencies follow the multinomial and product-multinomial laws; that sample proportions are ML point estimators of population proportions; and that these estimators are maximally consistent, decidedly sufficient, and relatively efficient, it is not surprising that both ML point estimation and interval estimation generally are preferred over ordinary least-squares estimation, and even weighted least-squares estimation, for the work to be described in this book.

Much of the work previewed above will be accomplished through the use of log-linear models. Even though log-linear models will not be presented until Chapter 4, it seems fitting to reinforce the point that maximum likelihood methods will be used to estimate parameters (the tau or lambda parameters) that will appear in these models. In all but simple cases, the estimation of log-linear parameters will be performed by computer programs. We will learn that some programs such as the LOG-LINEAR program in the SPSS[x] use a general computational technique known as the Newton-Raphson to generate ML estimates of log-linear parameters. Other programs such as the 4F program in the BMDP package use a computational technique known as the Deming-Stephan, which is also known as *iterative proportional fitting* (IPF). Incidently, both the Newton-Raphson and the Deming-Stephan are iterative procedures. That is, both methods begin by using trial estimates that are subsequently refined until consistent or convergent results are achieved. Obviously, this is not the place to discuss either the operations or relative merits of these two iterative computational techniques except to say that for a general class of log-linear models, called hierarchical models, the Newton-Raphson and the Deming-Stephan generate equivalent parameter estimates, estimates that make observed sample outcomes most likely.

NOTES

1. In working with Equation 2.3, one must realize that a number raised to the power of zero equals unity.

2. Should a reader with a command of the calculus attempt to do this on the density function for the binomial, calculations will be made more manageable by taking the natural log of this function and thereby transforming the multiplicative function into a linear function. The transformed function is termed the *log-likelihood function*.

3

Traditional Applications of Chi-Square

Since its invention in 1900 by Karl Pearson, the use of the χ^2, the chi-square statistic, has been extensive. A χ^2 statistic, for example, is commonly used when the variable or variables of interest are qualitative and a test of the agreement is desired between *observed* frequencies and the frequencies to be *expected* (theoretical frequencies) on the basis of some hypothesis. Because the chi-square distribution is so basic to theory in statistics, and because the χ^2 statistic is so ubiquitous and versatile in application, all who work directly with behavioral data or make decisions based on such data should be at least acquainted with its elemental theory and use.

However, as has been stated by Lohnes and Cooley, "χ^2 theory is as elusive as its applications are pervasive" (1968, 145). Nevertheless, knowledge of the chi-square is a sine qua non to the study of log-linear analysis. Hence, this chapter is designed to review the basic features of the chi-square, to outline the requisite conditions for the appropriate use of the χ^2 statistic, and to illustrate a number of the traditional applications of the chi-square. Readers who possess a working knowledge of basic chi-square applications, and therefore are understandably anxious to proceed to Chapter 4, are advised to examine at least the last two sections of this chapter, where an important alternative version of the chi-square will be introduced, namely the *likelihood-ratio chi-square*, and an introductory discussion of residual analysis, which is also important to our impending work, will be presented.

THE χ^2 AND ITS SAMPLING DISTRIBUTION

We begin by examining the χ^2 statistic somewhat removed from practical application. Hence, consider an infinitely large *population* of scores ($N \rightarrow \infty$)

that are distributed normally and independently. An unspecified score in this population will be denoted by X_1, where $i = 1, 2, \ldots, N$. The *variance* of population is represented by σ^2.

Now assume that a *sample* of size n is randomly drawn from the population and that the arithmetic mean $(\overline{X})$ and an unbiased variance estimate are calculated. The estimate of population variance is given by

$$\hat{\sigma}^2 = \frac{\sum_i^n (X_i - \overline{X})^2}{n - 1} \tag{3.1}$$

If σ^2, the population variance, is either known or assumed to be known under a null hypothesis, the following statistic is amenable to calculation:

$$\chi^2 = \sum_i^n z_i^2 = \sum_i^n \frac{(X_i - \overline{X})^2}{\sigma^2} = \frac{(n - 1)\hat{\sigma}^2}{\sigma^2} \tag{3.2}$$

This statistic, verbally described as the sum of n squared normal deviates is an *exact* χ^2 statistic—a statistic whose continuous probability distributions are well known.

Like the t statistic, the probability distribution of χ^2 is dependent on sample size. That is, the shape, mean (i.e., expected value), and variance error of sampling distributions of exact χ^2's depend on the number of degrees of freedom associated with the samples on which they are computed. To achieve economy of expression, in this section we will often use v as a general symbol for the number of degrees of freedom. Thus, with respect to a sample size of n and Equation 3.2, $v = n - 1$.[1]

The sampling distributions of χ^2's are solely determined by v. For example, the expected value (mean) of a distribution of χ^2 is the numeric value of its degrees of freedom. That is,

$$E(\chi^2) = v$$

The *standard error* (standard deviation) of a χ^2 distribution is also a function of v. Specifically, it is

$$S.E.(\chi^2) = (2v)^{1/2} = \sqrt{2v}$$

With respect to the underlying metric of these distributions, the lower bound is zero since the numerical value of the χ^2 cannot be negative, and the upper bound extends to infinity. In addition chi-square distributions are nonsymmetrical, except for large n's. Sketches of several distributions are presented in Figure 3.1.

Finally, the reader should know that the exact χ^2 given by Equation 3.2 has important applications for response measures that are interval or ratio in nature.

Figure 3.1
Chi-Square Distributions Associated with 2, 10, and 30 Degrees of Freedom

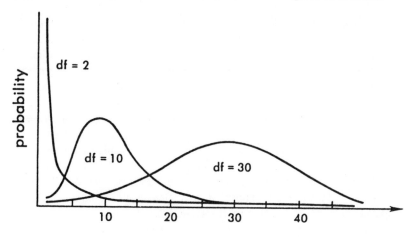

For example, Equation 3.2 is used to test a null hypothesis that the population variance (σ^2) is equal to a specified value (see Hays, 1988, 327–29). Furthermore, the χ^2 plays an important role in multivariate analysis, for the sampling distributions of multivariate normal distributions can be shown to be a function of the χ^2 (see Tatsuoka, 1988, 66–72). However, our present concern is not with the use of the χ^2 for interval data but rather with how χ^2 procedures are used with qualitative data.

APPLICATIONS AND REQUISITE CONDITIONS

There are at least three research situations in which the chi-square can be used with qualitative data. Each is defined by a different number of variables.

1. There is one qualitative variable and the researcher desires to compare the number of cases that are *observed* to fall into specific categories with the number of cases that are *expected* to fall into each category on the basis of some hypothesis. The situation calls for a one-variable test of *goodness-of-fit*.

2. There are two crossed categorical variables and the researcher desires to determine whether

   a. there is a significant association, or relationship, between the two variables, a situation which calls for a test on a null hypothesis of variable *independence* (i.e., a symmetrical analysis), or

   b. the pattern of response to one variable is similar over all categories of the second variable, a situation which calls for a test on a null hypothesis of *homogeneity of response* (i.e., an asymmetrical analysis).

3. There are more than two crossed qualitative variables and the intent is either to assess associations among these variables or to determine if there are differences in the

pattern of responding to one of these variables. Here, chi-square goodness-of-fit procedures are used, but within the context of log-linear contingency table analysis.

In this chapter, we limit discussion to the first two situations above: log-linear
analysis will be introduced in the next chapter. With respect to the first two
situations, we learned from Chapter 2 that exact sampling distributions are given
by the binomial, multinomial, or product-multinomial laws. However, the use
of equations given in Chapter 2 to construct these sampling distributions, or even
the tails of these distributions, will prove to be tedious, especially for larger
values of n. However, when n's are sufficiently large—say, large enough to
satisfy the rule of five—the construction of exact sampling distributions can be
circumvented, for we also learned that the more accessible distribution of chi-
squares can be used as an approximation to the binomial, multinomial, and so
forth. To use the χ^2 distribution as a proxy, however, a way must be found to
compute a χ^2 statistic (or an approximate χ^2 statistic) on qualitative data—not
on interval data, as is assumed by Equation 3.2.

Fortunately, in addition to introducing the *parametric* statistic given by Equation 3.2, Pearson also developed a *nonparametric* version of the chi-square for
use with qualitative data. The nonparametric version involved fewer assumptions
relating to the parameters μ and σ^2, and when a number of conditions reasonably
are satisfied, it is approximately distributed as an exact chi-square. Since discrete
multinomial distributions are approximated well be exact chi-square distributions,
and since exact chi-square distributions are under certain conditions approximated
by the nonparametric chi-square, Pearson's nonparametric statistic represented
a welcome solution to many problems formerly encountered when analyzing
qualitative data.

When applied to qualitative data, the nonparametric χ^2 is used to compare observed sample frequencies within categories of qualitative variables (i.e., np_i's or
f_i's) to frequencies that would be expected under a null population with population
proportions $P_1, P_2, \ldots, P_k$. This well known approximation is given by

$$\chi^2 = \sum_i^k \frac{(np_i - nP_i)^2}{nP_i} = \sum_i^k \frac{(f_i - F_i)^2}{F_i} \tag{3.3}$$

Although the derivation of the Pearsonian χ^2 approximation is well beyond the
scope of most books, including this one, the nature of its derivation is nonetheless
intuitively pleasing. Notice, for instance, that for each category of a qualitative
variable, we obtain first the difference between the observed frequency and that
which is expected for the category when assuming that the population proportion
was P_1. That is, for each of the k classes or categories, we compute

$$f_i = F_i$$

Now if we were to simply sum these differences over categories, the sum would
turn out to be zero since

$$\sum_{i}^{k} (f_i - F_i) = \sum_{i}^{k} f_i - \sum_{i}^{k} F_i = n - n = 0 \tag{3.4}$$

However, by squaring each observed/expected difference prior to summing, this problem can be circumvented. But before squared differences are summed, notice that each is divided by its *expected* frequency. By so doing, the squared discrepancy for each category is weighted by F_1 prior to summation. Even this weighting operation makes sense if one considers that a given discrepancy in a category in which few observations are expected (i.e., F_i is small) is more indicative of departure from a hypothesized population than it would be if it were associated with a category with a large expected frequency. Finally, note that the sum of weighted-squared observed/expected differences constitutes the test statistic, a statistic that we have said is approximately distributed as an exact chi-square possessing a number of degrees of freedom equal to the number of restrictions placed on sample calculations. As we shall see, in situations involving only one qualitative variable the number of restrictions is generally one, and hence, most often $v = k - 1$.[2]

Earlier it was noted that if the nonparametric chi-square is to serve as a good approximation to the exact continuous chi-square, a number of conditions must be satisfied. To ensure that the nonparametric Pearsonian statistic defined by Equation 3.3 does, in fact, approximate the multinomial, three general conditions relating to methods of data collection should be met.

1. Members of the sample who are to provide data should be independently sampled with equal probability from the population of interest. In theory, the validity of statistical inference based on the chi-square is predicated on the assumption that simple random sampling was used for a symmetrical analysis and either simple or stratified random sampling was used for an asymmetrical analysis. Obviously, in practice this condition often cannot be satisfied completely.

2. Members of the sample should be classified into categories of each and every variable such that the classification process can be said to be *independent, mutually exclusive,* and *exhaustive.* The first is important because distributions described by the multinomial law assume that each observation is independent of all other observations. The consequence of compliance with the independence of response condition is that members of the sample can only be assigned to one category of a variable; therefore, it follows that members can be placed into only one cell of a contingency table. Consequently, the use of a variable that is analogous to a repeated measurements variable as often seen in mixed-variable ANOVA designs is not appropriate here. The second member of the trio, mutual exclusivity, means that each variable should be structured and defined so that members drawn from the population are assigned to one and only one category. Finally, exhaustiveness implies that each and every variable has categories sufficient to accommodate all members of the population as defined by the researcher.

3. Members of the sample should be present in sufficient numbers (the n

should be sufficiently large) so that exact multinomial probability distributions approach exact chi-square distributions (under the central limit theorem) and, in turn, the distributions of Pearsonian χ^2's approach exact chi-squares. For the binomial situation, it has been established that approximate methods can be used when the *rule of five* is satisfied. In general, this rule is also applicable to polytomies and to cells comprising contingency tables. When generalized to these situations, the rule of five can be taken to mean that the size of the sample should be large enough to ensure that no category (or cell) contains an expected frequency (not an observed frequency) of less than five cases. Applying the χ^2 to tables in which expected frequencies fall below the level of five is thought by many to produce χ^2 values that are spuriously large, especially if the table is a fourfold table. For larger tables, however, the rule of five is generally conservative and hence may be relaxed somewhat without serious inflation of the Type I error rate as long as there are only a few cells with expectancies less than five (see Hays, 1988, 781). Sometimes it is possible to avoid small expected cell frequencies by combining neighboring categories so as to satisfy the rule, but this remedy must be implemented with caution, for not only can combining categories result in a loss of statistical power (Cochran, 1954), but, as we shall see, it can result in a marked distortion of findings.

With this much background, we are now in the position to review several traditional applications of the chi-square. We begin with a consideration of only one variable and the use of the Pearsonian χ^2 to perform a goodness-of-fit test. Our attention will then be directed to several multivariable situations to witness both a test of independence and a test of homogeneity of response.

SINGLE-VARIABLE GOODNESS-OF-FIT

Tests of this genre attempt to determine whether a distribution of observed sample frequencies (or corresponding proportions) is sufficiently well-fitted to some theoretical form. The theoretical form will be either a binomial or a multinomial distribution specified by the researcher when he or she posits a null hypothesis. Through the use of Equation 3.3, observed sample frequencies (f_i's) are compared to expected frequencies (F_i's) that have been posited under the null.

Consider the following simple example. Assume that the dean of a college of social work believes that graduate students are evenly divided with respect to their opinions on requiring statistics courses in their programs. To subject this belief to test, a modest but representative sample of graduate students (say $n = 30$) was polled, and subsequently students were classified into one of three mutually exclusive categories (i.e, $k = 3$). These categories were (1) in favor of requiring statistics, (2) opposed to requiring statistics, and (3) undecided.

The dean's belief concerning an equal division of opinion can be translated into the following null hypothesis:

$H_0: P_1 = P_2 = P_3 = .33$

where P_1 symbolizes the proportion of students in the population who favor statistics as a requirement, P_2 the proportion that is opposed, and P_3 the proportion that is undecided.

Turning to the sample, assume that 16 students favored a statistical requirement, 9 indicated that they were opposed to such a requirement, and 5 were judged to be undecided on this matter. These values constitute observed frequencies (f_i's) within levels of the polytomous opinion variable.

It is, however, the researcher's task to generate the *expected* frequencies for each level that are consonant with the null. Since $P_1 = .33$, the expected number of students in a sample size 30 that would favor a statistical requirement is $F_1 = nP_1 = (30)(.33) = 10$. By similar logic, F_2 and F_3 also would be 10 in this case. A working table for the goodness-of-fit test is shown below.

	Favor	Oppose	Undecided	Overall
Observed (f_i)	16	9	5	30
Expected (F_i)	10	10	10	30

Substituting working values into Equation 3.3 yields

$$\chi^2 = \sum_i^k \frac{(f_i - F_i)^2}{F_i}$$
$$= \frac{(16 - 10)^2}{10} + \frac{(9 - 10)^2}{10} + \frac{(5 - 10)^2}{10}$$
$$= 3.60 + 0.10 + 2.50 = 6.20$$

To complete the test, the χ^2 test statistic is related to a tabled distribution of chi-square statistics with degrees of freedom $k - 1 = 2$. Consulting a table of critical values for the chi-square distribution (given in Appendix B) reveals that a test statistic equal to or in excess of 5.99 is needed to be able to claim statistical significance at the .05 level. Since $\chi^2(2) = 6.20$, significance can be claimed.

The dean, therefore, can conclude that the null hypothesis of uniform distribution of opinion on this issue is not tenable. Moreover, for a simple problem like this, it is a simple matter to identify the categories where the discrepancy between observed and expected response is most pronounced. From an examination of the respective contribution made by each category to the numerical value of the χ^2 statistic (e.g., contributions were 3.60, 0.10, and 2.50, respectively) it is evident that the sample distribution does not depart from the hypothesized distribution in the "opposition" category, but rather that the "poorness-of-fit" is due to a greater than expected number of students with "favorable" opinions and a fewer than expected number of students who were classified as "undecided." There are still other techniques (e.g., the analysis of residuals) that can be of help when attempting to identify categories (or cells) that deviate markedly from the null distribution. Several of these techniques will be introduced in a slightly more challenging context later in this chapter.

To illustrate an earlier point that the χ^2 test can be effected by the reordering of categories, assume that the dean decides to redefine the opinion variable. That is, instead of a trichotomy, the opinion variable is now treated as a dichotomy consisting of (1) students in favor of requiring statistics and (2) students not expressly in favor of requiring statistics. To accommodate the new second category, the second and third categories of the previous example will be combined. The null hypothesis of uniform distribution is now H_o: $P_1 = P_2 = .50$. Regrouping the observed frequencies results in 16 students in favor of statistics and 14 students not in favor of statistics as a requirement. Performing the single-df χ^2 test gives $\chi^2(1) = .13$, a result that the reader is encouraged to verify. (Since $k = 2$ here, a z test such as was illustrated in Chapter 2 could have been performed with comparable results.) Because the computed test statistic falls far short of $X_\alpha^2 = 3.84$, the tabled critical value at the .05 level, there is no basis for rejecting the null. Thus, unless there is a strong theoretical justification for a certain grouping procedure, caution is advised, for as we have seen, arbitrary classification can affect results.

THE HYPOTHESIS OF VARIABLE INDEPENDENCE

In the two-variable case, the χ^2 test performed on a null hypothesis of variable independence is essentially an extension of the previous test of goodness-of-fit. In brief, the researcher (1) creates a hypothesis (i.e., a null hypothesis) that reflects a condition of variable independence between the two variables, (2) draws a sample of n members and jointly classifies members on the basis of the two variables, and (3) compares observed cell frequencies with those expected under the null for goodness-of-fit.

Independence in Fourfold Tables

In Chapter 1, two dichotomies were crossed to form a fourfold table. Recall that college students were jointly classified by gender and attitude toward an antiabortion amendment, henceforth referred to simply as the Attitude variable. In this section we desire to determine whether a statistically significant relationship (or association) exists between Gender and Attitude, which would suggest that if one had knowledge of a student's sex, one would be able to predict his or her attitude relative to the abortion issue (or vice versa) better than would be expected by chance. The mode of inquiry is decidedly symmetrical.

Assuming that we have familiarized ourselves with the contents of Table 1.1, we begin by advancing the null hypothesis that dichotomous Variables A (Gender) and B (Attitude) are independent. Symbolically, this may be expressed as

H_0: $A \otimes B$

It should be understood that this hypothesis relates to a *population* of college students who, in this instance, belong to one and only one of the following four variable combinations:

AB_{11} = females opposed to the amendment
AB_{12} = females in support of the amendment
AB_{21} = males opposed to the amendment
AB_{22} = males in support of the amendment

Now if the null hypothesis is precisely true and if two parameters are known, the exact *proportion* of students belonging to each of the four cells or variable combinations above can be determined. The first parameter to know is the proportional representation of females (or males) in the population, namely, P_1^a. The value of this parameter, of course, gives us the value of P_2^a, the proportion of males in the population. Second, we need to know the proportion of subjects in the population that fall into one of the categories of the Attitude variable, say P_1^b. With knowledge of these *marginal* parameters, if there is no relationship between Gender and Attitude, then the proportion of students belonging to the cell located in the ith row of A and the jth column of B is

$$P_{ij}^{ab} = P_i^a P_j^b \tag{3.5}$$

To illustrate this most important multiplicative principle, suppose that 50 percent of population members were females (i.e., $P_1^a = .50$) and that 60 percent of population members opposed the antiabortion amendment (i.e., $P_1^b = .60$). If Gender and Attitude are independent, then the proportion of females who oppose the amendment would be

$$P_{11}^{ab} = P_1^a P_1^b = (.50)(.60) = .30$$

Moreover, deviation from $P_{11}^{ab} = .30$ in this instance constitutes evidence in support of an association between the two variables, for knowledge of a student's gender would permit a better-than-chance prediction of that student's attitude toward abortion, or vise versa.

The identity given by Equation 3.5 represents, in effect, the state of variable independence at the population level. In actual practice, however, we rarely have access to populations, and, therefore, rarely know the numerical value of parameters. Instead, we try to obtain samples that are representative of populations and to estimate the unknown parameters of interest. For this example, therefore, assume as before that a sample of 100 college students has been randomly drawn and jointly classified by Gender and Attitude as indicated by Table 1.1.

The information provided in Table 1.1 will now be used to *estimate* (1) the marginal parameters P_i^a and P_j^b shown to the right of the equals sign in Equation 3.5 and, in turn, (2) P_{ij}^{ab}, the expected proportion (or probability) for the *ij*th cell. Recall from the last chapter that the ML estimators of parameters P_i^a and P_j^b are sample p_i^a and p_j^b, respectively. Moreover, it turns out that these ML estimators are unbiased (which often is not true of ML estimators), so we can say that $E(p_i^a) = P_i^a$ and $E(p_j^b) = P_j^b$.

Having found highly suitable estimators of the marginal parameters, we turn to the estimation of P_{ij}^{ab} which, under the null hypothesis of *independence*, is

$$\hat{P}_{ij} = p_i^a \, p_j^b \tag{3.6}$$

where the carat or "hat" ($\hat{P}$) over P_{ij} will again be used to designate a population estimator. However, since the conventional formula for the approximate χ^2 uses frequencies instead of proportions, we usually work with *expected frequencies* for the cells of the contingency table. These are given by

$$
\begin{aligned}
F_{ij} &= n\hat{P}_{ij} = np_i^a p_j^b \\
&= (n)(n_i^a/n)\,(n_j^b/n) \\
&= \frac{n_i^a n_j^b}{n}
\end{aligned}
\tag{3.7}
$$

For example, the expected frequency for females who are opposed to the antiabortion amendment is

$$F_{11} = \frac{n_i^a n_j^b}{n} = \frac{(40)(70)}{100} = 28$$

Only one F_{ij} need be computed by formula because in a fourfold table, if one F_{ij} is known, the remaining three may be obtained by subtraction from respective fixed marginal frequencies.

Our work to this point is summarized by Table 3.1, where we note that expected cell frequencies are contained within parentheses and that the size of the sample is sufficient to accommodate the chi-square approximation to the multinomial.

To apply Pearson's approximate chi-square to a contingency table, weighted-squared-cell differences are summed over rows ($i = 1, 2, \ldots, a$) and columns ($j = 1, 2, \ldots, b$). With this in mind, we compute

$$
\begin{aligned}
\chi^2 &= \sum_{ij}^{ab} \frac{(f_{ij} - F_{ij})^2}{F_{ij}} \\
&= \frac{(33 - 28)^2}{28} + \frac{(7 - 12)^2}{12} + \frac{(37 - 42)^2}{42} + \frac{(23 - 18)^2}{18} \\
&= .8929 + 2.0833 + .5952 + 1.3889 \\
&= 4.96
\end{aligned}
\tag{3.8}
$$

Table 3.1
Observed and Expected Frequencies for the Hypothetical Study Introduced in Chapter 1

	Attitude toward the Amendment		
Gender of Subject	Opposed	Support	Marginals
Female	33 (28)	7 (12)	40
Male	37 (42)	23 (18)	60
Marginals	70	30	100

Note: Expected or theoretical cell frequencies are contained within parentheses.

In general, the number of degrees of freedom that prescribe the relevant χ^2 sampling distribution for contingency tables is the product $(a - 1)(b - 1)$. Therefore, for fourfold contingency tables, $v = (2 - 1)(2 - 1) = 1$. Relating the computed χ^2 statistic to the tabled critical value associated with the .05 level of significance reveals that $\chi^2(1) = 4.96 > \chi^2_\alpha = 3.84$. Rejection of the independence hypothesis is justified; there is a statistically significant association between the two dichotomous variables.

Usually, however, the mere documentation of an association does not complete the analysis. Questions concerning the *directionality* and *intensity* of the association remain. For large, complicated tables, a residual analysis (to be discussed) can prove to be of assistance in determining the directional nature of an association. For relatively simple designs, an examination of differences between observed and expected cell frequencies will usually reveal the essential direction of the association. For the present simple example, such an examination reveals that males at this college are most supportive of the antiabortion amendment than are females. The strength or intensity of the association, however, is a separate matter. As a reading of the section on follow-up procedures in Chapter 4 will disclose, Yule's Q statistic will be a highly appropriate measure of the strength of the relationship in this fourfold table.

Independence in Larger Tables

As long as the previously discussed requisite conditions are satisfied, the test of variable independence can be extended to contingency tables of order greater than 2 × 2. Such a table has been constructed from data reported by O'Connor and Sitkei (1975). Briefly, these investigators conducted a national survey of

Table 3.2
Cross-Classification of Facilities by Type and Number of Retarded Residents Served

	Number of Residents (#R)			
Type of Facility	#R ≤ 10	10 < #R < 21	#R ≥ 21	Marginals
Public	67 (46)*	45 (48)	19 (37)	131
Nonprofit	98 (99)	98 (105)	88 (80)	284
Private Profit	48 (68)	83 (73)	65 (55)	196
Marginals	213	226	172	611

Source: This table has been constructed from data presented as bar graphs by O'Connor and Sitkei (1975) with permission of the publisher, the American Association on Mental Deficiency.
*Expected cell frequencies, rounded to the nearest whole number, are contained within parentheses.

community-based residential homes for retarded persons "to provide an initial profile of these facilities and their residents" (p. 35). One aspect of their research centered around the relationship between Type of Facility (public, private non-profit, or private profit) and Number of Residents served by the facility (up to 10, between 11 and 20, or over 20). The cross-classifications of the 611 institutions surveyed are presented in Table 3.2.

Although O'Connor and Sitkei did not subject their data to inferential analysis, we shall. Specifically, let us test the null hypothesis that there is no association between Type of Facility and Number of Residents. To obtain expected cell frequencies under the assumed condition of variable independence, Equation 3.7 is employed. The value of F_{11}, for example, is

$$F_{11} = \frac{n_i^a n_j^b}{n} = \frac{(131)(213)}{611} = 45.67$$

We need to use Equation 3.7 at least three more times because four expected cell frequencies must be known before the remaining F_{ij}'s can be obtained as residuals from appropriate marginals. (It follows, therefore, that $v = 4$ for this problem.) Using the F_{ij}'s given in Table 3.2, which have been rounded to the nearest whole number, Equation 3.8 is used to compute the chi-square test statistic.

$$\chi^2 = \frac{(67 - 46)^2}{46} + \frac{(45 - 48)^2}{48} + \ldots + \frac{(65 - 55)^2}{55}$$
$$= 28.88$$

Realizing that $v = (a - 1)(b - 1) = (3 - 1)(3 - 1) = 4$, reference to tabled values of chi-square reveals that $\chi^2(4) = 28.88$, $p < .001$. Evidence is sufficient to reject the null and conclude that there is an association between the two variables in question. Moreover, a preliminary study of discrepancies between observed and expected cell frequencies in Table 3.2 tends to support the finding advanced by O'Connor and Sitkei that "public facilities tend to have the fewest number of residents and to use small facilities while private profit facilities appear to be slightly larger than the non-profit or public facilities" (1975, 36). (The substantive implications of this finding were not addressed by the authors.) We will attempt a more thorough follow-up of this analysis in the forthcoming section devoted to residual analyses.

THE HYPOTHESIS OF HOMOGENEITY OF PROPORTIONS

Still another use of the χ^2 is to assess whether groups of subjects respond differently when response is viewed over levels of a categorical response variable. Consider, for example, an experiment that involved two groups: one that received a special treatment and one that served as a control group. At the end of the experiment, subjects in each group were administered a task and assigned a performance rating of either "pass" or "fail." In this instance, it is unlikely that the investigator is interested in exploring the relationship between the Group variable and the Response variable. Rather, inquiry is more likely to be asymmetrical in that the investigator probably wants to know whether members of the experimental and control groups (an explanatory variable) respond differently over levels of the outcome or response variable. More to the point, the investigator probably wants to know if the profiles of proportional response differ by group. To partially answer this question, a χ^2 test can be performed on the hypothesis of homogeneous proportional response.

Often the similarities and differences between χ^2 tests of independence and homogeneity of proportions are not well appreciated. Indeed, both use the Pearsonian χ^2, assuming, of course, that basic requirements are met. Differences, however, may be seen in the (1) sampling plans, (2) initial interpretation of results, and (3) procedures used to follow up an initial significant result.

Turning first to sampling, recall that, in theory, only the overall sample size is fixed by the investigator for a test of independence. Under ideal circumstances, the investigator defines a population of interest, proceeds to obtain a representative sample of size n, and cross-classifies sample members on the basis of selected qualitative variables. In contrast, for tests of homogeneity of proportions, the investigator may arbitrarily fix the marginal frequencies of the explanatory variable. We learned from the discussion of asymmetrical inquiry in Chapter 1, for example, that the investigator may wisely choose to make each category of the explanatory variable of equal size despite the fact that group n's may not be equal with respect to the background population. Having fixed the marginals of the explanatory variable, subjects within fixed groups are then classified according to their status on the response variable. Such a sample scheme, of course, would vitiate the value of a test of independence, but since our present concern centers around differences and similarities in group response, it is appropriate here.

After observed and expected frequencies have been established, a conventional χ^2 statistic is computed to test the null hypothesis of uniform proportional response. As a rule, the sampling distribution approximated by the Pearsonian χ^2 is given by the product-multinomial law, and not the multinomial law, which is the basis for tests of independence. Nevertheless, the computation of the χ^2 statistic is carried out in the usual way, but, as we shall see, the results are interpreted differently.

An example of a study that sought to test a hypothesis of homogeneity of proportional response has been reported by Goldsmid, Gruber, and Wilson (1977). The study examined selected attributes of "superior" college teachers in a large university. Sixty faculty members who were either awarded the honor of being a distinguished teacher or received a significant number of nominations for this award were identified. In addition, a group of 60 control members was randomly selected from the faculty at large. Hence, the explanatory variable, Type of Teacher, consisted of two levels: distinguished vs. control.

One of several hypotheses advanced in this study was that the quality of teacher will peak in mid-career. To determine if there was support for this hypothesis, teachers within each of the two levels of the explanatory variable were classified in turn on the basis of three levels of chronological age. The categories of the Age variable were: under 39, 40 to 49, and over 49.[3] Keep in mind that the intent here was not to investigate a possible relationship between Type of Teacher and Age but rather to determine whether distinguished teachers differed from control teachers with respect to age. To accommodate this intent, a sample drawn at random from the population of faculty members at this institution was not required. Instead, the faculty at large, in effect, was stratified on the basis of distinguished members and typical (control) members so that 60 of each type could be drawn, a sampling scheme that maximizes the sensitivity of comparisons between these two groups.

The frequencies of occurrence by level of the explanatory variable and by the three levels of the response variable turned out as shown in Table 3.3. Note that in addition to f_{ij}'s, the table also contains the F_{ij}'s that would be expected under the hypothesis of mutual variable independence. (The F_{ij}'s were calculated by methods discussed in the previous section; and even though we are not interested in variable independence per se, the F_{ij}'s will be shown to be relevant to the problem at hand.)

There is a perspective to be highly recommended for this and similar problems.

Table 3.3
Cross-Classifications by Type of Teacher and Age

	Age Categories (B)			
Type of Teacher	$B < 40$	$40 \leq B \leq 49$	$B > 49$	Marginals
Distinguished	30 (29.0)*	20 (18.5)	10 (12.5)	60
Control	28 (29.0)	17 (18.5)	15 (12.5)	60
Marginals	58	37	25	120

Source: Data reproduced with minor modifications from Goldsmid, C. A., Gruber, J. E., and Wilson, E. K., "Perceived attributes of superior teachers (PAST): An inquiry into the giving of teacher awards," *American Educational Research Journal, 14*, (1977), 423–40. Copyright 1977, American Educational Research Association, Washington, DC.
*Expected cell frequencies under the hypothesis of variable independence are contained in parentheses.

It is useful to view each level of the explanatory variable (e.g., Type of Teacher) as an intact entity, which may or may not contain the same number of subjects as other entities. This view readily accommodates the conversion of frequencies within these entities to proportions that sum to unity. That is, envision the standardization of response separately by levels of the explanatory variable by transforming frequencies to proportions such that, within levels, the proportions sum to 1.00. *Standardization to proportional unity* within groups facilitates the comparison of profiles of response between groups. Should the profile of proportional response to the Age variable provided by distinguished teachers turn out to be similar to the profile provided by the controls, the proportional response is said to be homogeneous. Should the profiles of proportions turn out to be decidedly different, however, the response profiles are said to be heterogeneous. Let us illustrate this with the data at hand.

Assuming Variable A to be explanatory, the profile of frequencies within a level of A can be standardized to proportional unity by

$$p_{ij} = f_{ij}/n_i^a \tag{3.9}$$

Thus, for distinguished teachers, observed proportions standardized to unity are

$p_{11} = 30/60 = .500$
$p_{12} = 20/60 = .333$
$p_{13} = 10/60 = .167$

Table 3.4
Proportional Response to Levels of Age by Type of Teacher

Type of Teacher	Age Categories (B)			
	$B < 40$	$40 \leq B \leq 49$	$B > 49$	Marginals
Distinguished	.500 (.483)*	.333 (.308)	.167 (.208)	1.00
Control	.467 (.483)	.283 (.308)	.259 (.208)	1.00

*Expected cell proportions under the hypothesis of homogeneity of proportional response are congained in parentheses.

For the controls, parallel operations yield $p_{21} = .467$, $p_{22} = .283$, and $p_{23} = .250$.

Having established the pattern of *observed* response for each group of teachers, we next determine *expected* patterns of proportional response for each group, assuming under the null that these patterns are homogeneous in the background populations. As the reader may have surmised, expected proportions standardized to unity within a group are a function of the F_{ij}'s in Table 3.3. They are given by

$$P_{ij} = F_{ij}/n_i^a \tag{3.10}$$

Thus, for distinguished teachers, expected proportions are

$p_{11} = 29.0/60 = .483$
$p_{12} = 18.5/60 = .308$
$p_{13} = 12.5/60 = .208$

Parallel calculations performed on control teachers yield an identical profile. That is, under the hypothesis of homogeneity of response, $p_{21} = .483$, $p_{22} = .308$, and $p_{23} = .208$. Our work to this point is summarized in Table 3.4.

Several inferences can be drawn from careful study of Tables 3.3 and 3.4. The first is that when the F_{ij}'s for a test of mutual independence are transformed to proportions within levels of an explanatory variable (such that they sum to unity), profiles of proportional response within levels of the explanatory variable will be identical. Hence, we conclude that the *expected distributions* for tests on the hypothesis of independence and tests on the hypothesis of homogeneity of proportional response are essentially the same—it is the perspective taken toward the research problem that is different. Second, if a Pearsonian χ^2 were applied to data in Table 3.3, a significant result would mean that observed proportions deviate from those expected, in the long run, under the hypothesis of homogeneity of proportions. Finally, unlike the earlier test of mutual independence, the present test on the hypothesis of homogeneity of proportions is clearly asymmetrical. The sampling scheme used in the Goldsmid et al. (1977) study, for example, would not permit us to reverse directions and conclude that the proportion of distinguished teachers and the proportion of control teachers are homogeneous (or heterogeneous) over levels of the age variable.

Before we take leave of the Goldsmid et al. study, it may be of interest to note that the application of Equation 3.8 to the data presented in Table 3.3 results in a chi-square test statistic that is obviously nonsignificant, namely, $\chi^2(2) = 1.31$, $p > .50$. The hypothesis that teachers who are identified as distinguished tend to be in mid-career finds little support in the data given in Table 3.4.

THE LIKELIHOOD-RATIO CHI-SQUARE

Many readers may be surprised to learn that there is an alternative to Pearson's goodness-of-fit χ^2 statistic. The alternative was developed by R. A. Fisher (1924) who, subsequent to developing the method of maximum likelihood that is described briefly in Chapter 2, derived a competing goodness-of-fit statistic based on the ML methodology. Despite differences in underlying method, however, Fisher's alternative, known as the maximum-likelihood-ratio chi-square, serves the same function as does the Pearsonian chi-square. The computational formula for the likelihood-ratio chi-square, symbolized by L^2 (although some writers perfer G^2), is

$$L^2 = 2\sum (f_{ij})(\ln\frac{f_{ij}}{F_{ij}}) \tag{3.11}$$

As before, the summation is over all cells of the table, but unlike the calculation of the χ^2 statistic, the calculation of L^2 uses *natural logarithms*, abbreviated "ln." Natural logarithms are logs to the base of e, where $e = 2.718282$, and should not be mistaken for common logarithms, which are logs to the base 10.

Like the Pearsonian χ^2, L^2 is distributed approximately as a chi-square distribution when samples are sufficiently large. In fact, as samples become increasingly large, the χ^2 and L^2 converge or become asymptotically equivalent. In practice, therefore, both statistics will lead to essentially the same conclusions relative to goodness-of-fit. Because the calculation of L^2 has been perceived to be more involved than the calculation of χ^2, the former is not often seen in the research literature. However, L^2 possesses several properties that are most desirable in log-linear work, and hence it will soon prove to be our preferred goodness-of-fit statistic.

Let us illustrate the computation of L^2 on the Goldsmid et al. data shown in

Table 3.3. To test the hypothesis that patterns of proportional response to the
Age variable are homogeneous over Teacher Types, the frequencies in Table
3.3 are entered into Equation 3.11 as follows:

$$L^2 = 2[(30)(\ln\frac{30}{29.0}) + (20)(\ln\frac{20}{18.5}) + \ldots + (15)(\ln\frac{15}{12.5})]$$

Performing the algebra yields:

$$
\begin{aligned}
L^2 &= 2[(30)(.0339) + (20)(.0780) + \ldots + (15)(.1823)] \\
&= 2(.6596) \\
&= 1.32
\end{aligned}
$$

This result compares well with the χ^2 value computed on the Goldsmid data.

To say that the likelihood-ratio chi-square is important in log-linear work is
an understatement. It will prove to be far more useful than the Pearsonian chi-
square. The L^2 statistic, therefore, is deserving of at least as much effort as was
expended on the Pearsonian χ^2 in developing an understanding of its nature that
goes beyond the direct application of the computational formula given by Equation 3.11.

Earlier we verbally defined the Pearsonian χ^2 as the sum (over all cells) of
weighted-squared differences between observed and expected frequencies. This
definition is embodied in Equation 3.3, the computational formula for χ^2. The
Fisherian likelihood-ratio chi-square may be defined as the natural log of squared
ratio comparisons of the likelihoods of observed to expected frequencies. Equation 3.12 embodies this definition.

$$L^2 = \ln[(\frac{L_{OBS}}{L_{EXP}})^2] \tag{3.12}$$

In Equation 3.12, L_{OBS} represents the numeric value of the likelihood function,
first introduced in connection with Equation 2.9, in which observed elementary
cell proportions are used as estimates of population proportions. L_{EXP} represents
the value of the likelihood function where cell frequencies under the null hypothesis (say the independence hypothesis) are substituted for population proportions. We offer a more manageable version of Equation 3.12 below:

$$
\begin{aligned}
L^2 &= 2\ln(\frac{L_{OBS}}{L_{EXP}}) \\
&= 2(\ln L_{OBS} - \ln L_{EXP})
\end{aligned}
\tag{3.13}
$$

Let us use the Goldsmid et al. data in Tables 3.3 and 3.4 to illustrate the view
of L^2 that is contained in Equations 3.12 and 3.13.

Since the Goldsmid et al. study is asymmetrical, the relevant sampling distribution is the product-multinomial. The relevant likelihood function for the 2×3 data set, therefore, is

$$L = \prod_{i=1}^{2} \frac{n_i^a!}{f_{i1}!f_{i2}!f_{i3}!} \, \hat{P}_{i1}^{f_{i1}} \, \hat{P}_{i2}^{f_{i2}} \, \hat{P}_{i3}^{f_{i3}} \tag{3.14}$$

where $\sum_i^a \hat{P}_{ij} = 1.00$ because standardization within levels of Variable A (Teacher Types) is appropriate here. Incidentally, since the first factor (i.e., the factorial factor) in Equation 3.14 will be constant in all ensuing calculations, it can be omitted without affecting the ensuing results.

Attending first to the simplified likelihood function where observed cell frequencies and corresponding proportions are used as population estimates we see that

$$\begin{aligned} L^*_{\text{OBS}} &= \prod_{i=1}^{2} \hat{P}_{i1}^{f_{i1}} \, \hat{P}_{i2}^{f_{i2}} \, \hat{P}_{i3}^{f_{i3}} \\ &= [(.500^{30})(.333^{20})(.167^{10})] \, [(.467^{28})(.283^{17})(.250^{15})] \end{aligned} \tag{3.15}$$

The calculations will be more tractable if we express Equation 3.15 in terms of logs, as is done below:

$$\begin{aligned} \ln L^*_{\text{EXP}} &= (30 \ln .500 + 20 \ln .333 + 10 \ln .167) \\ &\quad + (28 \ln .467 + 17 \ln .283 + 15 \ln .250) \\ &= (-60.684256) + (-63.573368) \\ &= -124.257624 \end{aligned}$$

Observe that log likelihood values are always algebraically negative due to the fact that the product of parameter estimates will always be less than unity. Moreover, increasing experience with likelihood functions will lead readers to the conclusion that for a given data set, the maximum value of a likelihood function is realized when observed elementary cell frequencies are used as parameter estimates.

Having computed the log likelihood from observed frequencies, we now compute the log likelihood from frequencies and corresponding proportions associated with the hypothesis of homogeneity of proportional response (or independence). Substituting the expected values appearing in Table 3.4 into the simplified likelihood expression given by Equation 3.15, and then expressing the simplified function in terms of logged likelihood as we did before, results in

$$\begin{aligned} \ln L^*_{\text{EXP}} &= (30 \ln .483 + 20 \ln .308 + 10 \ln .208) \\ &\quad + (28 \ln .483 + 17 \ln .308 + 15 \ln .208) \\ &= (-61.029156) + (-63.888420) \\ &= -124.917576 \end{aligned}$$

We now use Equation 3.13 to compute the log of the square of ratio of the likelihood of observed frequencies to the likelihood of expected frequencies.

$$
\begin{aligned}
L^2 &= (2)(\ln L^*_{\text{OBS}} - \ln L^*_{\text{EXP}}) \\
&= (2)[(-124.257624) - (-124.917576)] \\
&= (2)(.659953) \\
&= 1.3199
\end{aligned}
$$

By demonstration, therefore, we see that the L^2 statistic is essentially the difference between two logged likelihoods. Further, to the extent to which cell frequencies offered by the null hypothesis (independence or homogeneity of proportional response) approach the frequencies that are actually observed, the likelihood of expected frequencies under the null approaches the likelihood associated with observed frequencies; hence, differences in respective likelihoods become increasingly small, and consequently, the L^2 statistic becomes small. In time we will be able to discuss the likelihood-ratio chi-square in terms of log-linear models and will develop an even greater appreciation of this statistic.

RESIDUAL ANALYSIS AND OTHER FOLLOW-UP PROCEDURES

The statistical tests discussed so far are limited in that they only enable us to reject the hypothesis under test. They do not reveal to us either the direction or the intensity of the relationship between two variables, or the boldness of effects or differences between groups. For a test of mutual independence, a statistically significant χ^2 does not indicate the strength of the association between categorical variables or whether the association between categorical variables is significant in a practical sense. By the same token, the presence of a significant χ^2 associated with a test of homogeneity of proportions simply means that at least one group has demonstrated a response pattern that is different from the response pattern of at least one other group. The specific location and magnitude of difference remains unknown. Consequently, a thorough analysis of data usually requires additional follow-up procedures.

The Analysis of Residuals

Simply put, residuals are differences between respective f_{ij}'s and F_{ij}'s. In several prior instances we have looked at patterns of residuals to determine the directionality of a statistically significant association. Granted, these previous attempts at residual analysis were rather primitive, for they amounted to scarcely more than a casual visual examination of patterns of raw residuals. In this section, more sophisticated methods of residual analysis will be introduced which can facilitate the interpretation of results, especially results emanating from tables containing numerous cells. Though we are still operating within the context of two-dimensional tables, let it be said that the benefits to be derived from a serious analysis of residuals increase in direct relation to the dimensionality and complexity of tables. Moreover, as will become apparent in Chapter 9, the analysis of residuals is central to the conduct of configural frequency analysis (CFA).

Standardized Residuals. In his authoritative paper on residual analysis, Haberman (1973) presented a residual, termed the *standardized residual*, which, for the ijth cell of a two-dimensional table, is

$$R_{ij} = (f_{ij} - F_{ij})/(F_{ij})^{1/2} \qquad (3.16)$$

To compute R_{ij} on the cell in the upper left corner in Table 3.2, for example, we get

$$R_{11} = \frac{67 - 46}{\sqrt{46}} = 3.10$$

Since $R_{11} > 1.96$, the discrepancy between f_{11} and F_{11} is deemed statistically significant. The eight remaining R_{ij}'s, to be displayed later in Table 3.5, may be calculated accordingly.

Several immediate observations appear to be in order. The first is that the standardization accomplished by dividing the raw residual (i.e., $f_{ij} - F_{ij}$) by the square root of F_{ij} is intuitively pleasing. After all, to the extent to which an F_{ij} becomes large, a fixed raw residual becomes increasingly less indicative of a discrepancy between the sample result and the parameter posited by the null; therefore, the magnitude of the residual measure is adjusted downward. Of course, the converse results in a desirable upward adjustment.

A similarity in structure between the formula for standardized residuals and the formula for Pearson's χ^2 statistic prompts yet another observation. Compare Equations 3.3 and 3.16, and verify that, if the R_{ij}'s for all tabular cells are squared and then summed,

$$\chi^2 = \sum_{ij} (R_{ij})^2$$

But there is more to standardized residuals than this most interesting linkage to the χ^2. Haberman has shown that if the requisite conditions for the chi-square approximation are satisfied (conditions that were surveyed earlier in this chapter), then the probability distribution of R_{ij}'s tends toward the normal, with a mean of zero and an asymptotic variance approaching, but not quite achieving, unity. In short, if requisites are met,

$$R_{ij} \cap N(0, \sigma^2 < 1)$$

Though not distributed precisely as a unit normal, if used judiciously, the R_{ij}'s can function as standard normal deviates (i.e., z statistics), although they are apt to err in the direction of underestimating the nominal or "true" value of these deviates. Approximation to the standard normal is best when the numeric values of F_{ij}'s are relatively uniform and the number of levels comprising variables is large. All in all, standardized residuals possess great appeal. They are easily obtained with a hand calculator and are routinely given output by most computer programs.

   Freeman-Tukey Deviates. Prior to the introduction of standardized residuals, Freeman and Tukey (1950) showed that the quantity

$$\sqrt{f_{ij}} + \sqrt{f_{ij} + 1}$$

which is termed a *variance stabilizing transformation*, was distributed approximately as a normal distribution with a mean equal to $\sqrt{4F_{ij} + 1}$ and variance equal to 1. By subtracting the aforementioned mean, an approximate z statistic is obtained. Accordingly, Freeman-Tukey deviates are given by

$$D_{ij} = \sqrt{f_{ij}} + \sqrt{f_{ij} + 1} - \sqrt{4F_{ij} + 1} \tag{3.17}$$

When we compute D_{ij} on the cell in the upper left corner of Table 3.2, we get

$$D_{11} = \sqrt{67} + \sqrt{67 + 1} - \sqrt{(4)(46) + 1} = 2.83$$

Note that there is less than perfect agreement between the R_{11} and D_{11} computed on the cell in question; in other words, $R_{11} = 3.10$, whereas $D_{11} = 2.83$. However, inasmuch as these two statistics only purport to approximate standard normal deviates, and only under optimal conditions, some manner of discrepancy is to be expected. An empirical comparison between standardized residuals and Freeman-Tukey deviates has been reported by Bishop, Fienberg, and Holland (1975). When both residual measures were computed on data in a four-dimensional table following the fit of a log-linear model, the two sets of deviates were almost identical. However, as those authors point out, the extremely large size of the sample ($n = 7,653$) likely contributed in large measure to the near perfect agreement between measures.

   Let us emulate the work of Bishop et al. by comparing residuals on the much simpler data set provided by O'Connor and Sitkei (1975; see Table 3.2). R_{ij}'s and D_{ij}'s are juxtaposed in Table 3.5. It seems that, with the possible exceptions of cells $(AB)_{11}$ and $(AB)_{13}$, agreement between corresponding measures is quite good. Agreement is particularly good for those cells with high observed and expected frequencies. Further, a consideration of both measures leaves little doubt as to the location of significant discrepancies between observed frequencies and those expected under the hypothesis of independence. Using a minimum residual distance of ± 2.00 as a rough indicator of statistical significance at the .05 level, significant departure from independence is seen in cells $(AB)_{11}$, $(AB)_{13}$,

Table 3.5
Standardized Residuals (*R*s) and Freeman-Tukey Deviates (*D*s) as Applied to the O'Connor-Sitkei Data in Table 3.3

Type of Facility	Number of Residents (*n*)					
	$n \leq 10$		$10 < n < 21$		$n \geq 21$	
	R	D	R	D	R	D
Public	3.10	2.83	−.43	−.40	−2.96	−3.38
Nonprofit	−.10	−.08	−.68	−.67	.89	.99
Private Profit	−2.43	−2.59	1.17	1.16	1.35	1.32

and $(AB)_{31}$.[4] Thus, we can now conclude with even greater confidence that the O'Connor-Sitkei data indicate that it is in publicly supported institutions, not profit-making private institutions, that small numbers of retarded residents tend to be found.

As we shall see, residual analysis can be of greater usefulness with complex tables that are analyzed using log-linear models. A residual analysis, for example, can assist in the identification of highly deviant cell frequencies which may be due to a clerical error or an anomaly in data. Moreover, a residual analysis can sometimes provide insights into reasons for the failure of a log-linear model to fit certain cells in a table, insights that can point to a previously overlooked term which, if incorporated into the model, results in good fit (see Bishop et al., 1975, 138). Finally, the formal analysis of residuals will constitute the basis for our ensuing study of CFA.

A Note on Other Follow-up Procedures

If the mode of inquiry is symmetrical, there are a number of procedures that attempt to measure the *strength of association* between variables in 2 × 2 tables. Best known is the phi coefficient, a Pearson product-moment correlation coefficient computed on two dichotomous variables (Hays, 1988, 784–86). Unfortunately, the phi coefficient is extremely sensitive to skewed marginal distributions, a limitation that phi shares with many other measures of association. To be more specific, the maximum possible numerical value of the phi coefficient is attenuated as marginal frequencies depart from an even split. An alternative measure of association for 2×2 tables is Yule's Q. Yule's Q, to be treated in the next chapter, uses what is known as the *odds ratio*, which is not adversely affected by uneven marginal distributions.

For the symmetrical analysis of tables larger than 2×2, less satisfactory measures of association have been proposed. Those most frequently used are Cramer's V and the contingency coefficient. Both measures are predicted on the χ^2 statistic, and both approach zero to the extent to which variables are independent, and, at the other extreme, approach positive unity to the extent to which a perfect association is indicated. Both measures, however, are affected by the unequal marginals in a manner similar to that of the phi coefficient. In addition, they are adversely affected when the contingency table is not square. For a detailed discussion of the merits and limitations of measures of association, the reader is referred to a monograph authored by Reynolds (1984). The brief texts by Maxwell (1961) and Everitt (1977) are also recommended.

Following up the results of an asymmetrical analysis presents a different set of problems. However, in recent years there have been advances in this area which in many ways make the follow-up process more tractable than it is for tests of association. For example, multiple comparison tests, which are somewhat analogous to those used subsequent to an ANOVA, can be applied to groups to determine the specific nature of group differences with respect to their responses to a qualitative dependent variable. These comparisons, which have been termed *focused comparisons*, will be introduced in Chapter 6.

NOTES

1. The number of degrees of freedom is equivalent to $n - 1$ because, in the execution of Equation 3.2, the sample mean $(\overline{X})$ is used as an estimator of the population mean (μ), which need not be known. Since the sample mean has been "fixed" in its role as a parameter estimate, only $n - 1$ sample values are free to vary and hence to contribute to the variance estimate.

2. The calculation of the chi-square statistic in typical one-factor situations is restrained by the fact that the sum of F_i's equals n. Consequently, if $k - 1$ expected frequencies are known, the remaining frequency can be determined. There is, however, a special case: a goodness-of-fit test for a normal population where, in addition to the above restraints, two parameters (μ and σ) have to be estimated to perform the test. For this special case, $v = k - 3$.

3. In their report, Goldsmid, Gruber, and Wilson (1977) structured a four-level Age variable, which contained an "under 30" category. However, because this latter category contained a total of only four faculty, with permission, I have taken the liberty to combine these four youngsters with members of a group ranging in age from 31 to 39 to form the "under 39" group used in the present illustration.

4. It is somewhat difficult to state an exact numerical criterion for the statistical significance of a residual because there are a number of factors to be considered that are difficult to quantify precisely. For example, since in a 3×3 table there are nine residuals, and hence nine tests, good statistical practice would have us exercise some control over the Type I error rate which escalates with successive testing. The problems associated

with simultaneous testing will be treated at greater length in the last chapter. At this point I will simply point out that both standardized and Freeman-Tukey deviates tend to be conservative approximations of standard normal deviates, reducing somewhat the need for explicit control over an escalating alpha when the number of cells in a table is not too large, and that since residuals should be viewed as suggestive indicators of departure rather than definitive tests of departure, the compromise criterion of ± 2.00 seems reasonable here.

4

Log-Linear Analysis of
Two-Dimensional Tables

Because basic principles are best illustrated initially in simple contexts, we will begin our study of log-linear modeling within the context of two-dimensional tables. The reader should be forewarned, however, that the benefits associated with log-linear methods cannot be appreciated fully within this context. In fact, if behavioral researchers worked only with two-dimensional tables, there would be little or no need for the newer methods to be introduced here, for the older methods reviewed in the previous chapter would suffice. Keep in mind, therefore, that, like earlier chapters, this chapter is also preparatory to our study of log-linear modeling, which is most useful when contingency tables are defined by more than two variables.

MAJOR OPERATIONS

The performance of a log-linear analysis is not a discrete act but rather a process, that, like common factor analysis, is part art and part science. To understand a process, it often helps to identify, in proper sequence, its constituent steps or operations. We are going to begin, therefore, with an outline of the major operations that characterize a log-linear analysis, be it a simple analysis that might be applied to a two-dimensional table or a more comprehensive log-linear analysis that might be performed on a table of higher dimensionality.

Our outline will be organized under three headings. Under the first heading we will briefly review initial steps that are common to log-linear analyses, or, for that matter, traditional analyses of two-way tables as was entertained in the previous chapter. Subsequently, the major steps that are executed during the course of a typical symmetrical log-linear analysis will be presented. Finally, the third portion of the outline will list parallel steps that are associated with a typical asymmetrical analysis.

Initial Operations

Research procedures prefatory to a log-linear analysis—which have been discussed in earlier chapters—are briefly cited below.

1. Define two or more qualitative variables and structure the constituent categories (or levels) of these variables so that they are mutually exclusive and exhaustive.

2. Determine the essential nature of the ensuing inquiry. That is, determine if the research intent is to identify relations between or among variables (i.e., symmetrical inquiry) or if the intent is to identify differences between or among groups (i.e., asymmetrical inquiry).

3. Specify the target and accessible populations. *Target population* refers to the population to which the researcher would like to be able to generalize his or her findings. The researcher often does not have complete access to the target population, however, and must therefore use a subset of the target population to construct the sampling frame. This subset of the target population, the population from which the researcher is able to draw a sample, is the accessible population. Bear in mind that the reconciliation of differences between target and accessible populations is largely a matter of logic and argument, not statistical inference.

4. Obtain a sample that is representative of the accessible population. For symmetrical inquiry, the overall sample size should be fixed and, if feasible, the sample should be drawn at random. If inquiry is asymmetrical, however, give serious thought to fixing the size of respective levels of the explanatory variable such that level sizes are equal or approximately equal.

5. Cross-classify members of the sample on the basis of the qualitative/categorical variables, being sure to observe the requisite condition of response independence. Remember that a variable consisting of levels that are repeated observations on the same subjects will likely violate the independence assumption and hence cast suspicion on the integrity of the analysis. Assuming that the condition of response independence is satisfied, observed cross-tabulations then are displayed in a contingency table of proper dimensionality.

Major Steps in Symmetrical Analyses

As will become clear, when inquiry is symmetrical, our primary objective will be to identify and then interpret the *most acceptable log-linear model*: the most parsimonious model that appears to explain observed frequencies well. To this end, we will implicitly or explicitly do the following.

1. *Model Specification.* Specify a number of log-linear models consistent with

the intent of the research. If the research is designed to investigate a limited number of a priori hypotheses, then two or three models that are consonant with these planned hypotheses will be specified. On the other hand, if the research is of an exploratory nature, it is more than likely that a wide range of models will be specified.

2. *Generation of Expected Frequencies.* For each specified model, a set of *expected* elementary cell frequencies will be generated via the method of maximum likelihood. Normally, expected cell frequencies are provided on request by computer programs that utilize iterative computational algorithms (e.g., the Deming-Stephan or the Newton-Raphson).

3. *Comparison of Expected and Observed Frequencies.* For each specified model, chi-square procedures, preferably likelihood-ratio chi-square procedures, will be used to assess agreement between the frequencies generated by the model and those actually observed. The chi-square will be used in two different ways to accomplish two somewhat different objectives. We will first assess the ability of each model to provide expected cell frequencies that approach those that are observed; that is, to assess the overall goodness-of-fit of expected frequencies relative to observed frequencies. Chi-square test statistics used to assess overall model fit will be termed *residual chi-squares.* The second use of the chi-square will be to evaluate the relative importance of specific terms in log-linear models relative to their ability to promote an overall model fit. Intramodel evaluation of individual terms will be accomplished, in part, through the use of *component* chi-square statistics.

4. *Selection of the Most Acceptable Model.* Based on a careful consideration of both substantive and statistical criteria, a log-linear model will be selected and subsequently offered as the "best" explanation of data originally observed. (Interpret the word *best* to mean "most acceptable," and not necessarily as an adjective describing a model that fits observed data precisely.) In general, the model selected as being most acceptable will contain only those terms that are substantively or statistically deemed necessary to provide an acceptable fit. It merits repeating that in a symmetrical analysis, the goal is to select the most parsimonious model that can be shown to generate expected cell frequencies that fit observed frequencies well.

5. *Model Interpretation and Follow-Up.* A translation of the contents of the selected model will lead to the advancement of omnibus or overall findings relative to the subject matter of the research. If the log-linear analysis has been performed on a table of considerable size or dimensionality, additional follow-up techniques will likely be needed to explicate the omnibus relations posited as a result of interpreting the selected model.

Readers with little or no familiarity with log-linear modeling have undoubtedly been overwhelmed by the contents and implications in the list above. Do not be discouraged. Realize that the list is meant to serve as an advance organizer, and is meant to provide a global view of the major operations that will be addressed in greater detail in the chapters to follow.

Major Steps in Asymmetrical Analyses

Let us modify the five steps associated with a symmetrical analysis so that they conform more closely to the reconstructed operations involved in the conduct of an analysis that is asymmetrical.

1. *Model Specification*. Only certain log-linear models are suitable for formal specification in the asymmetrical case. In Chapter 5 we will learn that legitimate asymmetrical models must contain certain terms that represent higher-order interactions among explanatory variables. Consequently, from a potentially large list of general log-linear models, only a subset of models will be appropriate for use in the asymmetrical case.

2. *Generation of Expected Cell Frequencies*. As before, each specified log-linear model will produce a set of expected elementary cell frequencies. In practice, expected cell frequencies will be generated by a computer-driven computational algorithm (e.g., the Deming-Stephan or the Newton-Raphson).

3. *Comparison of Expected and Observed Frequencies*. Again likelihood chi-square testing is performed; however, in comparison to symmetrical inquiry, far greater emphasis is placed on the results of tests on component chi-squares.

4. *Identification of Significant Terms*. An essential difference between the symmetrical and asymmetrical occurs at this stage. Whereas the principal approach in symmetrical investigations is model fitting, followed by model selection, in the asymmetrical, classical hypothesis-testing strategies are adopted. Briefly, component chi-squares that are linked directly to specific terms in log-linear models are tested for statistical significance in a manner analogous to the testing of sources of variance (i.e., mean squares) in the ANOVA.

5. *Interpretation and Follow-Up*. If one or more log-linear terms should be found to be statistically significant, it will be interpreted in terms of significant *effects*, namely, differences between sample groups with respect to their profiles of response over levels of the designated categorical response variable. Often, however, additional scrutiny is required to clarify the exact nature of differences between and among sample groups. This is where the contents of Chapter 6, focused comparisons, assumes relevancy.

It is obvious that to perform the first step in either a symmetrical or asymmetrical analysis, namely, the specification of relevant models, knowledge of the structure and functioning of log-linear models is needed. Let us begin, therefore, to develop this knowledge.

A FIRST LOOK AT CONTINGENCY TABLE MODELS

Be prepared to appreciate the fact that contingency table models may be expressed in either multiplicative or additive form. Even so, comparable multiplicative and additive models can be made to yield the same results. Multiplicative models possess the advantage of being more closely linked to the multiplicative concepts that inherently underlie contingency table relations. On the other hand, additive models, which are specifically called *log-linear models*, possess the advantage of being more amenable to algebraic and iterative computations. Multiplicative and log-linear models should not be viewed as being in competition, however. Because both are useful, on the pages that follow we will often find ourselves "toggling" back and forth between multiplicative models and log-linear models to illustrate distinctive points.

In a number of respects, log-linear models in particular resemble models associated with the ANOVA. Since it is assumed that the majority of readers of this text are familiar with the ANOVA, a brief review of ANOVA modeling will be provided so that in the near future we will be able to exploit the synonymity between ANOVA and log-linear models.[1]

ANOVA Models as Analogues

To begin our background discussion, the reader is asked to consider a 2 × 2 table such as that given by Table 1.1, and to assume momentarily that the four elementary cells of the table contain arithmetic *means* instead of observed cell frequencies. That is, until further notice, assume that we are working with interval (or ratio) data within the context of a 2 × 2 factorial design (with one measure per cell), instead of a fourfold contingency table, and that the *observed* cell mean situated in the ith level of Variable A and jth level of Variable B is denoted by $\overline{X}_{ij}$.

In the ANOVA, $\overline{X}_{ij}$ can be "explained" by a linear combination of population parameters in an ANOVA model of the form

$$\overline{X}_{ij} = \mu + \alpha_i + \beta_j + (\alpha\beta)_{ij} \tag{4.1}$$

The first is the parameter μ; the latter three are *effects*, namely, differences between the population means. Specifically, $\overline{X}_{ij}$ may be expressed as the sum of:

1. The grand arithmetic mean of population cell means, symbolized by μ. This parameter is a component of all cell means, and it serves as an anchor point, or point of departure, so that cell means can be described ultimately in terms of effects.

2. The *main effect* associated with the ith level of Variable A. This effect is denoted by α_i, an abbreviation for $\mu_i - \mu$, and it represents the difference between the mean belonging to the ith level of A and the grand mean. Recall that if the independent Variable A is fixed (as opposed to random), then $\Sigma\alpha_i = 0$.

3. The *main effect* associated with the jth level of Variable B, symbolized by β_j, an abbreviation for $\mu_j - \mu$. Again, if B is fixed, $\Sigma\beta_j = 0$.

4. The effect associated with a particular cell, the ijth cell, due to the *interaction* of Variables A and B. The symbol for this effect is $(\alpha\beta)_{ij}$, and is defined by the identity

$$(\alpha\beta)_{ij} = (\mu_{ij} - \mu) - \alpha_i - \beta_j$$
$$= (\mu_{ij} - \mu) - (\mu_i - \mu) - (\mu_j - \mu) \qquad (4.2)$$
$$= \mu_{ij} - \mu_i - \mu_j + \mu$$

To the extent to which an interaction between Variables A and B is present, cell means will vary consequent to correcting for (or partialing out) the influences of the two main effects. Further, if both independent variables are fixed, the interaction term is also fixed, and hence,

$$\sum_i^a \sum_j^b (\alpha\beta)_{ij} = 0$$

Inasmuch as the model displayed as Equation 4.1 explains cell means, not multiple scores nested within cells, an error term representing the difference between individual scores and the cell mean (e.g., $\epsilon_{\cdot ij}$) does not appear in the model.

Thus far, the $\overline{X}_{ij}$'s have been explained exclusively in terms of parameters. However, unless we are conducting a census, we will not know the numerical values of the parameters. We know, however, that these unknown parameters may be estimated. We know that μ can be estimated by $\overline{X}..$, the grand mean of *sample* observations; that α_i can be estimated by $(\overline{X}_{i\cdot} - \overline{X}..)$, and so forth. Therefore, by systematically substituting appropriate sample estimators for the parameters contained in Equation 4.1, and by taking the liberty of expressing estimates of abbreviated effects as arabic letters (instead of Greek characters), the following *working models* result

$$\overline{X}_{ij} = \overline{X}_{\cdot\cdot} + a_i + b_j + (ab)_{ij} \qquad (4.3)$$
$$= \overline{X}_{\cdot\cdot} + (\overline{X}_{i\cdot} - \overline{X}_{\cdot\cdot}) + (\overline{X}_{\cdot j} - \overline{X}_{\cdot\cdot}) + (\overline{X}_{ij} - \overline{X}_{i\cdot} - \overline{X}_{\cdot j} + \overline{X}_{\cdot\cdot})$$

where we note that the estimate of the main effect for the ith level of A is a_i, an abbreviation for $(\overline{X}_{i\cdot} - \overline{X}..)$; the estimate for the main effect of the jth level of B is b_j, short for $(\overline{X}_{\cdot j} - \overline{X} ..)$; and the estimate of interaction is $(ab)_{ij}$, which, in extended form, is $(\overline{X}_{ij} - \overline{X}_{i\cdot} - \overline{X}_{\cdot j} + \overline{X}..)$.

Now if, in fact, we were to perform an ANOVA, we would be able to determine if the main effects for Variables A and B are statistically significant. We would obtain variance estimates (i.e., mean squares) for each variable and for the interaction between Variables A and B. Then, F tests on main effects for Variables A and B would be performed where the variance estimate for interaction (mean square for interaction) would serve as the *error term* in the denominator of the F ratio.[2] Tests of significance on the main effects of Variables A and B are available because we are willing to assume that one of the terms in the model, the interaction term, constitutes a reasonable estimate of sampling error. What would we do, however, if we did not possess a reasonable estimate of sampling error (if none of the terms in our model could serve as an error term against which to assess differences beyond chance)?

If an error term were not available, we could pursue an alternative strategy that involves the successive evaluation of models to determine which model contributes most to an explanation of observed means. Most likely, we would begin by assessing how well the grand mean (i.e., $\overline{X}..$) serves as an explanation of observed cell means. In effect, we would be working with a simple model that employs only the grand mean to represent, or estimate, observed cell means. The model in question is

$$\hat{\overline{X}}_{ij} = \overline{X}_{..} \tag{4.4}$$

where $\hat{\overline{X}}_{ij}$ denotes cell means furnished. If it should happen that only minuscule differences are seen between the means produced by the model and the means actually observed; that is, if the means furnished by Model 4.4 appear to fit observed cell frequencies well, then additional model fitting will not be needed and we will conclude that neither main effects nor interaction effects are present. If, however, noticeable differences are seen between the $\overline{X}..$'s and the $\overline{X}_{ij}$'s, then an additional term, or terms, should be entered into the model.

Assuming that Model 4.4 does not provide a good fit, a reasonable next step would be to evaluate the ability of the following model to explain observed cell means.

$$\hat{\overline{X}}_{ij} = \overline{X}_{..} + a_i \tag{4.5}$$

Be sure to realize that in Model 4.5 we will offer $\overline{X}_{1.}$ as a description of all cell means located in the first level of Variable A, and $\overline{X}_{2.}$ as a description of all means observed in the second level of Variable A. What would we conclude if the means given by Model 4.5 offered little or no improvement over the fit provided by Model 4.4? Under these circumstances, would we not conclude that main effects for Variable A are *not* present. On the other hand, if the means given by Model 4.5 should happen to fit all observed cell means exceedingly well—so well that further assessment does not appear warranted—then main effects for Variable A are indicated and the assessment process is terminated. If the means of Model 4.5 contribute markedly to an improved explanation of observed cell frequencies but considerable differences between expected and observed means remain, main effects for Variable A are indicated but the investigation should continue to see if remaining differences can be explained by terms that have yet to be incorporated in the model.

Let us assume that the expected cell frequencies given by Model 4.5 do not fit observed means sufficiently well and we are therefore encouraged to evaluate a model that uses both the overall means observed for Variable A and the overall means observed for Variable B, namely,

$$\hat{\overline{X}}_{ij} = \overline{X}_{..} + a_i + b_j \tag{4.6}$$

We deduce that to the extent to which the addition of the b_j term in Model 4.6 contributes to our ability to explain observed cell means, main effects associated with Variable B are indicated.

Finally, if Model 4.6 is unable to generate expected cell means that closely approximate those that have been observed, there is little recourse but to adopt a model that contains all possible terms,

$$\hat{\overline{X}}_{ij} = \overline{X}_{..} + a_i + b_j + (ab)_{ij} \tag{4.7}$$

Model 4.7 will give expected cell means that are identical to observed cell means. Moreover, the adoption of Model 4.7 means that the interaction term is needed to explain observed cell means; it means that Variable A interacts with Variable B.

Having concluded our review of ANOVA models and the brief presentation of an alternative strategy, bear in mind that the latter was offered as an alternative to formal testing in the ANOVA only when the identification of an error term to serve as a denominator in a F test cannot be found. It must be admitted, however, that rarely would we have to resort to such a strategy when performing ANOVAs because in almost all situations some manner of error term can be found to take full advantage of the F test. As the reader probably suspected, the strategy was not presented for serious consideration with the ANOVA, but rather, for imminent consideration with contingency table models, models that attempt to explain cell frequencies, and not cell means.

Simply put, contingency table models do not possess terms that can be used as indicators of sampling error. Within the pale of a given model, therefore, it will not be possible to compare principal terms to an error term to determine if principal terms embody effects (or relations) that exceed chance expectation. To evaluate whether all terms in a contingency table model are important (whether all terms are representing relations or effects that exceed chance expectation), a strategy of differential model specification and evaluation, similar to the strategy outlined above, will be implemented. Of course, during implementation, more rigorous criteria will be used to determine if a model, or individual terms within a model, contribute significantly to the explanation of observed cell frequencies.

We are now ready to consider models designed specifically to explain elementary cell frequencies that appear in a contingency table. Remember that these models share many features with ANOVA models and that they may be structured as either multiplicative models or log-linear models. Since models cast in the multiplicative are more compatible with the structure of hypotheses about qualitative data, we turn to these models first.

Multiplicative Cell Frequency Models

Multiplicative models contain factors, not terms. They yield products, not sums. Aside from basic probability theory, most behavioral researchers are not used to working with multiplicative models and therefore are likely to feel ill at ease on first exposure to these strange intellectual vehicles. Experience has shown, however, that with a little practice, multiplicative models will not only become vehicles of comfort, they will probably be preferred when working with contingency tables.

The Mutual Equiprobability Model. Turning first to the cell-frequency model that parallels the ANOVA working model of Equation 4.4, we have the single-parameter model

$$F_{ij} = \hat{\tau} \tag{4.8}$$

Interpret this model to mean that elementary cell frequencies given by this model are determined by only the parameter estimator $\hat{\tau}$ (Greek tau). The tau parameter is the multiplicative counterpart to μ, the grand arithmetic mean in ANOVA models. Specifically, the estimate of tau in Equation 4.8 is a *geometric* mean. As we will repeatedly see, it will turn out to be the grand geometric mean of the expected cell frequencies given by this model, and, for that matter, the geometric mean of expected cell frequencies generated by succeeding models.

Before proceeding, we pause to define and illustrate the geometric mean. Suppose that we had four scores (i.e., X_i's) with values of 33, 7, 37, and 23. Since $n = 4$ here, the arithmetic mean is $\overline{X} = \sum X_i/n = 100/4 = 25$. The geometric mean, however, is the nth root of the *product* of the four scores. That is,

$$\overline{G} = \left(\prod_i^n X_i \right)^{1/n} \tag{4.9}$$

where $\overline{G}$ is used as a convenient symbol to denote the geometric mean. Thus, for the specified values in question,

$$\overline{G} = \left(\prod_{i=1}^4 X_i \right)^{1/4}$$
$$= (33 \cdot 7 \cdot 37 \cdot 23)^{1/4}$$
$$= (196,581)^{1/4}$$
$$= 21.0565$$

Like μ, its counterpart in the ANOVA, the grand geometric mean will be the first factor in more complete models that follow, and it will serve as the anchor point about which subsequent factors are defined.

Returning to Model 4.8, by now it should be clear that the function to be performed by this model is the generation of an expected cell frequency for each cell of a contingency table. To appreciate the manner in which this is done, consider the following simple exercise. Suppose that you were asked to estimate the numerical values of four scores, but all you knew about the scores was that they summed to 100. Most likely you would estimate each of the scores to be 25, the arithmetic mean of the scores. Incidentally, these also happen to be the least-squares estimates, for in the long run, the sum of squared differences between actual values and estimated values will be a minima. Now let us modify the exercise slightly to state that the request is to estimate cell frequencies (not scores) in a two-dimensional or $a \times b$ table—more specifically, a fourfold or 2×2 table such as is depicted in Table 1.1. Assume that all that is known is that the sum of estimated frequencies is to be 100 (i.e., $n = 100$). Intuitively, we would again distribute the 100 cases such that 25 would be given to each of the four cells. When reconstructed, the general formulation that we just used to generate expected cell frequencies was

$$F_{ij} = n/ab \qquad\qquad\qquad (4.10)$$

which, when applied to the current exercise, is

$$F_{ij} = 100/4 = 25$$

In sum, we would deem that outcomes most likely in the long run are best obtained by distributing the n cases uniformly among the ab cells, such that, in this case, each cell contains 25 subjects. Essentially we have just done the work of Model 4.8. Using only one observed datum, total sample size, our intuitively based expectancies of 25 cases per cell were also maximum likelihood (ML) expectancies (see Chapter 2).[3]

Having generated the four F_{ij}'s, the tau parameter in Model 4.8 can be more readily defined. Specifically, $\hat{\tau}$ is the geometric mean of expected elementary cell frequencies produced by the model. In a more general sense, expected cell frequencies provided by Model 4.8 are given by

$$
\begin{aligned}
F_{ij} = \hat{\tau} = \overline{G} &= \prod_{ij}^{ab}\left(\sum_i^a \sum_j^b f_{ij}/ab\right)^{1/ab} \\
&= [(n/ab)]^{1/ab} \\
&= n/ab
\end{aligned} \qquad (4.11)
$$

Recapping our work to this point, the application of Model 4.8 to the data in Table 1.1 gives

$$F_{ij} = \prod_{ij}^{4} (100/4)^{1/4}$$
$$= [(100/4)^4]^{1/4}$$
$$= 100/4 = 25$$

a solution that we now recognize as the geometric mean of expected cell frequencies given by the model in question.

At this point the reader is asked to reflect on the earlier discussion of ANOVA model analogues, and specifically on the strategy of evaluating different models relative to their ability to fit observed data. Upon completion of this request, a question that is sure to arise is how well the F_{ij}'s produced by Model 4.8 fit observed cell frequencies, for example, the f_{ij}'s reported in Table 1.1. A direct answer to this question will not be given at this time. Shortly, however, we will perform a chi-square goodness-of-fit test between these expected and observed frequencies to determine adequacy of fit, and should it turn out that the fit is "good" (which is not going to be the case), Model 4.8 would be adopted as the best explanation for observed data.

If Model 4.8 were to be adopted, what kinds of conclusions could be advanced? From a symmetrical perspective, it is clear that we could conclude that there is no association between Variables A (Gender) and B (Attitude). Variables A and B are not only independent, since there are 25 fitted cases in each cell, this outcome can be characterized as *mutual equiprobability*, meaning that every sample subject has an equal probability of being assigned to any of the four cells in the table—a probability of .25 in this case. From an asymmetrical perspective, with Variable A as the explanatory variable, not only are there no differences between females and males relative to their proportional response to respective categories of Variable B, we can also say that their responses are equiprobable (i.e., distributed evenly) over categories of the response variable. Thus, should this model be selected for interpretation, it follows that we would either conclude that Variables A and B are clearly independent, or that there are no differences between females and males with respect to their attitudes concerning the anti-abortion amendment. For these reasons, single-parameter models will be called models of equiprobability from a symmetric perspective, or completely null models if the analysis is asymmetrical.

The Conditional Equiprobability Model. Consider next the multiplicative version of Model 4.5, which is

$$F_{ij} = \hat{\tau}\, \hat{\tau}_i^a \tag{4.12}$$

Before defining the two factors in this model, let us establish three requisite understandings.

First, whereas the previous model used only n to produce F_{ij}'s, this model uses $[A]$, the main marginal frequencies observed for Variable A. (Note that in Table 1.1, $[A]$ consists of $f_1^a = 40$ and $f_2^a = 60$.) As a rule, as models incorporate more factors (or terms), correspondingly more observed data is used to estimate model parameters. Second, when the frequencies in [A] are transformed into proportions ($p_1^a = .40$ and $p_2^a = .60$), the sample proportions are ML estimates of respective population proportions. Finally, the use of p_i^a's as estimators of P_i^a's is the only constraint that Model 4.12 imposes on the data. Therefore, given that $p_1^a = .40$ and $p_2^a = .60$, maximum-likelihood thinking holds that *all remaining cell entries are equiprobable*. Hence, the F_{ij}'s produced by Model 4.12 are:

	B_1	B_2	[A]
A_1	20	20	40
A_2	30	30	60

We now define the estimators appearing in Equation 4.12. The first parameter on the right represents the geometric mean of cell frequencies fitted by the model. More precisely,

$$\hat{\tau} = \overline{G} = \left(\prod_{ij}^{ab} F_{ij} \right)^{1/ab}$$
$$= (20 \cdot 20 \cdot 30 \cdot 30)^{1/4}$$
$$= (360{,}000)^{1/4}$$
$$= 24.4951$$

The second parameter estimate acknowledges main-marginal differences in [A]. In general, the estimate associated with the ith category of Variable A may be defined by

$$\hat{\tau} = \overline{G}_i^a / \overline{G} \tag{4.13}$$

where $\overline{G}_i^a$ is the geometric mean of all fitted cell frequencies appearing in the ith level of A. When $a = 2$, as it does for the current example, $\hat{\tau}_i^a$ represents two specific estimates, namely $\hat{\tau}_1^a$ and $\hat{\tau}_2^a$. When applied to a specific level of Variable A, say A_1, $\hat{\tau}_1^a$ is

$$\hat{\tau}_1^a = \frac{\overline{G}_1^a}{\overline{G}} = \frac{\left(\prod_{j=1}^{b} F_{ij} \right)^{1/b}}{\overline{G}}$$
$$= (20 \cdot 20)^{1/2}/24.4951$$
$$= 20/24.4951$$
$$= .8165$$

The second specific parameter estimate is

$$\hat{\tau}_2^a = \overline{G}_2^a/\overline{G}$$
$$= (30 \cdot 30)^{1/2}/24.4951$$
$$= 1.2247$$

Incidentally, it was not necessary to directly calculate the second specific parameter because the product of specific parameters in multiplicative contingency table models equals unity. That is,

$$\prod_i^a \hat{\tau}_i^a = 1.00$$

Exploiting this fact, $\hat{\tau}_2^a$ is easily obtained by taking the reciprocal of $\hat{\tau}_1^a$, as indicated below.

$$\hat{\tau}_2^a = 1/\hat{\tau}_1^a$$
$$= 1/.8165$$
$$= 1.2247$$

Pause to note that

$$\prod_i^a \hat{\tau}_i^a = (.8165)(1.2247)$$
$$= 1.00$$

Some readers may be experiencing difficulty in grasping the underlying meaning of the factors contained in the model. However, when we convert these multiplicative models to linear models, these factors will be shown to be analogous in meaning to their corresponding members in ANOVA models.

Since we have determined the numerical values of parameter estimates for Model 4.12 as they apply to data in Table 1.1, as an exercise let us use this acquired knowledge to generate at least one expected cell frequency in this table, say F_{11}. Substituting known values into the equation for Model 4.12, gives

$$F_{11} = \hat{\tau} \, \hat{\tau}_1^a$$
$$= (24.4951)(.8165)$$
$$= 20.0002$$

where a slight discrepancy is seen due to rounding error. Remaining frequencies fitted by this model can be generated by similar methods, and, as expected, they turn out to be those that we intuitively advanced and that are shown in the unnumbered table presented above.

Eventually, we will want to determine if the F_{ij}'s fitted by Model 4.12 constitute an "acceptable" fit. If they do (they will not) then Model 4.12 would be adopted and interpreted. Should this model be adopted, *conditional equiprobability* will be the omnibus conclusion that will be advanced. That is, if an adjustment is made for the inequalities in the marginals for Variable A, then both females and males in the sample have an equal probability (.50) of being placed in either the first or second categories of Variable B. To illustrate, suppose we adjust for unequal gender representation by regarding each gender group as an intact entity and examine not frequencies but rather proportional response *within* levels of A. To do this, set $p_1^a = 1.00$ and $p_2^a = 1.00$. Transforming the fitted frequencies *within* levels of A to proportions would result in $\hat{P}_{11} = .50$, $\hat{P}_{12} = .50$, $\hat{P}_{21} = .50$, and $\hat{P}_{22} = .50$. From a symmetrical perspective, the outcome indicated above represents a special case of independence between Variables A and B. By the same token, if the inquiry is asymmetrical, it is clear that females and males do not differ in response to Variable B; hence, the null hypothesis of no main effects due to gender should be retained.

The Mutual Independence Model. Consider next a model that fits both [A] and [B] and that is structurally analogous to the ANOVA Model 4.6.

$$F_{ij} = \hat{\tau} \, \hat{\tau}_i^a \, \hat{\tau}_j^b \qquad\qquad (4.14)$$

Looking ahead, should observed data in Table 1.1 turn out to be most consistent with this model, the two principal hypotheses tested by traditional chi-square procedures would be retained. That is, if the analysis were symmetrical, Variables A and B would be regarded as being independent; if the analysis were asymmetrical, the hypothesis of homogeneity of response would be retained.

To see why this is so, we use Model 4.14 to generate F_{ij}'s for our working example. As noted, this model employs only knowledge of [A] and [B]. In the example, [A] contains $f_1^a = 40$ and $f_2^a = 60$, and [B] is $f_1^b = 70$ and $f_2^b = 30$. Thus, with knowledge of only the observed marginals (marginals that can be readily converted into proportions and hence serve as ML estimates of respective population proportions), the probability that a member of the sample will be jointly classified in the ijth cell is

$$\hat{P}_{ij} = p_i^a \, p_j^b$$

which we recognize as a restatement of Equation 3.6.

Recall that Equation 3.6 is the mathematical definition of response independence in two-way tables. Clearly, independence is inherently a multiplicative concept, and hence is an argument in favor of working with models that are multiplicative in nature. For data at hand, F_{ij}'s are produced by Equation 3.6 or its equivalent, Equation 3.7, with the following result:

	B_1	B_2	[A]
A_1	28	12	40
A_2	42	18	60
[B]	70	30	100

If the reader has any doubt as to how these values were obtained, a review of the discussions in Chapter 3 associated with Equations 3.5, 3.6, and 3.7 is recommended.

Having used Model 4.14 to fit a set of F_{ij}'s, let us examine more closely the parameter estimates in the model. The first tau is the geometric mean of F_{ij}'s produced by the model.

$$\hat{\tau} = \overline{G}$$
$$= (28 \cdot 12 \cdot 42 \cdot 18)^{1/4}$$
$$= 22.4502$$

The estimate of the *marginal effect* associated with the first level of Variable A is:

$$\hat{\tau}_1^a = \overline{G}_1^a/\overline{G}$$
$$= (28 \cdot 12)^{1/2}/22.4502$$
$$= 18.3303/22.4502$$
$$= .8165$$

Hence, the marginal effect for the second level of A is

$$\hat{\tau}_1^a = \overline{G}_2^a/\overline{G}$$
$$= 1/\hat{\tau}_1^a$$
$$= 1/.8165$$
$$= 1.2247$$

The marginal effects for Variable B are obtained by parallel calculations:

$$\hat{\tau}_1^b = \overline{G}_1^b/\overline{G}$$
$$= (28.42)^{1/2}/22.4502$$
$$= 1.5275$$

$$\hat{\tau}_2^b = \overline{G}_2^b/\overline{G}$$
$$= 1/\hat{\tau}_1^b$$
$$= .6547$$

Note that unity is the product of the effects for both A and B.

Before considering the next model, let us put into perspective our work to this point. The three models that we have seen are relatively simple, and therefore we have been able to use elementary probability theory to advance the F_{ij}'s associated with each. Irrespective of the method used to obtain F_{ij}'s, once they are obtained, the effect parameters in the model can be determined by the formulas that we have been using. Moreover, we should be able to use the effect parameters to fit a frequency in any cell of the table. For example, the F_{21} given by Model 4.14 is

$$F_{21} = \hat{\tau} \, \hat{\tau}_2^a \, \hat{\tau}_1^b$$
$$= (22.4502)(1.2247)(1.5275)$$
$$= 42.0017$$

where it appears that we have an accumulated error of .0017 due to rounding. Finally, realize that the F_{ij}'s given by Equation 4.14 will be compared eventually to the f_{ij}'s contained in Table 1.1, and should the F_{ij}'s constitute an acceptable fit, one of two omnibus deductions will be made: either (1) Variables A and B will be considered mutually independent or (2) there is no evidence of a significant main effect in proportional response to Variable B due to Variable A.

The Saturated Model. The multiplicative analogue to the complete ANOVA model, Model 4.7, is termed the *saturated model*. This model is written as

$$F_{ij} = \hat{\tau} \, \hat{\tau}_i^a \, \hat{\tau}_j^b \, \hat{\tau}_{ij}^{ab} \tag{4.15}$$

Like Model 4.7, but unlike previous multiplicative models, the saturated model makes use of all observed tabular data. Therefore, the elementary cell frequencies produced by this model are identical to f_{ij}'s; that is, for this model, $F_{ij} = f_{ij}$ for all values of i and j, producing a perfect fit. Since no further work is needed to generate F_{ij}'s, we proceed immediately to an explanation of model parameters.

As expected, the first factor, $\hat{\tau}$, is the geometric mean of f_{ij}'s in Table 1.1:

$$\hat{\tau} = \overline{G}$$
$$= (33 \cdot 7 \cdot 37 \cdot 23)^{1/4}$$
$$= 21.0563$$

The marginal effects for Variable A are

$$\hat{\tau}_1^a = \overline{G}_1^a / \overline{G}$$
$$= (33 \cdot 7)^{1/2} / 21.0563$$
$$= .7218$$

$$\hat{\tau}_2^a = 1.3854$$

Similarly, effects for B are

$\hat{\tau}_1^b = \overline{G}_1^b/\overline{G}$
   $= (33 \cdot 37)^{1/2}/21.0567$
   $= 1.6595$

$\hat{\tau}_2^b = .6026$

This brings us to the third and new factor in the model, a factor that corresponds to first-order interaction in conventional ANOVA models. For now, we simply point out that interaction effects for cells of a contingency table may be estimated by

$$\hat{\tau}_{ij}^{ab} = f_{ij}/(\hat{\tau} \ \hat{\tau}_i^a \ \hat{\tau}_j^b) \tag{4.16}$$

To illustrate, we calculate the interaction effect for the cell in the first levels of Variables A and B.

$\hat{\tau}_{11}^{ab} = 33/[(21.0563)(.7218)(1.6595)]$
   $= 33/25.2218$
   $= 1.3084$

The remaining three effects need not be calculated directly, for, as in the case of a 2×2 ANOVA, once the value of one effect is known, the remaining three are determined. They are determined because the marginal products of multiplicative interaction effects turn out to be unity. That is, for all values of i,

$$\prod_j^b \hat{\tau}_{ij}^{ab} = 1.00$$

and for all values of j,

$$\prod_i^a \hat{\tau}_{ij}^{ab} = 1.00$$

Consequently, for fourfold tables, it follows that

$$\hat{\tau}_{11}^{ab} = \hat{\tau}_{22}^{ab}$$

$$\hat{\tau}_{12}^{ab} = \hat{\tau}_{21}^{ab} = 1/\hat{\tau}_{11}^{ab} = 1/\hat{\tau}_{22}^{ab}$$

Hence, for the working example, $\hat{\tau}_{11}^{ab} = \hat{\tau}_{22}^{ab} = 1.3084$ and $\hat{\tau}_{12}^{ab} = \hat{\tau}_{21}^{ab} = .7643$. A summary of our work with these interaction effects is displayed below:

	B_1	B_2	Marginal Products
A_1	1.3084	.7643	1.0000
A_2	.7643	1.3084	1.0000
Marginal Products	1.0000	1.0000	1.0000

Finally, since all parameter estimates for the saturated model have been calculated, as an exercise the reader is encouraged to use the model to produce the four expected cell frequencies. If done correctly, the F_{ij}'s will be equivalent to the f_{ij}'s appearing in Table 1.1.

A few words should be said about the consequences of selecting the saturated model as the best representation of the resultant data. Since interaction effects are, in effect, deviations from mutual independence, the adoption of this model indicates either the rejection of the independence hypothesis or the rejection of the hypothesis of homogeneity of proportional response. Thus, if the inquiry is symmetrical, acceptance of Model 4.15 means that Variables A and B are associated; if the inquiry is asymmetrical, main effects exist for levels of the explanatory variable—females and males do not respond similarly on the response variable.

Finally, it is not too early to begin to compare the methods just advanced to the traditional chi-square approach reviewed in Chapter 3. As will become increasingly clear, in the traditional approach, Models 4.14 and 4.15 are implicitly evaluated. In the traditional approach, when the conventional chi-square statistic is computed, Model 4.14—the independence or homogeneity of proportions model—is evaluated, and if the statistic is found to be significant, in effect, Model 4.14 is deemed unacceptable and the explanation offered by the saturated model, Model 4.15, is then accepted. Acceptance of the saturated model, of course, prompts the conclusion that the variables are associated, and so forth. The methods that we will continue to explore in this chapter will make more explicit what is implicit in the traditional approach.

Log-Linear Cell Frequency Models

Linear models that directly correspond to the multiplicative models of the previous section may also be written to explain cell frequencies in contingency tables. The linear models are simply the multiplicative models that become linear in their logarithms. Linearity is a ubiquity in the behavioral sciences. It is not surprising, therefore, that most behavioral researchers prefer to think and work with linear phenomena, particularly since the majority of our statistical techniques and most of our computer software are based on linear solutions. Thus, despite my own penchant for the multiplicative models of the last section, it must be conceded that by casting our models in the form of linear combinations, a number of advantages will be accrued.

To transform a multiplicative model into the linear, the numerical value of each constituent factor is expressed in terms of its natural logarithm (ln), a logarithm to the base e. (This explains the term *log-linear* as a description of these models.) Accordingly, instead of multiplying parameter estimates to obtain a product, log estimates will be placed in linear combination, yielding a sum. Moreover, the operations of raising a factor to a specified power or exponent, or of extracting from a factor a specified root, will be replaced by the corresponding operations of multiplication and division.

By way of illustration, consider the single-parameter model presented as Equation 4.8. Upon transformation, the log-linear version is

$$\ln F_{ij} = \hat{\lambda} \tag{4.17}$$

The right-hand term is the natural log of $\hat{\tau}$, namely, $\hat{\lambda} = \ln \hat{\tau}$. It follows that cell frequencies fitted by this model will also be expressed in terms of logs. (This means that actual cell frequencies will be respective antilogarithms, numbers corresponding to given logarithms.) Hence, for the example where the $\hat{\tau}$ of Model 4.8 was found to be equal to 25, the equivalent log-linear model is

$$\ln F_{ij} = \hat{\lambda} = \ln \hat{\tau} = \ln (25) = 3.2189$$

This model fits each cell with a value of 3.2189, the antilog of which is 25, and thus exhibits a condition that we earlier called mutual equiprobability.

If the three remaining multiplicative models—Models 4.12, 4.14, and 4.15—are each subjected to a logarithmic transformation, the following log-linear models are obtained:

$$\ln F_{ij} = \hat{\lambda} + \hat{\lambda}_i^a \tag{4.18}$$

$$\ln F_{ij} = \hat{\lambda} + \hat{\lambda}_i^a \hat{\lambda}_j^b \tag{4.19}$$

$$\ln F_{ij} = \hat{\lambda} + \hat{\lambda}_i^a \hat{\lambda}_j^b + \hat{\lambda}_{ij}^{ab} \tag{4.20}$$

The saturated model, Model 4.20, provides us with an opportunity to explore further the meaning of model parameters and effects. Recall that in the multiplicative, the following expression was used to obtain $\hat{\tau}_i^a$:

$$\hat{\tau}_i^a = \overline{G}_i^a/\overline{G}$$

Effecting a logarithmic transformation on the above results in

$$\hat{\lambda}_i^a = \ln \hat{\tau}_i^a$$
$$= \ln \overline{G}_i^a - \ln \overline{G}$$

Now, recall that in the ANOVA, the corresponding effect is

$$\hat{\alpha}_i = \hat{\mu}_i - \hat{\mu}$$
$$= \overline{X}_{i.} - \overline{X}_{..}$$

Hence, we may infer (correctly so) that the estimator $\hat{\lambda}_i^a$ is analogous to its corresponding member in conventional ANOVA models, notwithstanding the fact that these effects are expressed on different scales.

Let us see if this correspondence also holds for interaction effects. In the multiplicative an unspecified interaction effect was given by Equation 4.16,

$$\hat{\tau}_{ij}^{ab} = f_{ij}/(\hat{\tau} \; \hat{\tau}_i^a \; \hat{\tau}_j^b)$$

In the log-linear, an unspecified interaction effect is

$$\hat{\lambda}_{ij}^{ab} = \ln \hat{\tau}_{ij}^{ab} = \ln f_{ij} - (\ln \hat{\tau} + \ln \hat{\tau}_i^a + \ln \hat{\tau}_j^b)$$
$$= (\ln f_{ij} - \ln \overline{G}) - \hat{\lambda}_i^a - \hat{\lambda}_j^b \qquad (4.21)$$
$$= \ln f_{ij} - \ln \overline{G}_i^a - \ln \overline{G}_j^b + \ln \overline{G}$$

Now, recall that in the ANOVA, the interaction effect linked to the ijth cell may be defined as the difference between the μ_{ij} and μ, subsequent to partialing out appropriate main effects. That is, first-order interaction in the ANOVA is commonly defined as

$$(\hat{\alpha}\hat{\beta})_{ij} = (\hat{\mu}_{ij} - \hat{\mu}) - \hat{\alpha}_i - \hat{\beta}_j$$
$$= \hat{\mu}_{ij} - \hat{\mu}_i - \hat{\mu}_j + \hat{\mu}$$

Clearly, a comparison of the lines above with the lines of Equation 4.21 shows that aside from differences in underlying scales—logarithmic vs. equal-interval—effect parameters in log-linear models may be viewed, and hence interpreted, in a manner consonant with effects in conventional ANOVA models. Although alternative views and interpretations exist (e.g., an odds ratio interpretation), and these alternative views will be touched on in ensuing chapters, it is my belief that consciously exploiting the many synonymous features of the ANOVA and the log-linear has great merit, particularly for researchers in areas where historically the ANOVA has become well established.

Wrapping Up Some Loose Ends

In an earlier section I said that the first major operation peculiar to log-linear analysis was the specification of contingency table models. In this section, we surveyed models for two-dimensional tables. We began with a model that contained only one parameter estimator and, in a forward manner, added estimators so that each new model contained *all* the parameter estimates of the previous models plus the newly incorporated term (or factor). Normally, in the absence of strong a priori theory, the specification of models in this forward-addition manner is most defensible, for this manner of specification minimizes the chances of overlooking important effects and maximizes the ease of computing expected cell frequencies.

A summary of multiplicative models for two-dimensional tables is contained in Table 4.1. (Space limitations discourage a presentation in this table of corresponding log-linear models.) For future reference, be sure to notice that the models of Table 4.1 have been renumbered 1 through 4, a numbering system that conveniently reflects the number of *general* (not basic) parameters in the models.[4] Note too that carets (^) no longer appear over terms in the models because it is now well understood that all model terms are estimators of parameters and not parameters per se. Finally, observe that verbal descriptions of hypotheses associated with each model for both a symmetrical and an asymmetrical analysis are contained in Table 4.1.

Before we discuss the next operation, that of determining how well models are able to explain observed data, a number of important differences between conventional ANOVA models and contingency models will be reiterated. An obvious difference is that ANOVA models attempt to explain a dependent variable that is measured on either an interval or a ratio scale, whereas contingency table models describe cell counts or frequencies. Another obvious difference is that ANOVA models use all observed data to estimate parameter effects, whereas contingency table models use progressively more observed data as terms are added to them. Only the saturated model, Model 4 in Table 4.1, makes use of all data by fitting elementary cells in the [AB] configuration. But the most striking difference is seen in the way that parameter estimates or terms are assessed.

In the ANOVA, for example, a model is adopted and, during the analysis, an estimate of error variability (i.e., mean square error) is obtained which makes it possible to test each parameter estimate directly for statistical significance. Testing takes place *within* the system of analysis prescribed by the model. Estimates that do not achieve significance are excluded from the model only in the sense that they are generally ignored in subsequent substantive conclusions. A much different strategy, however, is employed in log-linear work because log-linear models do not have built-in error terms. It is not possible, therefore, to obtain estimates of error variability within the structure of the models per se. To overcome this apparent liability, a series of models is specified, with each

Table 4.1
Hierarchical Multiplicative Models for Two-Dimensional Tables

Model Number	Models	Fitted Marginals	Associated Omnibus Hypotheses	
			Symmetrical	Asymmetrical
(1)	$F_{ij} = \tau$	n	Equiprobability	
(2)	$F_{ij} = \tau\tau_i^a$	[A]	Conditional Equiprobability	
(3)	$F_{ij} = \tau\tau_i^a\tau_j^b$	[A], [B]	Mutual Independence	Null
(4)	$F_{ij} = \tau\tau_i^a\tau_j^b\tau_{ij}^{ab}$	[AB]	Nonindependence	Main effects for A

Note: For the asymmetrical case, it is assumed that Variable *B* is the response or logit variable. For this case, Models 1 and 2 are not relevant logit models.

model containing a different set of parameter estimates. A judgement as to which estimates are important is made by determining which model in the series gives F_{ij}'s that fit the observed data reasonably well.

When the analysis is symmetrical, the task becomes one of evaluating a number of competing models in an effort to identify the most parsimonious model that generates expected cell frequencies that fit observed cell frequencies well. When the analysis is asymmetrical, the focus will shift to individual terms within models where the task will become one of testing terms for statistical significance. In any event, before we can discuss these matters in greater depth, the roles played by the chi-square in symmetrical and asymmetrical analysis need to be surveyed.

COMPARING OBSERVED AND EXPECTED FREQUENCIES

Since the four models in Table 4.1 give different expected elementary cell frequencies, chi-square procedures (reviewed in Chapter 3) can be used to determine the extent to which expected frequencies correspond to observed frequencies. Chi-square procedures will be applied in two different ways. The first is a straightforward application of either Pearson's χ^2 statistic (Equation 3.3), the likelihood-ratio L^2 statistic (Equation 3.11), or both, to test for overall agreement between model F_{ij}'s and observed f_{ij}'s. This first use of the chi-square is often simply referred to as *goodness-of-fit*, although some writers refer to this application as *residual* chi-square testing. For the most part, the adjective residual will be used throughout this text to denote chi-square tests of overall agreement. The second use of the chi-square is peculiar to the likelihood-ratio (L^2) statistic (see Chapter 3). Because the likelihood-ratio L^2 possesses additive properties, the arithmetic difference between the residual L^2 statistics of two log-linear models can be obtained. The resultant difference between two residual chi-squares is called a *component* chi-square, and it can be subjected to statistical test. Component chi-square values can be used to great advantage to assess the relative importance of specific terms that are contained within a model, and, as briefly noted, they play a central role in asymmetrical analyses.

Residual Chi-Square Comparisons

The hypothetical data in Table 1.1 will again be used to illustrate how residual chi-squares are used to assess the extent of agreement between cell frequencies that are actually observed and those issued by a model or models. For the hypothetical data, the expected cell frequencies generated by each of the four models have been determined. Recall that Model 1, the completely null model, gave F_{ij}'s equal to 25 for all four cells; the results of Model 2 were $F_{11} = F_{12}$ = 20 and $F_{21} = F_{22} = 30$; and Model 3 yielded $F_{11} = 28$, $F_{12} = 12$, $F_{21} = $ 42, and $F_{22} = 18$. Of course, the F_{ij}'s of the saturated model, Model 4, perfectly reproduced the observed cell frequencies of Table 1.1. To make residual comparisons, we invoke Equations 3.3 and 3.11 to calculate the magnitudes of

Pearsonian and likelihood-ratio statistics, respectively. The results of these calculations for each model in Table 4.1 are summarized below:

	Residual Values	
Model	χ^2	L^2
(1)	21.44	25.68
(2)	20.17	21.65
(3)	4.96	5.19
(4)	0.00	0.00

As evidenced by its residual chi-square, the fit provided by the saturated model is perfect, namely, $L_4^2 = 0.00$. This does not necessarily mean, however, that this model will be chosen as "most acceptable" in a symmetrical analysis. Granted, observed frequencies are completely described by saturated models, but observed frequencies generally are redolent with sampling error and other complexities. Ultimately, our goal will be to try to identify and describe attributes affecting data in the fewest number of stable terms, in the simplest of structures, without distorting or sacrificing meaning. That is, our goal will be to seek parsimony of explanation; hence, we strive to choose models that contain only parameters that are essential to functional explanation. Thus, upon assessment of log-linear models, it might turn out that a model containing fewer terms (or factors) than the saturated may fit observed data almost as well. If this should be the case, because of its simplicity, it would be considered more acceptable.

Looking at the three unsaturated models above reveals that the model fit becomes increasingly less good as models contain fewer terms—as models exhibit, in effect, more terms that have been set to zero. A term that potentially could appear in a model but does not, because it has been set to zero, is said to be a *restricted* term. Understandably, the most restricted model, the completely null model, shows the poorest fit, $L_1^2 = 25.68$.

We now desire to statistically test for agreement between f_{ij}'s and the various sets of F_{ij}'s produced by the models above. First, however, the proper number of degrees of freedom must be determined for each residual chi-square test. A number of "rules of thumb" have been proposed to assist in this determination (see Goodman, 1970, 231; Fienberg, 1977, 36). Before we propose a most simple set of rules to determine the number of degrees of freedom, let us employ simple logic to discern them for residual tests in fourfold tables.

We begin by viewing the cell frequencies of the 2×2 table as a sample of observations of size four. For each model under test, we will determine the number of cell frequencies that are free to assume any numerical value, given the constraints imposed by the model in question. For example, if there were no model, there would be no constraints and the four cell frequencies would be free to assume any value. It follows, therefore, that the number of degrees of freedom (v) in this suppositional situation is four, namely, $v_0 = 4$. Not suppositional is Model 1, where F_{ij}'s have been fitted using knowledge of n. In theory, three of the cell frequencies are free to vary here; the fourth is not, for it must assume a specific value to make the sum of frequencies equal to n. Hence, the residual chi-square test for Model 1 will be made using $v_1 = 3$.

With respect to Model 2, since [A] is used to fit F_{ij}'s, cell frequencies *within* each level of Variable A must sum to an f_i^a. To comply with this, only one cell frequency within each level of A can be arbitrarily specified; consequently, $v_2 = 2$. Model 3 fits both the observed main marginals of Variables A and B. As a result, only one cell frequency can be arbitrarily assigned a value, for once this is done, the remaining three frequencies will have determined values under the constraint that levels of A sum to [A] and levels of B sum to [B]. Therefore, $v_3 = 1$. Finally, note that there are no degrees of freedom for the saturated model (i.e., $v_4 = 0$) since all elementary cell frequencies are completely determined by the observed sample outcome.

The foregoing intuitive approach for determining v can be extended to tables of greater dimensionality, though it becomes increasingly cumbrous and prone to error as the size and dimensionality of tables become large. Obviously, a rule or algorithm to assist in this determination would be desirable, and such a rule will be presented in the next chapter. For now, since the values of residual chi-square X^2 and L^2 are known, and since we also know v for each test, the probability of observing each respective test statistic can be routinely assessed. The outcome p-values associated with these tests can be found in Table 4.2.

Component Chi-Square Comparisons

In addition to the residual chi-square, a component L^2 value may be computed for all models. A component L^2 value is the difference between two residual L^2 statistics; hence, a component L^2 can be used to compare two models. For example, to compare the relative goodness-of-fit of Model 4 in relation to Model 3, a component L^2 is calculated by subtracting the residual L^2 observed for Model 4 from the residual L^2 found for Model 3. For the example, the component L^2 associated with Model 4 is

$$
\begin{aligned}
L^2_{3-4} &= L^2_3 - L^2_4 \\
&= 5.19 - 0.00 \\
&= 5.19
\end{aligned}
$$

One use of this component is to judge whether Model 3 should be chosen over Model 4. Granted, since Model 3 contains one less term than Model 4, Model 3 will probably not fit observed data as well as Model 4. But how much of a loss in ability to fit data would result from choosing Model 3 instead of Model 4? The answer, in part, is provided by L^2_{3-4}, which indicates that the adoption of Model 3 will result in an increased accumulation of 5.19 units of residual chi-square; and the greater the increase in residual chi-square, the poorer the fit. So by selecting Model 3 in favor of Model 4, one indeed sacrifices some ability to fit observed data. However, if the sacrifice is slight, the advantages of being able to advance a more parsimonious explanation—that offered by Model 3— will outweigh the slight loss of ability to fit observed data accurately. We will discuss this point at greater length in the next section. For now, we compute the remaining pairwise component L^2's. Respectively, the component L^2's for Models 3 and 2 are

$$
\begin{aligned}
L^2_{2-3} &= L^2_2 - L^2_3 \\
&= 21.65 - 5.19 \\
&= 16.46
\end{aligned}
$$

$$
\begin{aligned}
L^2_{1-2} &= L^2_1 - L^2_2 \\
&= 25.68 - 21.68 \\
&= 4.03
\end{aligned}
$$

Obviously, the greatest relative reduction in ability to fit observed elementary cells will occur should Model 2 be selected over Model 3.

Tests of Significance. Component L^2's can be subjected to tests of statistical significance. The number of degrees of freedom for a given test are given by the difference in number of degrees of freedom for respective residual chi-square tests. For example, the component chi-square for the saturated model ($L^2_{3-4} = 5.19$) is tested on a single degree of freedom since $v_3 - v_4 = 1 - 0 = 1$. The results of tests of significance on component L^2's are summarized in Table 4.2.

The Additive Properties of L^2. Additive properties of the likelihood-ratio chi-square enable us to make direct comparisons of models when they are arranged in pairs. More to the point, component L^2's permit us to assess the specific contribution made by each model parameter or term to the fit of observed data. To appreciate how this is typically done, consider the completely null model which has a residual L^2 equivalent to 25.68. Now, recall that this residual value reflects the magnitude of departure of observed f_{ij}'s about a fitted table where each cell of the fitted table contains an expected frequency of 25 (i.e., $F_{ij} = \tau = 25$). Because L^2's are additive, the residual L^2 and v for Model 1 can be partitioned into additive components as shown below:

Table 4.2
Summary of Log-Linear Analysis of Data Presented in Table 1.1

Model	Fitted Marginals	Residual L^2	df	p	Component L^2	df	p
(1)	n	25.68	3	.000			
(2)	[A]	21.65	2	.000	4.03	1	.045
(3)	[A], [B]	5.19	1	.023	16.46	1	.000
(4)	[AB]	0.00	0	1.000	5.19	1	.023

Model	Components	df
(2)	$L_{1-2} = 4.03$	$v_{1-2} = 1$
(3)	$L_{2-3} = 16.46$	$v_{2-3} = 1$
(4)	$L_{3-4} = 5.19$	$v_{1-2} = 1$
(1)	$L_1^2 = 25.68$	$v_1 = 3$

As we see, the component L^2's of Models 2, 3, and 4 sum to the residual chi-square for the completely null model, and the numbers of degrees of freedom manifest corresponding additivity.

Component L^2's enable us to identify terms in the model which, in a relative sense, appear not to be important. Relatively unimportant terms are those that contribute little to the reduction of residual chi-square. From another perspective, components enable us to identify specific terms that appear to be important: terms that have the effect of markedly improving the fit between expected and observed cell frequencies, as evidenced by prominent component values. Since this concept is often difficult to grasp initially, several concrete examples are offered.

As a starting point, consider the fit (or lack of fit) provided by the single-parameter completely null model, $L_1^2(3) = 25.68$, $p < .00001$. By adding $\hat{\tau}_i^a$ to this model, which takes into account observed differences in [A], the residual departure is reduced by 4.03 units. Moreover, as shown in Table 4.2, this reduction of the residual (or improvement of fit) is significant at the .05 level.

Let us now add $\hat{\tau}_j^b$ to the model to achieve Model 3, and a further reduction in the residuum. Notice that as a result of adding [B], we see a highly significant reduction of 16.46 units ($p < .00005$). Finally, let us contrast the residual L^2's of Models 1 and 3. The resultant component here is $L_{1-3}^2 = 25.65 - 5.19 = 20.49$, which, upon subjecting to test on two degrees of freedom (i.e., $v_{1-3} = v_1 - v_3 = 2$), is also found to be highly significant ($p < .00004$). This particular component tells us that differences are present in [A] or [B], or both. (Because of our previous work, we know that unequal distributions are present in both [A] and [B].)

In sum, the likelihood-ratio component L^2's provide us with the means to determine which specific effects, or groupings of effects, contribute significantly to the improvement of fit between expected and observed cell frequencies. This salutary feature will help us fine-tune models in symmetrical analyses and will prove to be of immense help in an asymmetrical analysis, for it will enable us to approach the analysis in a manner much like that seen in the ANOVA.

AN INITIAL DISCUSSION OF MODEL SELECTION

Our remarks in this section pertain primarily to analyses that are symmetrical and where the central achievement is the selection and subsequent interpretation of a substantively defensible log-linear model. "Unfortunately," as Fienberg has stated, "there is no all-purpose, best method of model selection" (1977, 47). Nevertheless, there is a guiding concept and there are two statistical procedures that, in the absence of strong a priori theory, generally lead to the selection of the most appropriate model. The guiding concept has been mentioned: *parsimony*.

The "law of parsimony" is fundamental to scientific inquiry. The law, in brief, holds that when confronted with a choice between competing explanations (hypotheses or theories), the best explanation is that which adequately explains existing data in the simplest terms. When applied to our work, this means that the most desirable explanation is that provided by the contingency table model that contains the fewest terms yet still fits the observed data reasonably well. To *assist* in the selection of this model, residual chi-square procedures, supplemented by component chi-squares, can be used to advantage.

Residual chi-squares are used to exclude from serious consideration unsaturated models that obviously do not fit observed data well. Referring to Table 4.2, both Models 1 and 2 can be eliminated immediately because of their highly significant L^2 values. The disposition of Model 3 depends on the level of significance that the researcher has adopted, cognizant of sample size, as the criterion for exclusion. Adoption of the .05 level, for example, would lead to the exclusion of Model 3. However, if the .01 level of significance was the criterion, Model 3 would be retained, although the fit provided by this model is suspect.

Following the use of residual chi-squares to eliminate poor-fitting models, component L^2's can be used to make determinations among remaining models. As we have learned, when hierarchical models are examined in pairs, the magnitude of the component L^2's belonging to the more complete model (i.e., the less restricted model) indicates the diminution in ability to fit observed data should the simpler model (i.e., the more restricted model) be selected. The examination usually begins with the saturated model and extends systematically until a component L^2 is observed that is decidedly statistically significant. When encountered, we proceed no further because the selection of a model with fewer terms than the model manifesting the significant component L^2 would result in a significant loss of fit.

To apply this strategy to the models of Table 4.2, we start at the bottom of the table and assess the component for the saturated model, that is, $L^2_{3-4} = 5.19$, $p < .023$. Whether we move upward to simpler, more restricted models depends on the chosen level of significance and on considerations rooted in the substance of the research problem. If the decision is to be made solely by statistical criteria and it happens that the a priori alpha level was established at .05, then L^2_{3-4} would be deemed statistically significant and the saturated model would be selected. After all, proceeding to Model 3 would result in a significant ($p < .05$) loss in ability to fit the observed data. On the other hand, if the a priori alpha level had been .01, the researcher would proceed to examine the component for Model 3. Since this component is highly significant, $L^2_{3-2}(1) = 16.46$, $p < .000$, further attempts to find a model would be terminated and Model 3 would be selected.

The reader may suspect (and correctly so) that the hypothetical data of Table 1.1 were deliberately constructed to yield an intricate result. Complex results occur frequently in log-linear work, and we should, therefore, begin to appreciate the fact that model selection is often as much an art as it is a science. Further, the failure of the working example to furnish us with a clean "textbook" result provides us with an excellent opportunity to mention briefly several additional considerations pertaining to the art of model selection.

If, as above, conventional statistical criteria do not point unequivocally to an acceptable model, it should go without saying that the researcher should select from among serious competitors the model that possesses the greatest subject-matter relevancy. Keep in mind always that statistical tests are merely tools— intended to assist, but not replace, substantive judgement. Unfortunately, it is most difficult to illustrate how substantive concerns would lead to the selection of a model for our working example because our example has no history, the data are not real, and there has been little or no intellectual investment in the problem. When dealing with an actual problem and real data, however, the researcher will find him- or herself in a better position to ensure that the statistical tail is not permitted to wag the substantive dog. Thus, we conclude our first of many discussions of model selection in the symmetrical case by reiterating the point that subject-matter relevancy is the ultimate criterion. Nevertheless, statistical considerations play an important role, and obviously the role played by residual and component chi-square testing, along with additional supplementary statistical procedures (e.g., the analysis of residuals), will be highlighted in this book.

MODEL INTERPRETATION AND FOLLOW-UP PROCEDURES

A well designed and executed log-linear analysis will prompt at least one overall or omnibus conclusion. As we know, the nature of the conclusion will depend on whether the analysis was symmetrical or asymmetrical, and on the specific log-linear model that was selected (see Table 4.1). For example, if the analysis were symmetrical and if Model 3 were chosen as most acceptable, one would conclude that independence constitutes the best explanation of Variables *A* (Gender) and *B* (Attitude) when they are considered in concert. This conclusion represents the most reasonable explanation among explanations that have been considered—the explanation most consistent with the data. Note that the conclusion is *not* a logically accepted alternative to a rejected null hypothesis. The model-fitting, model-selection approach that characterizes symmetrical inquiry often results in what appears to be the "acceptance of a null hypothesis," and thus, at first, presents intellectual problems for many classically trained researchers who have been taught to advance only those findings that emanate from clear rejection of a null hypothesis. Realize that good science is the intellectual pursuit of explanations for phenomena—it is not blind adherence to prescribed method. Following increased exposure to the model-fitting approach, it is hoped that the intellectual reservations currently held by some readers will be assuaged.

Should Model 4 be selected in a symmetrical analysis, then because $\hat{\lambda}_{ij}^{ab}$ is needed in the model to achieve reasonable fit, observed cell frequencies obviously deviate from cell frequencies expected under the hypothesis of variable independence. Consequently, Variables *A* and *B* are associated.

Should Model 3 be selected in the asymmetrical case, since Variables *A* and *B* cannot be said to be associated, it follows that there are no differences between females and males with respect to their respective responses to the abortion issue. However, if Model 4 best describes the observed data, main effects exist between levels of the explanatory variable; in other words, females and males differ in their response to the abortion-issue variable.

Interpreting omnibus findings, however, is only the first step if the saturated model is selected. Whereas the task of following up an omnibus result gleaned from a complex table can be exacting, following up initial results emanating from fourfold tables is relatively straightforward. If, for our fourfold working example, we were to accept the saturated model and thus were to conclude that the Gender and Attitude variables are related, we would be in a situation analogous to approaching a busy intersection and getting a green light to proceed with additional investigations.

If the mode of inquiry is symmetric, both variables are perceived as response variables; thus, additional investigations center not on *effects* (group differences) but rather on the *form* (or direction) and *strength* (or intensity) of the association. The form of the relationship is easily determined by the *interocular test*, a most underutilized statistical procedure. Simply put, for the working example, one visually contrasts the expected frequencies given by the saturated model (the f_{ij}'s) with the F_{ij}'s given by Model 3, the independence model. Before going any further, the reader is asked to perform this "test" on data in Table 3.2. Assuming compliance to this request, we conclude that females tended to assume a more negative posture toward the antiabortion amendment than did males; or, equally as valid, of those opposed to the amendment, females were represented to a greater degree than were males. The strength of the relationship can be assessed by *measures of association* such as a ratio of conditional odds or an adaption of this ratio known as Yule's Q.

If the mode of inquiry is asymmetric, results emanating from simple tables can be further illuminated by examining and testing relevant lambda (or tau) parameters. We will examine these parameters shortly. Explicating asymmetrical results based on more complex tables awaits Chapter 6.

Measures of Association

A most encouraging trend among behavioral researchers is the growing awareness that the "practical" significance of a relationship (or effect) is not provided by merely reporting a statistically significant test statistic with its associated p value. After all, the magnitude of a test statistic such as the L^2, and hence its p value, is, to a considerable extent, a function of sample size. In fact, to push this point to its extreme, it can be said that any null hypothesis can be statistically rejected if sample n's are sufficiently large. Consequently, subsequent to documenting a statistically significant relationship, it is desirable to assess the *intensity* of the relationship independently of sample size. A number of measures of association for contingency tables have been proposed for this purpose. It is not our intent here to examine all these measures, for this has been done well elsewhere (e.g., Reynolds, 1984). Two measures of association, however—the odds ratio and Yule's Q—have particular relevance in log-linear work and thus merit, if only briefly, our attention.

The Odds Ratio. A significant χ^2 test statistic means that certain intratabular cell proportions differ. One way to view these differences is to first fix on one of the variables. Then, for each level of that variable, compute the odds of responding to a specific level of that variable, compute the odds of responding to a specific level of that variable, compute the odds of responding to a specific level of the other variable (i.e., compute the conditional odds). Finally, compare the conditional odds over levels of the fixed variable. In fourfold tables, this

P 53

procedure is relatively simple and yields a most meaningful measure of association called the *ratio of conditional odds*, or, for short, the odds ratio.

Consider yet again the data in Table 3.1 and momentarily fix on Variable A. Consider specifically the A_1 condition (females) where the *conditional odds* of opposing the antiabortion amendment are $f_{11}/f_{12} = 33/7 = 4.71$, or almost 5 to 1. For males, however, the odds of responding negatively are $f_{21}/f_{22} = 37/23 = 1.61$, or only about 1½ to 1. Now, does it not follow that if there were no association between Sex and Attitude, the odds of opposing the amendment would be essentially the same for both females and males? By similar argument, to the extent to which the two variables are associated, the conditional odds will differ. Therefore, a comparison of respective conditional odds should yield a measure of the strength of the association.

The desired comparison, a ratio of conditional odds, is given by

$$\Omega_{1/2} = \frac{f_{11}/f_{12}}{f_{21}/f_{22}} \tag{4.22}$$

As seen, the numerical value of the odds ratio is symbolized by an uppercase Greek omega. Here, omega also carries the subscript ½ to reflect the *direction* of the conditional odds which, for the moment, are the odds of belonging to B_1 as opposed to B_2. If Variables A and B are independent, that is, if females and males have precisely the same odds of being opposed to the amendment, then the value of Ω will be 1. Conversely, deviation from unity in either direction is suggestive of an association between variables.

Incidently, should we multiply both the numerator and denominator of the ratio in Equation 4.22 by the quantity (f_{12}/f_{21}), upon simplification we would find that

$$\Omega_{1/2} = \frac{f_{11}/f_{12}}{f_{21}/f_{22}} = \frac{f_{11}/f_{21}}{f_{12}/f_{22}} \tag{4.23}$$

which demonstrates that the odds ratio is invariant with respect to the variable on which we initially fix.

Exercising Equation 4.22 on our working-example data gives an odds ratio that is deviant from unity.

$$\Omega_{1/2} = \frac{33/7}{37/23}$$
$$= \frac{4.714}{1.609}$$
$$= 2.93$$

As an additional exercise, let us reverse the direction of the conditional odds. That is, let us consider the odds of being classified in B_2 (or A_2) as opposed to B_1 (or A_1). Computing the value of $\Omega_{2/1}$ results in:

$$\begin{aligned} \Omega_{1/2} &= \left(\frac{37/23}{33/7} = \frac{37/33}{23/7} \right) \\ &= \left(\frac{1.609}{4.714} = \frac{1.121}{3.286} \right) \\ &= .34 \end{aligned}$$

which, we should note, is the reciprocal of $\Omega_{1/2}$. Thus, although the strength of the association between Variables A and B has not changed, by reversing the direction of the relationship, the value of the odds ratio here turns out to be less than unity instead of greater.

As a measure of association, Ω possesses both strengths and weaknesses. A principal strength is that the magnitude of Ω is independent of sample size, a fact that enables us to compare the strength of two or more associations computed on samples of different sizes; and just as desirable, the magnitude of Ω is not artificially reduced in the presence of unequal marginal distributions. Recall that in Chapter 3 it was noted that the values of many measures of association (e.g., the phi coefficient and the contingency coefficient) only achieve their maximum when the association is perfect and the marginal distributions within [A] and [B] are even. To the extent to which the latter condition does not hold, the maximum value of these measures is suppressed—just as the maximum value of a Pearson product-moment correlation is suppressed when variable distributions depart from normality. This limiting feature is not associated with the odds ratio.

The odds ratio, however, is not without its problems. Surely the reader experienced some discomfort a moment ago when the intensity of the association of the working example was first computed as $\Omega_{1/2} = 2.93$ and, subsequent to reversing the direction, then as $\Omega_{2/1} = .34$. The problem here is that the underlying metric of the odds ratio is partially unbounded and, to compound the problems of interpretation, the metric is not symmetric on a unit scale of unity. Granted, the substantive center of the metric is anchored about 1, indicating no relationship; however, as the association gains in intensity, the value of Ω approaches either 0 or infinity (∞), depending on the arbitrary choice of direction. In other words, the underlying metric occupies the entire range of the domain of nonnegative real numbers, but it is not symmetric about 1, its center. (Between 0 and unity, the metric spans only one interval unit while the metric between unity and ∞ occupies an infinite number of units.) Clearly, the interpretation of this measure would be greatly enhanced if the metric could be made symmetric about a point representing an absence of association. This has been done, at least for 2 × 2 tables, by Yule (1900).

Yule's Q Statistic. The Q statistic is a function of a rather well-known measure called the *crossproduct ratio* (CPR) which, in turn, is a function of the odds ratio. To appreciate these relations, we start with the odds ratio formula of Equation 4.22 and then simplify this ratio by "inverting the denominator" and multiplying the inverted denominator by the original numerator. The simplified results shown on the extreme right of Equations 4.24 and 4.25 below are the crossproduct ratio for fourfold tables:

$$\Omega_{1/2} = \frac{f_{11}/f_{12}}{f_{21}/f_{22}} = \frac{f_{11} f_{22}}{f_{21} f_{12}} \tag{4.24}$$

$$\Omega_{2/1} = \frac{f_{12}/f_{11}}{f_{22}/f_{21}} = \frac{f_{12} f_{21}}{f_{22} f_{11}} \tag{4.25}$$

Note that the CPR constitutes a more economical way of computing an odds ratio. Also, Yule found that by (1) subtracting 1 from the CPR, (2) adding 1 to the CPR, and (3) forming a ratio of these reduced and augmented quantities, a most meaningful measure of association is obtained. This measure, Yule's Q, is developed more fully below:

$$
\begin{aligned}
Q_{1/2} &= \frac{\Omega - 1}{\Omega + 1} = \frac{CPR - 1}{CPR + 1} \\
&= \frac{(f_{11} f_{22}/f_{12} f_{21}) - (f_{12} f_{21}/f_{12} f_{21})}{(f_{11} f_{22}/f_{12} f_{21}) + (f_{12} f_{21}/f_{12} f_{21})} \\
&= \frac{(f_{11} f_{22}) - (f_{12} f_{21})}{(f_{11} f_{22}) + (f_{12} f_{21})}
\end{aligned}
\tag{4.26}
$$

For the working example and from the perspective of being in the first level of B (or A), $Q_{1/2}$ is

$$
\begin{aligned}
Q_{1/2} &= \frac{2.93 - 1}{2.93 + 1} \\
&= \frac{(33 \cdot 23) - (7 \cdot 23)}{(33 \cdot 23) + (7 \cdot 23)} \\
&= .49
\end{aligned}
$$

From the opposite perspective, that of being in the second level of A or B, $Q_{2/1}$ is

$$
\begin{aligned}
Q_{2/1} &= \frac{.34 - 1}{.34 + 1} \\
&= \frac{(7 \cdot 23) - (33 \cdot 23)}{(7 \cdot 23) + (33 \cdot 23)} \\
&= -.49
\end{aligned}
$$

Yule's Q ranges in value from -1.00 to $+1.00$, and is symmetric, as demonstrated above, about zero. As Q approaches zero, the association becomes weaker; as Q approaches unity, in either direction, the association increases in intensity. Although not without faults (see Reynolds, 1984, 42), Yule's Q has much to recommend it as a measure of association, even though its use is restricted to fourfold tables. However, the odds ratio, which serves as the basis for Yule's Q, can be generalized to tables of greater size and dimensionality, as will be seen later.

Examination of Lambda Effects

As we have seen, the parameter estimates (lambdas or taus) in contingency table models determine the specific values of expected cell frequencies. They also may be used to (1) determine whether a given term in a log-linear model, or factor in a multiplicative model, is contributing meaningfully to the explanation of observed data; and (2) follow up omnibus results, particularly the results of asymmetrical analyses. To the extent to which lambda parameters approach zero (or as tau parameters approach unity), they become less important with respect to their ability to explain observed cell frequencies, and thus they can be eliminated from models without seriously sacrificing the model's ability to fit observed data. Conversely, prominent lambda parameters point to variables that appear to explain observed data. A careful study of prominent lambda parameters, therefore, often reveals the specific nature of effects associated with an influential variable.

Assessing the relative importance of lambdas in log-linear models (or tau parameters in multiplicative models) is greatly assisted by the fact that they can be subjected to tests of statistical significance. It is more convenient to test estimates of lambda while realizing that outcomes are equally applicable to corresponding estimates of tau parameters. Specifically, if the size of the table is reasonable large, say $n > 25$, for each lambda effect a statistic of the following form can be calculated

$$z(\lambda_i) = \frac{\lambda_i}{\text{S.E. } (\lambda_i)} \tag{4.27}$$

which we recognize as a normal deviate or z test.

There are a number of different computational strategies that may be used to obtain the numeric value of the standard error (S.E.) employed in the calculation of z. Historically, a strategy known as the *delta method* was used most frequently (see Goodman, 1970; Bishop, Fienberg & Holland, 1975). Briefly, an *exact* S.E. is computed for the saturated model and, if desired, used in the context of a z test to test all lambda parameters in the saturated model. However, in this method, the same S.E. is used again in desired tests of lambdas that appear in unsaturated or less restricted models. When used with less restricted models, the S.E. computed on the saturated model is not exact; rather, it is a conservative approximation. Because the standard error computed on a saturated model gives conservative bounds for unsaturated models, this strategy was, and continues to be, defensible.

Since the mid-1970s advances have been made such that exact S.E.s can be computed on a number of models other than the saturated model—models that will subsequently be called *direct models*—and better approximations can be used in connection with remaining models (see Lee, 1977). Modern computer programs reflect many of these advances. At this point, our discussion is of necessity limited to two-dimensional tables where the historic approach of calculating S.E.s for z tests on the saturated model will suffice.

Realize that for two-dimensional tables, follow-up is required only if the saturated model is selected. Further, for fourfold tables, extensive post hoc examination is not required in the asymmetric case because there are only two levels of the explanatory variable (say Variable A), and because acceptance of the saturated model suggests that the pattern on proportional response over levels of Variable B is not similar at A_1 and A_2. Consequently, only the algebraic signs of $\hat{\lambda}_{ij}^{ab}$ effects need be examined to determine the nature of differences between levels of A.

To illustrate, recall that calculations of interaction effects in the saturated model that were performed earlier in this chapter, turned out as follows:

	τ (tau)		λ (lambda)	
	B_1	B_2	B_1	B_2
A_1	1.308	.764	.269	-.269
A_2	.764	1.308	-.269	.269

Because the lambdas are slightly easier to interpret, they will be chosen for the ensuing discussions of post hoc procedures. From the algebraic signs of the lambdas, it can be seen that the odds of subjects at A_1 giving a B_1 response are greater than the odds of subjects giving this response at A_2; that is, females are more disposed to be against the antiabortion amendment than are males. Even though this uncomplicated result does not require further statistical scrutiny, as a pedagogic exercise we pursue our follow-up examination by subjecting the $\hat{\lambda}_{ij}^{ab}$ to statistical test.

In general, the null to be subjected to test is H_0: $\hat{\lambda}_{ij}^{ab} = 0$, for all values of i and j. But since there is only one *basic parameter* here (i.e., when a solution is achieved for one, the remaining three effects are determined), only one statistical test need be performed. With reasonably large samples (e.g., $n > 25$), under the null hypothesis, we have learned that the distribution of lambdas approaches the normal; hence, subsequent to calculating the standard error of the λ's, a conventional normal deviate test (i.e., z test) can be performed (Goodman, 1970). The standard error for the saturated model of a fourfold table may be computed as follows:

$$\text{S.E. } (\lambda) = \frac{\left(\sum_i^a \sum_j^b (1/f_{ij}) \right)^{1/2}}{ab} \qquad (4.28)$$

Substituting values peculiar to our example gives

$$\begin{aligned} \text{S.E. } (\lambda) &= (1/33 + 1/37 + 1/7 + 1/23)^{1/2}/(2 \cdot 2) \\ &= (2.437)^{1/2}/4 \\ &= .123 \end{aligned}$$

Having computed the S.E. that can be used to test all lambda parameters in the saturated model, and can be used as a conservative S.E. to assess lambdas in more restricted models, the z test on interaction effects is

$$z(\hat{\lambda}_{ij}^{ab}) = \hat{\lambda}_{ij}^{ab}/\text{S.E. } (\lambda) \qquad (4.29)$$

which, when applied specifically to the basic parameter estimate $\hat{\lambda}_{11}^{ab}$, results in

$$\begin{aligned} z(\hat{\lambda}_{11}^{ab}) &= .269/.123 \\ &= 2.19 \end{aligned}$$

Since this computed test statistic exceeds the two-tailed critical z value of 1.96, the null that $\hat{\lambda}_{ij}^{ab} = 0$ is rejected at the .05 level of significance. Moreover, since there is only one basic interactive parameter for the fourfold table, further testing would be redundant. A summary of our post hoc examination as it might appear in a journal article is presented in Table 4.3.

By way of concluding, earlier it was stated that the traditional chi-square procedures of Chapter 3 are generally sufficient for the analysis of two-dimensional tables. If researchers typically possessed information on only two qualitative variables, it would be difficult to justify the new approach ponderously outlined in this chapter, for, in retrospect, all we have done is make more explicit that which is implicit in the traditional approach. However, researchers often deal with more than two variables, and since the principles that were at times extensively deliberated in this chapter can be extended to situations in which there are more than two variables, our work here is justified. There is, of course, still much to learn about the application of log-linear analysis to two-dimensional tables. We could, for example, extend our methods to analyze data in two-way tables defined by two polytomous variables. However, it is advantageous to

Table 4.3
Observed [AB] Frequencies, Lambda Parameters, and Normal Deviate Tests for the Working Example

Attitude: Variable B	Gender: Variable A					
	Females			Males		
	f_{1j}	λ^{ab}_{1j}	z	f_{2j}	λ^{ab}_{2j}	z
Opposed	33	.269	2.19*	7	-.269	-2.19
Support	37	-.269	-2.19	23	.269	2.19
Marginals	70	0.000		30	0.000	

*$p < .05$.

proceed immediately to the analysis of three-dimensional tables so that the full benefits of log-linear methodology can be more fully seen.

NOTES

1. Readers who are not familiar with the models to be reviewed may desire undertake independent study. Texts prepared Hays (1988, ch. 12) and Kennedy and Bush (1985, chs. 4 and 6), among numerous others, contain extensive discussions of ANOVA models and related topics.

2. Since the ANOVA model under discussion is fixed, to the extent to which interaction that is independent of sampling error is present, the resultant F tests on main effects will be negatively biased. Therefore, if these overly conservative tests achieve statistical significance, they can be advanced with little hesitation.

3. Based on the supposition that if only the value of n is known (i.e., $n = 100$), the most reasonable cell expectancies are $F_{ij} = n/ab = 100/4 = 25$, it then can be shown that these reasonable expectancies are also ML expectancies by substituting reasonable expectancies for observed frequencies in the likelihood function

$$L^* = \prod \hat{P}^{n/ab}_{11} \, \hat{P}^{n/ab}_{12} \, \hat{P}^{n/ab}_{21} \, \hat{P}^{n/ab}_{22}$$

where it will be found that the maximum value of the function is realized when estimated parameters are $\hat{P}_{11} = \hat{P}_{12} = \hat{P}_{21} = \hat{P}_{22} = .25$.

4. The number of general parameters is equivalent to the number of terms (or factors) in the model. On the other hand, the number of basic parameters refers to the number of estimates and effects that are free to vary. Relative to a 3×2 table, for example, there are four general parameters but six basic parameters in the saturated model. This distinction will be discussed in Chapter 5.

5

The Analysis of
Three-Dimensional Tables

Prior to the decade of the 1970s, researchers who were able to cross-classify subjects on more than two variables and who desired to perform an analysis that considered all variables simultaneously were presented with serious problems. However, with the advent of log-linear theory and supporting computer programs, contemporary researchers can readily perform comprehensive analyses of higher-order tables. This chapter describes the application of log-linear methods to tables of three dimensions. Adhering to our earlier practice, log-linear methods will be described in a manner synonymic with multifactor ANOVA. Again, basic principles will be introduced using contrived data, but unlike before, refinements will be discussed subsequently within the context of an actual data set.

WORKING EXAMPLES

We turn first to the hypothetical data in the three-way table displayed in Table 5.1. In an effort to keep things simple, the three categorical/qualitative variables that define the contingency table are dichotomies and the total tabular count is 100 (i.e., $n = 100$).

Data in Table 5.1 are to be used in two working examples. The first contrived example will be called the *substance abuse study*, in which data in Table 5.1 will be subjected to a symmetrical log-linear analysis. The second example will be called the *adverse impact study*, in which these same data will be subjected to a *logit model*, or asymmetrical log-linear analysis. By and large, we will consider again the major operations surveyed in Chapter 4, but in somewhat greater depth and with somewhat greater emphasis on the distinction between the general application of log-linear models for symmetrical inquiry and the

Table 5.1

Observed Frequencies Associated with the Symmetric Substance Abuse Study and the Asymmetric Adverse Impact Study

Variable A	Variable B	Variable C	
		C_1 : Yes \ Failed	C_2 : No \ Passed
Abuse \ Impact	Abuse \ Impact		
A_1 : Yes \ Females	B_1 : Yes \ Majority	9	2
A_1 : Yes \ Females	B_2 : No \ Minority	5	4
A_2 : No \ Males	B_1 : Yes \ Majority	16	26
A_2 : No \ Males	B_2 : No \ Minority	10	28

application of a subset of models, called *logit models*, for use when the mode of inquiry is asymmetrical.

Notation for Three-Dimensional Tables

First, however, let us consider the 2 × 2 × 2 table and data in Table 5.1 in the abstract so that we can extend the notational system of earlier chapters to accommodate the introduction of the third and new variable, Variable C. Under either a fixed or random sampling plan, n sampling units (e.g., subjects) are cross-classified on the basis of three variables, Variables A ($i = 1, 2, \ldots, a$), B ($j = 1, 2, \ldots, b$), and C ($k = 1, 2, \ldots, c$). Observed elementary cell frequencies in the [ABC] configuration are denoted by f_{ijk}'s; therefore, expected cell frequencies fitted by a given model will be symbolized by F_{ijk}'s. Observed main marginals and two-variable (first-order) marginals are designated as follows:

Main Marginals	Two-Variable Marginals
$[A]: f_i^a$	$[AB]: f_{ij}^{ab}$
$[B]: f_j^b$	$[AC]: f_{ik}^{ac}$
$[C]: f_k^c$	$[BC]: f_{jk}^{bc}$

Applying this notation to data in Table 5.1, for the main marginals we have

[A]: $f_1^a = 20$ and $f_2^a = 80$
[B]: $f_1^b = 53$ and $f_2^b = 47$
[C]: $f_1^c = 40$ and $f_2^c = 60$

For the two-variable marginals (or first-order marginals), we observe

[AB]			[AC]			[BC]		
A	B	f^{ab}	A	C	f^{ac}	B	C	f^{bc}
1	1	11	1	1	14	1	1	25
1	2	9	1	2	6	1	2	28
2	1	42	2	1	26	2	1	15
2	2	38	2	2	54	2	2	32

Finally, realize that each of the 100 sampling units is classified into one, and only one, of the eight elementary cells of the $2 \times 2 \times 2$ table.

Three-Dimensional Working Examples

The Substance Abuse Study. The scenario that serves as the backdrop for our working symmetrical example involves the abuse of three potentially harmful substances: (1) "hard" drugs such as cocaine, heroin, and so forth, (2) "softer" drugs such as marijuana, prescription sedatives, and so on, and (3) alcoholic beverages. For this example, the reader is to assume that a representative sample of 100 juvenile offenders was clinically assessed with respect to the extent to which they used these substances. Subjects were classified dichotomously as either using the substance so frequently that they were abusing it, or as demonstrating a frequency of usage that was not so extensive as to merit classification as an abuser. Specifically, the three dichotomous variables for our symmetrical example are:

A: *Abuse of Hard Drugs*
A_1 = yes
A_2 = no

B: *Abuse of Soft Drugs*
B_1 = yes
B_2 = no

C: *Abuse of Alcohol*
C_1 = yes
C_2 = no

Following clinical assessment, the 100 juvenile offenders were cross-classified on the basis of the three aforementioned variables where it is assumed that resultant frequency counts turned out as depicted in Table 5.1.

Based on the brief description, where it should be noted that no reference was made to an outcome or response variable, this example would most likely lend itself to the type of analysis that we have defined as symmetrical. If the investigation were highly exploratory, an obvious question to be pursued would be whether there are significant associations between or among the three substance variables. A more focused question might be whether a significant association exists between alcohol and soft drug usage subsequent to partialing from this association relations associated with the use of hard drugs. In any event, we are to assume that the purpose of the substance abuse study is to identify relations; the purpose is not to detect differences between subjects placed in different categories on one variable with respect to usage patterns on another variable. This hypothetical investigation will be used to illustrate basic operations in the conduct of a symmetrical log-linear analysis.

The Study of Adverse Impact. This second working example will serve to illustrate an asymmetrical log-linear analysis. Here we are to assume that a large corporation has established a comprehensive testing program to identify the most qualified employees for promotion to management positions. Assume further that to comply with affirmative action guidelines, a special effort was made to ensure that approximately half of program participants were representatives of minority groups. A total of 100 employees participated in the testing program, and 60 were ultimately deemed qualified and hence promoted. Because management was concerned that the testing program might screen out a disproportionate number of female and minority applicants, thus rendering the company vulnerable to the charge that their testing procedures were having an "adverse impact" on these particular groups, a statistical assessment was sought.

Program participants were cross-classified on the basis of the following three dichotomies:

A: *Gender*
A_1 = females
A_2 = males

B: *Ethnic Group*
B_1 = majority
B_2 = minority

C: *Outcome at Termination of Testing*
C_1 = failed to qualify for a position
C_2 = qualified for a position

As before, we assume that the resultant data turned out as shown in Table 5.1.

Unlike before, however, the adverse impact example presents us with a response variable, Variable C. This example, therefore, lends itself to the type of analysis that we have defined as asymmetrical. Typical questions to be asked of data in Table 5.1 are whether differences are present between females and males and between majority and minority participants with respect to the response variable. If differences between females and males are present, another question might be whether the gender effects are comparable for both majority and minority employees or whether gender effects are moderated by ethnic classification. In other words, does Gender interact with Ethnic Group with respect to program failure and success? Questions such as these will be entertained in the middle of the chapter when the adverse-impact example will be used to illustrate basic operations in the conduct of an asymmetrical analysis.

HIERARCHICAL MODELS FOR SYMMETRICAL INQUIRY

The synonymity between conventional ANOVA models and log-linear models was discussed in Chapter 4. That discussion, however, was confined to tables defined by two qualitative variables. Relative to three-variable situations, the ANOVA analogue is a model that explains elementary cell *means* (i.e., μ_{ijk}'s) by a linear combination containing (1) a grand mean parameter μ, (2) main effects of each of the three principal variables, (3) three first-order (or two-variable) interaction effects, and (4) a second-order (or three-variable) interaction. The ANOVA model is

$$\mu_{ijk} = \mu + \alpha_i + \beta_j + \gamma_k + (\alpha\beta)_{ij} + (\alpha\gamma)_{ik} + (\beta\gamma)_{jk} + (\alpha\beta\gamma)_{ijk} \qquad (5.1)$$

The grand mean μ, the main effects for Variables A and B, and the first-order interaction between A and B have been defined previously. Moreover, from discussions associated with Equation 4.1, the reader can readily deduce the definitions for the main effects of Variable C and the first-order effects involving Variable C. The second-order interaction term Equation 5.1, however, merits special attention because its meaning is not universally appreciated either within the ANOVA or in a log-linear analysis.

In an ANOVA, the presence of second-order interaction indicates that elementary cell means manifest variability subsequent to correcting these means for main effects of Variables A, B, and C, and subsequent to correcting the means for the three first-order interactions. Put another way, the variability among cell means cannot be totally explained by the additive influences exerted by single variables (i.e., the main effects) or variables in dual combination (first-order interaction effects) because there are other sources promoting variability among cell means that are operative only when the three principal variables act in concert. The appearance of second-order interaction can also be understood to mean that there is a change in the *nature* (or pattern) of *simple* first-order

Table 5.2
Hierarchical Multiplicative Models for Three-Dimensional Tables

Model Number	Multiplicative Model	Fitted Marginals
(1)	$F_{ijk} = \tau$	n
(2)	$F_{ijk} = \tau\ \tau_i^a$	$[A]$
(3)	$F_{ijk} = \tau\ \tau_i^a\ \tau_j^b$	$[A],\ [B]$
(4)	$F_{ijk} = \tau\ \tau_i^a\ \tau_j^b\ \tau_k^c$	$[A],\ [B],\ [C]$
(5)	$F_{ijk} = \tau\ \tau_i^a\ \tau_j^b\ \tau_k^c\ \tau_{ij}^{ab}$	$[AB],\ [C]$
(6)	$F_{ijk} = \tau\ \tau_i^a\ \tau_j^b\ \tau_k^c\ \tau_{ij}^{ab}\ \tau_{ik}^{ac}$	$[AB],\ [AC]$
(7)	$F_{ijk} = \tau\ \tau_i^a\ \tau_j^b\ \tau_k^c\ \tau_{ij}^{ab}\ \tau_{ik}^{ac}\ \tau_{jk}^{bc}$	$[AB],\ [AC],\ [BC]$
(8)	$F_{ijk} = \tau\ \tau_i^a\ \tau_j^b\ \tau_k^c\ \tau_{ij}^{ab}\ \tau_{ik}^{ac}\ \tau_{jk}^{bc}\ \tau_{ijk}^{abc}$	$[ABC]$

Note: To fit a particular model on many "canned" computer programs, the capital letters representing the marginals that are fitted by the model are specified, separated by commas, and terminated with a period. For example, to fit Model 6 using the BMDP/4F, one requests a fit for: *AB, AC*. In ensuing tables, therefore, the brackets will be omitted when specifying marginals that are fitted by particular models.

interactions if they are viewed over levels of the third (or excluded) variable. Should we choose, for example, to examine the interaction between Variables *A* and *B* peculiar to each level of Variable *C*, the pattern of these simple *AB* interactions will manifest some degree of change over levels of Variable *C*. Consequently, if the first-order interaction between *A* and *B* is substantively meaningful, simple first-order interactions must be interpreted independently at respective levels of *C*. As we shall see, an analogous situation will present itself in log-linear work whenever the saturated model is selected for interpretation.

Again we choose to discuss multiplicative models prior to log-linear models. Eight multiplicative models for three-dimensional tables are displayed in Table 5.2.

Several observations can be made from an examination of Table 5.2. First, the numbering system used to identify models is consistent with the number of general parameters within each model. Second, proceeding from Model 1 to the saturated model, note that more observed marginal information is used by succeeding models to generate F_{ijk}'s. Model 1, for example, uses only n to generate F_{ijk}'s, whereas the saturated model uses all observed information to generate elementary cell frequencies. (The latter model, therefore, will generate F_{ijk}'s identical to observed f_{ijk}'s.) Finally, yet nonetheless important, Models 5 through 8 may be described as *hierarchical* models.

When used in connection with contingency table models, the term *hierarchical* indicates that the lower-order "relatives" of all higher-order terms (or factors) are present in the model. Consider Model 5, a model that contains the first-order factor τ_{ij}^{ab}. Model 5 can be said to be a hierarchical model because also present in the models are the lower-order constituents of τ_{ij}^{ab}, namely τ_i^a and τ_j^b. The same hierarchical property is seen in Models 6, 7, and the saturated model. There are a number of computational advantages associated with the specification of models in hierarchical form. Aside from computational convenience, we will work primarily with hierarchically structured models because they are meaningful, in a substantive sense, in most practical research situations, and because a number of computer programs permit only the specification of hierarchical models (e.g., BMDP/4F).

Before leaving Table 5.2, the reader should appreciate the linkage between the parameters within a model and the marginal information used by that model. The relevance of the "Fitted Marginals" column in Table 5.2, to both theory and computer application, cannot be overstated. As a case in point, to obtain the fit of a specific model on most current computer programs, say the fit produced by Model 5, one requests that the following observed marginals be used: [A], [B], [C], and [AB]. If as with BMDP/4F, the specification of models in hierarchical form is understood; then the specification can be shortened by requesting only [C] and [AB], since the fitting of [AB] also provides for the fitting of its lower-order relatives [A] and [B]. Incidentally, if only [AB] were requested, rather than fitting Model 5 to observed data, the following model would instead be fitted:

$$F_{ijk} = \tau \, \tau_i^a \, \tau_j^b \, \tau_{ij}^{ab}$$

It follows that to specify Model 6, [A], [B], [C], [AB], and [AC] are fitted; or, more simply, [AB] and [AC] are fitted. Finally, to produce results associated with the saturated model, observed frequencies in the [ABC] configuration are fitted.

From Chapter 4, we know that the multiplicative models of Table 5.2 are linear in their logarithms. The log-linear versions of multiplicative models are displayed in Table 5.3. Again, notice that log-linear models produce expected cell frequencies that correspond to the natural logs of F_{ijk}'s produced by their multiplicative counterparts. And whereas linear models are more amenable to existing computational routines, realize that there is no significant difference between corresponding multiplicative and log-linear models.

INTERPRETING GENERAL MODELS IN SYMMETRICAL INQUIRY

In this section, the *general* log-linear models in Table 5.3 will be examined within the context of the substance abuse scenario for the purpose of determining

Table 5.3
Hierarchical Log-Linear Models for Three-Dimensional Tables

Model Number	Log-Linear Models

(1) $\ln F_{ijk} = \lambda$

(2) $\ln F_{ijk} = \lambda + \lambda_i^a$

(3) $\ln F_{ijk} = \lambda + \lambda_i^a + \lambda_j^b$

(4) $\ln F_{ijk} = \lambda + \lambda_i^a + \lambda_j^b + \lambda_k^c$

(5) $\ln F_{ijk} = \lambda + \lambda_i^a + \lambda_j^b + \lambda_k^c + \lambda_{ij}^{ab}$

(6) $\ln F_{ijk} = \lambda + \lambda_i^a + \lambda_j^b + \lambda_k^c + \lambda_{ij}^{ab} + \lambda_{ik}^{ac}$

(7) $\ln F_{ijk} = \lambda + \lambda_i^a + \lambda_j^b + \lambda_k^c + \lambda_{ij}^{ab} + \lambda_{ik}^{ac} + \lambda_{jk}^{bc}$

(8) $\ln F_{ijk} = \lambda + \lambda_i^a + \lambda_j^b + \lambda_k^c + \lambda_{ij}^{ab} + \lambda_{ik}^{ac} + \lambda_{jk}^{bc} + \lambda_{ijk}^{abc}$

Note: Consult Table 5.2 for observed marginal configurations that are used for parameter estimation and model specification.

the omnibus conclusion that can be advanced should the model in question be deemed acceptable. The mode of inquiry will be assumed to be symmetrical—asymmetrical inquiry (logit models) will be discussed in the next section. The didactic strategy adopted for the ensuing discussion is as follows:

1. Models will be successively identified, and basic probability theory, where appropriate, will be used to generate expected elementary cell frequencies.
2. Expected cell frequencies for each model will be presented in tabular form.
3. We will momentarily assume that the expected cell frequencies fit observed data extremely well, thus rendering the model acceptable for interpretation.
4. A general interpretation or conclusion, in terms of symmetrical concepts, will be inferred.
5. For selected models, the numerical values of parameter estimates will be calculated.

Before we begin, however, note that I have just said that elementary probability theory will be used to generate the expected cell frequencies whenever possible. Probability theory can and will be used to produce F_{ijk}'s for all models in Table

5.2 except Model 7, the full two-variable model. When this model is entertained, we will be forced to exercise one of the iterative computational routines (e.g., the Deming-Stephan or the Newton-Raphson) to produce the desired F_{ijk}'s; that is, we will be forced to generate F_{ijk}'s as do computer programs. Because expected cell frequencies of Model 7 cannot be computed directly, and can only be obtained by iterative computational algorithms, Model 7 is sometimes called an *indirect* model, as opposed to the remaining models, which may be termed *direct* models.

Model 1: Mutual Equiprobability

The multiplicative version of this model contains only the estimate of τ and uses only n to determine its value. Since there are no other restrictions (i.e., no other parameters to estimate) in the model, the n counts will be distributed uniformly throughout the cells of the table. Therefore, for the substance abuse study, the F_{ijk}'s may be computed directly by

$$\begin{aligned} F_{ijk} &= n/abc \\ &= 100/8 \\ &= 12.5 \end{aligned} \qquad (5.2)$$

which, for the $2 \times 2 \times 2$ table in question, yields the following expected cell frequencies:

A	B	C_1	C_2
1	1	12.5	12.5
1	2	12.5	12.5
2	1	12.5	12.5
2	2	12.5	12.5

Assuming that the fitted frequencies in the table above describe observed data extremely well, what omnibus conclusion could be advanced relative to the symmetric relations between and among the three variables? It is obvious that not only are the three variables mutually independent (i.e., $A \otimes B \otimes C$), but an equal number of cases falls into each cell as well. Hence, the adoption of Model 1 would connote *mutual equiprobability*.

Turning to the numerical value of the sole parameter, from Chapter 4 we learned that τ is analogous to μ, the grand mean in ANOVA models. More precisely, τ is equivalent to the geometric mean of F_{ijk}'s given by the model in question. Hence,

$$\tau = \overline{G} = (\prod F_{ijk})^{1/abc}$$
$$= [(12.5)^8]^{1/8}$$
$$= 12.5$$

or, should the log-linear estimator be desired,

$$\lambda = \ln \tau$$
$$= \ln 12.5$$
$$= 2.5257$$

Model 2: Conditional Equiprobability

This two-parameter model uses [A] to generate expected cell frequencies. In our example, $f_1^a = 20$ and $f_2^a = 80$. Hence, subsequent to the requirement that the main marginals for A must sum to the respective values above, counts within levels of A are independently or uniformly distributed. Expected cell frequencies, therefore, may be directly computed by

$$F_{ijk} = f_i^a/bc \qquad\qquad (5.3)$$

which, if carried through, yields the following F_{ijk}'s:

A	B	C_1	C_2
1	1	5	5
1	2	5	5
2	1	20	20
2	2	20	20

From the table it is clear that $A \otimes B \otimes C$. In addition, responses are equiprobable if observed differences in f_1^a and f_2^a are taken into account. Therefore, if Model 2 fits observed data well, *conditional equiprobability* best describes the outcome. In other words, responses are equally probable on the condition that adjustments are made for the observed inequalities in the main marginals of Variable A.

Let us calculate the values of the two parameters in this model. As always, the first parameter is the geometric mean of F_{ijk}'s. Consequently,

$$\tau = \overline{G}$$
$$= (5 \cdot 5 \cdot 5 \cdot 5 \cdot 20 \cdot 20 \cdot 20 \cdot 20)^{1/8}$$
$$= 10.00$$

In the log-linear, the first parameter is

$$\lambda = \ln \tau$$
$$= \ln 10.00$$
$$= 2.3026$$

Now, recall that the generic expression for the second parameter is

$$\tau_i^a = \overline{G}_i^a / \overline{G}$$

The specific effects for the abuse and nonabuse of hard drugs are

$$\tau_1^a = \overline{G}_1^a / \overline{G}$$
$$= (5 \cdot 5 \cdot 5 \cdot 5)^{1/4} / 10.00$$
$$= .50$$

$$\tau_2^a = \overline{G}_2^a / \overline{G}$$
$$= (20 \cdot 20 \cdot 20 \cdot 20)^{1/4} / 10.00$$
$$= 2.00$$

Note that $\prod \tau_i^a = 1.00$; hence, for dichotomies, $\tau_1^a = 1/\tau_2^a$, or $\tau_2^a = 1/\tau_1^a$. For readers familiar with ANOVA, more insightful definitions of these effects are provided by the linear expressions:

$$\lambda_1^a = \ln \overline{G}_1^a - \ln \overline{G}$$
$$= 1.6094 - 2.3026$$
$$= -.6932$$

$$\lambda_2^a = \ln \overline{G}_2^a - \ln \overline{G}$$
$$= 2.9957 - 2.3026$$
$$= .6932$$

The "ANOVA-like" effects above sum to zero, as do fixed effects in the analysis of variance, which should not come as a complete surprise because the log of the product of multiplicative effects (i.e., unity) is zero.

Operational versions of Model 2 for the substance abuse study are

$$F_{1jk} = (10)(.50)$$

and

$$F_{2jk} = (10)(2.00)$$

Exercising these models for all values of i and k will yield the expected cell frequencies shown earlier.

Model 3: Conditional Equiprobability

The conditional equiprobability model fits both [A] and [B]. If we were dealing with a two-dimensional table, F_{ij}'s would be the products of $np_i^a p_j^b$. However, we are working with a three-dimensional table and, since the third variable (Variable C) is not fitted, frequencies will be evenly distributed over this variable. It follows, therefore, that

$$F_{ijk} = np_i^a p_j^b / c \qquad (5.4)$$

The expected cell frequencies are

A	B	C_1	C_2
1	1	5.3	5.3
1	2	4.7	4.7
2	1	21.2	21.2
2	2	18.8	18.8

Not only do we see that $A \otimes B \otimes C$, but additionally, we observe another instance of *conditional equiprobability*—equal probabilities over levels of Variable C following adjustments for the main marginals of Variables A and B. Relative to the three parameters in this model, the reader is encouraged to calculate these values. The values should turn out to be:

$\tau = 9.982$

$\tau_1^a = .500$ (hence, $\tau_2^a = 2.000$)

$\tau_1^b = 1.062$ (hence, $\tau_2^b = .942$)

Notice that the numerical value of τ has changed from that computed for Model 2 but the main-marginal effects for Variable A (i.e., τ_i^a's) are as they were in Model 2.

Model 4: Mutual Independence

Since the mutual independence model contains all three main-marginal parameters, it can be called the *full main-marginal* model. Equation 5.5 below can be used to fit main-marginals [A], [B], and [C]:

$$F_{ijk} = np_i^a p_j^b p_k^c = f_i^a f_j^b f_k^c / n^2 \qquad (5.5)$$

The resultant frequencies are:

A	B	C_1	C_2
1	1	4.24	6.36
1	2	3.76	5.64
2	1	16.96	25.44
2	2	15.05	22.56

The fitted frequencies reflect a condition of *mutual independence*; namely, $A \otimes B \otimes C$. Should Model 4 fit the observed data extremely well, there is no evidence of a relationship between any pair of variables. For Model 4 it turns out that $\tau = 9.780$, the τ_i^a's and τ_j^b's have the same values as seen for Model 3, and $\tau_1^c = .816$; hence, $\tau_2^c = 1.225$.

Model 5: Marginal Association Between A and B

This model contains a first-order interaction parameter, namely τ_{ij}^{ab}. To fit this model, frequencies in [AB] (presented earlier) are used. Consequently, for hierarchical models, the main marginals [A] and [B] are also fitted. Main marginal [C], however, must be fitted directly. Using basic probability theory, this is accomplished by

$$F_{ijk} = f_{ij}^{ab} p_k^c \tag{5.6}$$

which gives the following expectancies:

A	B	C_1	C_2
1	1	4.4	6.6
1	2	3.6	5.4
2	1	16.8	25.2
2	2	15.2	22.8

If Model 5 is deemed most acceptable, indicating that τ_{ij}^{ab} is needed in the model to achieve respectable fit, then not only is the hypothesis of mutual independence *not* tenable, it can also be said that there is a *marginal association* between Variables A and B. To be more precise, if we ignore Variable C by simply collapsing over its levels to form the [AB] configuration, in this two-dimensional table Variables A and B will manifest an association—as evidenced by a conventional chi-square test. The intensity of the marginal relationship between A and B, of course, will depend on the extent to which τ_{ij}^{ab} is needed to achieve an acceptable fit. Equally as important is the fact that the factors (or terms) associated with AC, BC, and ABC are not present in this model which, we are momentarily assuming, fits the observed data extremely well. Interpret these omissions as indications that associations between Variables A and C, and B and C, and mutual associations among Variables A, B, and C, are not present, at least to the extent to which they merit serious consideration.

Model 5 offers us a good opportunity to reinforce our understanding of model-parameter estimates. Consider first the geometric mean of F_{ijk}'s, which turned out to be 9.767 here (hence, $\lambda = 2.279$). Now it should have been noticed that since models generate different F_{ijk}'s, the first parameter is numerically different for each model discussed to this point. But what changes, if any, have occurred in main-marginal parameter estimates? For the present model, it can be shown that $\tau_1^a = .499$, $\tau_1^b = 1.078$, and $\tau_1^c = .816$. A comparison with earlier models reveals that the τ_i^a's and τ_j^b's have changed, but the τ_k^c's have not changed from Model 4. This was to be expected since, by fitting $[AB]$, we have effected a change in the main-marginal effects for Variables A and B relative to Model 4; however, main-marginal effects for Variable C were not effected by fitting $[AB]$, hence the τ_k^c's are identical in Models 4 and 5.

Let us take a hard look at the first-order effects for Model 5. The point was made in Chapter 4 that these effects are analogous to first-order interaction effects in the ANOVA. In that chapter, the analogy between interaction in the ANOVA (see Equation 4.2) and contingency table interaction (see Equations 4.16 and 4.21) was developed when τ_{ij}^{ab}, defined in Chapter 4 as

$$\tau_{ij}^{ab} = f_{ij}^{ab}/(\tau \, \tau_i^a \, \tau_j^b)$$

was converted to λ_{ij}^{ab} and then shown to be

$$\lambda_{ij}^{ab} = \ln f_{ij}^{ab} - \lambda - \lambda_i^a - \lambda_j^b$$
$$= \ln f_{ij}^{ab} - \ln \overline{G}_i^a - \ln \overline{G}_j^b + \ln \overline{G}$$

Although the formulas above were developed within the context of two-dimensional tables, they can be generalized to tables of three dimensions. Consider first that the number of F_{ijk}'s in a combination (cell) formed by the crossing of Variables A and B is, in general, c. For the working example, $c = 2$. Thus, it follows that we can extend the definition of first-order interaction between A and B to mean variability among the logs of the ab geometric means in $[AB]$ after partialing out the effects of $(\ln \overline{G}_i^a - \ln \overline{G})$ and $(\ln \overline{G}_j^b - \ln \overline{G})$. Stated mathematically, for three-dimensional tables,

$$\tau_{ij}^{ab} = \frac{\left(\prod_k^c F_{ijk} \right)^{1/c}}{\tau \, \tau_i^a \, \tau_j^b} = \overline{G}_{ij}^{ab}/(\tau \, \tau_i^a \, \tau_j^b) \qquad (5.7)$$

or,

$$\lambda_{ij}^{ab} = \ln \overline{G}_{ij}^{ab} - \ln \overline{G}_i^a - \ln \overline{G}_j^b + \ln \overline{G}$$

Using the multiplicative formula to compute the interaction effect for the first level of A and B in the working example, we find

$$\begin{aligned}
\tau_{11}^{ab} &= [(4.4)(6.6)]^{1/2}/[(9.767)(.499)(1.708)] \\
&= 5.389/5.254 \\
&= 1.026
\end{aligned}$$

The corresponding linear estimate is

$$\begin{aligned}
\lambda_{11}^{ab} &= 1.684 - 1.584 - 2.354 + 2.279 \\
&= .025
\end{aligned}$$

Since we know that marginal products of interaction effects in the [AB] configuration are unity (or marginal sums are all zeros in the linear), the remaining three interaction effects for the 2×2 table can be calculated most easily as residual quantities.

Model 6: Marginal Association Between A and C

The F_{ijk}'s given by hierarchical Model 6, a model that fits both [AB] and [AC] and thereby automatically fits the three main marginals, may be obtained from Equation 5.8:

$$F_{ijk} = np_{ij}^{ab}(p_{ik}^{ac}/ p_i^a) \tag{5.8}$$

with the result:

A	B	C_1	C_2
1	1	7.70	3.30
1	2	6.30	2.70
2	1	13.65	28.35
2	2	12.35	25.65

If Model 6 is selected as most acceptable, thereby indicating that τ_{ik}^{ac} is needed to obtain a good fit, it follows that Variables A and C are associated. More precisely, a *marginal* association is present between Variables A and C. There may or may not be a marginal association between A and B. This is a matter for subsequent investigation. Moreover, because factors (or terms) representing

BC and *ABC* are not needed to explain the observed data, we can deduce that associations between or among *BC* and *ABC* are not present to a significant degree.

Model 7: Full First-Order

Model 7 contains all three first-order parameters, and therefore it is sometimes called the *full first-order model*. It differs markedly from previous models in that direct calculation of F_{ijk}'s is not possible. Instead, as mentioned, we must call on either the Newton-Raphson or the iterative fitting algorithm developed by Deming and Stephan (1940), which has been described for use in the log-linear literature by Fienberg (1970b) and Goodman (1970), and has been translated into Fortran for computer application by Haberman (1972). The Deming-Stephan computations as they pertain to Model 7 for the working example are illustrated in Appendix A of the first edition of this book (Kennedy, 1983). Resultant expectancies are shown below:

A	B	C_1	C_2
1	1	8.411	2.589
1	2	5.589	3.411
2	1	16.589	25.411
2	2	9.411	28.589

Acceptance of this model over the previous model indicates the presence of an association between Variables *B* and *C*, but the nature of the association is different from the associations that were mentioned in connection with Models 6 and 7. Here we can claim that evidence points to a *partial association* between Variables *B* and *C*, and not "just" a marginal association. That is, we can claim that *B* and *C* are related subsequent to partialling from this association the influences of associations between Variables *A* and *B* and Variables *A* and *C*. The distinction between partial and marginal associations is important and, as such, will be discussed at greater length below. Continuing with the assumption that Model 7 has been selected as most acceptable, because τ_{ijk}^{abc} is *not* in the model, it can be deduced that the nature or pattern of the *simple* associations between *B* and *C* will be relatively consistent over the various levels of *A*.

If evidence suggests that the τ_{jk}^{bc} factor (or λ_{jk}^{bc} term) is needed in Model 7 to adequately explain data, how is it that a partial association between Variables *B* and *C*, as opposed to a marginal association, can be claimed? The answer is twofold. First, the trio of first-order factors (or terms) are not orthogonal; they do not reflect associations that are independent of each other. Second, the claim in question can be made for the *BC* association because of the ordered position in which the *BC* factor (τ_{jk}^{bc}) or term (λ_{jk}^{bc}) appears in Model 7, the seven-parameter model as specifically defined in Tables 5.2 and 5.3. Notice that the *BC* factor is entered as the seventh or last factor in the model, or, from a related perspective, it is entered third or last among first-order factors. As we shall see, when Model 7 is compared to Model 6, should Model 7 demonstrate an enhanced ability to explain the observed data, the enhancement can be attributed to an association between Variables B and C over and above previously offered explanations associated with the marginal associations between A and B and between A and C.

To reinforce the latter point, suppose that we wanted to determine if a claim could be made for the presence of a partial association between Variables A and B. To assess this claim, we would place the AB factor (or term) in the seventh or last position in a seven-parameter model, as suggested below:

$$F_{ijk} = \tau \, \tau_i^a \, \tau_j^b \, \tau_k^c \, \tau_{ik}^{ac} \, \tau_{jk}^{bc} \, \tau_{ij}^{ab}$$

and compare this model—using methods that will be discussed—to a six-parameter model that contains all factors that appear in the seven-parameter model except the AB factor. The six-parameter model to which the seven-parameter model is compared is given below:

$$F_{ijk} = \tau \, \tau_i^a \, \tau_j^b \, \tau_k^c \, \tau_{ik}^{ac} \, \tau_{jk}^{bc}$$

If over and above the contributions made by τ_{ik}^{ac} and τ_{jk}^{bc}, it is determined that the seventh parameter (τ_{ij}^{ab}) is needed to achieve an acceptable fit, then a partial association between Variables A and B is indicated.

Having had our first exposure to the significance of order of variable entry in log-linear models, we turn next to the difference between marginal and partial associations. The former, a marginal association between two variables such as B and C, is the association between B and C when the third variable (Variable A) is ignored—that is, when we collapse the three-way table over levels of Variable A to view exclusively the association in the two-way $[BC]$ table or configuration. One could subject the marginal association to statistical test by computing a χ^2 or L^2 statistic on the frequencies in the $[BC]$ configuration, as was done in Chapter 3. A marginal association between two qualitative variables is analogous to a zero-order correlation, when the latter is calculated between two continuous measures.

Realize, however, that a marginal association may be conditioned by the third variable. For example, should we deliberately adjust the association between B and C to take into account the influences exerted on this association by Variable A, and should there remain an association subsequent to this adjustment, then what remains is the partial association between B and C. We could exercise control over the influence of the third variable by examining the *simple* associations at separate levels of the third variable. If simple associations are seen at each level of the third variable, a partial association exists. However, if simple associations are not observed at separate levels of the third variable, a partial association does not exist. As can be inferred, a strong analogy can be drawn between the association under discussion and a first-order partial correlation when variables are continuous.

Model 8: The Saturated Model

The saturated model is perhaps the least interesting model in that F_{ijk}'s are completely determined by observed f_{ijk}'s (see Table 5.1). Parenthetically, the number of degrees of freedom associated with a residual chi-square test of this model is zero, a number that reflects the fact that the F_{ijk}'s are completely constrained. If it happens that restricted models are unable to fit the observed data adequately, then attempts to advance a parsimonious explanation must be abandoned, leaving us with no recourse but to accept and interpret the saturated model.

In general, acceptance of the saturated model indicates that *simple* associations between variable pairs are present but that the nature (pattern or direction) of simple bivariable associations changes in some manner when viewed over levels of the third variable. With respect specifically to $2 \times 2 \times 2$ tables, the direction (positive vs. negative) of simple associations between any two variables is reversed over levels of the third variable. Marginal associations may or may not be present; only an examination and comparison of more restricted models will reveal the presence or absence of marginal relationships. It almost goes without saying that the interpretation and follow-up of a saturated model in the symmetrical case can be somewhat complicated. However, when interpreted within the context of an asymmetrical analysis, Model 8 will present fewer difficulties.

MODEL SELECTION IN THE SYMMETRICAL CASE

The most important yet least prescribed process in a symmetrical analysis is the selection of a model for subsequent interpretation. The cornerstones of this process are subject-matter relevance, parsimony, and goodness-of-model fit. From Chapter 4 we know that the objective is to choose a substantively meaningful model that on the one hand is parsimonious, yet on the other hand is complete enough to fit observed elementary cell frequencies reasonably well. We also know that choosing a model is not exclusively a statistical decision; however, both residual and component chi-square procedures, among other statistical considerations, can be used to great advantage in the model-selection process.

The aim of this section is to apply and extend our knowledge of model selection to tables of three dimensions. We will begin by illustrating the use of residual and component chi-square testing on substance abuse data to compare models for acceptability-of-fit. An additional statistical procedure that involves a modification of what is known as Akaike's Information Criterion (AIC) statistic will be introduced shortly. Subsequently, a general strategy for model selection will be outlined. Finally, we will attempt to select and interpret the model that appears to offer the most defensible explanation of the data given in Table 5.1.

Comparing Models for Acceptability-of-Fit

It has been said repeatedly that the objective of a symmetrical analysis is the identification and interpretation of the most *acceptable* log-linear model. Unfortunately, there is no single criterion or definitive statistical test that will unequivocally lead us to that model. Nevertheless, we do have a conception of the ideal acceptable model and, further, we possess a number of statistical tools that, if properly used, will lead us close to, if not directly to, the model itself.

Ideally, we seek the most parsimonious (restricted) model that is capable of providing a reasonable, defensible fit. The model should not be so restricted, however, that the discrepancies between observed frequencies (f's) and the expected frequencies given by the model (F's) are conspicuously large, for this would indicate that one or more important terms have been omitted. Looking ahead, the results of residual chi-square testing will help us to determine if the discrepancies between f's and F's are too large.

On the other hand, the model to be adopted should not be overly specified, it should not contain higher-order terms that represent minuscule variable effects that will only serve to adulterate scientific explanation or, possibly worse, terms that, for the most part, conceal sampling error. Remember, observed elementary cell frequencies are not sacrosanct; they are generally imperfect measures endowed with error due to sampling as well as error due to uncontrolled extraneous influences that we assume (or hope) are distributed randomly throughout the table. This is why we are reluctant to automatically accept the saturated model in symmetrical inquiry. Granted, the saturated model fits observed frequencies perfectly, but when we are "forced" to accept this model, we do so knowing that extraneous factors are likely to prejudice the resultant explanations. Looking ahead again, the use of component chi-square testing will help us identify *terms* that do not make a substantial contribution to the explanation of observed data.

In sum, from among competing models we seek to adopt a model that contains only terms that are substantively meaningful and that neither underfits nor overfits the observed data. All things being equal, we seek a meaningful model that will yield a residual chi-square statistic whose numeric value is in the general vicinity of its expected value, that is, a chi-square value that is approximately equal to the number of degrees of freedom (df) associated with the model. Hence we seek a model whose residual chi-square is not so large as to achieve significance at, say, the .20 level ($p < .20$), nor so small, in a relative sense, as to be associated with an outcome p value larger than, say, .80 (i.e., $.80 < p < 1.00$). Let us survey the statistical tools that can assist us with the selection of this model.

Residual Test Statistics. A principal use of the residual chi-square statistic is to identify models that fit observed data so poorly that they can be eliminated

Table 5.4
Adequacy-of-Fit of General Log-Linear Models for the Substance Abuse Data

	Residual				Component		
Model	L^2	df	p	AIC	L^2	df	p
(1)	55.16	7	.000	57.16			
(2)	16.61	6	.011	20.61	38.55	1	.001
(3)	16.25	5	.006	22.25	0.36	1	.548
(4)	12.22	4	.016	20.22	4.03	1	.045
(5)	12.18	3	.007	22.18	0.04	1	.841
(6)	2.91	2	.234	14.91	9.27	1	.002
(7)	0.43	1	.512	14.43	2.48	1	.115
(8)	0.00	0	1.000	16.00	0.43	1	.512

immediately from further consideration. Consider the fit offered by Model 1 to the data observed in Table 5.1. Model 1 fits a value of 12.5 to each elementary cell in the $2 \times 2 \times 2$ table. To assess the extent to which the frequencies fitted by Model 1 deviate from observed frequencies, a residual likelihood-ratio chi-square statistic is calculated:

$$L_1^2 = 2\sum_i \sum_j \sum_k (f_{ijk}) [\ln (f_{ijk}/F_{ijk})]$$
$$= 2[9 \cdot \ln (9/12.5) + \cdots + 26 \cdot (28/12.5)]$$
$$= 55.16, \ p < .000$$

Obviously, Model 1 does not provide a good fit.

Should a residual chi-square be computed for Model 2, it will be $L_2^2 = 16.61$ ($p < .011$). Granted, the fit provided by this model is better than that offered by Model 1, but it is still far from being satisfactory. Moreover, as residual statistics are calculated successively on models in the hierarchy, their values tend to decrease monotonically until a perfect fit is realized (hence, $L_8^2 = 0.00$) for the saturated model. This can be seen in Table 5.4 where, for the working example, resultant residual chi-squares are displayed.

Degrees of Freedom for Residual Chi-squares. To test for statistical significance, the number of degrees of freedom for each residual chi-square must be determined. In Chapter 4, these determinations were made intuitively. It was promised, however, that a rule of thumb would be offered to assist researchers with these decisions when complexities arise. The rule of thumb for complete tables, stated as an equation for unspecified Model X, is presented below:

$$df\,\{\text{Model }(X)\} = N - \kappa\{\text{Model }(X)\} \tag{5.9}$$

where N represents the total number of elementary cells in the contingency table and κ (lowercase Greek kappa) represents the number of *basic* (or free) parameters in Model X, the model in question.

Obviously, the definition of basic parameters is key to the use of the rule. Basic parameters are parameters representing specific effects that are free to vary. When all qualitative variables are dichotomies, the number of basic parameters associated with a model is equal to the number of general parameters in that model. For example, the saturated model for a $2 \times 2 \times 2$ table has eight general parameters, and it also has eight basic parameters, hence $\kappa = 8$. Consider, however, a saturated model for a table of size $3 \times 2 \times 3$. To count the number of basic parameters here, we begin the count with λ, the log of the geometric mean; continue to λ_i^a, where we find that two of the three specific effects are free to vary since $\sum \lambda_i^a = 0$; continue to λ_j^b, where only one of the two effects can assume any value since $\sum \lambda_j^b = 0$; continue to λ_k^c where two effects again are free to vary, and so on. In sum, the number of basic parameters for this particular saturated model would be 18, as is illustrated below:

$$\lambda \quad \lambda^a \quad \lambda^b \quad \lambda^c \quad \lambda^{ab} \quad \lambda^{ac} \quad \lambda^{bc} \quad \lambda^{abc}$$
$$1 + 2 + 1 + 2 + 2 + 4 + 2 + 4 = 18$$

Having defined and illustrated κ, as an exercise, let us use the rule to determine the number of degrees of freedom for Model 2 of the working example. First, the reader is reminded that there are eight elementary cells in the table and that $\kappa = 2$ for Model 2. Restating Equation 5.12 and substituting into the equation gives

$$df\,\{\text{Model }2\} = N - \kappa\{\text{Model }2\} = 8 - 2 = 6$$

Because df is known, tests of the significance of residual departure can be made routinely for each model. For our example, the resultant p values associated with these tests can be found in Table 5.4.

Component Chi-Squares. Notice that Table 5.4 also contains component chi-squares for models of the working example. Components, recall, are differences between residuals. The number of degrees of freedom used to test a component chi-square is also a difference—the difference between the df's of respective residual chi-squares. Observe the component associated with the saturated model, which in Table 5.4 is

$$L_7^2 - L_8^2 = 0.43 - 0.00 = 0.43$$

and when assessed on a single df is obviously nonsignificant ($p < .512$). One way to view this component is from the perspective of the ability of the λ^{abc} term to enhance fit. That is, if we add the λ^{abc} term to the seven terms in Model 7 to produce Model 8, how much of an improvement in fit is realized? The reduction in residual chi-square from 0.43 to 0.00 reflects this improvement, an improvement that cannot be said to be satistically significant ($p < .571$). From another perspective, if we delete the λ^{abc} from the saturated model in favor of choosing Model 7, how much diminution in ability to fit will be realized? Again, it will be an insignificant ($p < .512$) amount. Simply put, the second-order term is inconsequential relative to explaining the substance abuse data. As can be seen, component chi-squares can be used to assess the relative importance of individual terms in models. Furthermore, if a term is judged to be inconsequential, it will be excluded from the model of choice.

AIC Procedure. Hirotugu Akaike (1976) proposed a simple procedure that can be used to great advantage when selecting either hierarchical or nonhierarchical models in the symmetrical case. The procedure, based on the principle of entropy from information theory, involves the computation of *an information criterion*, the statistic AIC for short, for each model under consideration, and directing most serious attention to the model or models that yields the smallest AIC statistic. The AIC procedure attempts to identify the optimum balance between goodness-of-fit, as measured by a model's maximized likelihood function (review the discussion associated with Equation 2.9) and the number of parameter estimates that appear in models. As the number of parameters is increased, the expected cell frequencies given by a model approximate more closely the observed cell frequencies, but this resultant improvement in fit is at the expense of parsimony. The AIC statistic computed on a model may be viewed as a relative indicator of fit where the number of parameters used to achieve fit has been considered. For a log-linear model, the generic definition of the AIC statistic (Sakamoto & Akaike, 1978, 186) can be modified (see Agresti, 1990, 251) so that for a given model it can be computed as a function of its residual L^2 and associated number of degrees of freedom, as follows:

$$\text{AIC} = L^2 - 2(df) \tag{5.10}$$

or, to avoid negative statistics, by the equivalent formula

$$\text{AIC} = L^2 + 2\kappa \tag{5.11}$$

where, as before, κ = number of basic model parameters. When computed on competing models, all things being equal, the preferred model by this criterion is the model that yields the smallest AIC statistic.

We illustrate AIC computations by comparing working Models 4 and 5. Using Equation 5.11, where the reader should verify that $\kappa = 4$ for Model 4 and

$\kappa = 5$ for Model 5, and where respective residual chi-squares are obtained from Table 5.4, we have

AIC (Model 4) $= 12.224 + (2)(4) = 20.224$

AIC (Model 5) $= 12.184 + (2)(5) = 22.184$

Based on AIC, we choose Model 4 over Model 5. AIC statistics are given for the general models summarized in Table 5.4.

A Strategy for Model Selections

Model selection in the symmetrical case is far from being the mechanical application of a singular technique. It is instead a challenging process, which is abetted by the researcher's experience with log-linear applications and his or her knowledge of the subject matter. Moreover, although oversimplification usually characterizes attempts to describe a process in terms of salient steps, for new students of log-linear methods, the following step-by-step reconstruction, based on the substance abuse example, is offered.

Step 1. For every model that has been specified, one obtains from a log-linear application program (e.g., BMDP/4F, SPSSX LOG-LINEAR, SAS CATMOD, etc.) residual likelihood-ratio chi-square statistics along with their respective df's and outcome p values. With this information, respective component chi-squares and AIC statistics can be readily obtained with a hand calculator. The outcome p values for component chi-squares may need to be approximated from the table of critical L^2 values given in Appendix B. In any event, the first task is to marshal relevant computer-generated and hand-calculated information such that it can be summarized in a table like Table 5.4.

Step 2. Examine the residual chi-squares for the purpose of eliminating from serious consideration all highly restricted models that obviously do not fit the observed data well. Proceeding from the bottom left-hand side of Table 5.4, we entertain the residual L^2's of increasingly simple models until we encounter an L^2 that is large enough to be statistically and practically significant. Since the encountered model does not fit the observed data well, we will eliminate this model and, in general, all more restricted models from further consideration. In the working example, the application of residual chi-square screening would result in the elimination of only Model 1. Although Models 2 through 5 also are not providing a good fit, they do appear to exhibit a modest ability to explain data, and hence, during this initial screening phase, these models will be retained for further study.

Step 3. Examine the component chi-squares for the purpose of identifying specific terms that obviously do not have the capacity to enhance fit. Again, proceeding from the bottom of Table 5.4 but this time on the right-hand side, we move upward in search of components that are so small and nonsignificant (say $p > .20$) that their corresponding terms will not be included in viable models. For the working example, we would immediately exclude the second-order term since the component associated with λ^{abc} is clearly not contributing to fit, $L^2(1) = 0.43, p < .512$. Another candidate for immediate elimination is the first-order AB term since $L^2(1) = 0.04, p < .841$. Finally, even though the component associated with main-marginal differences between levels of Variable B is also conspicuously nonsignificant ($p < .548$), it is best during screening to retain all main-marginal terms.[1]

Step 4. Identify the most promising set of competing models for intensive study. Up to this point, the execution of Steps 1 and 2 has served to screen out the most unlikely models and terms. We now regroup, so to speak, so that our remaining intellectual and statistical tools can be applied to those models that qualify as serious candidates for selection. If the investigation is exploratory, it is often necessary to obtain the residual fit of models that now appear to hold promise but that were not analyzed initially. Since initial screening has suggested that the main-marginal terms for Variables A and C and the first-order terms for AC and BC are salient, we specify all reasonable models involving combinations of salient terms and, if necessary, approach the computer again for their respective residual chi-squares. The results of a second pass for hierarchical models that are deemed to be most promising for the working example are as follows:

Model	Marginals Fitted	L^2	df	p	AIC
(4a)	[A], [C], [AC]	3.31	4	.506	11.31
(5a)	[A], [B], [C], [AC]	2.95	3	.399	12.95
(6a)	[A], [B], [C], [AC], [BC]	.52	2	.770	21.52

Step 5. Using the previously illustrated tools (residual and component testing) in conjunction with the ardent use of the AIC statistic, we assess competing models in an effort to find the most restricted model containing meaningful terms that shows a residual L^2 that is in the vicinity of its expected value (i.e., number of degrees of freedom). Here is where information provided by the AIC procedure can be most helpful. All things considered (the resultant AIC statistics among them), Models 4a and 5a appear to be prime candidates for adoption. As we see, the only difference between these two models is the acknowledgement by Model 5a that insignificant ($p < .548$) main-marginal differences exist relative to Variable B. Now, if Variable B had been deliberately fixed as a part of our sampling plan (as we will assume it to be when we turn to the study of adverse impact), then the term for Variable B would be retained in the model. If, however, the main marginals for this variable were free to represent the main marginals of the background population from which the sample was drawn, then this

inconsequential term could be omitted from the final model. Since the latter is assumed for the substance abuse example, we choose to adopt Model 4a.

Finally, the adopted model is interpreted. Aside from the presence of main-marginal differences between levels of Variable A, significantly fewer subjects were classified as hard drug abusers than as nonabusers ($p < .001$), and main-marginal differences between levels of Variable C ($p < .045$), the paramount finding is that Variables A and C are significantly associated.[2] The nature of the relationship may be seen by comparing observed frequencies in the collapsed [AC] configuration against the expected frequencies given by Model 4a in the [AC] configuration. Alternatively, one can request as computer output the values of the λ^{ac}'s as they are estimated in Model 4a, our model of choice. Such a request would provide the following lambda parameters for the AC term:

	C_1	C_2
A_1	.395	-.395
A_2	-.395	.395

As anticipated, the approximate z tests on these parameter estimates are statistically significant, $\pm z = 2.91$. Hence, the association is such that abusers of hard drugs tend also to abuse alcohol, or vice versa. However, remaining associations such as those between hard drug and soft drug use, or between soft drug use and use of alcohol, cannot be documented by the existing data.

We have completed our discussion of symmetrical inquiry for this chapter. We will return to this manner of analysis again in Chapter 7 where we will have an opportunity to augment our model-selection skills in the more challenging setting of four dimensions and where we will be introduced to screening procedures that greatly facilitate the identification of models that are worthy of serious study.

INTERPRETING EFFECTS IN ASYMMETRICAL INQUIRY

This section deals with a special application of log-linear models. Specifically, log-linear models can be specified, and constituent terms within these special models can be evaluated, to determine if sampling groups differ with respect to their response pattern over levels of a designated response variable. Such a manner of analysis is consistent with the scenario associated with the study of adverse impact described earlier in this chapter. Often the asymmetrical application of log-linear models is called a *logit-model analysis* (see Goodman, 1972b), and the variable that is designated as response (e.g., Outcome at Termination of Testing) is called the *logit variable*.[3]

In many respects, a logit-model analysis is similar to an ANOVA. The study of adverse impact, for example, lends itself to a logit-model analysis that can be loosely compared to a two-way ANOVA. In the study, the two explanatory variables (Gender and Ethnic Group) have been crossed to form a 2 × 2 factorial arrangement and the intent is to perform an ANOVA-like analysis on a categorical response variable, namely, Outcome at Termination of Testing.

Most behavioral investigations lend themselves to asymmetrical inquiry, yet, unfortunately, most current expository writings place the greatest emphasis on symmetrical inquiry. An exception is the compiled writings of Goodman (1978). Goodman, in fact, has greatly advanced the use of the logit-model approach by demonstrating that distinctively different formulations and models are not needed to perform an asymmetrical analysis. Instead, in most cases, a logit-model analysis can be performed by generating, evaluating, and interpreting a subset of the models with which we have been working. Our immediate aim is to identify those models in Table 5.2 (or Table 5.3) that are legitimate logit models and to indicate why they are so designated. Subsequently, we will point out the omnibus interpretation associated with legitimate logit models as we did in the previous section for general log-linear models.

Legitimate Logit Models

A clue as to what constitutes a legitimate logit model can be gleaned from our work with two-dimensional tables in Chapter 4. Examine again the models presented in Table 4.1, and note that only Models 3 and 4 have meaningful interpretations in the asymmetrical case. It may be recalled that in the working example of the last chapter, Variable A (Gender) was the explanatory variable, whereas Variable B (Attitude) was the logit or designated response variable. The central question was whether females and males responded in equal proportions to each category of the attitude variable.

Since we were concerned with patterns of proportional response over levels of Variable B within levels of Variable A, the fact that there happened to be fewer females in the sample ($f_1^a = 40$) than males ($f_2^a = 60$), and that, overall, more members of the sample opposed the amendment ($f_1^b = 70$) than supported it ($f_2^b = 30$) was not relevant to the central question. After all, it is the investigator who determines $[A]$ (i.e., frequencies in the main marginal of Variable A) by his or her choice of sampling scheme. Moreover, frequencies seen in $[B]$, per se, have no bearing on differences in proportional response between females and males. Indeed, main-marginal differences in $[A]$ and $[B]$ are not only irrelevant to the manner of response under consideration, but to the extent to which they exist, they should not be permitted to distort the picture of proportional response to the logit variable by gender.

For two-dimensional tables, therefore, irrelevant main-marginal differences should be both acknowledged and controlled by incorporating their respective terms in all models that are to be assessed asymmetrically. In other words, at the very least, a legitimate logit model should contain τ_i^a and τ_j^b, as does Model 3. If Model 3 should be chosen, we can conclude that there may be differences in $[A]$ and $[B]$, but that beyond these differences the proportional response of females and males to levels of the logit variable cannot be said to be different. However, if Model 4 should prove to be the model of choice, we can say that there are differences in the proportional response of females and males to levels of the logit variable, differences that are over and above arbitrary differences in the main marginals of A and B. To be a legitimate logit model, the model must contain all parameters that reflect potential differences not relevant to proportional response over the logit variable. The model must contain these parameters so that they can be controlled in a manner analogous to that seen in the analysis of covariance. In sum, Models 3 and 4 are legitimate models for an asymmetrical analysis in the two-dimensional situation, an analysis of the hypothesis of homogeneity of proportional response.

Let us return to a three-variable situation, a situation characterized by two explanatory variables and one logit variable. Here again, a logit model should contain all the parameters that are linked to irrelevant or arbitrary differences in the main marginals, but in addition, the model must contain the first-order parameter associated with the fixed (hence, irrelevant) two-variable configuration.

Consider specifically the study of adverse impact where it is clear that Variables A (Gender) and B (Ethnic Group) are explanatory and Variable C (Outcome at Termination of Testing) is the response variable.[4] The intent is to determine whether there are effects due to gender or ethnic group status with respect to the outcome of testing. To pursue this intent, a sample of 100 workers was obtained, a sample in which males far outnumbered females, as a consequent of representative sampling, and Variable B was deliberately structured so that majority and minority group members were approximately equal. Irrespective of the sampling plan associated with a particular study in which Variable C is the designated response, we certainly do not want the uneven distributions in either $[A]$ or $[B]$ to influence logit-variable response. By the same token, differences in observed cell frequencies in the $[AB]$ configuration are not relevant to logit response, hence they too should not be permitted to influence logit response and they too must be controlled. It follows that we must fix the $[AB]$ configuration—and by doing so, we can automatically fix upon both $[A]$ and $[B]$—in order to standardize to unity the proportional response to Variable C within each cell of the $[AB]$ configuration. Consequently, present in any and all logit models for the working example must be the parameter estimate τ_{ij}^{ab} (or λ_{ij}^{ab}).[5] The models in Table 5.2 that qualify as legitimate logit models are Models 5, 6, and 7 and the saturated model.

In general, and in conclusion, log-linear models that are evaluated in asymmetrical inquiry contain at least: (1) terms representing all main-marginal effects and (2) terms that represent all higher-order interactions that are exclusively defined by the explanatory variable. As an exercise, consider a four-dimensional table defined by Variables A, B, C, and D, and where the investigator has designated Variable A as the response variable. Here, legitmate logit models must contain the four main-marginal terms (i.e., terms for A, B, C, and D), plus first-order terms where both constituents are explanatory (i.e., terms for *BC*, *BD*, and *CD*), as well as the second-order *BCD* term.

Based on the foregoing discussion, where it has been established that Models 5, 6, 7, and 8 are legitimate models for an asymmetrical analysis (where Variable *C* has been deemed response), let us examine these models with an eye toward their interpretative implications. During the examination, remember that in the asymmetrical mode our approach to the analysis will be more akin to classical hypothesis testing. That is, our primary concern will not center on how well a given model appears to fit observed data, though a number of model-fitting features will still apply, but rather on how well certain terms in logit models contribute to data fit.

Model 5: The Completely Null Model

Model 5 contains the minimal requisite terms discussed immediately above. The elementary cell frequencies given by Model 5 have been calculated by Equation 5.6 and displayed previously. The most meaningful view in an asymmetrical analysis, however, is that of proportional response over levels of the logit variable (Variable *C* here) from within cells of the fixed [*AB*]. Accordingly, we take the F_{ijk}'s given by this model for the cells of [*AB*], and within these cells we standardize to unity the proportional response to levels of *C*. Mathematically, for the cell situated in the *i*th level of *A* and the *j*th level of *B*, the *fitted* proportion for the *k*th level of *C* is

$$P_{ijk} = F_{ijk}/f_{ij}^{ab} \tag{5.12}$$

The use of Equation 5.12 for Model 5 on working data gives us the following view of proportional response by Gender and Ethnic Group:

A	B	C_1	C_2	[AB]
1	1	.400	.600	1.000
1	2	.400	.600	1.000
2	1	.400	.600	1.000
2	2	.400	.600	1.000

As before, the reader is asked to assume for the moment that the expected cell frequencies produced by Model 5 provided an extremely good fit to the observed data. If this were so, clearly, no logit-model effects of any kind are present. The pattern of response is the same for females and males and the same for majority and minority subjects. By analogy, the outcome is like that given by a two-way ANOVA when the *F* tests for both main effects and the interaction are found to be nonsignificant. Therefore, to the extent that Model 5 fits the observed data, and to the extent to which the residual chi-square for this model is small and statistically nonsignificant, evidence pointing to logit-model effects due to Gender or Ethnic Group is not present.

Model 6: Main Effects for Variable A

In addition to obligatory λ_{ij}^{ab}, Model 6 contains λ_{ik}^{ac}. To obtain patterns of proportional response to levels of the logit variable we again use Equation 5.9, but now the F_{ijk}'s in the numerator are the F_{ijk}'s produced by, and previously tabled for, Model 6. Fitted cell proportions turn out to be

A	B	C_1	C_2	[AB]
1	1	.700	.300	1.000
1	2	.700	.300	1.000
2	1	.325	.675	1.000
2	2	.325	.675	1.000

Should this model fit the observed data well, what ANOVA-like conclusion can be drawn? Can we not conclude first that the female and male profiles of logit-variable response are different? Moreover, if it can be shown that the observed response profiles are statistically different, it can be said that logit-model main effects have been observed for Variable A. In short, the fact that λ_{ik}^{ac} is needed to achieve a good fit indicates that the "difference" between C_1 and C_2 will, in turn, be different at A_1 and at A_2. Notice, however, that profiles of response to C do not change over levels of B; hence, at this time, no main effects are indicated for levels of the Ethnic Group variable. Also, profiles do not differ within the cells of [AB] after adjustments are made for the main effects due to A, and hence, there is no evidence of interaction.

Model 7: Main Effects for Variable B

The selection of Model 7 in the symmetrical case implies that λ_{jk}^{bc} is needed to achieve a reasonable fit. Let us assume in the asymmetrical case that we have determined that λ_{jk}^{bc} is similarly important. To the extent to which this first-order term is needed, response profiles over levels of C can be expected to vary over levels of B. That is, from an asymmetrical perspective, one would expect to observe main effects for Variable B. To see whether our expectation is correct, and to eliminate the confounding effects due to λ_{ik}^{ac}, the following logit model was fit:

$$\ln F_{ijk} = \lambda + \lambda_i^a + \lambda_j^b + \lambda_k^c + \lambda_{ij}^{ab} + \lambda_{jk}^{bc}$$

and Equation 5.12 was used on F_{ijk}'s produced by the model immediately above with the following result:

B	A	C_1	C_2	[AB]
1	1	.472	.582	1.000
1	2	.472	.582	1.000
2	1	.319	.681	1.000
2	2	.319	.681	1.000

Be sure to notice that the indices for Variables A and B above have been reversed so as to better accommodate a visual comparison between levels of B. Although it is apparent that response profiles are dissimilar over levels of Variable B (suggesting logit-model main effects due to this variable), the profiles are not as different as those seen above in connection with main effects due to Variable A. When we evaluate the "boldness" of main effects due to Variable B by subjecting its component chi-square to test, not surprisingly, it will *not* be found to be statistically significant.

Model 8: Interaction Between Variables A and B

For Model 8, the fitted proportions over levels of C for each cell in [AB] are given by $P_{ijk} = f_{ijk}/f_{ij}^{ab}$. For the adverse impact data, these proportions are

A	B	C_1	C_2	[AB]
1	1	.818	.182	1.000
1	2	.556	.444	1.000
2	1	.381	.619	1.000
2	2	.263	.737	1.000

If the saturated model is adopted in a symmetrical analysis, it means that the second-order λ_{ijk}^{abc} term is needed to explain the data. Translated into the asymmetrical, a prominant λ_{ijk}^{abc} term indicates the presence of logit-model first-order interaction between Variables A and B. Unfortunately for our immediate purpose, the first-order interaction term was not prominent in our working example ($p <$ .512), and hence, the proportions presented in the unnumbered table above, proportions that also reflect the confounding influences of main effects due to Gender and Ethnic Group, do not clearly reveal the nature of the interaction between Variables A and B. Nevertheless, we can deduce the consequences of a logit-model first-order term in situations where it is found to be substantively and statistically significant.

The appearance of a significant λ_{ijk}^{abc} term means that the observed data cannot be adequately explained in terms of the additive main effects of Variables A and B. As noted, the interaction between Variable A and B is analogous to first-order interaction in a two-way ANOVA. (Incidentally, meaningful main effects for

Variables A and B either may or may not be present.) If this term was found to be prominent in the study of adverse impact (it will not be), it could be interpreted in several ways. It could be said, for example, that the pattern of response to the logit variable given by females and males who belong to the majority is distinctively different from the pattern of response observed for females and males of the minority. It could also be said that the pattern of logit-variable response observed for majority and minority applicants is moderated by the Gender variable. In either case, interaction connotes complexity, which should be acknowledged during the interpretation of results.

ASSESSING EFFECTS IN THE ASYMMETRICAL CASE

In an asymmetrical analysis the objective is to identify and subsequently interpret terms that appear to be promoting discrepancy about the null-logit model, namely, Model 5 in the study of adverse impact. To accomplish this objective, residual chi-squares are obtained for all legitimate models. Whereas residual chi-squares are central to the selection of models in the symmetrical case, in the asymmetrical case they serve as a means to an end. Residual chi-squares are used primarily to obtain relevant component chi-squares. Relevant component chi-squares are then subjected to statistical test to determine if significant logit-model effects can be documented. The approach to be illustrated is parallel in many respects to that taken when performing an ANOVA.

The information needed to analyze the results of the adverse impact study is currently available in Table 5.4. It will be to our advantage, however, to obtain from Table 5.4 selective information that pertains only to the four legitimate logit-models and to present this information in a table that is similar in both appearance and function to the summary of a two-factor ANOVA. This logit-model summary table is shown below as Table 5.5.

Table 5.5 is interpreted in a manner not unlike an ANOVA table. In the ANOVA, recall that an overall measure of variability about the grand mean (total sum of squares) may be partitioned into two general additive components: a component explained by the factors incorporated into the design (explained or regression sum of squares) and a residual component. Moreover, the relative size of the explained component (the magnitude of the R^2) can be subjected to statistical test. If significance is *not* achieved, further analysis is discouraged unless there is defensible a priori argumentation to the contrary. On the other hand, if the explained composite component is found to be statistically significant, the researcher is encouraged to examine specific components for statistical significance.

Comparable features are found in analyses involving asymmetrical models. Notice first in Table 5.5 that the component chi-squares for effects due to Variables A and B and the interaction of Variable A with B sum to the residual chi-square for the null-logit model. The ability to partition the residuum about the null-logit model into additive component chi-squares will be addressed in greater

Table 5.5
Summary Table of the Logit-Model Analysis of Adverse Impact Data

Model/Source		L^2	df	p
(6)	Due to Gender	9.27	1	.002
(7)	Due to Ethnic Group, Given Sex	2.48	1	.115
(8)	Due to Interaction	.43	1	.512
(5)	Null/Total	12.18	3	.007

length shortly. For the moment, realize that the size of the residual chi-square for the null-logit model represents the degree to which observed cell frequencies do *not* conform to those offered by the null model. In other words, the size of the residual reflects the extent to which design factors (Variable A, Variable B, etc.) are operative. From a different perspective, the residual chi-square for Model 5 can be viewed as a component chi-square defined as $L^2_{5-8}(3) = 12.18 - 0.00 = 12.18$, $p < .007$. From this perspective, the composite influence of specific effects, analogous to the sum of squares regression in the ANOVA, can be examined and tested for statistical significance. Usually, this composite test is considered first in an exploratory analysis.

The Composite Test

Taken together, are the main and interaction effects specified in Table 5.5 strong enough to render Model 5 a poor fit? Since $L^2_5(3) = 12.18$, $p < .007$, and since this residual is statistically significant (at, say, the .05 level), the answer is *yes*. Encouragement to examine specific constituent components associated with Gender, Ethnic Group, and so forth has been provided. Be alert to the fact, however, that the test in question is a composite test, and that composite tests tend to be more conservative than tests performed on constituent components. It is possible, therefore, for the composite test to fail to achieve significance yet for significance to be achieved for tests performed on specific components. Should this occur, it is generally advisable to ignore the significant results associated with specific effects. After all, if the overall test is not significant, collectively, tests on specific components carry with them a higher Type

I error rate than is nominal. Even so, an exception is frequently seen when the results of component tests are consistent with strong a priori predictions. That is, if, on the basis of theory, predictions made in advance of data analysis happen to be supported by the results of specific tests, then despite the outcome of the composite test, the investigator is justified in pursuing specific results. In any event, since the composite testing resulted in statistical significance for the working example, suggesting in general that the testing program is having some manner of adverse impact on employees, specific effects will be assessed to clarify the nature of this overall finding.

Tests on Specific Effects

Main Effects Due to Variable A. We consider next in Table 5.5 the component associated with the λ_{ik}^{ac} term in Model 6, a component that is observed to be significant, $L_{5-6}^2 = 9.27, p < .002$. We know that in symmetrical inquiry, this outcome denotes a significant marginal association between Variables A and C. From our reading of the previous section, we also know that a significant association between A and C can be interpreted as indicating that the pattern of proportional response over levels of Variable C is significantly dissimilar for females and males. In short, evidence is sufficient to support a finding of significant main effects due to Gender. We will follow up this omnibus finding shortly.

Main Effects Due to Variable B. The component associated with the λ_{jk}^{bc} term in Model 7 has failed to achieve significance at the .05 level, the level of significance adopted for this example, namely, $L_{6-7}^2 = 2.48, p < .115$. Therefore, significantly different response patterns due to ethnic group differences cannot be professed.

Consider for a moment, however, a situation in which these effects were found to be statistically significant. Not only could we claim significant main effects due to Variable B in this situation, it could also be said that these effects are significant after adjustments have been made for Variable A, the Gender variable. Such a claim is permitted because of the way in which we have fashioned our models. Notice that among the three two-variable terms (or first-order terms, in the nomenclature of asymmetrical inquiry), the λ_{jk}^{bc} term was the last term entered and assessed. The component that was subjected to test, therefore, represents the strength of the partial association between Variables B and C, the association between B and C subsequent to accounting for associations between Variables A and B and Variables A and C. If the BC component was significant, response differences between majority and minority group members, where effects due to gender differences have been controlled, would be indicated. A concrete illustration of partialed main effects will be offered in the ensuing study of reflective teaching.

Interaction Between Variables A and B. The component associated with the λ_{ijk}^{abc} term in the saturated model was clearly not significant, $L_{7-8}^2 = .43$, $p <$ .512. Since we have documented significant effects due to gender, one implication prompted by the failure of the interaction to achieve significance is that gender differences are not moderated by ethnic group status. Though we will not have to grapple with an interpretation of first-order interaction for the adverse impact study, we will interpret such an interaction in Chapter 7 in connection with the McLean (1980) study.

Follow-Up Procedures

Because statistical significance was observed only for main effects due to gender, and because we need only to examine the 2×2 tabular configuration defined by Gender and Outcome of Testing, the task of explicating omnibus results is relatively straightforward. Two strategies come to mind. The first and most obvious is to compare *observed* frequencies in the 2×2 tabular configuration to their respective *expected* frequencies under the conventional hypothesis of homogeneity of proportional response (or independence). The table in question that presents expected frequencies in parentheses is shown below:

	Outcome of Testing		
Gender	Failed	Passed	[A]
Females	14 (8)	6 (12)	20
Males	26 (32)	54 (48)	80
[C]	40	60	100

Since the marginal association between Variables *A* and *C* was observed to be significant ($\chi^2 = 9.38$ or $L^2 = 9.27$, $p < .002$), and because the table is fourfold, among the several conclusions that can be drawn is that proportionately more females failed ($p = 14/20 = .70$) than did males ($p = .325$).

A second strategy is to examine lambda parameters associated with the λ_{ik}^{ac} term. To implement this strategy, however, a model must be selected since lambda parameters are model-dependent. In other words, an acceptable *follow-up* model must be adopted. The situation is comparable to the search for an acceptable model in symmetrical inquiry, only here our choice is limited to logit models. Even so, the principles and operations that were discussed in connection with model selection in the symmetrical case apply to the selection of the most acceptable follow-up model in the asymmetrical case.

In this regard, since it was obvious that the interaction term was not significant ($p < .512$), it can be excluded immediately from the follow-up model. Though some would argue, I would also exclude the λ_{jk}^{bc} from the follow-up model not only because it did not approach significance ($p < .115$) but also because its presence in the follow-up model would only serve to obscure (albeit only slightly) the nature of the marginal association under study. Hence, the following model has been selected to assist us in our efforts to clarify differential effects due to the Gender variable:

$$\ln F_{ijk} = \lambda + \lambda^a + \lambda^b + \lambda^c + \lambda^{ab} + \lambda^{ac} \tag{5.13}$$

Having selected a follow-up model, with additional computer assistance we solve for the F_{ijk}'s and estimates of lambda. Should this be done, the lambda parameters for the λ^{ac}_{ik} in the model above will be found to be

| | Outcome of Testing | |
Gender	Failed	Passed
Females	.395	-.395
Males	-.395	.395

It will also be found that the accompanying z statistics are ± 2.91, therefore permitting the rejection of the null hypotheses that lambdas are equal to zero.

Though it is clear that the lambda parameters support the finding that tested females were not as successful as males, if technical accuracy is desired, one should be careful when attempting to verbally interpret lambda parameters. A review of Equation 4.21 reminds us that lambda parameters reveal differences between geometric means expressed on a log scale, and their multiplicative counterparts, tau parameters, indicate differences in geometric means. Lambda parameters may also be interpreted in terms of logged odds ratios, called log odds. The latter, tau parameters, may be interpreted more simply in terms of differential odds. The point to be made here is that neither lambda nor tau parameters, per se, directly reflect proportional differences between or among groups.

Since lambda parameters are often used as vehicles to follow up a log-linear analysis in complex analyses, an attempt to clarify their meaning might be useful. Let us begin by considering the lambda estimate from Equation 5.13, the follow-up model, for females who failed, specifically $\lambda^{ac}_{11} = .395$. To avoid the mention of logarithms at this point, we begin with an examination of the multiplicative counterpart, specifically τ^{ac}_{11}. Using Equation 4.21 as a basis for generalization, the tau parameter in question may be expressed as

$$\begin{aligned} \tau^{ac}_{11} &= \frac{\overline{G}^{ac}_{11}}{\tau\,\tau^a_1\,\tau^c_1} \\ &= \frac{(\overline{G}^{ac}_{11})}{\overline{G}} \cdot \frac{1}{\tau^a_1} \cdot \frac{1}{\tau^c_1} \\ &= \frac{\overline{G}^{ac}_{11}}{\overline{G}} \cdot \frac{\overline{G}}{\overline{G}^a_1} \cdot \frac{\overline{G}}{\overline{G}^c_1} \end{aligned} \tag{5.14}$$

where the geometric mean of expected frequencies from Equation 5.13 for females who failed would be found to be

$$\overline{G}_{11}^{ac} = (7.70 \cdot 6.30)^{1/2}$$
$$= 6.9649$$

As a check, we substitute other computed values from the follow-up model into the right-hand expressions of Equation 5.14.

$$\tau_{11}^{ac} = \frac{6.9649}{9.2368} \cdot \frac{1}{.4936} \cdot \frac{1}{1.0294}$$
$$= \frac{6.9649}{9.2368} \cdot \frac{9.2368}{4.5596} \cdot \frac{9.2368}{9.5095}$$
$$= 1.484$$

Having obtained tau, the corresponding lambda estimate for females who failed is obtained by taking its log as follows:

$$\lambda_{11}^{ac} = \ln \tau_{11}^{ac}$$
$$= \ln 1.484$$
$$= .395$$

Do not lose sight of our central purpose here, which is to gain an interpretative insight into the nature of resultant log-linear parameter estimates, an insight that is provided from a careful examination of the right-hand expressions in Equation 5.14. Here it can be seen that the statistically significant tau parameter indicates that with respect to the tabular average (i.e., $\overline{G}$), the odds are greater that females will fail—subsequent, of course, to affecting a correction for the unfavorable tabular odds of belonging in the average (geometric) female cell (i.e., .49 to 1), and affecting an adjustment for the somewhat favorable odds of being in the average (geometric) failure cell (i.e., 1.03 to 1). The lambda parameter represents the log of the aforementioned odds.

It will be conceded that the interpretation that has been offered is both cumbrous and complicated. And whereas lambda and tau parameters can be, and have been, used to great advantage to interpret results, interpretations couched in odds, especially log odds, often present difficulties to lay audiences. Fortunately, as will be shown in Chapter 6, through the use of focused comparisons it will be possible to explicate the results of an asymmetrical analysis with greater precision and to speak of effects in terms of proportional differences, a metric with which most consumers of research are more comfortable.

THE EFFECTS OF REFLECTIVE TEACHING:
A DIDACTIC EXAMPLE

We will now attempt to reinforce and extend our knowlege of log-linear methods by exercising them within the context of an educational experiment, the *reflective teaching study* reported by Holton and Nott (1980). Aside from my desire to expose readers to an example that is unequivocally asymmetrical and experimental—so as to assuage the impression that log-linear methods are only used for descriptive research—another reason for choosing this study is to show how these researchers handled a potentially troublesome pre- and posttest variable to minimize violations of the assumption of response independence. This experiment is also of interest due to a number of additional features. The research was conducted to test a specific a priori hypothesis—it was not an exploratory investigation—and the three-dimensional table of observed frequencies will contain a zero cell frequency.

An Overview of the Reflective Teaching Experiment

The 101 subjects in this experiment were teachers in training enrolled in a large midwestern university. Subjects were enrolled in four intact classes, two of which were assigned at random to be exposed to *reflective teaching*, a new form of on-campus laboratory teaching experience, while the remaining two classes served as controls. The principal planned hypothesis was that exposure to reflective teaching would enhance the ability of the students to express themselves in an analytical manner when discussing the process of learning.

Data were obtained from the written responses of students to the stimulus "When I think about learning," which were gathered prior to and following the experiment. Pretest responses to the stimulus sentence were subjected to a grammatical structural analysis, which ultimately led to each student being placed into one of four categories based on his or her predominant mode of response. The grammatical categories were: (1) analytical, (2) evidential, (3) declarative, and (4) indeterminate, with the latter containing subjects whom judges could not reliably classify into one of the three other categories. Identical methods were used with respect to the posttest responses provided by subjects. There were, therefore, three variables, namely:

Variable *A*, a polytomy, was the *pretest* response variable. On the basis of their judged predominant mode of response, subjects were assigned to one of the four categories mentioned above. This variable was an explanatory variable in the logit-model analysis.

Variable *B*, a dichotomy, was the *treatment* variable; it consisted of 55 subjects from the experimental group that were exposed to reflective teaching and 46 students who were members of the control groups. This variable, obviously, was the principal explanatory variable in the experiment.

Variable *C* was the *posttest* variable, and in this experiment it was the response

Table 5.6
Cross-Classification of Subjects in the Reflective Teaching Experiment by Pretest Response, Treatment Groups, and Posttest Response

Pretest Response	Treatment Group	Posttest Categories			
		C_1	C_2	C_3	C_4
A_1	B_1	8	2	1	4
A_1	B_2	1	2	2	4
A_2	B_1	6	4	2	5
A_2	B_2	1	14	5	3
A_3	B_1	1	2	2	1
A_3	B_2	1	0	1	3
A_4	B_1	8	4	1	4
A_4	B_2	2	4	1	2

variable. As noted, subjects were classified into one of the four grammatical categories.

Before we look at the data, consider the way that these researchers handled pre- and posttest responses. At first, it might seem desirable to combine these two sets of data to form a repeated measurements variable, as is often done in classical experimental design work. Such a combination would not constitute good practice here, however, since it would result in each subject appearing twice in the contingency table, a result that would likely lead to a violation of the basic assumption that tabulations are independently determined. Instead, pretest and posttest responses were treated as separate variables, variables that were crossed with the treatment variable to form a $4 \times 2 \times 4$ contingency table in which subjects were placed into one—and only one—of the 32 elementary cells. It must be admitted, however, that these researchers were fortunate in that the correlation between pretest and posttest response was not so strong as to result in an excessive number of empty cells in the $[AC]$ configuration.

Observed tabulations for the study are shown in Table 5.6. Note that there is a void cell, a zero, in the table. The discussion of void cells will be presented in Chapter 7; for now, we simply state that the presence of void cells does not preclude a log-linear analysis if these cells are a result of sampling artifacts (i.e., sampling zeros)—as opposed to structural artifacts (i.e., structural zeros; for example, pregnant males)—and if void cells are not overly numerous. Both

Table 5.7
Residual Chi-Squares Computed on Logit-Models for the Reflective Teaching Experiment

Model	Marginals Fitted	L^2	df	p
(5)	[AB], [C]	29.31	21	.107
(6)	[AB], [AC]	18.40	12	.104
(7)	[AB], [AC], [BC]	8.09	9	.524
(8)	[ABC]	0.00	0	1.000

requisites are satisfied in this experiment. To proceed mathematically, however, a small numerical quantity, called a *delta value*, must be added to each cell count to facilitate the computation of chi-square statistics for the saturated model. A reexamination of Equation 3.11, the formula for the L^2 statistic, will reveal why a zero observed cell frequency (i.e., $f_{ijk} = 0$) is intractable. The problem of a zero dividend is circumvented by adding a small constant delta value—usually in the amount of 0.5, though some analysts prefer a smaller quantity—to all f_{ijk}'s. Incidentally, the effect of employing a delta adjustment is typically inconsequential; it simply tends to reduce slightly and systematically the magnitudes of residual chi-squares.

Summary of the Asymmetrical Analysis

A delta value of 0.5 was added to the 32 observed frequencies that appear in Table 5.6, and Models 5 through 8, as defined in Table 5.3, were fitted to these augmented frequencies. Resultant residual chi-squares are reported in Table 5.7. Be reminded, however, that for an asymmetrical analysis, residual chi-squares are a means to an end; they are needed primarily to calculate by hand component chi-squares that reflect the strength of effects.

Component chi-squares reported by Holton and Nott (1980) are seen in the summary Table 5.8. We first look at the summary table to see if the residual chi-square for the null-logit model is statistically significant. At the .05 level, it is not: $L_5^2(21) = 29.31, p < .107$. Thus, it would seem that the results of this composite test would discourage rejection of the null logit as an explanation for the observed frequencies. However, since the investigators posited strong predictions in advance of data collection, they felt justified in examining tests on specific effects.

If the investigators' hypothesis that the reflective teaching treatment promotes "higher-level" written responses is, in fact, viable, then the λ_{jk}^{bc} in Model 7

Table 5.8
Summary Table of the Logit-Model Analysis of the Reflective Teaching Experiment

Model/Source	L^2	df	p
(6) Due to Pretest	10.92	9	.282
(7) Due to Treatments, Given Pretests	10.31	3	.016
(8) Due to Interaction	8.09	9	.524
(5) Null/Total	29.31	21	.106

Note: The sum of reported effect components is not exactly equivalent to 29.31 due to rounding error.

should be prominent. The component chi-square for Model 7 reported in Table 5.7 was deemed to be significant, namely, $L^2_{6-7}(3) = 10.31$, $p < .016$. Furthermore, since λ^{bc}_{jk} was entered last in this full first-order model, the significant component here meant that differences exist between treatment groups with respect to how they responded to Variable C even after pretest differences have been taken into account. The situation is analogous to an analysis of covariance (ANCOVA) in which posttest differences between treatment groups are evident after adjustments are made for initial pretest differences. Finally, note that there is no support for the contentions that pretest groupings differed significantly in their patterns of posttest response ($p < .282$) or that treatment groups interacted with the pretest variable ($p < .524$).

Alternative Partitions of the Residuum

Before considering follow-up procedures, let us look at several alternative approaches to the partitioning of

$$L^2_{5-8} = 29.32 - 0.00 = 29.32$$

the residuum about the expected cell frequencies given by Model 5, the null-logit model. We know that the order in which higher-order terms are introduced in a model determines whether its associated component represents a marginal or partial association. For example, to test for a partial association between Variables B and C, λ^{bc}_{jk} would be entered last in a seven-parameter model, and the component for this partial association would be the difference in residuals between the model in question and a six-parameter model except for the λ^{bc}_{jk} term. This specific order was adopted by Holton and Nott; hence, finding λ^{bc}_{jk} to be statistically significant ($p < .017$), they were able to document treatment group effects adjusted for pretest effects.

Had they chosen to do so, the λ_{jk}^{bc} term could have been introduced as the sixth term and this model could be assessed against the null-logit model. The models in question are shown below:

Model 5a: $\ln F_{ijk} = \lambda + \lambda^a + \lambda^b + \lambda^c + \lambda^{ab}$

Model 6a: $\ln F_{ijk} = \lambda + \lambda^a + \lambda^b + \lambda^c + \lambda^{ab} + \lambda^{bc}$

The component for treatment effects given this model arrangement would be found to be

$$
\begin{aligned}
L_{5a-6a}^2 &= L_{5a}^2 - L_{6a}^2 \\
&= 29.31 - 16.86 \\
&= 12.45
\end{aligned}
$$

which, when related to a chi-square distribution predicated on $df = 21 - 18 = 3$, yields an outcome p value of .006. In short, the effects of the treatment variable where no attempt has been made to partial out pretests effects are also significant and, not surprisingly, somewhat stronger than the adjusted treatment effects reported in Table 5.8. Incidentally, the component associated with the λ_{ik}^{ac} term reported in Table 5.8 is a marginal component. However, by repositioning this term along the lines suggested above, a component that would reflect pretesting effects adjusted for treatment group effects is obtainable.

To make a long story short, there are several ways to calculate and report the results of a generalized logit-model analysis just as there are several options available for the reporting of a nonorthogonal (unbalanced) two-way ANOVA. The results of pretesting and treatment effects could each be reported as unadjusted effects or, as is seen in Table 5.8, one term could be unadjusted (pretests) while the other is adjusted (treatment), or both could be reported as adjusted effects. The strategy adopted by Holton and Nott, as revealed in Table 5.8, is essentially hierarchical in that the residuum explained by treatment groups is calculated subsequent to accounting completely for the residuum that can be explained by the pretesting variable. The latter strategy, whereby both terms are reported as partials, is a conservative strategy that is analogous to what is sometimes termed a *full regression approach* in the ANOVA (e.g., Type III analysis using PROC GLM in SAS). These three approaches as applied to the Holton-Nott data are illustrated in Table 5.9.

Following-Up the Logit-Model Analysis

To this point, all that can be said is that experimental group members did not respond to the logit variable in the same way as did members of the control

Table 5.9

A Comparison of Three Approaches to the Calculation, Interpretation, and Reporting of Effects in the Holton-Nott Study

Model Number	Order in Which Terms are Entered					
	AB→ AC→ BC→ ABC		*AB→ BC→ AC→ ABC*		Both Orders	
	Source	L^2	Source	L^2	Source	L^2
(6)	*A*	10.92	*B*	12.45	*A │ B*	8.77
(7)	*B │ A*	10.31	*A │ B*	8.77	*B │ A*	10.31
(8)	*AB*	8.09	*AB*	8.09	*AB*	8.09
(5)	Total	29.31		29.31		

Note: The sum of component chi-squares for the conservative approach, where partialed main-effects are reported, does not equal the residual for the null-logit model.

group. But unlike our earlier prior example, the response variable in the Holton-Nott study was a polytomous variable. It consisted of four categories of posttest grammatical response: (1) analytical, (2) evidential, (3) declarative, and (4) indeterminate. Hence, we do not know whether experimental and control subjects responded differently in one, two, three, or all four posttest categories; nor do we know the direction of the difference or differences. Obviously, the analysis is not complete until some manner of explication is undertaken. The next chapter will be devoted to a discussion of relatively new methods, generically termed *focused comparisons*, that are designed to clarify results. These new methods will be applied in the next chapter to the Holton-Nott experiment.

The remaining pages of the current chapter, however, will be devoted to a more traditional follow-up strategy, the interpretation of relevant lambda parameters. This strategy was employed by Holton and Nott and possesses considerable merit even in view of newer methods. The identification and study of relevant lambda parameters will often yield insights as to the specific nature of observed omnibus effects. Relative to the Holton-Nott analysis, of immediate interest are the λ_{jk}^{bc}'s, the estimated logit-model effects between the treatment and the posttest variable. However, what model would be selected to provide the λ_{jk}^{bc}'s that should be studied?

This is not a trivial question, for the numerical values of λ_{jk}^{bc}'s are model-dependent; they will frequently increase or decrease in value as additional terms

Table 5.10
Observed Frequencies, Lambdas, and Tests on Lambdas for a Follow-Up Model Fitted to the Holton-Nott Data

Posttest Variable	Experimental			Control		
	f^{bc}	λ^{bc}	z	f^{bc}	λ^{bc}	z
Analytical	23	.527	2.57	5	-.527	-2.57
Evidential	12	-.280	-1.50	20	.280	1.50
Declarative	6	-.221	-1.07	9	.221	1.07
Indeterminate	14	-.026	-0.15	12	.026	0.15
Totals	55	0.000		46	0.000	

are added to or deleted from the model. In sum, the task at hand is to select a follow-up model that contains the most relevant λ^{bc}_{jk}'s. Although there are few definitive rules of conduct in this work, it is, nevertheless, recommended that, at the very least, the lambdas of interest be examined in two different models: the most parsimonious model that constitutes an acceptable fit and, if the table is not of extremely high dimensionality, the saturated model. The former will generally prove to be most useful and informative because the effects that appear in this model will be relatively "pure." That is, the effects of interest in the most acceptable logit model will reflect the state of affairs given that the most acceptable model happened to fit the observed data perfectly. On the other hand, the effects of interest in the saturated model will reflect the "contaminating" influences of additional sources. Should there be *serious* discrepancies between the effects of interest in these two models, it is likely that an important term or terms has been omitted from the logit model deemed acceptable.

In the current example, since the interaction term (i.e., λ^{abc}) was found to be inconsequential, and since it was desired to assess treatment effects given effects due to pretests, the most restricted model that appears to provide a reasonable fit is one that fits marginals [AB], [AC], and [BC], namely, Model 7 in Table 5.7. The saturated model, in this table of course, is Model 8. The suggestion is that both models should be fitted so that the λ^{bc}_{jk}'s in each can be studied to determine the nature of the main effects for levels of the treatment variable; however, for economy of expression, only the λ^{bc}_{jk}'s associated with Model 7, the selected follow-up model, are displayed in Table 5.10.

In the table, the lambda effects suggest that a differential response by experimental and control members to the posttest variable was least pronounced in the indeterminate category and most pronounced in the analytical category. Moreover, the algebraic signs of the lambdas for the latter category suggest that the *odds* are greater that experimental subjects had their remarks judged as analytical than was the case for control subjects. Notice that in accordance with our earlier discussion, we have been careful to interpret the lambda effects in terms of odds.

Thus we see that estimates of lambdas can help us discern the magnitude of group difference and are most useful in determining the direction of difference. By themselves, however, they do not tell us if suspected differences are statistically significant. To establish significance, estimates of effects must be subjected to test in a manner similar to that seen in the last chapter. Z tests were performed on the null hypotheses that λ_{jk}^{bc} are equal to zero, and the results are reported in Table 5.10. Although a total of eight z statistics are reported, realize that only three tests, in effect, are being performed, for in each 2×4 table the results of five tests will be determined by the outcomes of three basic tests.

Essentially, the z tests reported in Table 5.10 are of the same form as noted in the previous chapter (see Equation 4.27). That is

$$z(\lambda_{jk}^{bc}) = \lambda_{jk}^{bc}/\text{S.E.} \ (\lambda_{jk}^{bc})$$

The computation of the standard error (S.E.), however, is not as straightforward as it was before because we are no longer dealing with a simple fourfold table. If we were, then Equation 4.28 would still suffice. In fact, as long as we are dealing exclusively with dichotomous variables, then a simple extension of Equation 4.28 can be used with tables of higher dimensionality to obtain the S.E. of *all* estimated effects in the saturated model. For example, for a $2 \times 2 \times 2$ table, where there are a total of seven *basic* effect parameters, the S.E. common to all basic effects is

$$\text{S.E.} \ (\lambda) = \frac{\left(\sum (\frac{1}{f_{ijk}}) \right)^{1/2}}{(abc)} \tag{5.15}$$

where the summation is understood to be over all elementary cells of the table. Goodman (1970) and Bishop, Fienberg, and Holland (1975), among others, have used Equation 5.15 to calculate the S.E. of lambdas for the saturated model of tables defined by dichotomies and then have used this S.E. to assess the significance of lambdas appearing in unsaturated models. This procedure, described earlier as the delta method, can be defended on the grounds that the S.E. computed for all λ's on the saturated model represents a conservative estimate of exact standard errors for more restricted models.

Since the conservative methods of Goodman and Bishop et al., improvements in the calculation of standard errors for lambda estimates have been proposed and incorporated into most modern computer programs (e.g., BMDP/4F). The work of Lee (1977), which advanced computational algorithms for calculating exact asymptotic standard errors for unsaturated models that are direct—for models where expected cell frequencies can be computed directly from observed marginal frequencies—is particularly important in this regard. Briefly, the calculation of standard errors for unsaturated models involves collapsing or reducing the full table to the dimensionality of the unsaturated model and subsequently computing standard errors on the "saturated model" of the reduced table. These procedures apply to tables defined by both dichotomies and polytomies. Moreover, Lee (1977) showed that conservative bounds for the standard errors of indirect (e.g., Model 7) are obtainable by employing the standard errors of the most parsimonious direct model of which the model in question is a proper subset (e.g., Model 8). Despite these welcomed improvements, one would do well to remember that z tests on lambda parameters are exact only under large sample conditions and because a number of such tests are typically performed, they are susceptible to the excessive commission of Type I errors. In short, they are better used as indicators of significant effects rather than as definitive tests of effects.

Returning to the research of Holton and Nott (1980), results of significant testing on the λ_{jk}^{bc}'s associated with the follow-up model revealed that effects associated with the analytical category were statistically significant at the .05 level. Holton and Nott, therefore, appropriately confined their conclusions to differences between treated groups with respect to posttest analytical response, conclusions that were consistent with their a priori hypothesis. A more detailed exposition of findings produced by the method of focused comparisons will be offered in the next chapter.

NOTES

1. Although the component for the main-marginal term for Variable B is also obviously nonsignificant, $L^2(1) = 0.36$, $p < .548$, we choose not to exclude the main-marginal term for B—at least not at this point—because our discussion is centered on hierarchical models. Should a hierarchical model be chosen that contains either the AB or CB, the main-marginal B term, by construction, will be incorporated into that model.

2. Speaking technically, the statistically significant association between A (hard drugs) and C (alcohol) that can be advanced as a result of our work to this point is a marginal association, the strength of which is reflected by the marginal component for the AC term that can be observed in Table 5.4, namely, $L^2 = 9.27$, $p < .002$. Should it be desired to evaluate the strength and significance of the partial association between Variables A and C, adjusted for Variable B, a component based on a residual chi-square comparison of the following two models would need to be calculated:

Model 6a: $\ln F_{ijk} = \lambda + \lambda^a + \lambda^b + \lambda^c + \lambda^{ab} + \lambda^{bc}$

Model 7a: $\ln F_{ijk} = \lambda + \lambda^a + \lambda^b + \lambda^c + \lambda^{ab} + \lambda^{bc} + \lambda^{ac}$

This comparison results in $L^2_{6a-7a} = L^2_{6a} - L^2_{7a} = 9.75 - .43 = 9.32, p < .002$. It can be concluded, therefore, that the association between the abuse of hard drugs and alcohol is significant subsequent to partialing from this association influences due to soft drug usage.

3. According to Aldrich and Nelson (1984, 37), the etiology of the term *logit* is found in the abbreviation of "logistic probability unit," which, in turn, represents a common description (or model) of outcome probabilities associated with dichotomous choices. The common mathematical description of dichotomous outcomes in question is the logistic function (Aldrich & Nelson, 1984, 32; Agresti, 1990, 90), a continuous S-shaped curve that resembles the cumulative normal distribution.

4. I have a decided preference for structuring models such that the designated response variable is introduced last alphabetically. For a three-variable study, the response variable would be Variable C. In a four-variable analysis, the response variable would be Variable D, and so forth.

5. Assuming A and B to be explanatory and C to be response, any model that does *not* contain λ^{ab} will not fit the observed $[AB]$ configuration in the process of generating F_{ijk}'s. Instead, such a model will generate *expected* cell frequencies for $[AB]$ that will most likely be at variance with observed cell frequencies in $[AB]$. And since frequencies in $[AB]$ are determined by sampling, any model that does not reproduce these fixed frequencies is not a legal model for logit analysis.

6

Following Up
Asymmetrical Analyses

In the opening chapter, it was conceded that problems can arise when attempts are made to follow up the results of a log-linear analysis (see Clogg & Elison, 1987). In the last chapter, for example, we found that reliance on lambda parameters to explicate the results of the asymmetrical analysis of the Holton-Nott (1980) data left much to be desired. However, explication that is more precise and more focused is possible. In this chapter methods will be proposed that will enable log-linear analysts to pursue omnibus results with greater precision—to pursue results with a rifle instead of a shotgun.

The methods to be described permit analysts to implement specific comparisons among classes of a polytomous response variable that may be tested for statistical significance on a single degree of freedom. The comparisons, to be called *focused comparisons*, resemble specific *t*-test contrasts that are frequently performed following an ANOVA (see Rosenthal & Rosnow, 1985).

The focused comparisons of this chapter should not be confused with the follow-up methodology proposed by Bock (1975, 531–35) and accessible to advanced users of SPSSX LOG-LINEAR. Bock's approach is regression-based (i.e., the Newton-Raphson) whereby contrast-coded vectors representing comparisons are entered and assessed in a forward addition manner. Focused comparisons, in contrast, can generally be performed with a hand calculator. Comparisons performed using Bock's approach are a function of the order in which they are performed. Focused comparisons, on the other hand, yield *unique* solutions; that is, their solutions are not dependent on the order in which they are performed. Moreover, focused comparisons are readily interpretable in terms of either differences in log odds (logged odds ratios) or proportions. In short, the methods to be described afford log-linear analysts a degree of flexibility in analyzing response that previously (as we noted in Chapter 1) could be achieved only with the GSK approach.

Focused comparisons are rooted in a methodology proposed some years ago by Lancaster (1949), in which larger contingency tables of two dimensions are reformulated into smaller local tables (i.e., subtables) such that the ordinary (Pearsonian) chi-square statistic for the larger table can be recovered by summing the chi-squares computed on local subtables. Reformulating two-way tables to achieve an *exact* partitioning of the ordinary chi-square statistic has been the subject of considerable scholarship (Irwin, 1949; Kimball, 1954; Kastenbaum, 1960; Castellan, 1965; Bresnahan & Shapiro, 1966). The focused comparisons developed by Kennedy and Bush (1988), to be presented herein, constitute an extension of the Lancaster tradition of cross-table and chi-square partitioning, an extension into the arena of log-linear analysis, where the dimensionality of tables is generally greater than two.

Focused comparisons will be developed initially in a three-variable setting using contrived data. These data were generated to yield statistical significance for both logit-model main effects and logit-model interaction; statistical significance of approximately equal boldness. The analysis of these data will also enable us to highlight several complexities that are encountered occasionally in log-linear work such as the appearance of partial relationships that exceed corresponding marginal (or zero-order) relationships. Following their exposition within a fictitious working example, the methodology of focused comparisons will be applied to the results of Holton and Nott (1980) reported in Chapter 5.

A WORKING EXAMPLE

Consider 100 females and 100 males who were asked to record their marital status (e.g., single, married, or divorced) and then asked to indicate if they were generally happy, unhappy, or neither happy nor unhappy. Therefore, the three variables with which we will be working are:

A: *Gender*

A_1 = females

A_2 = males

B: *Marital Status*

B_1 = single

B_2 = married

B_3 = divorced

C: *Dispositional Response*

C_1 = happy

C_2 = neutral

C_3 = unhappy

Table 6.1

Observed Frequencies by Gender (Variable A), Marital Status (Variable B), and Response (Variable C)

Gender	Marital Status	Response Happy	Response Neutral	Response Unhappy	[AB] Marginals
Female	Single	26	14	9	49
	Married	6	12	4	22
	Divorced	10	10	9	29
Male	Single	15	19	8	42
	Married	9	11	17	37
	Divorced	11	2	8	21
[C] Marginals		77	68	55	200

Assume that the three-dimensional table produced by crossing the variables turned out as shown in Table 6.1. The marginals of explanatory Variable A are deliberately fixed, Variable B is to be treated as a fixed explanatory variable, and Variable C is the response variable in the asymmetrical analysis to be performed.

The observed frequencies displayed in Table 6.1 were subjected to a generalized logit-model analysis as described in the previous chapter. Four hierarchical models were fitted to observed frequencies and residual chi-squares were used to compute the component chi-squares that are given in Table 6.2. To demonstrate the ability of methods to affect an exact partitioning or decomposition of relevant components, all calculations associated with this example are reported to four-place accuracy in the tables and text of this section.[1]

Verify first that the residuum about the null model is considerable as evidenced by its significant residual chi-square, $L^2(10) = 24.5506$, $p < .006$; or, viewed differently, by a significant component given by subtracting the residual L^2 of the saturated model from the residual L^2 of the null logit model, namely, 24.5506 − 0.0000 = 24.5506. The null logit model does not explain observed data well, hence further testing of specific effects is justified.

Additional study of Table 6.2 reveals that whereas the marginal component for the $A\overline{C}$ term failed to achieve significance (at .05), $L^2(2) = 3.0876$, $p < .281$, the partial component for $B\overline{C}$ was significant, $L^2(4) = 10.6397$, $p < .031$. The latter significance suggests the presence of at least one difference

Table 6.2
Summary of Asymmetrical Analysis of Response (Variable C) by Gender (Variable A) and Marital Status (Variable B)

Model/Source	Marginals Fitted	Component Chi-Square	df	p
(5) Null/Total	$[C]$, $[AB]$	24.5506	10	.006
(6) Due to Gender	$[AB]$, $[AC]$	3.0876	2	.281
(7) Due to Status, Given Gender	$[AB]$, $[AC]$, $[BC]$	10.6397	4	.031
(8) Due to Interaction	$[ABC]$	10.8233	4	.029

Note: The marginal component for the $\overline{BC}$ term (Marital Status) obtainable by computing a L^2 on the two-way $\overline{BC}$ table was $L^2(4) = 11.1859$, $p < .025$.

between or among marital statuses with respect to patterns of dispositional response. There is more, however. Because of its order of entry in Model 7—third in the trio of bivariate terms—the component for $\overline{BC}$ is the partial component, and, as such, denotes effects due to Variable B subsequent to partialing from $\overline{BC}$ the effects associated with $\overline{AC}$ (i.e., $B|A$). The strength of effects due to Variable B in the absence of adjustments for $\overline{AC}$ is expressed by the marginal component for $\overline{BC}$, $L^2(4) = 11.1859$, $p < .025$, as reported in the table footnote. Clearly, the analysis indicates the presence of logit-model main effects for Marital Status both prior to and following adjustments for main effects due to Gender.

Table 6.2 also reveals that the component for $AB\overline{C}$ was significant, $L^2(4) = 10.8233$, $p < .029$. As already learned, this outcome may be interpreted in a manner analogous to the interpretation of first-order interaction in the ANOVA. Several verbal interpretations, therefore, are possible. Let us say that the outcome suggests that *simple* main effects due to Marital Status are present for each gender, but the nature of these simple effects are not consistent for males and females.

Having observed significant omnibus effects due to Marital Status and the interaction between Marital Status and Gender, the current task is to describe these effects in greater detail. If the analysis had been an ANOVA, we would be encouraged to follow up the interaction first. Such advice also is appropriate in a post–log-linear environment. However, since following up main effects is less complex than it is for interaction, the methodology of focused comparisons will be applied first to main effects due to Marital Status.

THE METHODOLOGY OF FOCUSED COMPARISONS

The structure of a focused comparison, abbreviated FC, consists of two elements: sample subgroups that are to be compared, and categories of response that constitute the object of comparison. Each element will be expressed by a set of numeric contrast coefficients—strictly speaking, they should be termed *pseudo-numeric coefficients*—that indicate the nature of the comparison. An FC, therefore, consists of two separate designs, a *sample design* and a *response design*. Contrast coefficients associated with a sample and a response design are crossed to produce the design of a specific comparison. As will be seen, FC_{jk} denotes a focused comparison formed by the crossing of contrast coefficients associated with the jth sample design with coefficients associated with the kth response design.

Designing Focused Comparisons

Before we proceed, let it be said with strong emphasis that the FCs that we are about to design belong to a special class known as *orthogonal comparisons*. Recall that comparisons of this genre are mutually independent. Orthogonal comparisons will be performed here for one compelling reason: to demonstrate that the methodology of focused comparisons possesses the capacity to affect an *exact* decomposition of an overall chi-square, a decomposition into additive comparison chi-squares. With this capacity, in actual practice, the liberal use of nonorthogonal comparisons can be defended more convincingly (see Rosenthal & Rosnow, 1985, 21).

Designs on Response. Let us first construct response designs on Variable C. For reasons already stated, the comparisons to be illustrated will be orthogonal, and since there are three categories of response ($r = 3$), two sets of independent numeric contrasts may be written. Let the two response designs for Variable C be:

Focused Comparison	Classes of Response Variable C ($r = 3$)		
FC_{jk}	C_1	C_2	C_3
FC_{j1}	+1.0	0.0	-1.0
FC_{j2}	+ .5	-1.0	+ .5

Notice that the contrast coefficients sum to zero within sets, and also that the sum of between-set cross-products is zero. A requisite condition for orthogonality, therefore, has been satisfied.

The coefficients in the set for FC_{j1} posit a comparison between "happy" and "unhappy" respondents, ignoring subjects who said that they were neither. The coefficients for FC_{j2} denote a comparison between happy and unhappy respondents, combined into one group, against neutral respondents in the other group. Incidentally, some readers may have observed that selected coefficients mimic the polynomial coefficients that are used to perform a trend analysis in the ANOVA. Strictly speaking, a formal trend analysis is precluded here because levels of Variable C are not ordered on an interval scale. These coefficients may be used in an initial quasi-analysis of contracting trends, however.[2]

Designs on the Sample. Reverse Helmert coefficients have been selected to illustrate sample designs. Since there are three sample categories ($s = 3$), two independent sets of coefficients, displayed below, are permissible.

Sample Variable	Focused Comparison	
Variable B ($s = 3$)	FC_{1k}	FC_{2k}
B_1 - Single	+1.0	+ .5
B_2 - Married	-1.0	+ .5
B_3 - Divorced	0.0	-1.0

The first set, FC_{1k}, specifies a comparison between single and married subjects; divorced subjects are excluded. FC_{2k} suggests a contrast between nondivorced (single and married subjects combined) and divorced subjects.

The Design of an FC. The design of a specific comparison is achieved by selecting a set of coefficients imposed on the sample and combining it with a set of coefficients imposed on the response variable. For example, by combining coefficients FC_{1k} and FC_{j1}, focused comparison FC_{11} is formed, a comparison of single and married subjects in terms of whether they said they were "happy" or "unhappy." A view of FC_{11} may be obtained by crossing the two sets of coefficients, and performing the multiplication that is implied, as has been done below:

Sample	Response FC_{j1}		
FC_{1k}	+1.0	0.0	-1.0
+1.0	+1.0	0.0	-1.0
-1.0	-1.0	0.0	+1.0
0.0	0.0	0.0	0.0

The matrix of coefficients above not only serves to identify the subjects who will participate in FC_{11} but also suggests that divorced subjects as well as "neutral" respondents will not enter into the calculation of this *FC*. A modified version of this coefficient matrix, to be called an *identification matrix*, will be

Table 6.3
General Types of *FC*s Used to Explicate Main Effects for *B* and Interaction in the Working Example

Type of *FC*	Partitioned Component	Contributing Effects	Relevant Frequencies
Marginal	$L^2(3a)-L^2(4a)= 11.1859$	$A + B$	f^{bc}
Confounded	$L^2(6)-L^2(8)\ \ = 21.4630$	$B \mid A + AB$	f^{abc}
Partialed	$L^2(6)-L^2(7)\ \ = 10.6397$	B	f^{abc}
Interaction	$L^2(7)-L^2(8)\ \ = 10.8233$	AB	f^{abc}

constructed shortly for the purpose of identifying the specific 2×2 subtable that will be used to calculate FC_{11}.

FC_{11} is but one of the four orthogonal comparisons that are produced by cross-merging the two $(s - 1)$ sample designs with the two $(r - 1)$ response designs. Another comparison would result from crossing the coefficients associated with FC_{2k} with coefficients for FC_{j1}. FC_{21} compares nondivorced subjects who said that they were either "happy" or "unhappy" to divorced subjects with the same reported dispositions.

Looking ahead, each *FC* will prompt a reformulation of the master $2 \times 3 \times 3$ contingency table into a fourfold *comparison subtable*. Then, on each 2×2 comparison subtable, a *comparison chi-square* will be calculated. Finally, assuming mutual orthogonality, it will be shown that comparison chi-squares can be summed to produce the omnibus component chi-square, the component for $B\overline{C}$ in this case.

Types of Focused Comparisons

Recall that the initial analysis revealed two significant omnibus findings: logit-model main effects due to Marital Status, (Variable *B*) and interaction effects due to Gender and Marital Status ($A \times B$). When this happens, one can decide to follow up the main effects, the interaction, or both. Be prepared, therefore, to be exposed to different types of *FC*s; namely, marginal, fully partialed, confounded, and interaction comparisons. Table 6.3 attempts to summarize the salient features of each type of comparison.

A central distinction underlying the different types of *FC*s is the component chi-square that is amenable to *exact* partitioning if implemented comparisons should happen to be orthogonal. Consider this distinction as it pertains to orthogonal marginal and partialed *FC*s. Marginal comparisons can partition the marginal component chi-square, a chi-square that indicates the strength of effects due to Marital Status in the BC table per se, and which was found to be $L^2 = 11.1859$ in our example. Fully partialed comparisons can recapture the partial component; for example, $L^2 = 10.6397$. Comparisons of this latter type, therefore, indicate differences between marital status groups after adjustments are made for effects due to Gender.

There is, in addition, a less obvious component that is amenable to exact partitioning. The component is given by the subtraction of the residual chi-square for the saturated model from the residual chi-square of Model 6, that is,

$$L^2_{6-8} = 21.4630 - 0.0000$$
$$= 21.4630, \ p < .006$$

Note that the sum of components for $B|A$ and AB in Table 6.2 equals the component in question; thus, in theory, main effects due to Variable B given Variable A (Marital Status|Gender), and the interaction between A and B, contribute to this component. Comparisons based on the partitioning of this confounded component chi-square will be independent of Variable A (Gender), but it cannot be said that they will be unaffected by effects due to the interaction between Variables A and B. Since these comparisons may be determined both by main and interaction effects, the adjective *confounded* will be used to address FCs of this genre.

A Procedural Overview

In general, the basic procedural operations underlying the implementation of marginal, partialed, and confounded comparisons are:

Step 1. Formulate one or more FC by crossing response and sample designs as was illustrated previously. In practice, the number and nature of FCs will be determined by the substance of the research. We state again that orthogonal comparisons will be performed on the working example so that the exact decomposition of omnibus components can demonstrated.

Step 2. Construct an *identification matrix* for each FC to use as an aid in tabular reformulation. Though optional, identification matrices become increasingly helpful as FCs become more complex.

Step 3. For every FC, reformulate the BC table (or AC table, if pursuing effects for A) into a fourfold *comparison subtable*.

Step 4. Subject the cell frequencies in each comparison subtable to a conventional test of the hypothesis of homogeneity of proportional response using the likelihood-ratio chi-square.

Step 5. Interpret significant results in terms of differences in proportional response or differences in log odds. Since analyses are based on fourfold tables, the strength of effects independent of local table size may be estimated by calculating phi coefficients or Yule's Qs.

These steps will be illustrated first to perform marginal comparisons, then they will be modified accordingly to implement fully partialed, confounded, and inter-action comparisons. Each type of FC in its own way contributes to an enhanced understanding of how sample groups differ with respect to defined outcome.

Marginal Comparisons

The original table is of size $2 \times 3 \times 3$, but only frequencies in the collapsed 3×3 table for BC are used for marginal comparisons. The working context, therefore, has been reduced to two dimensions. The omnibus chi-square that is potentially partitionable is the marginal component for $\overline{BC}$, where relevant two-dimensional log-linear models are

Model 3a: $\ln F_{ijk} = \lambda + \lambda_j^b + \lambda_k^c$

Model 4a: $\ln F_{ijk} = \lambda + \lambda_j^b + \lambda_k^{2c} + \lambda_{jk}^{bc}$

Model 3a fits only the main marginals of the BC table, whereas the less restricted Model 4a fits f_{jk}^{bc}s, the frequencies observed in the BC table. For our example, the marginal component is

$$L_{3a-4a}^2(4) = 11.1859 - 0.0000$$
$$= 11.1859, \ p < .025$$

which will be decomposed into four comparison components, each distributed on a single df. Of the four orthogonal comparisons defined, FC_{11} has been chosen for exposition on the pages that follow.

The Design of FC_{11}. Recall that the pseudo-numeric coefficients that constitute the sample design and the response design for this FC were

Sample Variable B				Response Variable C			
Class: B_1	B_2	B_3		Class: C_1	C_2	C_3	
FC_{1k} +1.0	-1.0	0.0		FC_{j1} +1.0	0.0	-1.0	

By crossing the sample and response designs, the design of FC_{11} is achieved. If respective sample and response coefficients are multiplied, the coefficient matrix that was presented earlier will result.

However, the coefficient matrix shown earlier was meant to be illustrative; technically, the numeric values presented in this matrix have limited value because our work involves the comparison of frequencies (or proportions) between sample groups, and not the comparison of metric effects. Features of the implied multiplication, however, can be used to identify cell frequencies that will be used in the comparison. To be specific, the pattern of algebraic signs associated with each implied product can be used to select frequencies belonging to an FC, and to properly organize them in the comparison subtable.

The Identification Matrix for FC_{11}. If we consider only the algebraic signs that would govern the multiplication, specifically the multiplication of a sample (row) coefficient by a response (column) coefficient, and display each pair of signs in a matrix such as

Sample Variable B		Response Variable C Class: C_1	C_2	C_3
Class FC_{1k}		FC_{j1} +1.0	0.0	-1.0
B_1	+1.0	++	+0	+-
B_2	-1.0	-+	-0	--
B_3	0.0	0+	00	0-

an identification matrix for FC_{11} is formed. As will be made more obvious below, the patterns of algebraic signs within cells of the identification matrix reveal the composition of comparison subtables, the local tables that will be subjected to analysis.

The Comparison Subtable for FC_{11}. This fourfold table which will be subjected to analysis is defined by a dichotomous *sample* (row) *variable*, where the first level is labeled "$+$" and the second level "$-$," and a dichotomous *response* (column) *variable*, with two levels similarly labeled "$+$" and "$-$," respectively. Frequencies that will populate this 2×2 table are suggested by simple rules based on the sign patterns appearing in the identification matrix. Pick a cell in the identification matrix: say, the BC_{11} cell. Because the first algebraic sign is "$+$," frequencies associated with BC_{11} will be placed in the positive or first row of the comparison subtable. Because the second algebraic sign is "$+$," BC_{11} will be further assigned to the first, or positive, column (in the positive row) of the comparison subtable. Frequencies in the 3×3 table for BC that are associated with identification-table pattern "$+ -$" will be placed in the positive row and negative column of the comparison subtable. It is important to note, however, that if either the first or second sign is "0," the corresponding frequency is omitted from the subtable. Accordingly, divorced subjects and subjects who offered a neutral response will not be represented in the comparison subtable for FC_{11}. In sum, cell frequencies in the original BC table that will appear in the comparison subtable for FC_{11} are

Sample Classes	Classes of Response R(+)	R(-)
S(+)	BC_{11}	BC_{13}
S(-)	BC_{21}	BC_{23}

Calculating the L^2 for FC_{11}. To test FC_{11}, expected cell frequencies are generated under the hypothesis of homogeneity of proportional response (or independence), and then a likelihood-ratio chi-square is computed in the usual way. Find below the comparison subtable that presents observed f_{jk}^{bc}s —identified with the help of the identification matrix and compiled from Table 6.1—and frequencies (in parentheses) expected under the null.

Sample Classes	Classes of Response	
	R(+)	R(-)
S(+)	41 (34.5532)	17 (23.4468)
S(-)	15 (21.4468)	21 (14.5532)

Substituting subtable values into Equation 3.11 for the likelihood-ratio L^2 gives the single-*df* chi-square for FC_{11}:

$$L_{11}^2(1) = 2[(41)\ln(41/34.5532) + \ldots$$
$$\ldots + (21)\ln(21/14.5532)]$$
$$= 7.7732, \ p < .005$$

Statistical significance can be claimed for the comparison. Moreover, since the result is predicated on the analysis of a fourfold table, differences in response can be interpreted either in terms of proportions or log odds. It can be said, for example, that the proportion of single subjects ($p = .71$) who reported themselves to be "happy" exceeded the proportion of married subjects ($p = .42$) who said that they were "happy." In addition to clarity of interpretation, be reminded that measures of effect size (or association), such as phi coefficients (Hays, 1988, 784–86), are readily calculable.

FC_{11} is but one of four orthogonal comparisons that we set out to perform. The results of the remaining three single-*df* marginal comparisons are displayed in Table 6.4. The most important observation to make when studying Table 6.4 is that the marginal chi-square for $B\overline{C}$ ($L^2 = 11.1859$) was explained by summing the four comparison chi-squares. Since the partitioning of the marginal chi-square was exact, a foundation has been established for the sagacious use of nonorthogonal comparisons in normal practice.

Finally, if comparisons are many and decidedly of an exploratory nature, some thought should be given exercising control over the experimentwise Type I error rate since the overall rate of falsely rejecting a viable null hypothesis increases in relation to the number of comparisons that are made. A modification of the Bonferroni approach, proposed by Holm (1979), is recommended when the need to protect the overall rate of committing Type I errors is felt. Holm's procedure will be illustrated shortly in connection with the use of *FCs* on the Holton-Nott data and later in our discussion of CFA in the last chapter.

Table 6.4
Summary of Orthogonal Marginal Comparisons and the Partitioning of the Component L^2 for the *BC* Term

Focused Comparison	Subtable Size	df	Comparison Chi-Square	p Value	Phi
FC_{11}	94	1	7.7723	.005	.29
FC_{21}	132	1	.2962	.650	.04
FC_{12}	150	1	.1131	.737	.03
FC_{22}	200	1	3.0944	.079	.12
Marginal *BC* Component	200	4	11.1859	.025	

Fully Partialed Comparisons

Though informative, marginal comparisons ignore the fact that there is a third variable (e.g., Gender) in the picture. To the extent to which third-variable main effects are operative, marginal comparisons project results that are surreptitiously influenced by the third variable. However, unlike the methods of old, log-linear methodology accommodates multiple variables. Indeed, the ability to document partial associations (in symmetrical analyses) and effects (in asymmetrical analyses) constitutes a major advantage of log-linear methods. It follows, then, that focused comparisons free from the confounding influences of extraneous variables are of both theoretical interest and practical importance.

Maintaining the established system of orthogonal comparisons, we expand our consideration to all three working-example variables to implement *FC*s among Marital Status groups from which effects due to Gender (Variable *A*) have been fully partialed. Realize that these *FC*s will be independent of both logit-model main effects due to Gender and interaction effects due to the crossing of Gender and Marital Status. To accomplish these ends, two procedural modifications are required. First, to remove logit-model main effects due to Gender, *simple comparison subtables* and *simple comparison chi-squares* will be calculated at respective levels of Gender, the extraneous variable in our example. Second, to remove interaction effects between Gender and Marital Status, the frequencies to be analyzed will be those provided by Model 7, a model that contains all terms (or factors) with the exception of the second-order, or $AB\overline{C}$, term.

Before we begin, however, it should be understood that the omnibus component that will be decomposed as a consequent of the two aforementioned procedural modifications is that given by the difference in residual chi-squares between Model 6 and Model 7, restated below:

Model 6: $\ln F_{ijk} = \lambda + \lambda_i^a + \lambda_j^b + \lambda_k^c + \lambda_{ij}^{ab} + \lambda_{ik}^{ac}$

Model 7: $\ln F_{ijk} = \lambda + \lambda_i^a + \lambda_j^b + \lambda_k^c + \lambda_{ij}^{ab} + \lambda_{ik}^{ac} + \lambda_{jk}^{bc}$

The partial component for $B\overline{C}$ is

$$
\begin{aligned}
L_{6-7}^2(4) &= L_6^2(8) - L_7^2(4) \\
&= 21.4630 - 10.8233 \\
&= 10.6397
\end{aligned}
$$

Model 6, in effect, is the base model for partialed comparisons due to the fact that separate computations (simple chi-squares) will be performed at the various levels of Variable A. Model 7, in effect, is the "saturated model" in the current system because the F_{ijk}s generated by this model, and not the observed f_{ijk}s, will be subjected to analysis. Since Model 7 does not contain an $AB\overline{C}$ term, and inasmuch as expected cell frequencies from Model 7 are to replace observed elementary cell frequencies, effects due to interaction will be physically withheld from ensuing comparisons. (Interaction effects will not be present in the sense that they have been removed in a "backward elimination" sense.) Thus, an alternative view of the component chi-square that underlies fully partialed comparisons is

$$
\begin{aligned}
L_{6a-7a}^2(4) &= L_{6a}^2(4) - L_{7a}^2(0) \\
&= 10.6397 - 0.0000 \\
&= 10.6397
\end{aligned}
$$

In sum, if FCs are properly orthogonal, the tabular-reformulation procedures to be illustrated will decompose the partial $B\overline{C}$ component into four additive comparison components, each of which will be associated with a comparison between Marital Status groups. Moreover, FCs will be independent of Gender ($A\overline{C}$) and the interaction between Gender and Marital Status ($AB\overline{C}$).

The Design of FC_{22}. To illustrate, the FC produced by crossing sample coefficients for FC_{2j} with response coefficients for FC_{j2} has been selected. In sample terms, this comparison pits nondivorced subjects against divorced subjects. Dispositional response has been cast in terms of either nonneutral (happy and unhappy combined) or neutral. Although FC_{22} may lack substantive significance, it nevertheless presents us with a challenge relative to its formulation and analysis.

The Identification Matrix for FC_{22}. As before, this matrix is formed by crossing contrast coefficients in respective sample and response designs. For FC_{22}, such crossing and the use of algebraic signs (instead of integer values) results in

Sample		Response Variable C		
Variable B		Class: C_1	C_2	C_3
Class FC_{2k}		FC_{j2} + .5	-1.0	+ .5
B_1	+ .5	++	+-	++
B_2	+ .5	++	+-	++
B_3	-1.0	-+	--	-+

Because the algebraic signs of BC_{11}, BC_{13}, BC_{21}, and BC_{23} exhibit the pattern "+ +," subjects in these variable combinations will be pooled and assigned to a cell in the first row (the positive row) and first column (the positive column), or SR_{11} cell, of the fourfold comparison subtable. By similar construction, subjects in BC_{12} and BC_{22} will be combined and placed in the SR_{12} cell of the comparison subtable. Since there are no zero entries in the matrix, all subjects will be represented in the comparison subtable. At this interim point, the reformulated subtable contains the following variable combinations:

Sample Classes	Classes of Response	
	$R(+)$	$R(-)$
$S(+)$	$BC_{11} + BC_{13}$ $BC_{21} + BC_{23}$	$BC_{12} + BC_{22}$
$S(-)$	$BC_{31} + BC_{33}$	BC_{32}

The Comparison Subtable for FC_{22}. Whereas the entries suggested by the identification matrix would suffice for marginal comparisons, several adaptations are needed to affect fully partialed comparisons. Since we are working with all three factors, and desirous of exercising control over Variable A, simple subtables, composed along lines suggested in the matrix above, will be constructed and analyzed at each level of Variable A. Also, be reminded that F_{ijk}s from Model 7, and not observed elementary frequencies, occupy the master $2 \times 3 \times 3$ table that will be apportioned into simple comparison subtables. Expected frequencies from Model 7 are obtainable from all major log-linear programs, and are presented to four-place accuracy in Table 6.5.

Selecting cell frequencies from Table 6.5, for females at A_1, the simple subtable is

Table 6.5
Expected Elementary Cell Frequencies Generated by the Full Main-Effects Model (Model 7)

Gender	Marital Status	Response Happy	Response Neutral	Response Unhappy	[AB] Marginals
Female	Single	22.8626	18.7764	7.3610	49
	Married	6.1341	9.6633	6.2026	22
	Divorced	13.0033	7.5603	8.4364	29
Male	Single	18.1374	14.2236	9.6390	42
	Married	8.8659	13.3367	14.7974	37
	Divorced	7.9967	4.4397	8.5636	21
[C] Marginals		77	68	55	200

Note: Computer programs (e.g., BMDP/4F) generally do not output expected cell frequencies to four-place accuracy. This desired degree of accuracy may be obtained, however, by multiplying original cell frequencies by 10 (for SPSSX) or by 100 (for BMDP/4F) prior to model fitting.

Sample Classes	Classes of Response $R(+)$	$R(-)$
$S(+)$	42.5603	28.4397
$S(-)$	21.4397	7.5603

For males at A_2, the simple subtable is

Sample Classes	Classes of Response $R(+)$	$R(-)$
$S(+)$	51.4397	27.5603
$S(-)$	16.5603	4.4397

Calculation of L^{2}'s for FC_{22}. For simple subtables, theoretical cell frequencies under the hypothesis of homogeneity of response (or independence) are determined in the usual way. Assuming that they have been determined, for females the simple chi-square is

$L^2\{@A_1\} = 2[42.5603 \ln(42.5603/45.4400) + \ldots$
$\qquad \ldots + 7.5630 \ln(7.5603/10.4400)]$
$\qquad = 1.8042$

For males, the simple chi-square is

$L^2\{@A_2\} = 1.5242$

Summing simple chi-squares gives the fully partialed comparison chi-square, distributed on 1 df, which is

$L^2_{22}(1) = L^2\{@A1\} + L^2\{@A_2\}$
$\qquad = 1.8042 + 1.5242$
$\qquad = 3.3284, \ p < .079$

We conclude, therefore, that subsequent to extracting influences exerted by the Gender variable, the examined difference in dispositional response between divorced and nondivorced subjects did not achieve significance at the .05 level.

If the remaining three partialed comparisons are performed along parallel lines, simple and comparison chi-squares will turn out as shown in Table 6.6, where it can be seen that the partial component for BC has been partitioned into four single-df comparison components. Realize that the results summarized in Table 6.6 differ from the results of marginal comparisons in Table 6.4 in that the magnitudes of partialed results indicate the extent to which response differs by Marital Status independent of all effects associated with Gender—a potentially informative accomplishment in contingency table work.

While comparing Tables 6.4 and 6.6, several additional observations should be made. First, since the methodology of partialed comparisons involves the establishment of simple subtables at respective levels of a tertiary variable— Variable A in our example—we may be tempted to subject simple subtables to single-df tests of statistical significance. The appropriateness of such testing, however, is questionable. When the $AB\overline{C}$ term was removed from the model that produced the frequencies that were analyzed, Model 7, the 4 df associated with that term were also, in effect, removed from the system of analysis. Simple arithmetic will show that only 4 df remain for apportionment to the four partialed comparisons to be tested, 1 df per comparison chi-square. Though not amenable to formal testing, the magnitudes of simple chi-squares, and even the results of informal testing of these simple components, should not be dismissed completely, for at the very least, they serve as indicators of differential response as a function of the tertiary variable.

It is also instructive to observe that for two FCs, partialed components were slightly larger than corresponding marginal components. This is most obvious in connection with FC_{22}, where the partialed component was found to be $L^2 =$

Table 6.6
Summary of Orthogonal Fully Partialed Comparisons Based on the Partitioning of the Partial Component for BC

Focused Comparison	Subtable Size	df	Comparison Chi-Square	Observed p Value	Phi
FC_{11}	94	1	6.6363	.010	.27
@ A_1	42.5		2.6167	.106	
@ A_2	51.5		4.0170	.046	
FC_{21}	132	1	0.4390	.508	.06
@ A_1	64		0.3503	.657	
@ A_2	68		0.0887	.766	
FC_{12}	150	1	0.2387	.629	.04
@ A_1	71		0.1976	.657	
@ A_2	79		0.0411	.840	
FC_{22}	200	1	3.3284	.079	.12
@ A_1	100		1.8042	.180	
@ A_2	100		1.5242	.217	
Partial $B\hat{C}$ Component	200	4	10.6397	.031	

3.3284; yet as seen in Table 6.4, its marginal component was $L^2 = 3.0944$. At first, this disparity appears to be incongruous. How could a component that reflects the removal of Gender effects (3.3284) be of greater magnitude than a component (3.0844) that does not reflect the removal of Gender effects?

Familiarity with multiple regression when applied to metric response will help to resolve this apparent paradox. Like multiple regression models, log-linear models are often redolent with dependencies (i.e., multicollinearity). They therefore are susceptible to the many vagaries associated with variable order of entry and suppression artifacts. Since we have long since adopted an order of entry, we turn to the latter, suppression effects (Cohen & Cohen, 1975, 87–91), to account for the apparent paradox. Stated simply, because Marital Status and Gender are themselves statistically related, in some (but not all) instances, by introducing Gender into the relationship between Marital Status and response (Disposition), as is done in the method of partialed comparisons, it is possible that Gender can have the effect of ''suppressing'' some of the irrelevant, nonpredictive elements in Marital Status's relationship with response so as to enhance the ability of Marital Status to explain the response variable. This occurred with respect to FC_{21} and FC_{22}. Suppression effects will return to haunt us when we consider interaction comparisons. For now, realize that analysts rely heavily on the interpretation of partial components (and partial regression coefficients) when the intent is to acknowledge the contributing presence of the tertiary variable (e.g., Gender) in a variable system but shift their attention to marginal components when there is good reason to ignore the active presence of the tertiary variable in the system.

Confounded Comparisons

Though similar, the steps to perform confounded focused comparisons are less involved than those for partialed comparisons. The principal difference is that observed elementary cell frequencies, f_{ijk}s, and not the expected frequencies generated by Model 7, are used to implement confounded comparisons. The interpretation of confounded comparisons, however, can be more involved. This is because the omnibus component that is potentially partitionable is given by the difference in residual chi-squares between Model 6—the consequent of our ensuing computations of simple chi-squares on f_{ijk}s at respective levels of Variable A—and the saturated model. These models are presented again below:

Model 6: $\ln F_{ijk} = \lambda + \lambda_i^a + \lambda_j^b + \lambda_k^c + \lambda_{ij}^{ab} + \lambda_{ik}^{ac}$

Model 8: $\ln F_{ijk} = \lambda + \lambda_i^a + \lambda_j^b + \lambda_k^c + \lambda_{ij}^{ab} + \lambda_{ik}^{ac} + \lambda_{jk}^{bc} + \lambda_{ijk}^{abc}$

Model 6 contains terms for AB and $A\overline{C}$; hence, logit-model main effects attributable to Gender will not contribute to the component, to be partitioned, that follows:

$$L_{6-8}^2(8) = L_6^2(8) - L_8^2(0)$$
$$= 21.4630 - 0.0000$$
$$= 21.4630$$

Interaction effects, however, will enter into the component. In sum, differential response that we are about to assess will be influenced by: (1) main effects due to Marital Status, adjusted for Gender, and (2) the interaction between Gender and Marital Status.

Before the interpretative consequences are considered, let us perform the calculations associated with a confounded comparison. Specifically, let us calculate FC_{22} but now as a confounded comparison. Besides being familiar, the selection of FC_{22} for illustration will affect economies of tabular presentation since the design of this comparison and the identification matrix have already been presented and discussed.

Calculating Relevant L^2'*s.* Again, separate subtables are constructed and analyzed at each level of Variable A. However, as just noted, simple subtables contain original frequencies presented in Table 6.1. For females at A_1, the simple subtable (with expected cell frequencies in parentheses) is

Sample Classes	Classes of Response	
	R(+)	R(-)
S(+)	45 (45.44)	26 (25.56)
S(-)	19 (18.56)	10 (10.44)

For males at A_2, the simple subtable is

Sample Classes	Classes of Response	
	R(+)	R(-)
S(+)	49 (53.72)	30 (25.28)
S(-)	19 (14.28)	2 (6.72)

At A_1, the single-*df* chi-square is

$$L^2\{@A_1\} = 2[45 \ln(45/45.4400) + \ldots$$
$$\ldots + 10 \ln(10/10.4400)]$$
$$= .0410, \; p < .840$$

At A_2, the single-*df* chi-square is

$$L^2\{@A_2\} = 7.2627, \; p < .007$$

Summing gives the comparison chi-square for confounded FC_{22}:

$$L^2_{22}(2) = L^2\{@A_1\} + L^2\{@A_2\}$$
$$= .0410 + 7.2627$$
$$= 7.3037, \; p < .026$$

In general, the *df* for a confounded *FC* is equivalent to the number of constituent simple chi-squares; hence, $df = 2$ for L^2_{22} above.

Assuming that the remaining three orthogonal comparisons have been computed as above, simple and comparison chi-squares will materialize as shown in Table 6.7. Again, the most important outcome is that the confounded component ($L^2 = 21.4630$) has been decomposed into four additive comparison chi-squares, or from a different perspective, into eight single-*df* simple chi-squares.

It should come as no surprise that the interpretation of these comparisons can be approached in two ways. If desired, under certain conditions, confounded comparisons can be used to explicate logit-model main effects—as marginal and partialed comparisons have been interpreted on preceding pages. On the other

Table 6.7

Summary of Orthogonal Compound Comparisons and the Partitioning of the Component for $B\overline{C}$ and $AB\overline{C}$

Focused Comparison	Subtable Size	df	Comparison Chi-Square	Observed p Value	Phi
FC_{11}	94	2	5.3864	.068	
@ A_1	45	1	.7403	.390	.13
@ A_2	49	1	4.6461	.031	.31
FC_{21}	132	2	2.4134	.299	
@ A_1	64	1	1.9761	.160	.18
@ A_2	68	1	.4373	.508	.08
FC_{12}	150	2	6.3596	.042	
@ A_1	71	1	4.3331	.037	.25
@ A_2	79	1	2.0265	.155	.16
FC_{22}	200	2	7.3037	.030	
@ A_1	100	1	.0410	.840	.02
@ A_2	100	1	7.2627	.007	.27
$B\overline{C} + AB\overline{C}$ Component	200	8	21.4630	.006	

hand, confounded comparisons can be interpreted in a manner that formally recognizes the interaction component, an approach that parallels a common strategy used following an ANOVA to interpret interaction.

The Main-Effects Interpretation. Main-effect interpretations are sweeping interpretations. If not stated explicitly, they nevertheless imply that a response difference of similar size and direction exists at all levels of remaining explanatory variables. Consider, for example, FC_{22}. A main-effects interpretation of this comparison would focus exclusively on *overall* differences in dispositional response between nondivorced ($B_1 + B_2$) and divorced (B_3) subjects, a comparison that was found to be significant, namely, $L_{22}^2 = 7.3037$, $p < .030$. Following an examination of observed and expected frequencies in the comparison subtable, it would be concluded that divorced subjects were less likely to advance a neutral response. On average, this was true. However, since this conclusion is not moderated by Gender, by itself, one can only surmise that a greater proportion of both divorced females and divorced males give a definitive (nonneutral) response. (However, this was not true.) Such is the nature of main effects and their ensuing interpretation.

Main-effect interpretations are warranted in several situations. Obviously, the first is where relevant interactions have been assessed and deemed to be either statistically or substantively insignificant. Relative to FC_{22}, had interaction between Gender and Marital Status not materialized (it did), a main-effects interpretation of the confounded comparison would have been justified. In fact, confounded FC_{22} might well be the preferred interpretation since confounded comparisons are based on *all* observed data (f_{ijk}s), not just f_{jk}^{bc}s (for marginal FCs) or the F_{ijk}s (for partialed FCs) given by Model 7.

Another situation where main-effects interpretations are warranted is where the answer to an a priori research question (or hypothesis) specifically requires that a main effect be interpreted. Still another circumstance, usually encountered in highly applied research, is where research-based decisions have to be made "for the greater good," irrespective of complicating conditions. In education, for example, if a new textbook is shown on average to be more desirable than an established book (main effect)—but this finding is due largely to the fact that the new book appears to work more successfully for male students—female students appear to be at a slight disadvantage when using the new text (interaction). Nonetheless, circumstances demand that only one text be adopted. In that case, a decision based on the resultant main effect will serve the greatest good.

An Interactive Interpretation. A main-effects interpretation of confounded FC_{22} would be misleading, at best, in our example because no acknowledgment is given to the significance ($p < .029$) of the interaction between Gender and Marital Status. To remedy this, simple main effects due to the variable of principal interest (Marital Status) can be examined, tested, and interpreted at each level of the variable of secondary interest (Gender). The objective, of course, is to determine if simple main effects, more appropriately termed *conditional* main effects (Hays, 1988, 467), vary over levels of the secondary or additional variable.

Whenever combined main and interactive effects are to be examined seriously, a graphical display of response is recommended. And as Marks (1975) has shown, cell mean graphs that are routinely employed for this purpose in the ANOVA can be adapted for similar use in log-linear work. Log odds are simply substituted for cell means.[3] The log odds that will be plotted to depict FC_{22} are computed and displayed in Table 6.8.

To better explain the contents of Table 6.8, consider the 71 nondivorced females, 45 of whom did *not* offer a neutral response (they were happy or unhappy), and 26 of whom did offer a neutral response. Their odds of being nonneutral (happy or unhappy) are 45 to 26, or approximately 1.7 to 1.0. Odds ratios, though useful, are limited as a practical response measure because they occupy a scale that is not symmetrical. Essentially, the center of the scale is 1.0, representing an odds ratio = 1.0. Ratios greater than 1.0 occupy a place on the scale between 1.0 as a lower bound and infinity as an upper limit. However, in all cases where the numerator is less than the denominator, ratios occupy a

Table 6.8
FC_{22}: **Log Odds of Giving a Nonneutral Response as Opposed to a Neutral Response, by Marital Status and Gender**

Gender	Marital Status	Non-Neutral	Neutral	Odds Ratio	Log Odds
Female	Nondivorced	45	26	1.7308	.5486
	Divorced	19	10	1.9000	.6419
Males	Nondivorced	49	30	1.6333	.4906
	Divorced	19	2	9.5000	2.2513

place on the scale between zero as a lower bound and 1.0 as an upper bound. This "awkwardness" can be overcome by taking the logarithms of ratios which will cause the underlying scale to be centered at zero, since ln 1.0 = 0.0, and cause the scale to be unbounded in both directions. For these good reasons, we will plot the log odds that were computed in Table 6.8 in the graph appearing in Figure 6.1.

It is difficult not to appreciate how well the plot of log odds clarifies the results of confounded FC_{22}. Whereas the main effects for Marital Status were found to be significant, $L^2(2) = 7.30, p < .03$, the plot of log odds in Figure 6.1 points to the interaction between Gender and Marital Status as the key feature of this result. Divorced males are distinctly less neutral than are nondivorced males, $L^2(1) = 7.26, p < .007$, whereas there is no discernable difference between divorced and nondivorced females, $L^2(1) = .04, p < .884$.

It is hoped that the utility of plotting log odds in conjunction with the use of confounded comparisons as vehicles for the explication of findings in the presence of interaction has been demonstrated. Relative to their joint use, keep in mind that (1) log odds are graphically displayed on a logarithmic scale, a scale that is not coincidental to more familiar equal-interval scales (e.g., proportional response); (2) simple effects are amenable to testing on a single df; and (3) resultant findings should be attributed to both main and interaction effects operating in concert. In the next chapter we will have another opportunity to construct a plot of log odds to assist in the interpretation of a second-order interaction in a four dimensional setting.

Figure 6.1
Plot of Log Odds (from Table 6.8) Associated with FC_{22}, by Marital Status and Gender

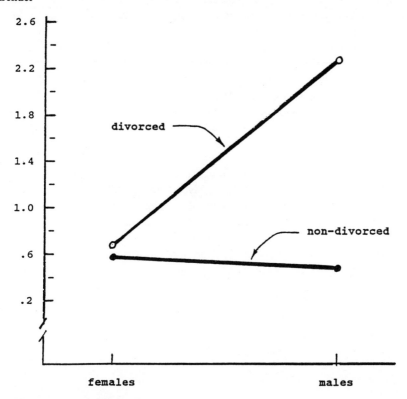

Interaction Comparisons

Our next task is to perform FCs similar to those of previous sections but at the level of first-order interaction in a logit-model analysis. Consider again the comparison between nondivorced and divorced subjects with respect to their response as defined by FC_{22}, but for the moment, adopt the view that the comparison was to be evaluated in two distinct studies, a study in which only females participated and a study that involved only males. A potentially relevant question is whether the outcome observed in the first study with females is comparable to the outcome observed in the second study with males. If the two comparisons in the two studies showed essentially the same results, no discernable interaction is indicated. If, however, findings vary significantly by Gender, first-order logit-model interaction is indicated. Note that by our construction, effects associated solely with Marital Status and Gender are precluded from our evaluation. Comparisons of this ilk performed within the context of a single study are termed *interactive comparisons*.

A direct parallel to interactive comparisons is found in the ANOVA. In the ANOVA, to evaluate conditional effects at the level of second-order interaction, contrasts associated with the first comparison design (e.g., females) are crossed with contracts associated with the second design (e.g., males) to produce a three variable matrix of *interaction contrasts* that is used to assess changes in simple first-order interaction (Marital Status and Response) as a function of an additional variable (Gender). Such an approach also can be undertaken in the log-linear (Kennedy & Bush, 1988). However, for our purposes, simpler methods based on our earlier work with confounded and fully partialed *FC*s will be used to determine if interactive comparisons are statistically significant, and to determine if orthogonal comparisons are capable of reproducing the interactive component chi-square.

Calculating FC$_{22}$. With *FC*$_{22}$ specifically in mind, verify that the comparison chi-square for the *confounded* version of this comparison was $L_{22}^2(2) = 7.3037$, $p < .030$. Effects due to Marital Status given Gender (*B*|*A*) and the interaction between Marital Status and Gender ($A \times B$) contribute to this chi-square. Verify next that the comparison chi-square for the fully partialed version of *FC*$_{22}$ was $L_{22}^2(1) = 3.3284$, $p < .079$. This chi-square was produced by effects exerted by Marital Status given Gender (*B*|*A*). Does it not follow that the extent to which unadulterated interaction characterizes the comparison may be assessed through subtraction? That is,

$$L^2 \{\text{interaction}\} = L^2 \{\text{confounded}\} - L^2 \{\text{partialed}\}$$

which, when specifically applied to the comparison under discussion, is

$$L_{22}^2(1)\{\text{interaction}\} = L_{22}^2(2)\{\text{confounded}\} - L_{22}^2(1)\{\text{partialed}\}$$
$$= 7.3037 - 3.3284$$
$$= 3.9753, \ p < .046$$

a significant outcome (at .05) that we will now attempt to interpret more precisely.

Interpreting FC$_{22}$. Let us first review conditions under which interaction would *not* be present in the current context. Speaking in terms of errorless data, neither main effects or interaction effects would be present if there is no difference between nondivorced and divorced females and males relative to response as defined; that is, if *FC*$_{22}$ is nil for both sexes. If, however, a difference between sexes exists, and the difference is comparable in magnitude and direction for both females and males, effects due to Marital Status are indicated but effects due to interaction are not. Finally, should there be a response difference between nondivorced and divorced subjects, but the difference observed among females is not the same as it is for males, interaction effects are present. Overall effects due solely to Marital Status may or may not be present; these effects are independent of effects associated with the interactive comparison.

Thus, the significant result realized for interactive *FC*$_{22}$ ($p < .046$) reinforces, and, in fact, justifies, our prior evaluation of FC_{22} as a confounded comparison. As a confounded comparison, single-df chi-squares based on the subtables for females ($p < .840$) and males ($p < .007$) strongly suggested that the responses of the nondivorced and the divorced individuals were dependent on gender. This indication received further support upon our examination of plotted odds ratios in Figure 6.1. Nevertheless, the finding emanating from our prior analysis had to be qualified somewhat because observed effects were the product of both Marital Status and the interaction between Marital Status and Gender. The present analysis, however, negates the need for qualification for it indicates that if overall effects for Marital Status are controlled, the difference represented by FC_{22} is still dependent on gender.

In practice, therefore, unless directed to the contrary by a priori considerations, it behooves the data analyst to undertake relatively independent assessments of FC_{22} at each level of Gender and consequently to advance relatively distinct interpretations of outcome. In most instances, interpretations along the lines suggested in connection with our earlier discussion of confounded FC_{22} will suffice. However, should a detailed evaluation of intemperate interaction effects be desired, the simple subtables commonly used as the basis for independent interpretations will need to be modified accordingly. For example, to evaluate interactive FC_{22} per se, the simple 2×2 subtable for females should contain the F_{ijk}'s given by Model 7 and observed f_{ijk}'s in proper juxtaposition. A comparison of residuals about the F_{ijk}'s across levels of Gender will reveal the manner in which differences between nondivorced and divorced subjects vary as a function of Gender.

Decomposition of the Interaction Component. A reoccurring theme in this chapter has been that focused comparisons yield results that are unique, and, under certain orthogonal conditions, explain exactly a relevant omnibus chi-square. To complete a demonstration of the latter, interactive comparisons FC_{11}, FC_{12}, and FC_{21} have been performed, and these results, along with those just observed for FC_{22}, are presented in Table 6.9. Not surprisingly, the sum of interactive comparison chi-squares reported in Table 6.9 will be found to be equal to the omnibus component for interaction. Again, the methodology of focused comparisons has achieved an exact decomposition of the initial component chi-square. However, Table 6.9 also presents a "surprising" outcome, namely, the algebraically negative chi-square for interactive FC_{11}: $L_{11}^2(1) = -1.2473$. This outcome merits explanation.

Explanation is approached from two perspectives: (1) a macro perspective, whereby a negative interactive comparison L^2 is viewed as an interim calculation in a more comprehensive process of calculating an omnibus component; and (2) a micro perspective, whereby the focus is on operations that directly account for the negativity associated with a particular interactive comparison. Relative to the former, such a perspective would be inconceivable had we been calculating ordinary (Pearsonian) chi-squares because all additive constituents of this statistic, that is, $(f - F)^2/F$, must be nonnegative. However, we have not been

Table 6.9
Summary of Orthogonal Interactive Comparisons and the Partitioning of the Component Chi-Square for *ABC*

Focused Comparison	Subtable Size	Confounded L^2	df	Partialed L^2	df	Interaction L^2	df	p Value
FC_{11}	94	5.3864	2	6.6336	1	-1.2473	1	
FC_{21}	132	2.4134	2	.4390	1	1.9744	1	.160
FC_{12}	150	6.3596	2	.2387	1	6.1209	1	.013
FC_{22}	200	7.3037	2	3.3284	1	3.9753	1	.046
Overall	200	21.4630	8	10.6397	4	10.8233	4	.029

computing ordinary chi-squares; rather, likelihood-ratio chi-squares have been used exclusively in our work with focused comparisons. Moreover, we have long since become accustomed to working with negative constituents of L^2, for they have occurred whenever observed frequencies (in a cell or grouping of cells) are less than corresponding expected frequencies. Hence, generalizing this feature of the likelihood-ratio chi-square, and realizing that in our work with interactive comparisons, the composite interaction observed for the master $2 \times 3 \times 3$ table (e.g., $L^2 = 10.8233$) is apportioned among four "additive" $2 \times 2 \times 2$ comparison subtables, finding that one (or more) subtables yields a negative chi-square is mathematically plausible.

From a micro perspective, with particular reference to interactive FC_{11}, the fact that the confounded chi-square ($L^2 = 5.3864$) for this comparison was less than its partialed chi-square ($L^2 = 6.6336$) caused the interactive chi-square to be algebraically negative. Admittedly, this could not happen if we were working within an integrated system of models where models differed only in terms of the number of imposed restrictions. In actuality, we have been working with dual model systems, a system of models that fits F_{ijk}'s given by Model 7 and a system that fits observed f_{ijk}'s. When models in each system are fit employing data exclusive to the $2 \times 2 \times 2$ configuration for FC_{11}, frequencies in the AB and AC configurations differ—hence, the lambdas associated with the AB and $A\overline{C}$ terms in like models differ. With respect to models that fit F_{ijk}'s, the residuum about the expectancies given by the *base model*, the model that fits [AB] and [AC], was greater than the residuum about the base model in the system where observed f_{ijk}'s were fit. Said differently, when interaction effects embodied in observed f_{ijk}'s were merged with effects due to Marital Status given Gender, instead of witnessing an enhancement of residuum, which is the typical result, for FC_{11} the result was a diminution in residuum. In a very real sense, the incorporation of a specific pattern of interaction, which was dealt to FC_{11} as a function of how we chose to reformulate the master table, had the effect of suppressing effects due to Marital Status given Gender as they were observed in models that fit F_{ijk}'s.

How should an interactive comparison such as FC_{11} be interpreted? If a priori considerations dictate that FC_{11} must be interpreted as an interactive comparison, in light of the complexities associated with negative chi-squares, reason dictates that the chi-square, in effect, be set to zero and the interaction be regarded as nil.[4] In the absence of such considerations, the most reasonable approach would be to acknowledge that interaction effects peculiar to this comparison operate to suppress effects due to Marital Status, and then proceed to assess the joint operation of these effects by evaluating the confounded version of FC_{11}. A more general discussion of factors to be considered when presented with decisions regarding the selection and interpretation of FCs is offered in the concluding section of this chapter.

THE HOLTON-NOTT STUDY REVISITED

To reinforce our nascent appreciation of focused comparisons, we return to the asymmetrical analysis reported by Holton and Nott (1980). Overall results were shown in Table 5.12. Recall that main effects due to the treatment variable (Variable B) were deemed to be present, but our initial attempts to posit specific differences between experimental and control groups, predicated largely on the interpretation of lambda parameters presented in Table 5.13, lacked the fecundity that we would have expected had we been following up an ANOVA instead of a logit-model analysis. In this section, let us see if FCs can be used to enhance the precision of findings.

The first step is to select the type of FC to perform. Whereas confounded FCs were most instructive for the earlier working example, they are not attractive candidates for selection here because the interaction between Pretesting and Treatment failed to approach significance—in fact, all indications point to an interactive result that is strictly the product of chance ($p < .525$). Admittedly, marginal comparisons are viable candidates, but because the presence of pre-testing effects were suggested ($p < .282$) and complications associated with suppression were not suggested (see Table 5.10), fully partialed comparisons appear to be the best choice of focused comparison for the Holton-Nott study.

Having selected partialed comparisons, the next step is to design the specific FCs to be performed. The task of structuring sample designs is made simple due to the fact that treatment variable (i.e., experimental vs. control) is dichotomous. Hence, for all FCs, the sample design coefficients are, FC_{1k}: $+1.0$ and -1.0. Decisions regarding response designs rest, at least initially, with the original investigators, but the following three designs seem reasonably consistent with the inferred intent of the experiment:

Focused Comparison FC_{jk}	Classes of Response Posttest Variable C			
	C_1	C_2	C_3	C_4
FC_{11}	+1.0	-1.0	0.0	0.0
FC_{12}	+1.0	+ .5	+ .5	0.0
FC_{13}	+ .5	+ .5	-1.0	0.0

Notice that the three FCs do not constitute an orthogonal set; hence, do not expect comparison chi-squares to sum to 10.31, the partialed component L^2 for the treatment variable.

Because the selected FCs are of the fully partialed variety, it will be necessary to request as computer output the expected cell frequencies from Model 7 so that outputed F_{ijk}s can be organized into simple subtables and subsequently analyzed. The reader should assume that this request has been executed and that the F_{ijk}s from Model 7 needed to perform the desired comparisons are at hand. With this, we will execute FC_{11} to test the null hypothesis that no difference exists between experimental and control group subjects relative to their analytical-evidential (C_1 vs. C_2) response profile.

Calculating FC_{11}

The tertiary Pretesting variable presents four levels; therefore, simple subtables are established at each level of Variable A. Below is the simple subtable showing the F_{ijk}s from Model 7 that was mounted at A_1. Theoretical frequencies are in parenthesis.

Sample Classes	Classes of Response	
	$R(+)$	$R(-)$
$S(+)$	7.94 (6.74)	2.17 (3.37)
$S(-)$	2.06 (3.26)	2.83 (1.63)

The simple chi-square at A_1 is

$$L_{11}^2 \{@A_1\} = 2[2.94 \ln(7.94/6.74) + \ldots$$
$$+ 2.83 \ln(2.83/1.63)]$$
$$= 1.92$$

Table 6.10
Selected (Nonorthogonal) Partial *FC*s Applied to Results Reported by Holton and Nott

Focused Comparison	Comparison Chi-Square	df	Observed p Value	Criterion p Value	Phi
FC_{11} ($n = 68$)	8.83	1	.003	.025	.36
FC_{12} ($n = 87$)	10.08	1	.001	.017	.34
FC_{13} ($n = 87$)	1.29	1	.257	.050	.12
Partial $B\tilde{C}$ Component	10.31	3	.016	.050	

Remaining simple chi-squares computed along similar lines were found to be

$$L_{11}^2 \{@A_2\} = 3.37$$
$$L_{11}^2 \{@A_3\} = .86$$
$$L_{11}^2 \{@A_4\} = 2.68$$

Summing over levels of Variable A, as we do below, yields the comparison chi-square for FC_{11}

$$L_{11}^2(1) = \sum L_{11}^2 \{@A_i\}$$
$$= 3.37 + \ldots + 2.68$$
$$= 8.83$$

The null hypothesis under test is rejected ($p < .003$). Upon examination of F_{ijk}s (from Model 7), one can conclude that in terms of analytical vs. evidential response, the proportion of analytical response observed among experimental subjects exceeded that observed among control subjects. Said differently, the likelihood or odds that a control subject issued an evidential response was greater than that observed for an experimental subject.

Synthesizing Results

Results emanating from all partialed comparisons are collected and presented in Table 6.10. In addition to FC_{11}, FC_{12} was also significant ($p < .001$). When response is defined as analytical vs. nonanalytical (i.e., evidential and declarative combined), experimental group members were more likely to have responded analytically than members of the control condition.

Because three post hoc comparisons were executed, at this point some individuals would argue that some manner of control should be exercised over the increased possibility that the positive results reported in Table 6.10 were Type I errors. To accommodate this concern, Holm's (1979) procedure has been used to calculate the *criterion p values* that appear in Table 6.10. Holm's procedure is a modification of the familiar Bonferroni approach, which is sometimes called Dunn's test in the field of experimental design. However, instead of establishing a criterion p value by dividing the desired experimentwise alpha (say, .05) by the number of comparisons performed (say, m), comparisons are rank-ordered on the basis of their observed p values from m, the boldest comparison, to $m - (m - 1)$, the weakest comparison; then, for each comparison, the desired overall level is divided by its corresponding rank ordering.

By way of illustration, of the three comparisons performed, FC_{12} was found to be most prominent ($p < .001$). Its rank value, therefore, is $m = 3$. Assuming a desired experimentwise alpha level of .05, the criterion p value for this comparison is $.05/3 = .017$. To be deemed statistically significant in the sense that the probability of committing one or more Type I errors for the collection of three tests does not exceed .05, this particular comparison must achieve significance at the .017 level, which it did. The next most prominent comparison was FC_{11} ($p < .003$). Its criterion p value is $.05/(m - 1) = .05/2 = .025$. Therefore, conservatively speaking, significance also can be claimed for FC_{11}.

At this point, it is hoped that readers are convinced that the methodology of focused comparisons has the potential to enhance the number and precision of findings that can be coaxed from the data. The fact that specific findings can be cast in terms of differences either in log odds or proportions, and that associated measures of effect size are readily calculable, make FCs particularly attractive. As with any methodology, however, the use of FCs, particularly in an exploratory environment, can be abused. The ability of FCs to coax additional findings from data not only invites the commission of Type I errors, a problem that can be attenuated through the use of the Holm's or similar procedure (see Holland & Copenhaver, 1988), but also can enable pedantic analysts to pursue substantively insignificant results. With these new tools, log-linear analysts would do well to be reminded of the advice offered to experimental researchers by Hays, who stated specifically that analysts "should not pay too much attention to the isolated results that happen to be significant. Rather, the pattern and interpretability of results, as well as the strength of association represented by the findings, form a more reasonable basis for the overall evaluation of the experiment" (1988, 471).

CONCLUDING COMMENTS

Four types of focused comparisons were demonstrated, but only with regard to their use in the Holton-Nott Study was serious thought given to the appropriateness of the FCs that were performed. In general practice, uncritical execution of FCs, especially comparisons that involve the fitting of models within different systems, can produce incommensurate results. Our experience with the negative chi-square for the interactive FC observed in connection with the contrived data set serves as a case in point. Informed selection of the type of FC that is appropriate for a given situation requires that informed judgments be made concerning the model or models—call them *follow-up models*—on which comparisons are based.

Informed judgments concerning follow-up models can be made if the way of thinking, fostered earlier in connection with selecting *acceptable* models in the symmetrical analyses, is adopted for the section of follow-up models in asymmetrical analyses. To be more specific, omnibus results such as were summarized in Table 5.11 for the Holton-Nott study or Table 6.2 for the contrived working example should be examined with an eye toward identifying the most parsimonious logit model that offers an acceptable explanation of observed data. For the Holton-Nott study, where the $AB\overline{C}$ term was substantively and statistically insignificant, previously defined Model 7 represents a defensible selection. For the working example, Model 8, the saturated model is the obvious selection. Returning to the Holton-Nott Study, because omnibus interaction has been deemed to be nil, interactive FCs are clearly negated and confounded FCs are of questionable value. Since the best representatives of experimental outcome appear to be those offered by the F_{ijk}'s given by Model 7, our attention is confined to FCs of either the marginal or fully partialed variety. To push the point further, suppose that conditions warranted the dismissal of the $A\overline{C}$ term in the Holton-Nott or a comparable analysis, then strong justification would be afforded the use of marginal FCs to explicate results.

The omnibus results observed for the working example present a different context for decisions concerning FCs. To the extent to which the analysis is exploratory, the intricacies associated with the prominent $AB\overline{C}$ term ($p < .029$) should not be ignored. FCs based on the saturated model generally will take precedence over FCs that directly involve the fittings given by the less acceptable Model 7. The decision to be made is whether to invest interest in confounded comparisons or interactive comparisons. Of course, this decision should be guided by the substance of the research but, having said that, it can also be said that confounded comparisons possess a number of advantages that make them most attractive candidates for consideration. For example, the fact that confounded FCs reflect influences exerted by both the principal variable (e.g., Marital Status) and interaction (Marital Status × Gender) presents a manner of outcome that is most often of greatest interest to the substantive researcher. In addition, confounded FCs are essentially composites of "wired-in" single-df contrasts, contrasts that are immediately available to test simple logit-model main effects.

Understandably, in this chapter we have discussed FCs only within the context of three-dimensional problems, but the methodology of focused comparisons can be generalized to tables of higher dimensionality. Following a presentation of how log-linear models are applied to tables of four and five dimensions, at the end of Chapter 7 we will return briefly to FCs to see how they may be used in these situations.

NOTES

1. Calculations were actually carried out to eight-place accuracy, but to effect economies of expression, they are reported only to four-place accuracy in this chapter.

2. For example, if single members of the sample are being contrasted to married members, and the substantive hypothesis is that a positive linear trend in response to ordered categorical Variable C will be observed for singles but a *contrasting* negative trend characterizes response for married members, then the use of response coefficients in the first set ($+1$, 0, -1) will permit an assessment of whether necessary (but not sufficient) conditions in support of the hypothesis are present.

3. Often, as will be done in Chapter 7, log odds are divided by 2 to produce *binomial logits*, and binomial logits are plotted in graphical displays of interaction. As will be noted, binomial logits are linked to lambda estimates in log-linear models. This additional transformation will not be shown in Table 6.8 nor used in Figure 6.1 since it will have no effect on the interpretation of the present outcome.

4. If a logit-model analysis is performed on observed frequencies in the $2 \times 2 \times 2$ table upon which FC_{11} is based, the confounded component, $L^2(2) = 5.39$, was found to be partitionable by a significant partialed component for Marital Status, $L^2(1) = 4.98$, and a minuscule component, $L^2(1) = 0.40$, for interaction, thus reinforcing the nil outcome for this interaction.

7

Tables of High Dimensionality

The power of log-linear methodology is realized most fully when contingency tables are of high dimensionality. It is hoped that this chapter, which is designed to show how the principles and procedures of previous chapters can be applied to tables of four and five dimensions, will provide readers with the experience and confidence needed to tackle the analysis of these tables and tables of higher dimensionality.

The concrete example to be used to illustrate the analysis of four-dimensional tables is based on the doctoral research of McLean (1980). Each of the four variables in the McLean study was a dichotomy, and the analysis was asymmetrical. So that we will not have to devote the additional space needed to introduce an additional data set, we will assume that the McLean study also lent itself to a symmetrical analysis so that screening procedures and subsequent model-selection procedures can be illustrated. The latter sections of this chapter are devoted to an overview of log-linear procedures as they are applied to five-dimensional tables. The example to be used in these latter sections is based in part on the doctoral research of Peters (1981), where for instructional purposes I have taken many liberties relative to data modification so as to highlight salient features of the asymmetric analyses.

THE SYMMETRICAL ANALYSIS OF FOUR-DIMENSIONAL TABLES

To analyse tables defined by four crossed qualitative variables, our system of notation must be extended to accommodate the new variable, that is, the fourth. Adhering to earlier practice, the first three variables and their respective subscripts remain A ($k = 1, 2, \ldots, a$), B ($j = 1, 2, \ldots, b$), and C ($k = 1, 2, \ldots, c$).

The fourth variable will be denoted D, with subscript m where $m = 1, 2, \ldots,$ d.[1] An unspecified *observed* elementary cell frequency will be f_{ijkm}. Accordingly, F_{ijkm} denotes the corresponding *expected* elementary frequency.

For tables defined by four variables, there are four main marginals, six distinct two-variable (first-order) configurations, four three-variable (second-order) configurations, and, of course, the observed four-variable configuration $[ABCD]$. Finally, realize that n subjects are cross-classified on the basis of the four variables, respecting the requisite conditions discussed in Chapters 3 and 4, so that each subject belongs to one (and only one) of the elementary cells in the $a \times b \times c \times d$ contingency table.

General Models for Four-Dimensional Tables

When models are arrayed hierarchically by ascending complexity as before, we have: (1) a one-parameter completely null model, (2) four main-marginal models, (3) six two-variable models, (4) four three-variable models, and (5) a sixteen-parameter saturated model. In its linear form, the saturated model is

$$\ln F_{ijkm} = \lambda + \lambda_i^a + \lambda_j^b + \lambda_k^c + \lambda_m^d + \lambda_{ij}^{ab} + \lambda_{ik}^{ac} + \lambda_{im}^{ad}$$
$$+ \lambda_{jk}^{bc} + \lambda_{jm}^{bd} + \lambda_{km}^{cd} + \lambda_{ijk}^{abc} + \lambda_{ijm}^{abd} + \lambda_{ikm}^{acd} + \lambda_{jkm}^{bcd} + \lambda_{ijkm}^{abcd} \quad (7.1)$$

Due to the size of models with which we will be working, some abbreviation and even abridgement will be needed in ensuing presentations. Table 7.1, for example, attempts to display a particular hierarchical arrangement of models by using only the superscripts associated with lambdas to denote all but the first parameter in each model.[2] Before proceeding to the discussion of model screening and subsequent model selection, Table 7.1 should be studied carefully.

Screening General Models for Acceptability of Fit

There are numerous ways that general models (models in the service of symmetrical inquiry) can be structured. Thus, when inquiry is symmetrical, the task of narrowing the range of models to a promising few can be both time consuming and costly—especially if the table is large and there is little a priori theory to guide the search. For three-way tables, for example, there are 72 different hierarchical arrangements which can generate a total of 142 distinct models. For four-way tables, the number of possible arrangements and distinct models is even greater. Just consider the effort required to fit and evaluate the 16 models presented in Table 7.1—never mind the effort that would be required to evaluate individually the hundreds of distinct models not explicitly presented in Table 7.1. Clearly, as has been pointed out by Brown, "Some screening of the effects or interactions in the log-linear model is necessary in order to limit the number of models whose tests-of-fit need to be evaluated" (1976, 38). Brown, moreover,

Table 7.1
A Hierarchical Arrangement of Models for Tables of Four Dimensions

Model No.	Log-Linear Models	Marginals Fitted
(1)	λ	n
(2)	λ + a	A
(3)	λ + a + b	A,B
(4)	λ + a + b + c	A,B,C
(5)	λ + a + b + c + d	A,B,C,D
(6)	λ + a + b + c + d + ab	AB,C,D
(7)	λ + a + b + c + d + ab + ac	AB,AC,D
(8)	λ + a + b + c + d + ab + ac + ad	AB,AC,AD
(9)	λ + a + b + c + d + ab + ac + ad + bc	AB,AC,AD,BC
(10)	λ + a + b + c + d + ab + ac + ad + bc + bd	AB,AC,AD,BC,BD
(11)	λ + a + b + c + d + ab + ac + ad + bc + bd + cd	AB,AC,AD,BC,BD,CD
(12)	λ + a + b + c + d + ab + ac + ad + bc + bd + cd + abc	ABC,AD,BD,CD
(13)	λ + a + b + c + d + ab + ac + ad + bc + bd + cd + abc + abd	ABC,ABD,CD
(14)	λ + a + b + c + d + ab + ac + ad + bc + bd + cd + abc + abd + acd	ABC,ABD,ACD
(15)	λ + a + b + c + d + ab + ac + ad + bc + bd + cd + abc + abd + acd + bcd	ABC,ABD,ACD,BCD
(16)	λ + a + b + c + d + ab + ac + ad + bc + bd + cd + abc + abd + acd + bcd + abcd	ABCD

Note: To promote economy of expression, parameter estimates are designated by only their respective superscripts (with the expression of λ), and fitted marginals are expressed without brackets.

has proposed two screening procedures that can help reduce the number of possible models and conserve effort, time, and money.

The first screening procedure is to evaluate kth *order models* for goodness-of-fit so that choice can be narrowed to a "family" of specific models. The designations "kth order" is applied to a full model; it is *not* used as a description for terms within a model. For example, Model 1 appearing in Table 7.1 may be termed a zero-order ($k = 0$) model. Model 5, the independence model, may be termed a first-order ($k = 1$) model because it not only contains all four main-marginal terms but, in addition, should this model *not* fit observed data well, associations of at least the first-order of magnitude (e.g., λ^{ab}, λ^{ac}, etc.) are indicated. Model 11 is a second-order ($k = 2$) model, for not only does it contain all two-variable terms (or first-order terms), its inability to fit the data implies the need to incorporate an additional term or terms that is at least of the second order of magnitude (e.g., λ^{abc}, λ^{abd}, etc.). Parenthetically, kth order model designations appear on screening tables produced by BMDP/4F, and they will frequently appear in the screening tables presented in this book.

The focus of the second screening procedure is directed towards the component chi-squares that are associated with kth order models. As we shall learn, kth order components are used to evaluate the marginal and partial associations linked to interaction terms for the purpose of determining which terms are needed and which terms are not needed in the model. It is most fortunate that these two screening procedures have been incorporated as options in the BMDP/4F computer program.[3] However, the screening information provided directly by BMDP/4F can be obtained from other computer programs if the user specifies and evaluates the specific models that will be discussed on the pages that follow.

As noted in the opening, the data to be used to illustrate model screening were obtained by McLean (1980). The McLean study will be discussed in greater detail in the next section. For now, we need only know that each of the four variables in the study was a dichotomy, the size of the sample was very respectable ($n = 896$), and the 4F program in the BMDP package was used to print out screening tables of residual and component chi-squares, facsimiles of which will be reproduced on ensuing pages.

Full Model Goodness-of-Fit. To effect economy, models can be grouped into sets according to the presence of like-order terms. These sets will be called *families*. As a prefatory exercise, consider the arrangement of models for three-way tables shown in Table 5.2 (or Table 5.3). Here models can be grouped into four families. Obviously, the one-parameter zero-order model constitutes a special case, a family containing only one model. Models that, in addition to the geometric mean parameter, also contain main-marginal parameters comprise another family. In this family, Model 4 is designated the full or first-order model because it contains all three main-marginal effects. Next, Models 5, 6, and 7 contain at least one two-variable term, and thus, they belong to the family of first-order models where the most complete model, Model 7, is the second-order model. Finally, there is the saturated model, the third-order model. Observe that

Table 7.2
Screening Tests on Full Models Applied to the McLean Data

Model*	K FACTOR	Residual			Component		
		D.F.	LR CHISQ	PROB	D.F.	LR CHISQ	PROB
(1)	0	15	929.64	.000			
(5)	1	11	829.83	.000	4	99.81	.000
(11)	2	5	10.06	.074	6	819.77	.000
(15)	3	1	2.53	.112	4	7.53	.110
(16)	4	0	0.00		1	2.53	.112

Note: The design of this table resembles the screening tables produced by the 4F program in the BMDP package.
*The models of this table correspond by number to the models displayed in Table 7.1.

we have reduced a number of specific models into a fewer number of "full" models, a reduction that is more pronounced in arrangements for tables of four and five dimensions.

With respect specifically to tables of four dimensions, models can be grouped into five families whereby each family is most completely specified by a full or kth-order model. By examining Table 7.1, the first family is represented by Model 1, the completely null model or the *zero-order* model. The second family is represented by Model 5, the full main-marginal model, which is alternatively labeled the *first-order* model. The third family is represented by Model 11, the *second-order* model, and so forth.

The first screening operation, therefore, is to request the residual fit of all kth-order models. The residual chi-squares for the kth-order models fitted to McLean's $2 \times 2 \times 2 \times 2$ table are presented in the middle portion of Table 7.2. Notice that corresponding component chi-squares, which may need to be computed by hand, are also displayed to the right in Table 7.2.[4]

The table is approached as before. That is, simple kth-order models that fit observed data poorly are identified by their large residual chi-squares and immediately excluded from serious consideration. Often, the results of residual screening will point immediately to a family of models where acceptability will be found. Examining residual chi-squares, from the bottom to the top of the table, reveals that the first significant chi-square is that associated with Model 5, namely, $L_5^2(11) = 829.83$, $p < .000$. Therefore, all main-marginal models and the completely null model can be excluded from further consideration.

Assessing Components of kth-Order Models. To evaluate tests on components, we start at the bottom of the table and entertain the component for the λ^{abcd} term, $L_{15-16}^2(1) = 2.53$, which is not significant at the .05 level, and which

Table 7.3
Residual and Component Chi-Squares for Selected Models Fitted to the McLean Data

	Residual			Component		
Model	df	L^2	p	df	L^2	p
(5)	11	829.83	.000			
(6)	10	714.24	.000	1	115.59	.000
(7)	9	628.32	.000	1	85.92	.000
(8)	8	610.01	.000	1	18.31	.000
(9)	7	18.96	.008	1	591.05	.000
(10)	6	12.47	.052	1	6.49	.025
(11)	5	10.06	.074	1	2.41	.121
(12)	4	8.80	.066	1	1.26	.262

Note: Models correspond by number to those presented in Table 7.1.

prompts us to suspect strongly that the saturated model will not be a serious candidate for adoption. The next component, $L_{11-15}^2(4) = 7.53$, is also not prominent ($p < .110$), which prompts us to look at the family of second-order models for acceptability. The component for second-order models, $L_{5-11}^2(6) = 819.77$, $p < .000$, is unquestionably significant, which precludes any suspicion that a first-order model might be acceptable. In sum, to this point, it appears that a model in the second-order family will approach acceptability for a symmetrical analysis, but it is too early to exclude the possibility that a three-variable term (e.g., λ^{abc}, λ^{abd}, etc.) may be needed to achieve acceptable fit.

Selecting an Acceptable General Model

To exercise our ability to select and interpret general models, let us assume for the moment that the inquiry of the McLean study was symmetrical. From knowledge gleaned from the screening table (Table 7.2), we would likely execute a computer run designed specifically to fit (1) second-order Models 6 through 11; (2) Models 5 and 12, so as to establish the outer boundaries of acceptability; and (3) the saturated model, a model that is always informative. The computer output will only provide residual chi-squares, but with these, component chi-squares can be hand-calculated. We suggest that these statistics be organized in tabular form as shown in Table 7.3.

We approach the task of choosing a model without benefit of knowledge of the variables and substantive theory. Appreciating these limitations, let us begin by evaluating the residual L^2's given in Table 7.3, the results of which support the rejection of Models 6, 7, and 8. Next, an examination of component chi-squares confirms our earlier suspicion that third-order models, represented here by Model 12, also can be rejected as serious candidates for selection. Our search, therefore, will begin in earnest with Model 11, and will likely terminate by choosing a model that contains at least one two-variable parameter estimate. Before we begin, however, a few words should be said about the order in which two-variable terms are entered in these models.

Recall from Chapter 5 that the order in which the three first-order terms appear in the second-order model affects not only the magnitudes of respective components but also the nature of the relationships (e.g., marginal or partial) associated with these components. Predictably, in this chapter, order of entry will also be found to influence the size and meaning of components but in a more complex manner. It is important to realize, however, that the magnitude of specific effects (lambdas or taus) is *not* affected by order of entry. That is, for a model containing a given set of two-variable terms, changing the order of appearance will not alter either the numerical value of effect parameters or the tests of significance (z tests) performed on these effects. In a sense, then, statistical tests performed on component chi-squares are somewhat like the partial F test performed on semipartial coefficients in multiple regression equations, where the latter are performed to determine whether a variable is making a significant contribution to the R^2. On the other hand, z tests performed on specific lambda effects in a log-linear model are analogous to t tests (or corresponding F tests) on specific coefficients (e.g., beta weights) in a multiple regression equation.

It is hoped that a number of these points will be clarified during the course of the survey of the models presented in Table 7.3 that we are about to undertake. The purpose of the survey is twofold: first to illustrate a number of the complexities associated with the order of variable entry and, secondly, to narrow the range of terms that "should" appear in the most acceptable model.

Model 11. Consider the component for this model: $L^2_{10-11}(1) = 2.41$, $p <$ .121. This component is linked to λ^{cd}, the term that has been entered sixth or last in the array of two-variable terms. The magnitude of the component is related to the strength of a *full partial association*—the full partial association between Variables C and D in this case—and a test on this component will indicate whether the full partial association is statistically significant. Here, *full partial* refers to the association between Variables C and D subsequent to effecting an adjustment for the potential confounding influences of Variable A, Variable B, and the association between Variables A and B which, in the full second-order model (unlike other second-order models) is *not* independent of the association between C and D.[5] Thus, the statistical test of this component tends to be extremely conservative, for it is a test of an association following the removal of the effects of all previously entered two-variable terms.

Notice in Table 7.3 that the test of the component for the *CD* association failed to achieve significance at the .05 level, despite the fact that respectable power was afforded the test by the reasonably large sample. Nevertheless, due to the conservative nature of the test and the fact that we are still engaged in a screening activity, λ^{cd} should not be excluded immediately from future consideration unless test results were decidedly nonsignificant, say $p > .25$. If we are to err during this tentative phase of model delimitation, it is best to err in the direction of inclusion rather than exclusion.

Additional insight can be obtained by examining the magnitudes of λ^{cd} effects in the full second-order model, Model 11, since these effects are invariant with respect to their ordering in this model. It turns out that the four effects are $\pm .093$, which, when divided by their standard errors, give z statistics greater than unity ($z = \pm 1.29$). Though not impressive, effects with z statistics greater than unity are of passing interest, at least during this initial phase.

Before considering Model 10, study Table 7.4, which is obtainable from BMDP/4F and contains (1) component chi-squares that reflect the magnitude of marginal associations between variable combinations (the association between two variables subsequent to collapsing or summing over the two unspecified variables); (2) components that reflect full partial associations, obtained by entering a variable combination in the sixth position in a full second-order model and then contrasting that model with one that contains all terms belonging to the full second-order model except the term in question; and (3) z tests on estimated lambda effects contained in the full second-order model. The component for a marginal association is obtained by entering the corresponding term first or second in the array of two-variable terms and then contrasting the five- (or six-) parameter model with an appropriate four- (or five-) parameter model. (Notice, for example, that the components for *AB* and *AC* given in Table 7.3 are the marginal components listed for these combinations in Table 7.4.) As was just noted, the component reflecting a full partial association is obtained by entering the corresponding term in the final position in a full second-order model, creating an eleven-parameter model, and then contrasting this model with a ten-parameter model where the latter is identical to the former except for the term in question. Needless to say, the availability of tests of marginal and full partials as output from BMDP/4F constitutes a salutary feature of this program.

Model 10. The component $L^2_{9-10}(1) = 6.49$, $p < .025$, represents what we shall term a *half-partial association*. Here it is an association between Variables *B* and *D* subsequent to the partialing of influences exerted by Variable *A* but not Variable *C*. Hence, when we refer to a half-partial association, control or adjustment has been exercised over only one variable (e.g., Variable *A* above), and not both.

The nature of the association reflected by a component is dictated by preceding terms in a model. Consider specifically λ^{bd} and what might precede it in a model. If λ^{ac} is found prior to λ^{bd}, the association between *A* and *C* has no effect on the association between *B* and *D* because they are independent of each other

Table 7.4

Tests of Marginal and Full Partial Associations and Tests of Lambda Parameters for the McLean Data

Effects	df	Marginal L^2	p	Partial L^2	p	z test[*]
AB	1	115.59	.000	30.05	.000	4.39
AC	1	85.92	.000	.83	.364	.77
AD	1	18.31	.000	9.37	.002	1.61
BC	1	675.81	.000	584.69	.000	15.42
BD	1	15.09	.000	.13	.723	.31
CD	1	16.93	.000	2.41	.121	1.29

*The absolute value of z statistics resulting from tests on lambda effects for the full second-order model, Model 11, are displayed in this column.

except in the highly dependent full second-order model. If, however, it should happen that *both* λ^{bc} and λ^{cd} have been entered prior to λ^{bd}, Variable C will be partialed from the association between B and D. Suppose, however, that λ^{ab} and λ^{ad} were entered before λ^{bd}, as is the case for current Model 10; what variable, if any, would be partialed out of the association between Variables B and D? Variable A is the answer, because A is common to the prior association involving Variables B and D. Since there must be at very least two common prior associations, documentation of half-partial associations can occur only for associations represented by terms entered third, fourth, or, as we have just seen, fifth.

At this point, it appears that λ^{bd} is a likely candidate for inclusion in the final model. First appearances, however, can be deceiving. A little additional probing, for example, will reveal two informational items that cast serious suspicion on the importance of λ^{bd}. First, the component associated with its full partial association (see Table 7.4) will be found to be minuscule ($p < .72$). Second, the size of lambda effects in the full first-order model are also relatively unimpressive ($z = \pm.31$). Apparently, the association between Variables B and D diminishes markedly when Variable C is taken into account, a deduction that can be confirmed by testing the component for the half-partial association controlling for Variable C, the results of which are $L^2(1) = .91$, $p < .33$. Needless to say, even though λ^{bd} remains a candidate for inclusion, we should be most suspicious and critical of this term, which cannot stand independently of Variable C.

Model 9. Simply put, the component for this model is huge. What does it say about the association between B and C, however? The fact that λ^{ad} precedes

λ^{bc} tells us nothing, since the association between A and D is independent of that between B and C. Notice, however, that two nonindependent terms involving Variable A—λ^{ab} and λ^{ac}—are present and prior to λ^{bc}. This arrangement points to a relationship between Variables B and C which is substantial even after the influences of Variable A have been taken into account.[6] Additional probing reveals that the component for the full partial association, $L^2(1) = 584.69$, is substantial and significant. Without doubt, λ^{bc} will be included in the model to be selected.

Model 8. The term in "third position" is similar to a term in the "fourth position" in that its component represents either a half-partial, incomplete, or marginal association. Now, we know that if either λ^{ab} and λ^{bd} or λ^{ac} and λ^{cd} were to precede λ^{ad}, a half-partial would be indicated. Should λ^{ab} and λ^{cd} (or λ^{ac} and λ^{bd}) be found prior to λ^{ad}, the component would reflect an incomplete partial, and, as indicated in note 5, incomplete partials are difficult to interpret substantively. However, the component in question reflects neither a half nor an incomplete association; instead, by default, it reflects the strength of the marginal association between Variables A and D, which is statistically significant. In Table 7.4, significance also is seen for a full partial association, $L^2(1) = 9.37, p < .002$. Although short of significance, the tests on the λ^{ad}'s in the full second-order model produce respectable results ($z = \pm 1.61$). In sum, the λ^{ad} term appears to be most promising.

Model 7. The component for a term in "second place" is readily interpreted: The component always reflects the strength of a marginal association. Here, the marginal association is between Variables A and C, and is significant: $L^2_{6-7}(1) = 85.92, p < .000$. The numerical value of this component would result from computing a likelihood-ratio chi-square on $[AC]$, subsequent to collapsing over Variables B and D. Table 7.4, however, informs us that the full partial association between A and C is not statistically significant ($p < .364$). Moreover, corresponding lambda effects in the full first-order model are quite small. In fact, the z statistics associated with these effects fail to exceed unity. All things considered, it is not likely that λ^{ac} will be found in the final model.

Model 6. The component linked to a first-order term that is entered first reflects the strength of a marginal association. This association is shown in Table 7.3 to be statistically significant. Also, both the complete partial association and z test on the λ^{ab}'s are statistically significant. This term undoubtedly belongs in the final model.

What have we learned from our survey of first-order models? From all the evidence, it is clear that λ^{bc} and λ^{ab} are important and certainly belong in the model that will eventually be adopted. Though not as impressive, λ^{ad} is promising, and λ^{cd}, though questionable, should not be discarded yet. Candidates for exclusion appear to be λ^{bd} and λ^{ac}. Even though the former term showed a significant component in Table 7.3, suggesting an association between Variables B and D after adjustments are made for Variable A, when this association was viewed at respective levels of Variable C, it vanished. Furthermore, recall that

Table 7.5
Final Fit of General Models to the McLean Data

		Residual				Component		
Model	Marginals Fitted	df	L^2	p	AIC	df	L^2	p
(7.2)	BC , AB	9	38.43	.000	52.43			
(7.3)	BC , AB , AD	8	21.50	.006	37.50	1	16.93	.000
(7.4)	BC , AB , AD , CD	7	10.96	.141	28.96	1	10.54	.001
(11)*	BC , AB , AD , CD , AC , BD	5	10.07	.074	32.07	2	.90	.639

Note: Fitted marginals are presented without brackets in this table.
*This is the full second-order ($k = 2$) model described in Table 7.1 and subsequent tables.

the test on its component for a full partial fell far short of statistical significance ($p < .72$); and tests performed on lambda estimates were similarly unimpressive ($z = \pm.31$). The latter term, λ^{ac}, appears to be almost as impotent, and for comparable reasons. (Incidentally, investigation of half-partials revealed that when examined at respective levels of B, the relationship between A and C was nonsignificant, specifically $L^2(1) = 1.16$, $p < .20$.) Hence, at this point, we cautiously hypothesize that the most acceptable model will, in addition to main-marginal terms, contain λ^{bc}, λ^{ab}, λ^{ad}, and possibly λ^{cd}.

To assess and possibly fine-tune our working hypothesis, an additional computer run will be required. At the very least, the following models should be fit:

$$\ln F_{ijkm} = \lambda + \lambda^a + \lambda^b + \lambda^c + \lambda^d + \lambda^{bc} + \lambda^{ab} \tag{7.2}$$

$$\ln F_{ijkm} = \lambda + \lambda^a + \lambda^b + \lambda^c + \lambda^d + \lambda^{bc} + \lambda^{ab} + \lambda^{ad} \tag{7.3}$$

$$\ln F_{ijkm} = \lambda + \lambda^a + \lambda^b + \lambda^c + \lambda^d + \lambda^{bc} + \lambda^{ab} + \lambda^{ad} + \lambda^{cd} \tag{7.4}$$

Results, combined with those seen earlier for the full second-order model, are summarized in Table 7.5.

As expected, the full second-order model can be bypassed in favor of the nine-parameter model given by Equation 7.4 since the adoption of the latter more parsimonious model results in a minimal loss of ability to fit observed data, namely, $L^2(2) = .90$, $p < .639$. The significant component ($p < .001$) aligned with the nine-parameter model, however, discourages us from dropping λ^{cd} and adopting Equation 7.3. Moreover, an examination of AIC statistics, calculated from Equation 5.11, points to the model expressed as Equation 7.4 as being optimal. Our exercise has resulted in the choice of Equation 7.4 as being the best explanation for the McLean data. Three strong relationships can be claimed, and a fourth—that between C and D—is present but may need to be advanced with qualification. Unfortunately, the substantive vacuum in which we have been operating makes it difficult to be more specific.

THE ASYMMETRICAL ANALYSIS OF FOUR-DIMENSIONAL TABLES

In reality, the McLean study was asymmetrical. In this and other four-variable logit-model investigations, the majority of general models shown in Table 7.1 do not apply. If we arbitrarily make Variable D the response variable, then the major requisite for a logit model is that, in addition to all main marginals, it also fits $[ABC]$. The model must contain λ^{abc} (or the corresponding tau parameter), for observed frequencies in the $[ABC]$ configuration can either be the result of sampling or can be deliberately fixed by the researcher. In either event, differing values of f_{ijk}^{abc}'s bear no relevance to response patterns over levels of Variable D, and consequently, these differences must be controlled. Control can be exercised over irrelevant, potentially contaminating differences among f^{abc}'s by insisting that λ^{abc} be in any models where D is the response variable. Main-marginal differences in $[D]$ also should not be permitted to influence response patterns to levels of D; thus, λ^d should appear in every logit model. Table 7.6 presents logit models for the layout under discussion.

Table 7.6 merits careful study. Notice that we have abandoned the practice of numbering logit models according to the number of terms that they contain. The numbering system now reflects the number of contained interaction terms that involve the response variable. In addition, notice that every model in Table 7.6 fits the $[ABC]$ configuration and that only logit models 4, 5, 6, and 7 are in the listing of general models appearing in Table 7.1; the null-logit model, Model 0, and Models 1, 2, and 3 have no counterpart in Table 7.1. Finally, note the bars over superscript d in all interaction terms. This is simply a convenient notation device to indicate that Variable D is the response variable and, if superscripts do *not* carry a bar, to indicate corresponding effect designations, as in the ANOVA.

In a number of respects, Table 7.6 is similar to the summary table for three-way ANOVAs, ANOVAs in which Variables A, B, and C are independent variables and Variable D is the dependent variable. Not surprisingly, therefore, we will conduct the logit-model analysis in a manner much like that of a three-way ANOVA. We will determine first whether there is a significant residuum observed about the F_{ijkm}'s provided by the null-logit model. If the residuum about the null-logit model is significantly large, then the residual L^2 for this model will be partitioned into seven additive components, each component being associated with a logit-model effect that is potentially responsible for the poor fit of the null-logit model. Statistically significant components will indicate statistically significant main or interaction effects.

Table 7.6
Hierarchical Logit Models for Four-Way Tables Where D Is the Logit Variable

Model No.	Log-Linear Logit Models	Marginals Fitted
(0)*	$\lambda + a + b + c + d + ab + ac + bc + abc$	ABC,D
(1)	$\lambda + a + b + c + d + ab + ac + bc + abc + a\bar{d}$	ABC,AD
(2)	$\lambda + a + b + c + d + ab + ac + bc + abc + a\bar{d} + b\bar{d}$	ABC,AD,BD
(3)	$\lambda + a + b + c + d + ab + ac + bc + abc + a\bar{d} + b\bar{d} + c\bar{d}$	ABC,AD,BD,CD
(4)	$\lambda + a + b + c + d + ab + ac + bc + abc + a\bar{d} + b\bar{d} + c\bar{d} + ab\bar{d}$	ABC,ABD,CD
(5)	$\lambda + a + b + c + d + ab + ac + bc + abc + a\bar{d} + b\bar{d} + c\bar{d} + ab\bar{d} + ac\bar{d}$	ABC,ABD,ACD
(6)	$\lambda + a + b + c + d + ab + ac + bc + abc + a\bar{d} + b\bar{d} + c\bar{d} + ab\bar{d} + ac\bar{d} + bc\bar{d}$	ABC,ABD,ACD,BCD
(7)	$\lambda + a + b + c + d + ab + ac + bc + abc + a\bar{d} + b\bar{d} + c\bar{d} + ab\bar{d} + ac\bar{d} + bc\bar{d} + abc\bar{d}$	ABCD

Note: To promote economy of expression, parameter estimates are denoted by their respective superscripts (with the exception of the first term, λ), and fitted marginals are presented without brackets.

*Numbers assigned to logit models in this table no longer reflect the number of constituent terms. They do, however, reflect the number of interaction terms that involve the logit variable.

Bear in mind, however, that the approach just described may also be viewed as selecting the most acceptable logit model. Before we compute and test relevant components, let us briefly survey the omnibus interpretations associated with the logit models that are seen in Table 7.6.

Interpretations of Logit Models

If it happens that Model 7, the saturated model, is, in effect, chosen, second-order (three-variable) interaction effects, much like those seen in a three-way ANOVA, are indicated. That is, *simple* first-order interactions exist, but they undergo modifications upon examination at separate levels of the third variable. Granted, interpreting a second-order interaction may appear complicated. However, if Variable D, our assumed logit variable, is dichotomous, the interpretation is no more difficult than it is in a three-way ANOVA. Incidentally, adoption of the saturated model does not preclude the existence of overall main effects or overall first-order interaction effects.

Acceptance of Model 6, 5, or 4 indicates that at least one overall first-order (two-variable) interaction is present. For example, if Model 5 were deemed most acceptable, we would conclude that Variables A and C interact with respect to the logit variable. In addition, there does not appear to be an interaction between B and C or a second-order interaction because they are not in the model. There is more, however. Because λ^{abd} precedes λ^{acd}, the interaction between Variables A and C is present over and beyond an interaction that might exist between Variables A and B. For the same reason, if Model 6 were to be selected, we would conclude that there is a first-order interaction between Variables B and C subsequent to partialing out the interaction between A and B, and that between A and C. We will have the opportunity to select and follow up a model in this family later in this chapter.

The family of main-effects models consists of Models 3, 2, and 1. Consider for a moment what it means to select Model 1. First, its adoption indicates that λ^{ad} is needed to achieve a reasonable fit to the observed data. Second, if our perspective were symmetrical, the presence of λ^{ad} would suggest a marginal association between A and D. But our perspective is not symmetrical, and hence, the presence of λ^{ad} suggests that the response profile over levels of Variable D is different when examined over levels of Variable A. Suppose Model 2 were to be chosen. From a symmetrical perspective, the presence of λ^{bd} would indicate a half-partial association, an association between B and D adjusting for Variable A. In a logit model, however, the need to incorporate λ^{bd} means that there are differences in the pattern of response to the logit variable when examined at different levels of Variable B even after adjustments have been made for main effects due to Variable A. Finally, suppose that Model 3 happened to be the model of choice. In the symmetrical, λ^{cd} would point to a full partial association between C and D; but in the asymmetrical, this can be translated to mean that main effects are present among levels of Variable C subsequent to correcting for the main effects of both Variables A and B. Again, the order of variable entry is important to interpretation and merits careful a priori consideration.

The remaining model in Table 7.6 is the null-logit model, appropriately designated Model 0. If this model fits the observed data reasonably well, we must conclude that there are no effects of sufficient magnitude to be entertained. Adoption of the null model is analogous to performing a three-way ANOVA and discovering that, of the seven omnibus F tests, not one has achieved statistical significance.

Let us make one more attempt to relate a logit-model analysis to an ANOVA. In the ANOVA, the sum of squared deviations about the grand mean (i.e., the total sum of squares) is calculated and then partitioned into specific components (i.e., SS_A, SS_B, etc.) associated with factors (e.g., Variables A, B, etc.) that explain variability about the grand mean. In a logit-model analysis, we attempt to explain the discrepancy between observed cell frequencies and those offered by the null-logit model. The size of the discrepancy is reflected by the size of the residual chi-square for Model 0. This residual chi-square can then be partitioned into specific components (e.g., L_{0-1}^2, L_{1-2}^2, etc.) associated with factors (e.g., Variables A, B, etc.) that appear to be promoting discrepancy about the expected cell frequencies generated by the null. Moreover, in the ANOVA, if cell n's are unequal and disproportionate, component sums of squares are not independent; they are nonorthogonal, and ANOVA methods based on comparisons between regression models need to be evoked. Methods not dissimilar to those used for unequal-n ANOVA's will be illustrated in the next section.

An Example of an Omnibus Logit-Model Analysis

McLean (1980) sought to investigate the graduation rates of black and white students in two southern universities: historically, one was black and the other white. Research indicated that, in general, black students tend to complete their undergraduate degree programs at a lower rate than white students. McLean, however, suspected that the differential rate of program completion was moderated in part by the type of institution attended. Specifically, he suspected that differences between blacks and whites in completion would be more pronounced in historically white universities than in historically black universities, whereas in the latter, differences might not exist.

Selected for study were 896 first-time, full-time students who enrolled in degree programs in either the white or the black university during the fall of 1975. Due to the small numbers, during the autumn all blacks entering the white university were included in the sample. Remaining black and white sample members at the respective universities were drawn at random. Data pertaining to high school performance were used in regression equations to predict college success; samples within universities were subdivided into a group that had prediction scores above the average (termed high-ability students by McLean) and a group with below-average predictors (termed low-ability students). At the end

Table 7.7
The McLean Data: Observed Frequencies by Race, Type of University, Ability Level, and Completion Status

			Completion Status	
Race	University	Ability	Graduation	Nongraduation
Black	White	High	10	22
		Low	4	18
	Black	High	55	90
		Low	71	222
White	White	High	114	146
		Low	46	66
	Black	High	5	5
		Low	3	19

of the fourth academic year (spring 1979), it was determined whether each sample member had graduated or had failed to graduate during the four-year period. Thus, this research involved the study of three dichotomous explanatory variables and a dichotomous response variable, completion status. The variables were:

A: *Ability Groups*
A_1 = high (f_1^a = 447)
A_2 = low (f_2^a = 449)

B: *Type of University*
B_1 = historically white (f_1^b = 426)
B_2 = historically black (f_2^b = 470)

C: *Race of Student*
C_1 = black (f_1^c = 492)
C_2 = white (f_2^c = 404)

D: *Completion Status, Spring 1979*
D_1 = graduated (f_1^d = 308)
D_2 = did not graduate (f_2^d = 588)

The elementary cell frequencies reported by McLean are reproduced in Table 7.7.

Prior to considering a logit-model analysis of these data, it is of interest to note the results of analyses of racial group by completion status when these analyses are performed separately within institutions. If the tabulations of the 426 students matriculating at the historically white institution are organized into a fourfold table defined by Race (black and white) and Completion Status (graduation and nongraduation), and a Pearsonian chi-square is calculated, significance is observed; specifically, $\chi^2(1) = 5.76, p < .016$. At the white university, fewer black students than expected under the null graduated during the period under study. In contrast, a similar analysis performed on the 470 observations peculiar to the historically black university failed to attain significance, $\chi^2(1) = .64, p < .424$. Thus, an insular analysis of these data would tend to support McLean's initial suspicion that Race and Type of University *interact* with respect to completion status.

A summary of the fit of models shown in Table 7.6 is presented on the left side of Table 7.8, where it is seen that the null-logit model does not fit observed data well: $L_0^2(7) = 36.00, p < .000$.[7] We have, therefore, a "green light" to proceed to specific sources to see which effects are most responsible for the residuum observed about the null.

Starting at the bottom in the left-hand portion of Table 7.8, we find the component for second-order interaction and the three first-order components are not significant at the .05 level. This means that interaction between or among explanatory variables can be ruled out. Somewhat of a surprise was the fact that the interaction between B (University) and C (Race) was not significant, namely, $L_{5-6}^2(1) = 2.89, p < .089$. After all, McLean suspected that retention by race was a function of the type of institution and, furthermore, the Pearsonian chi-squares mentioned a moment ago for the white university ($\chi^2 = 5.76$) and the black university ($\chi^2 = .64$) suggested that the retention rates of blacks and whites were different at the respective institutions. The more comprehensive logit-model analysis, however, has shown that the interaction between B and C is not prominent if the main effects of ability and other first-order interaction effects are taken into account. Incidentally, had McLean chosen not to effect the adjustments just mentioned but instead had entered λ^{bcd} in Model 4 in place of λ^{abd}, the resultant component (a component not adjusted for the remaining two first-order interactions) would still fall short of statistical significance, namely, $L^2(1) = 3.08, p < .079$.

Examining main effects in Table 7.8 reveals that significance can be claimed for ability level ($p < .007$) and universities subsequent to correcting for levels of ability ($p < .011$). However, if components reflecting full partials are examined—components reflecting full partials are given to the right in Table 7.8— university effects become minuscule. In the final analysis, since the .05 level was adopted as the criterion for significance at the outset, McLean only posited the commonsense finding that high-ability students are more likely to graduate than low-ability students.

Table 7.8
Summary of Two Approaches to the Logit-Model Analysis on the McLean Data

Model*	Hierarchical Components Source	L^2	df	p	Full-Partial Components Source	L^2	df	p
(0)	Null-Logit	36.00	7	.000				
(1)	Due to A	18.31	1	.007	Due to A | B & C	9.37	1	.002
(2)	Due to B | A†	6.49	1	.011	Due to B | A & C	.13	1	.723
(3)	Due to C | A & B	2.40	1	.122	Due to C | B & C	2.40	1	.112
(4)	Due to AB	3.06	1	.108	Due to AB | AC & BC	1.26	1	.262
(5)	Due to AC | AB	.32	1	.540	Due to AC | AB & BC	.02	1	.886
(6)	Due to BC | AB & AC	2.89	1	.089	Due to BC | AB & AC	2.89	1	.089
(7)	Due to ABC	2.53	1	.112				

*The hierarchical models specified in this table are those defined in Table 7.6.

†Read: Variation from the null-logit model due to effects of Variable B, subsequent to affecting adjustments for Variable A.

EXPLICATING INTERACTION IN A
LOGIT-MODEL ANALYSIS

Recall from the example that McLean believed that he would be able to document an interaction of given form between universities (Variable B) and student's race (Variable C). To do this, $\lambda^{bc\bar{d}}$ would first have to be statistically prominent. Subsequently, the pattern of first-order interaction between Variables B and C with respect to logit Variable D—an interaction that we shall term a *first-order-logit interaction*—would need to be examined to see if it were consistent in form with that which had been hypothesized. Neither of these events occurred since the component chi-square for the term in question was not statistically significant at the .05 level: $L^2(1) = 2.89$, $p < .089$. The interaction, however, did "approach" significance, and since we are familiar with the McLean study and desirous to learn how to handle a first-order-logit interaction, for the sake of pedagogy let us assume that the interaction of interest turned out to be significant so that it can be followed up.

Examining the Size and Patterns of Effect Parameters

Assuming $\lambda^{bc\bar{d}}$ to be significant, we know only that black and white students have different rates of graduation at the two different universities. Obviously, the nature of the "differences between differences" needs to be studied. Some of the same steps that were taken to explicate the main effects discovered in the reflective teaching example of Chapter 5 will be taken here to follow-up the first-order-logit interaction. Recall that these steps were: (1) identification of the most appropriate logit model to serve as the follow-up model and (2) examination of the size, direction, and pattern of relevant effects ($\lambda^{bc\bar{d}}$'s in the present instance) in the follow-up model and, for good measure, in the saturated model.

In terms of selecting a follow-up model, a strong case can be made for the adoption of a 13-parameter model that fits configurations [ABC], [BCD], and [AD]. For reasons previously discussed, the fitting of [ABC] is mandatory for all logit models pertaining to this example. In addition, [BCD] is needed because it represents the first-order-logit interaction that we are assuming to be significant, and [AD] should be fitted because of the prominent and significant main effects for Variable A seen in the McLean study. In an effort to lend additional support to the selection of the 13-parameter model, an analysis was undertaken of the residuum about the F_{ijkm}'s produced by this model along the lines discussed in Chapter 4. There were no instances where the standardized or Freeman-Tukey deviates either achieved or approached statistical significance (at the .05 level), nor were there apparent patterns in the algebraic signs of the deviates that might indicate the absence of an important term in the model.[8]

Having selected a follow-up model, estimates of effect parameters need to be requested as computer output. The $\lambda^{bc\bar{d}}$'s associated with the follow-up model and those associated with the saturated model are displayed in Table 7.9.

Table 7.9
Estimates of Logit Interaction Effects Between Variables B and C in the McLean Data

Var. B Univer.	Var. C Race	Accepted Model		Saturated Model	
		Grad.	Nongrad	Grad	Nongrad
White	Black	-.114*	.114	-.119†	.119
	White	.114	-.114	.119	-.119
Black	Black	.114	-.114	.119	-.119
	White	-.114	.114	-.119	.119

*The z tests on effects associated with the most acceptable logit model were $z = \pm 1.58$, $p < .12$, two-tail.
†z tests on effects from the saturated model were $z = \pm 1.64$, $p < .10$, two-tail.

Before the $\lambda^{b\bar{c}d}$'s in Table 7.9 are examined, let us be sure that we understand what they mean. $\lambda^{b\bar{c}d}$, an unspecified first-order-logit interaction (or a second-order interaction in a general model) may be defined verbally as a difference between the log of the geometric mean of F_{ijkm}'s in the jkmth combination of $[BCD]$ and the log of the grand geometric mean of F_{ijkm}'s (i.e., $\ln \bar{G} = \lambda$), subsequent to correcting that difference six times: three times for main-marginal effects and three times for relevant two-variable associations or interactions. Defined mathematically,

$$\lambda^{b\bar{c}d}_{jkm} = (\ln \bar{G}^{b\bar{c}d}_{jkm} - \ln \bar{G}) - \lambda^b - \lambda^c - \lambda^d - \lambda^{bc} - \lambda^{b\bar{d}} - \lambda^{c\bar{d}}$$

Because different models generate different F_{ijkm}'s, the numerical values of $\ln \bar{G}^{bcd}$ and $\ln \bar{G}$ can be expected to vary, and hence the numerical values of $\lambda^{b\bar{c}d}$'s will often vary from model to model. However, more important is the realization that for a given model, and from a logit-model perspective, the $\lambda^{b\bar{c}d}$'s in Table 7.9 constitute relatively pure estimates of the interaction between Variable B (University) and Variable C (Race), estimates that are unaffected by the logit main effects of Variables B and C. An examination of $\lambda^{b\bar{c}d}$'s, therefore, will provide us with a clear view of first-order-logit interaction.

The $\lambda^{b\bar{c}d}$'s belonging to the follow-up model and the saturated model, plus the z statistics resulting from tests on these estimates, are seen in Table 7.9 to be very similar. Since there is only one *free* $\lambda^{b\bar{c}d}$ effect, in effect only one independent test is being run for each model. That aside, the results of all testing failed to achieve significance at the .05 level, an outcome to be expected considering that the composite test reported earlier in Table 7.8 did not satisfy the .05 criterion, namely, $L^2(1) = 2.89$, $p < .089$. But since we are still assuming that the interactions are worthy of interpretation, we note that the pattern exhibited by $\lambda^{bc\bar{d}}$'s permits us to say that at the historically white university, a greater proportion of black students tend not to graduate "on time." Put differently, at the historically black school, a higher proportion of white students in attendance tend not to graduate on time. Strictly speaking, these conclusions are only appropriate subsequent to making adjustments for logit main effects—subsequent to making an adjustment for the fact that a higher percentage of students (black and white) in the black university did not graduate on time when compared to all students attending the predominantly white university (71% vs. 59%), and the fact that a higher percentage of black students, as compared to whites, combined over both schools did not graduate on time (72% vs. 58%).

Examining and Plotting Binomial Logits

While not meaning to depreciate the value of our work to this point, remember that in the actual conduct of inquiry we are apt to be more interested in the aggregate impact of effects on groups than in the analysis of specific effects per se. For example, in the McLean study, subsequent to analyzing pure interactions we would likely want to examine the combined influence of interaction and main effects as it affects the two student groups in the two universities. Combined influence may be examined and communicated to others through the use of a plot of log odds, as was earlier illustrated in Figure 6.1 in connection with focused comparisons.

The graphing of log odds, or a variant of log odds called *binomial logits*, is a straightforward procedure when the response variable is a dichotomy. The basic idea is to reduce a three-variable configuration to a two-variable config- uration and to transform the dichotomous response variable to a single variable measured on a log metric. In terms of the McLean study, the idea is to reduce [BCD] to [BC] and, for each of the cells in [BC], to transform Variable D to log-odds or binomial logits. The latter measure, the binomial logit (or half-logit), is symbolized by Ψ and for the current task can be defined by

$$\Psi^{bc\bar{d}}_{1/2} = \frac{\ln \omega_{1/2}}{2} = \frac{\ln (f^{bc\bar{d}}_{jk1}/f^{bc\bar{d}}_{jk2})}{2} \tag{7.5}$$

which will not be as intimidating a definition as it may appear to be at first glance. As we shall see, Equation 7.5 yields unbounded log-metric values that can be plotted like cell means in the ANOVA.

We again use data gathered by McLean, and shown in Table 7.10, to illustrate. The reader should undertake to find in the table the $f^{bc\bar{d}}$'s observed in [BCD]. Note that the column headed $\omega_{1/2}$ contains *conditional odds*, the observed odds of being classified in D_1 (graduated) as opposed to D_2 (did not graduate) for each combination in [BC]. If our point of reference were the odds of being in D_2 as opposed to D_1, the column heading would read $\omega_{1/2}$. Notice how the

Table 7.10

Odds and Binomial Logits from Response Variable *D* as Observed in Configuration (*BC*) of the McLean Data

University	Race	D_1	D_2	$\omega_{1/2}$	$\ln \omega_{1/2}$	$\psi_{1/2}$
White	Black	14	40	.350	-1.049	-.525
	White	160	212	.755	- .281	-.141
Black	Black	126	312	.404	- .907	-.453
	White	8	24	.333	-1.099	-.550

Note: Observed odds, logits, and binomial logits reflect the odds of being classified in D_1 (on-time graduation) as opposed to D_2 (did not graduate).

dichotomous response variable has been converted into a univariate metric variable for reduced configuration [*BC*].

Incidentally, Goodman and many other prominent developers of log-linear analysis have a penchant for viewing qualitative response in terms of odds and odds ratios, for they believe that odds constitute the least ambiguous vehicles for understanding and interpreting log-linear results (see Goodman, 1978). Proponents of the use of odds also make extensive use of log-linear models that yield *expected odds*—as opposed to the models used extensively herein which yield expected cell frequencies. In all candor, there is much to recommend odds as a vehicle for comprehension and interpretation. They have received little attention in this book, however, because a major objective of this work is to expose more fully the many similarities between the ANOVA and log-linear analysis. Therefore, the approach followed in these chapters, while not deliberately intending to eschew the use of odds, in effect does so due to the deliberate emphasis given to perceiving qualitative response in terms of ANOVA-like effects.

We did, however, discuss conditional odds in Chapters 4 and 6, where we learned that they possess a minor, yet vexatious, problem: Their distribution is not symmetric about a midpoint of unity. That is, the distribution of ω's is nonsymmetric about $\omega = 1.00$. We overcome this problem, as before, by working instead with the natural logs of the odds. The logs of the $\omega_{1/2}$'s can be found in Table 7.10.

Finally, in the right-most column of Table 7.10 are located the binomial logits. Frequently, Greek psi is used as a general symbol for these special logits, which are obtained by simply dividing the logs of the odds by 2. They can also be computed from Equation 7.5, a fact that should be verified and an equation that now should have increased meaning. The $\psi_{1/2}$'s are negative in this table because the odds of on-time graduation are less than unity for the four groupings of students. On the other hand, by reversing the perspective and using Equation

Figure 7.1
Plot of Binomial Logits by Race of Student and Type of University

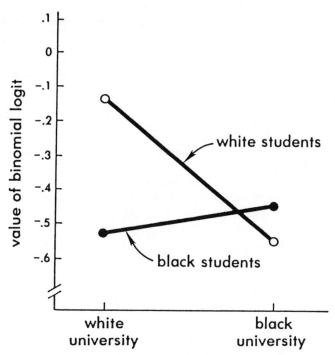

7.5 to calculate $\psi_{2/1}$'s instead of $\psi_{1/2}$'s, we would find no change in the numerical values of the binomial logits but their algebraic signs would be reversed: they would all be positive.

Another interesting characteristic of binomial logits is that they are equivalent to corresponding lambda effects in the absence of confounding. For the McLean situation, if it had turned out that there were no differences in [D] (i.e., $f_1^d = f_2^d$), and no logit main effects for either Variable B or Variable C, the binomial logits would be equal to the λ^{bcd}'s. To the extent to which these effects are operative, however, binomial logits and lambdas will not be equivalent. This is because the former will reflect the confounding of the aforementioned effects and interaction, while the latter will reflect pure interaction. Nevertheless, the confounded outcome often is of greater practical interest, and hence, the plotting of binomial logits has been offered as a meaningful device to use subsequent to detecting first-order-logit interaction (Marks, 1975).

Figure 7.1 contains a graphical display of binomial logits by Race of Students as a function of Type of University. The pattern of interaction is disordinal but it is not symmetric, in the sense that the difference between black and white students is greater at the white university than it is at the black university. At the white university, for example, the odds of graduating on time are higher for white than for black students. Though not as pronounced, at the black university, the opposite is observed. However, aside from a degree of distortion or lack of symmetry in the pattern of interaction, substantive conclusions are similar to those advanced following an examination of pure interaction effects in Table 7.9.

The binomial logits appearing in Figure 7.1 are susceptible to the confounding influences noted earlier. Notice, for example, where the pattern or configuration is located on the graph. Notice particularly where the configuration is centered: It is entirely in the negative realm, centered well below zero, centered well below the point that is indicative of even odds. Differences in the main marginals of Variable D (i.e., $f_1^d = 308$, while $f_2^d = 588$) are responsible for this. If instead of plotting $\Psi_{1/2}^{bcd}$'s, we instead decided to plot the $\Psi_{2/1}^{bcd}$'s, the configuration would reside in the positive realm.

Distortion in the symmetry of the configuration is due to the confounding of logit main effects for Variables B and C. Observe that the interaction configuration appears to be "tilted" in a downward direction when viewed from left to right. In part this tilt reflects the fact that, overall, the odds of graduating on time were observed to be greater at the historically white university. Furthermore, the higher odds of graduating on time for white students (as opposed to black students) is causing the difference between blacks and whites to be greater at the white university than it is at the historically black institution.

In sum, there are a number of factors mixed in with interaction effects that determine the algebraic values of binomial logits. When graphed, therefore, binomial logits reveal net influences and reflect a substantively meaningful picture of results. Incidentally, the pattern of results depicted in Figure 7.1 comes close to the initial suspicions held by McLean. Clearly, in practice, there is much to recommend the plotting of binomial logits.

THE ANALYSIS OF FIVE-DIMENSIONAL TABLES

Offered in this section is an illustration of a five-variable problem that lends itself to an asymmetrical analysis and in which we see a polytomous response variable. The illustration is based in part on the work of Peters (1981), although both the design and the resultant data have been altered somewhat to effect a more complex teaching example.

A Study of Preferred Styles of Inquiry

The sample for this teaching example consisted of 296 students pursuing doctoral degrees in psychology. Participating students were administered the Myers-Briggs Type Indicator (MBTI) (Myers, 1962), a well-established clinical and research instrument that can be used to classify examinees on four personality dimensions, the majority of which were advanced by the Swiss psychiatrist Carl Jung. The four dichotomous classifications constitute four explanatory variables in the emended Peters' study (1981). Specifically, following administration of the MBTI, subjects were cross-classified on the basis of the following:

A: *Extroversion (E) or Introversion (I)*
A_1 = classified as an E $(f_1^a = 134)$
A_2 = classified as an I $(f_2^a = 162)$

B: *Intuition (N) or Sensing (S)*
B_1 = classified as an N $(f_1^b = 123)$
B_2 = classified as an S $(f_2^b = 173)$

C: *Thinking (T) or Feeling (F)*
C_1 = classified as a T $(f_1^c = 150)$
C_2 = classified as an F $(f_2^c = 146)$

D: *Judging (J) or Perceiving (P)*
D_1 = classified as a J $(f_1^d = 139)$
D_2 = classified as a P $(f_2^d = 157)$

Peters, attempting to subject to test a hypothesis advanced by Mitroff and Kilmann (1978), sought to determine whether subjects' personality type, as measured on the MBTI, influenced their preference for certain styles of knowledge production. To assess subject preference, four published articles that address the topic of faculty development were identified. Each article approached the topic using a distinct "style of inquiry." Subjects were asked to select one of the four articles, namely the article that in their view possessed the "greatest potential for contributing to educational understanding." Choice of article, therefore, was the response variable. A brief description of this polytomous variable follows:

E: *Choice of preferred style of inquiry*
E_1 = choice of the *ST* article, and article that represented the *ST* mode of inquiry as described in the work of Mitroff and Kilmann. This article approached the topic of faculty development in an inductive, molecular, and experimental manner and was redolent with tabular material and quantitative analyses.
E_2 = choice of the *NF* article, an article that assumed an "action-oriented" approach to the common topic through the implementation, but not development, of a theoretical model.
E_3 = choice of the *NT* article, which approached the topic from a theoretical perspective. It represented an effort to advance a conceptual framework for the understanding of faculty growth.
E_4 = choice of the *SF* article, an article that approached the topic in a highly personal, concrete, affective manner with little recourse to theory or research.

Table 7.11

A Hierarchical Arrangement of Logit Models for Four Explanatory Variables

Model No.	Source of Variance About the Null Model		Marginal Configuration Fitted
(0)	Null Logit		ABCD, E
(1)	A		ABCD, AE
(2)	B	A	ABCD, AE, BE
(3)	C	A & B	ABCD, AE, BE, CE
(4)	D	A, B & C	ABCD, AE, BE, CE, DE
(5)	AB	ME*	ABCD, ABE, CE, DE
(6)	AC	ME & AB	ABCD, ABE, ACE, DE
(7)	AD	ME, AB, & AC	ABCD, ABE, ACE, ADE
(8)	BC	ME, AB, AC, & AD	ABCD, ABE, ACE, ADE, BCE
(9)	BD	ME, AB, AC, AD, & BC	ABCD, ABE, ACE, ADE, BCE, BDE
(10)	CD	ME, AB, AC, AD, BC, & BD	ABCD, ABE, ACE, ADE, BCE, BDE, CDE
(11)	ABC	ME, & FOE†	ABCD, ABCE, ADE, BDE, CDE
(12)	ABD	ME, FOE, & ABC	ABCD, ABCE, ABDE, CDE
(13)	ACD	ME, FOE, ABC & ABD	ABCD, ABCE, ABDE, ACDE
(14)	BDC	ME, FOE, ABC, ABD, & ACD	ABCD, ABCE, ABDE, ACDE, BCDE
(15)	ABCD		ABCDE

Note: Variable E is assumed to be the response variable.
*The letters ME stand for all main effects as specified in Models 1 through 4.
†The letters FOE stand for all first-order interaction effects as specified in Models 5 through 10.

It is, of course, well known that if the response variable for the foregoing study was measured on either an interval or a ratio scale, the appropriate analysis would be a four-way ANOVA. But Variable E is neither interval nor ratio; it is decidedly qualitative. Therefore, a four-variable generalized logit-model analysis—an analysis that parallels a four-way ANOVA—will be performed.

As a point of departure, realize that all asymmetrical hierarchical models that apply to this study must at least fit $[ABCD]$ and $[E]$. These requisite fittings will make adjustments for potential inequalities in f^{abcd}'s and f^e's, inequalities that are not only irrelevant to logit-variable response but that if left uncontrolled, would distort logit-variable response. Hence, notice that all logit models in the hierarchical arrangement presented in Table 7.11 contain these two requisite fittings.

One last attempt at an intuitive explanation of logit models seems warranted. Consider first Model 0, the null-logit model, which contains the two requisite fittings mentioned above and thus, in its extended form, contains 17 terms, none of which stands for an interaction involving Variable E. The 64 expected elementary cell frequencies generated by Model 0 represent a state of affairs that assumes that frequencies in all configurations other than $[ABCD]$ and $[E]$ are equiprobable. Therefore, should Model 0 be deemed to fit the observed data well, differences between respective estimated and observed elementary cell frequencies would be assumed to be due to chance, an assumption that precludes the mention of significant effects between or among explanatory variables.

Suppose, however, that, in addition to [ABCD], it was found that [CE] was needed to achieve reasonable congruence between expected and actual frequencies. (Incidentally, this particular model is not shown in the table of logit models.) What can this be taken to mean? Given the current problem, it would mean that if we focused our attention on any one of the 15 variable combinations in [ABCD], and if within this selected combination we examined patterns of proportional response over levels of Variable E, a statistically meaningful difference in response patterns would be seen between subjects classified as T's and those classified as F's on Variable C. Moreover, since we are assuming that no additional parameters are required in the model, the difference between T's and F's relative to their patterns of response to the logit variable is similar, at least within chance expectation, within all the remaining 14 combinations in [ABCD]. In short, adoption of this model would indicate significant main effects for Variable C.

Let us extend this line of thinking by momentarily assuming that, in addition to [ABCD], [BCE] was needed to achieve reasonable fit. Fitting [BCE], of course, also implies the fitting of [BE] and [CE] irrespective of whether these configurations contain beyond-chance differences. In any event, the need to incorporate [BCE] in the model is an acknowledgment that there are discernable differences among the f^{bce}'s. Therefore, if a particular variable combination in [ABCD] is selected again for study, a difference between T's and F's with respect to their pattern of proportional response to the logit variable will be observed. However, because of the indicated interaction between Variables B and C, unlike before we will not expect the difference between patterns to be similar in the 14 remaining combinations of [ABCD]. To be more specific, the *simple* main effects between T's and F's viewed at the first level of Variable B will be different from the simple main effects viewed at the second level of Variable B. Looking ahead, it is precisely this type of interaction that will be encountered in our teaching example.

Returning to the example, data that were generated by this writer and analyzed by the 4F program in the BMDP package are summarized in Table 7.12. We look first at Table 7.12 to see how well the null-logit model fits the observed data. The residual chi-square for this model was substantial: $L^2(45) = 113.75$, $p < .00$. Clearly, the poorness-of-fit offered by this model invites an examination of component chi-squares for the purpose of identifying specific effects most responsible for the significant residual discrepancy between expected frequencies of the null and observed frequencies.

Further examination of Table 7.12 reveals that only two component chi-squares are statistically significant at the .05 level: the component associated with main effects for Variable C (subsequent to adjusting for Variables A and B) and the component for the interaction between Variables B and C (after adjustments for all main effects and three first-order interactions).

Table 7.12
Summary of Logit-Model Analysis of MBTI Data

Model No.	Residual			Component		
	df	L^2	p	df	L^2	p
(0)	45	113.75	.00			
(1)	42	111.45	.00	3	2.30	.51
(2)	39	110.60	.00	3	.85	.84
(3)	36	27.58	.84	3	82.02	.00
(4)	33	27.47	.74	3	.11	.99
(5)	30	25.23	.71	3	2.24	.52
(6)	27	21.22	.78	3	4.01	.27
(7)	24	20.93	.64	3	.29	.96
(8)	21	11.52	.95	3	9.41	.02
(9)	18	5.75	.99	3	5.77	.12
(10)	15	5.47	.99	3	.28	.96
(11)	12	3.75	.99	3	1.72	.64
(12)	9	2.88	.97	3	.87	.83
(13)	6	2.25	.90	3	.63	.89
(14)	3	1.53	.68	3	.72	.87
(15)	0	0.00	–	3	1.53	.68

Note: Models correspond by number to those appearing in Table 7.11.

Selecting the Follow-Up Model

Before we follow up the two sets of effects that are obviously significant, at this tentative stage we should not arbitrarily dismiss the interaction between Variables B and D for it is not altogether inconsiderable ($p < .12$). Thus, prior to the final selection of a follow-up model, the 22-parameter model defined by the fitting of [ABCD], [BCE], and [BDE] was compared to a 20-parameter model defined by fitting [ABCD] and [BCD]. The residual chi-square for the 22-parameter model was $L^2(30) = 12.56$, $p < .99$; for the more restricted 20-parameter model, it was $L^2(36) = 18.83$, $p < .99$. Contrasting respective residual chi-squares gave a component of 6.27 which, when taken to a table of chi-squares distributed on six degrees of freedom, was not significant ($p > .394$). An examination of standardized residuals and Freeman-Tukey deviates also failed

Table 7.13
Estimates of Main Effects for the Dimensions of Thinking (*T*'s) Versus Feelings (*F*'s)

Article Preference	[*f*]	Thinking			Feeling			z
		λ	f^{ce}	p	λ	f^{ce}	p	
ST	61	.465	48	.32	−.465	13	.09	3.87
NF	71	−.675	14	.09	.675	57	.39	5.80
NT	70	.610	58	.39	−.610	12	.08	5.09
SF	94	−.400	30	.20	.400	64	.44	3.88
Totals	296	0.000	150	1.00	0.000	146	1.00	

to provide evidence that would suggest that the more restricted model was not an acceptable fit. The 20-parameter model, therefore, was chosen over the 22-model for further study of the logit main effects of Variable *C* (*T*'s versus *F*'s) and the first-order-logit interaction between Variables *B* and *C*.

Following Up Main Effects

Having detected significant main effects for Variable *C*, and thus having found that subjects who were classified as either *T*'s or *F*'s differed in their preference for at least one of the four articles, the next step is to specify the exact nature of differences. Two follow-up strategies that are not mutually exclusive present themselves. The first is the traditional strategy of examining and interpreting relevant lambda parameters, the $\lambda^{\bar{c}e}$'s in this instance. The second is to compute one or more substantively meaningful focused comparisons based on the contents of Chapter 6.

Though I favor the focused comparison approach, much can be learned about the specific nature of this difference, or differences, by examining relevant $\lambda^{\bar{c}e}$'s. For example, the resultant lambdas can serve as a basis for the formulation of exploratory focused comparisons. Hence, in Table 7.13, we can find, among other statistics, the $\lambda^{\bar{c}e}$'s associated with the 20-parameter follow-up model. (Corresponding lambdas associated with the saturated model were found to be sufficiently similar to those given in the table, and thus their presentation was deemed unnecessary.) The algebraic signs of the lambda effects in question suggest that the odds of preferring the *ST* article and the *NT* article are greater for *T*'s than they are for subjects classified as *F*'s. In contrast, *F*'s preferred the *NF* and *SF* articles.

Additional support for the tentative findings based on an examination of lambda parameters can be found in the table. Specifically, both the f^{ce}'s and patterns of proportional response to articles computed *within* groups of T's and F's are compatible with the stated observation. Technically speaking, however, we know that the λ^{ce}'s and the profiles of within-group proportional response do not convey exactly the same message. The former are *effects* (literally, differences between geometric means on a log scale) that have been adjusted for a very slight main-marginal inequality in $[C]$ and again for differences in $[E]$ which are shown in the second column of the table. The latter, the profiles of proportional response, are only adjusted for main-marginal differences in $[C]$—an adjustment that is a consequence of computing proportions such that they sum to unity within groups. The within-group proportions are influenced by main-marginal differences in $[E]$, however. Nevertheless, both views of these logit main effects are meaningful. The lambda effects depict a pure, unconfounded picture of simple main effects on a log scale for T's and F's with respect to their article preference, while within-group proportions reflect simultaneously both simple main effects and overall article preference.

So far, our discussion of differences between T's and F's has been confined to description. These main effects are amenable to statistical test, namely, to z tests. These tests are provided by most log-linear computer programs and, for our study, are shown in Table 7.13. To claim two-tailed statistical significance at, say, the .05 level, we know that conventional practice holds that the computed z statistic must exceed the 97.5-centile value (critical value) of 1.96. Notice that each test reported in Table 7.13 satisfies this criterion.

The use of focused comparisons constitutes a second follow-up strategy. Briefly, the 64 expected cell frequencies produced by the 20-parameter follow-up model would be organized into a 2×4 table for the CE configuration.[9] Then, a sample design and a response design would be specified to reflect the focused comparisons that are desired. Since the sample variable, Variable C, is dichotomous, sample-design contrasts are simply $+1.0$ (for C_1) and -1.0 (for C_2). A reasonable, but not inclusive, set of contrasts imposed on the response variable might be

Focused	Classes of Response			
Comparison	Variable E $(r = 4)$			
FC_{ko}	E_1	E_2	E_3	E_4
FC_{11}	+.5	-.5	+.5	-.5
FC_{12}	+1.0	0.0	0.0	-1.0
FC_{13}	0.0	+1.0	-1.0	0.0

The three suggested focused comparisons could be performed on the collapsed [CD] configuration, or to view comparisons that are independent of the confounding effects of Variables A and B (and the interaction between A and B), simple comparisons could be performed and summed at respective levels of these variables. The results would go a long way toward exploring the differences between F's and T's relative to their article preferences.

Follow-Up Interactions

In addition to the logit main effects for Variable C, the summary presented in Table 7.12 also revealed a significant chi-square component for Model 8. This revelation prompted the conclusion that $\lambda^{b\bar{c}\bar{e}}$ made a significant contribution ($p < .02$) to the explanation of the residuum about the fitted frequencies produced by the null logit model. It can be said, therefore, that in addition to main effects for Variable C, there remained differences between T's and F's, but these remaining differences were not uniform over all levels of the response variable. In other words, differences in article preference between T's and F's varied as a function of how they are classified on Variable B, the Intuition (N) versus Sensing (S) variable.

Explaining the nature of a first-order logit-model interaction when the logit variable is a dichotomy was a challenge in our earlier discussion of the McLean study. Since the logit variable here consists of four levels, the challenge is ever greater. As we now know, the first step in the interpretive process is to marshal and summarize relevant tabular information. The first-order-logit effects ($\lambda^{b\bar{c}\bar{e}}$'s) from the follow-up model selected earlier, and profiles of proportional response to the logit variable made by subjects within combinations in [BC], are basic; thus, they are given in Table 7.14.

Because the response variable is polytomous, we next identify the level or levels of Variable E that are associated with a significant interactive response. The z tests reported in the right-most column of Table 7.14 can assist here. It can be seen that the z's are minuscule for both the NF and the NT articles. Obviously, preference for the inquiry reflected in these two articles is not interactive. The observation is reinforced by the patterns of proportional response where the table shows that approximately 40 percent of both NT's and ST's favor the NT article and about 10 percent in each of these groupings favor the NF article. Relative to preference to these same two articles, a similar absence of interaction is evident in the NF and SF groups. Thus, it follows that our earlier conclusions concerning the direction of main effects for Variable C need not be qualified; it can still be said that proportionately more T's prefer the NT article while more F's favor the NF article. Notice, however, that z tests on effects for the ST article ($z = \pm 2.05$) and the SF article ($z = \pm 2.87$) either approach or attain statistical significance at the .05 level. It is with respect to the choice of the SF article, and possibly the ST article, that Variables B and C interact.

To be studied first are the strongest-appearing first-order-logit interaction ef-

Table 7.14
First-Order-Logit Interaction Effects for Variables B and C

	MBTI Personality Types									
	NT		ST		NF		SF			
Article Preference	λ_{11m}^{bce}	p	λ_{12m}^{bce}	p	λ_{21m}^{bce}	p	λ_{22m}^{bce}	p	z test
ST	-.246	.23	.246	.40	.246	.13	-.246	.07	2.05
NF	-.022	.09	.022	.10	.022	.43	-.022	.37	.19
NT	-.027	.39	.027	.38	.027	.09	-.027	.08	.23
SF	.295	.29	-.295	.12	-.295	.35	.295	.49	2.87
Total	0.0	1.00	0.0	1.00	0.0	1.00	0.0	1.00	

fects, those associated with the *SF* article. When the 30 *T*'s who chose this article are subdivided into groupings of *NT*'s ($f_{114}^{bce} = 20$) and *ST*'s ($f_{214}^{bce} = 10$), the algebraic signs of corresponding lambdas reveal greater odds in favor of *NT*s' preference for the article in question—subsequent, of course, to adjustment for all prior effects in the selected follow-up model. Moreover, of the 64 *F*'s who also happened to select the *SF* article, more *SF*'s ($f_{224}^{bce} = 45$) than *NF*'s ($f_{124}^{bce} = 19$) chose this article—subsequent to correction for prior model effects. In sum, the overall or main-effects preference of *F*'s for the inquiry embodied in "feeling" articles requires qualification for, as we have just observed, proportionately fewer *NF*'s preferred the *SF* article than did *SF*'s.

Although not as pronounced, interaction also appears to characterize preference for the *ST* article. The algebraic signs of the lambda effects suggest that when the 48 *T*'s who chose this article are additionally classified as *NT*'s ($f_{111}^{bce} = 16$) or *ST*'s ($f_{211}^{bce} = 32$), a greater proportion of the latter seem to have preferred the *ST* article. In point of fact, 40 percent of *ST*'s chose this article against 23 percent in the *NT* group. Looking at *F*'s, subjects of this persuasion tended to eschew the *ST* article—only 13 of the 146 subjects classified as an *F* selected it. Even so, differences between *NF*'s and *SF*'s appear to be present. Specifically, more *NF*'s (13 percent) chose the article than did subjects in the *SF* (7 percent) classification.

Interactions can be complex. The experience of having to struggle through the foregoing paragraphs should have convinced most readers that even interactions of the first order can often be difficult to describe and communicate verbally. Fortunately, description can be clarified and communication enhanced through the use of graphical representations in the delivery of presentations and the preparation of research reports. Recall the graphical representation of binomial logits in Figure 7.1 and how well that graph facilitated our understanding of the first-order-logit interaction that almost achieved significance in the McLean study. The plotting of binomial logits constituted a relatively straightforward procedure in that study because McLean's response variable was a dichotomy. When response is polytomous, as is the case presently, to construct a graph or graphs similar to Figure 7.1, the researcher must find a meaningful way to reduce a polytomy to a dichotomy. The researcher must define one or more sets of conditional odds, translate these odds into binomial logits, and plot the logits.

Essentially, the task may be accomplished by imposing the desired comparison contrasts on the polytomous response variable, as we have repeatedly done in connection with the response designs of focused comparisons. In the Peters' study, for example, one approach would be to focus primary interest on the selection of a particular level of the response variable, say the selection of the *SF* article, and then proceed to calculate the odds of choosing that article over not choosing that article—that is, the odds of selecting *SF* as opposed to any one of the remaining three articles. Alternately, the odds of favoring one article as opposed to another specific article may be of interest.

At any rate, there are many ways to (1) redefine four levels of response so that response is couched in dichotomous terms, (2) compute conditional odds within the combinations of [BC] as was done previously (see Table 7.10), (3) transform the multiplicative odds to linear binomial logits, as was also done previously (Table 7.10), and (4) plot the resultant binomial logits in a manner parallel to that shown in Figure 7.1. Aside from their salutary communicative value, recall that an advantage of such graphs is that they depict net influences. In the present case, for example, a plot of binomial logits would reflect the aggregate influence of first-order-logit interactions (as defined in Table 7.14), the influence of main-marginal differences in [E], and the influence of logit main effects of Variable B and C. Finally, for communication to lay audiences, do not overlook the fact that interactive findings can also be depicted with graphs of within-group proportional response to selected levels of the response variable. The graphs in question are direct, uncomplicated, and well suited for polytomous response variables because the reduction of a polytomy to a dichotomy is not required.

NOTES

1. The lowercase letter m is preferred over the lowercase letter l as the subscript for Variable D because the appearance of l too closely resembles the numeral 1, therefore providing too many opportunities for confusion.

2. In addition to the aforementioned tabular abridgements, since an isomorphic relationship has been established between superscripts and subscripts for model terms, to promote economy of expression, subscripts will be omitted whenever it is obvious from the context which term is being addressed.

3. The screening tables produced by BMDP/4F in connection with the McLean study were obtained by specifying the ASSOCIATION option in the Fit paragraph as follows: /FIT ASSOCIATION IS 4. Consult the most recent edition of the *BMDP Statistical Software Manual* for details on the use of this most informative optional feature.

4. Table 7.2 as presented was constructed by combining the residual and component chi-square screening tables produced by BMDP/4F. As noted, however, comparable output may be obtained from other programs by requesting the fit of kth-order models and marshaling the resultant information in a table similar to that displayed as Table 7.2.

5. Logically, it can be inferred that the association between A and B would be orthogonal to that between C and D. This inference is generally true, but not in the full first-order model in which multicollinearity abounds. Often, in fact, in the nonorthogonal environment of the full first-order model, the AB association can exert an influence on the CD association similar to that associated with suppressor variables in multiple regression.

6. Of course, had it been found that λ^{bd} and λ^{cd} preceded λ^{bc}, a half-partial in which control was effected over Variable D would be indicated. Should the necessary conditions for the two types of half-partials not be present in a model, then the component for a term in the third, fourth, or fifth place would reflect either a marginal association or an association in which incomplete partialing has taken place; the latter type of association in nonsystematic and most difficult to interpret substantively.

7. The results of Table 7.8 are not identical to those reported by McLean (1980, 71–

72). McLean used BMDP/3F, but in doing so, specified "delta = .5," which is used when tables contain sampling zeros, despite the fact that sampling zeros were not present in his data. The results in Table 7.8 are those analyzed by me without the delta option.

8. Bishop, Fienberg and Holland (1975, 137–39) illustrate that patterns in the algebraic signs of deviates can provide insights into why a particular model is not fitting data well and what new term might be added to improve the fit.

9. As an alternative, expected frequencies from a model defined by fitting [ABCD] and [CE] could be used as base frequencies. Focused comparisons that would not be influenced by any of the effects associated with terms not present in this model would result.

8

Additional Applications
and Concerns

The contents of this penultimate chapter are varied. Since the adjectives *versatile*, *general*, and *comprehensive* have been used frequently in this book to describe log-linear methodology, brief discussions of additional applications of this method in support of these adjectives appear to be in order. In the first discussion, one of our working examples will be emended to show that a logit-model analysis need not be limited to one variable of response. Specifically, it will be shown that two or more response variables, called, respectively, two-dimensional logits or multidimensional logits, can be examined simultaneously in a manner loosely analogous to a MANOVA. In a second section we will again encounter problems inherent with repeated measurements—or, more accurately, *repeated observations*—and we will be introduced to a strategy that on occasion can successfully accommodate a repeated-observation variable. The major intent of this section, however, will be to introduce several new models designed to assess symmetrical change over two observational periods. The third new area of application deals with the use of log-linear analogues to causal models that are seen in metric path analysis. It is hoped that these discussions, although brief, are sufficiently ample to convey essential ideas and a direction for further study.

As with all relatively new research tools, there are a number of real problems, soft spots, and issues that have yet to be resolved fully. Two of these are of particular concern and were encountered in this manuscript, although they were allowed to slip by almost unnoticed. It will be acknowledged here that empty cells can cause problems under certain circumstances and, since statistical significance is largely a function of sample size, using only statistical criteria to judge the adequacy of model fit also can be problematic.

Finally, we conclude with a discussion that typically one would expect to find in the introductory chapter of a book such as this. The discussion centers about the need for log-linear analysis, particularly the need for analyses that use logit models. The discussion is offered primarily because there are still some who would argue that existing techniques such as multiple regression and discriminant analysis can adequately perform the types of analysis that have been described in this book. The discussion has been postponed to the very last so that the arguments advanced in support of the study and use of log-linear methods can be more fully appreciated by the reader.

Thus, the contents of this chapter should give the reader a better idea as to what to pursue next, what problems to avoid in practice, and whether the study of log-linear analysis has been a worthwhile investment.

MULTIDIMENSIONAL LOGITS

Let us modify the example that we have been calling the Peters (1981) study so that it can accommodate two response variables. To keep things simple, assume that there are only two explanatory variables. The variables, formerly Variables B and C, will be relabeled Variables A and B. Specifically, the explanatory variables are:

A: *Intuition (N) vs. Sensing (S)*
A_1 = subjects classified as N's on the MBTI
A_2 = subjects classified as S's on the MBTI

B: *Thinking (T) vs. Feeling (F)*
B_1 = subjects classified as T's on the MBTI
B_2 = subjects classified as F's on the MBTI

As before, assume that participants were requested to select one of the four articles reflecting a preferred style of inquiry. (The articles were described in Chapter 7.) However, unlike before, subject preference for a particular article will not be handled as a four-level composite variable. Instead, a particular preference will be jointly classified and entered into a contingency table defined by the crossing of dichotomous Variables C and D. That is:

C: *Preference for an article with an N component vs. an S component*
C_1 = choice of either the *NT* or *NF* article
C_2 = choice of either the *ST* or *SF* article

D: *Preference for an article with a T component vs. an F component*
D_1 = choice of either the *NT* or *ST* article
D_2 = choice of either the *NF* or *SF* article

The result, of course, is a 2×2 table, and a response is a tabulation entered into one (and only one) of the cells of the fourfold *response table*. Notice that each cell of the response table corresponds to one of the four types of articles.

The intent of the hypothetical study would be to determine whether (1) the 2 × 2 response table is sufficiently different between subjects who have been labeled N's as opposed to S's (i.e., main effects due to Variable A); (2) the response table is dissimilar for T's and F's (i.e., main effects for Variable B); and (3) differences in resultant tabular response between, say, N's and S's (or T's or F's) are a function of whether subjects are T's or F's (or N's or S's). We recognized the latter as an assessment of first-order interaction between the explanatory Variables A and B. By analogy, the situation is like the layout for a two-way factorial ANOVA in which Variables A and B are independent variables, but the dependent "variable" is a 2 × 2 response table. The proposed analysis may be of inherent interest, or it might be performed to see if it is prudent to examine each response variable separately—just as a MANOVA is sometimes performed to justify the conduct of a series of ANOVAs. From what we know of the Peters study, a strong case could be made for the former intent.

Adhering to our decided preference for general logit models (in contrast to models that yield expected odds) and our slight preference for casting models in the multiplicative, the null-logit model—Model 0—for the situation under discussion is

$$F_{ijkm} = \tau\, \tau^a\, \tau^b\, \tau^c\, \tau^{ab}\, \tau^{ac}\, \tau^{ad}\, \tau^{bc}\, \tau^{bd}\, \tau^{\overline{cd}}\, \tau^{abc}\, \tau^{abd} \tag{8.1}$$

Model 0 is specified by fitting observed marginals [ABC], [ABD], and [CD].

The need to include τ^{ab} in the above model, and hence both τ^a and τ^b, has been discussed at length in connection with earlier logit models. However, there are additional factors (terms) that are also mandatory in this model. With the notable exception of $\tau^{\overline{cd}}$, notice that all interactions that do *not* portray logit Variables C and D *acting jointly* are also built into the model. These six interactive parameters serve to estimate effects that are not relevant to the desired response, which is a fourfold table defined by the crossing of C and D. The six parameter estimates, therefore, must be incorporated into this and other logit models to effect control over these extraneous effects. The estimated parameter $\tau^{\overline{cd}}$ also belongs in this and other models, but for a different reason. If the interaction symbolized by $\tau^{\overline{cd}}$ should turn out to be prominent, this would mean that subsequent to the fitting of a model, differences are manifest among the four geometric means in the cells of the [CD] configuration, even after corrections are made for main effects due to C and D. But are we really concerned with differences among cell *frequencies* within the response tables? No. Strictly speaking, our concern is limited to the *expected proportions* within the four cells of the response table and whether such tables are similar over levels of Variables A, B, and so on. Thus, just as we earlier put $\tau^{\overline{cd}}$ into the unidimensional null-logit model for this study (see Table 7.11), extending our logic will have us put $\tau^{\overline{cd}}$ in the null-logit model for the current version of the study.[1]

Table 8.1

Two-Dimensional Logit Models Where Variables *A* and *B* Are Explanatory

No.	Logit Model	Marginals Fitted
(0)	Null Logit	ABC, ABD, $\overline{CD}$
(1)	Due to Variable A	ABC, ABD, A$\overline{CD}$
(2)	Due to Variable B, Given Variable A	ABC, ABD, A$\overline{CD}$, B$\overline{CD}$
(3)	Due to Interaction	AB$\overline{CD}$

Note: Crossed Variables *C* and *D* define the logit response table.

Presented in Table 8.1 are hierarchical models for a two-dimensional logit analysis where crossed Variables *C* and *D* define response. Model 0 is given by Equation 8.1 and, as we have noted, it does not contain a second-order or third-order interaction that simultaneously involves *C* and *D*. Model 1 contains the 13 parameters seen in Model 0, but, in addition, it has a fourteenth parameter, the second-order interaction $\tau^{a\overline{cd}}$. Model 2 possesses the 14 parameters of Model 1 plus $\tau^{a\overline{cd}}$. Finally, the addition of third-order $\tau^{ab\overline{cd}}$ to the aforementioned factors gives the saturated model. When fitted by a computer program such as BMDP/4F, residual L^2's are produced for each model. With a pocket calculator, component L^2's are obtained and then subjected to test, as we have done on numerous occasions in this book.

Typically, the residual L^2 for Model 0 is examined first because it is a composite indicator of the residuum about the fit of the null. If the composite residual is significant, further testing is warranted. Relative to further tests, suppose the component chi-square for Model 1 was shown to be large and significant. This would indicate that $\tau^{a\overline{cd}}$ is making a significant contribution to the reduction, and hence the explanation, of the residuum about the null-logit model. Such a reduction points to significant main effects due to Variable *A*. In other words, the standardized-to-proportional-unity table of response for subjects classified as *N*'s (i.e., $\sum_k \sum_m p_{1km}^{a\overline{cd}} = 1.00$) is in some significant way different from the corresponding response table produced by *S*'s.

Tabular differences, of course, would need to be explored. A first step in this exploration would be a study, at each level of *A*, of the algebraic signs and distribution pattern of the $\tau^{a\overline{cd}}$ effects belonging to the model selected for follow-up, and a study of subsequent *z* tests performed on these effects. Following explication of the conservative multidimensional result, if it should be of interest, a series of unidimensional logit models analyses can be conducted along the lines by which multiple ANOVAs are sometimes used to follow-up a MANOVA.

Should the component L^2 belonging to Model 2 be judged to be significant, main effects due to Variable B are indicated. Because $\tau^{\overline{bcd}}$ comes after $\tau^{\overline{acd}}$ in the model, main effects for B are evident over and above those that might be due to Variable A.

Finally, if significance is observed for $\tau^{\overline{abcd}}$ in the saturated model, then, in addition to main effects which might have been detected, an interactive pattern in response tables is present. This interaction can be approached in several ways. For example, by plotting the $\tau^{\overline{abcd}}$'s, it might be of interest to first describe differences in the 2×2 response tables between T's and F's who are S's. The stronger the interaction, the greater the discrepancy to expect between these two descriptions. With a little ingenuity, the graphical procedures used to display earlier interactions can be extended to describe and communicate the interaction in question.

Within reason, general log-linear models can be constructed to accommodate any number of explanatory and response variables. As an example, imagine a four-dimensional contingency table in which only one variable, say Variable A, is considered explanatory. Rather than performing a series of unidimensional logit-model analyses, a sagacious initial analysis would be one in which Variables B, C, and D are crossed to form a three-dimensional response table. The analysis would in some ways resemble a one-way ANOVA and would require the fitting of only two models. The first, the null-logit model, would contain 16 general parameters and would fit the observed configurations $[ABC]$, $[ABD]$, $[ACD]$ and $[BCD]$. The saturated model would constitute the second model. Acceptance of the latter, which acknowledges the need to fit $\tau^{\overline{abcd}}$, can be taken to mean that there is a difference in the three-dimensional response table between at least two levels of Variable A. Examination of the $\tau^{\overline{abcd}}$'s at different levels of A will point to the location of the difference or differences. Following the multidimensional analysis, separate unidimensional logit-model analyses can be undertaken with greater insight and respect for alpha.

REPEATED OBSERVATIONS AND
RESPONSE INDEPENDENCE

Repeated measurement variables, which are common to ANOVA designs, are encountered occasionally when working with qualitative variables. Moreover, as a rule, when multiple observations are made on the same subjects, the assumption of response independence, which is basic to both the F and multinomial distributions, is contradicted. For the ANOVA, contradiction of the independence assumption leads to a positively biased F test, whereas violation of this assumption for the chi-square approximation to the multinomial leads to the retention of null hypotheses, at a given level of significance, more often than it should (Maxwell, 1961, 26). Over the years a number of strategies have been developed for the ANOVA that, for the most part, have overcome the difficulties associated with repeated measures. Unfortunately, similar comprehensive strategies have yet to be developed for the log-linear. There are, however, several less direct approaches that on occasion can be used to minimize difficulties associated with repeated observations.

Approaches to Problems of Repeated Observations

It may be recalled (Chapter 5) that Holton and Nott (1980), in their study on reflective teaching, encountered a common repeated observations situation. They wanted to measure change in the complexity of written response both prior and subsequent to an instructional intervention. Before experiencing reflective teaching or control group activities, the writings of subjects were classified into one of four response modes: analytical, evidential, declarative, or indeterminate. Following three weeks of intervention, written responses were obtained again from the same subjects and again subjected to the above classifications.

Experience with the ANOVA might tempt an investigator to structure a two-level pre-/posttest variable and to cross that variable with the four-level mode of response variable. The result would be a 4×2 table. For a moment, let mode of response be Variable A and pre-/posttest be Variable B. Now, if there were little or no change in the way in which written specimens were classified from pretest (B_1) to posttest (B_2), one consequent would be that $f_{i1} = f_{i2}$ for all levels of A, and the model that would fit these data well would be $F_{ij} = \tau \, \tau_i^a$. If change did occur, and if the result of change was that $f_{i1} \neq f_{i2}$ for two or more levels of A, then the model would become $F_{ij} = \tau \, \tau_i^a \, \tau_{ij}^{ab}$. Unfortunately, this appealing analysis is flawed because by counting a subject twice in the table, the independence assumption (discussed in Chapter 4) is most likely being violated.

Recall that Holton and Nott avoided the problem by crossing the four-level pretest variable (Variable A) with its replicate, the posttest variable (Variable C). The outcome was a 4×4 table in which subjects were counted only once. Had there been three or four testing periods, this approach would likely be intractable. Also, the degree of correlation between the crossed variables determines the feasibility of this approach. For example, had there been little change between testings, and hence a high correlation, the approach used by Holton and Nott would not be advisable because most frequencies would be found in cells on or near the principal diagonal, leaving off-diagonal cells either empty or with few frequencies. As we will learn later in this chapter, a few zero cell frequencies do not constitute a major problem if they are related to sampling procedures (i.e., sampling zeros). Holton and Nott had an empty cell in their $4 \times 2 \times 4$ table (see Table 5.6), yet the overall distribution of frequencies did not, in their view, militate against the approach in question. In fact, if it is permissible, the approach has much to recommend it. It is direct, it lends itself to straightforward applications of log-linear models, and, as we saw in their study, it permitted Holton and Nott to test for treatment effects on posttest response subsequent to adjusting for initial pretest effects.

Table 8.2
Hypothetical Data Sets for the Holton-Nott Study

Pre-test	Posttest a	e	d	i	Posttest a	e	d	i	Posttest a	e	d	i
a	15				4	5	2	4				15
e		17			5	5	1	6		17		
d			6		2	1	2	1			6	
i				17	4	6	1	6	17			

| No Change | Uniform Change | Extreme Change |

Other ways to measure change have been proposed for situations in which a group is tested or observed on two separate occasions. We are referring here to models used to describe *symmetry* and *quasi-symmetry*. Suppose, for example, that it is evident that changes have occurred in classifications made at two points in time. This may prompt a question concerning the nature or direction of this change. Change in the table may have been random and hence diffuse, or systematic and channeled in one direction.

Before pursuing this matter further, let us set up a one-group pre-posttest design (called a *panel study* in sociology) using the familiar data from Holton and Nott, so that we can use these data to explore some of the problems of trying to detect change in such a design. Of data reported in Table 5.6, we will consider only those belonging to one group, the group of 55 subjects who received the reflective teaching treatment. With respect to this group, we want to know if significant change in mode of responding took place between the pretest and posttest.

As mentioned, a *direct* assessment of this central question appears to be beyond the reach of log-linear methods at this time. To appreciate the problem better, three hypothetical data sets have been created in Table 8.2 that preserve values in [A] for the 55 treated subjects in the Holton-Nott study. The data on the left, where all frequencies are found on the *principal diagonal*, depicts absolutely no change from pretest to posttest. Change is seen in the middle set, however. Note that the change is distributed somewhat uniformly throughout the table; that is, students assigned to a particular pretest category tend to distribute themselves evenly over levels of the posttest variable. On the right we see the opposite of that shown to the left, namely dramatic change. To the extent to which we give ourselves permission to regard the testing variable as an *ordered* variable, a negative correlation between testing variables can be said to exist in the data to the right.

At first thought, it would seem that conventional log-linear models such as those summarized in Table 4.1 could be used effectively to detect departure from the pattern shown by data on the left. After all, such departure would be indicative of change between testings. However, the near-perfect fit of *any* model for two-way tables, even the one-parameter model, would indicate deviation from the no-change pattern on the left. The independence model, in particular, would appear at first thought to be the most informative, for in the absence of change, the pretest and posttest variable would be highly correlated and the independence model would not fit the data well. Consequently, the saturated model would be accepted. Will a good fit be realized for the independence model if it is applied to the extreme-change data on the right? The residual chi-square for this model, when applied to the extreme-change data, turns out to be $L^2(4) = 168.88$, $p <$ .00. In short, for both situations we would have no choice but to accept the saturated model and its interpretation that the pretest and posttest variables are correlated, yet in the latter situation, change *has* transpired. Finally, to make matters even more confusing, the independence model fits the uniform-change data fairly well, $L^2(9) = 4.47$, $p < .88$, but again, change is indicated. In short, a simple set of rules for the detection of change using log-linear models in the present context does not appear to exist.

Log-Linear Models for Symmetry

If it can be assumed, however, that change has taken place, as evidenced by ample frequencies in cells off the principal diagonal, one can ask whether the change in one direction is the same as the change in the other direction. If so, the "quantity" of change given by nonzero entries in off-diagonal cells located in the upper-right portion of the square table will be mirrored in the lower-left portion of the table. Put differently, to the extent to which change takes place, frequencies will be found in cells that do not reside on the principal diagonal, and to the extent to which $f_{ij} = f_{ji}$, when $i \neq j$, change is balanced, bilateral, and said to be symmetrical. Moreover, if change can be described as symmetrical, then it cannot be said that the state of affairs at the second testing is different from that observed at the first testing. Relative to Holton-Nott, where it was hypothesized that exposure to reflective teaching would result in students being more *analytic* in their posttest performance, symmetry would militate against support for their hypothesis. Rejection of symmetrical change, however, could be taken as first evidence in support of the hypothesis, for rejection would suggest that posttest performance is different from performance on the pretest. Rejection, therefore, would justify further study into the nature of the change.

We will subject to test the hypothesis of symmetrical change using data obtained on the 55 treated subjects in the study by Holton and Nott (1980). First, however, find the 4 × 4 table on the left of Table 8.3 which contains observed

Table 8.3
Observed Frequencies and Those Expected Under the Hypothesis of Symmetrical Change

Pre-Test	Posttest					Posttest				
	a	e	d	i	[A]	a	e	d	i	[A]
a	8	2	1	4	15	8	4	1	6	19.0
e	6	4	2	5	17	4	4	2	4.5	14.5
d	1	2	2	1	6	1	2	2	1	6.0
i	8	4	1	4	17	6	4.5	1	4	15.5
[B]	23	12	6	14	55	19	14.5	6	15.5	55.0
	Observed Frequencies					Symmetric Frequencies				

frequencies organized by levels of the pretesting variable (Variable A) and the relabeled posttest variable (Variable B). Because we are only concerned with the amount and nature of change from pretest to posttest, ignore from now on the cell entries in the principal diagonal. Now if the change that transpired had been symmetric, what would we expect to see in the off-diagonal cells to the upper right and lower left? The expected outcome is also presented in Table 8.3.

The expected frequencies appearing in Table 8.3 may be obtained in one of two ways. One way is to calculate them directly by averaging observed frequencies in corresponding off-diagonal cells. That is, for cells not on the principal diagonal,

$$F_{ij} = F_{ji} = (f_{ij} + f_{ji})/2 \qquad (8.2)$$

Alternately, the F_{ij}'s for expected symmetry can be given by a log-linear model that will yield F_{ij}'s identical to those computed directly with Equation 8.2.

Before we formulate and fit a log-linear model for symmetry, preparatory comments concerning expected main marginals, chi-square, and degrees of freedom are in order. First, examine the main marginals of the 4 × 4 table of expected frequencies in Table 8.3 or, for that matter, any $k \times k$ table that satisfies the criterion of symmetry. Note that under symmetry, $F_i^a = F_j^b$ when $i = j$. In other words, symmetry will produce *homogeneous marginal distributions*. By the same token, if observed marginals are not homogeneous, then, to the extent to which they are not, the potential of achieving symmetry is reduced. Second, a comparison of a $k \times k$ table of observed frequencies with a conformable table of frequencies to be expected under symmetry can be routinely accomplished through the use of a goodness-of-fit chi-square. However, since the cells on the principal diagonal are not involved in our thinking, they should not be involved in the tabular comparison. Consequently, the L^2 is computed using only $k(k - 1)$ cells. Since $k = 4$ in our example, only 12 cells will participate in the calculation. For the example, the likelihood-ratio statistic is

$$L_2 = 2\sum_{i\neq j} (f_{ij}) [\ln (f_{ij}/F_{ij})]$$
$$= 2[\ln (2/4) + \ldots + \ln (1/1)]$$
$$= 3.56$$

Finally, the number of degrees of freedom also needs to be modified. Granted, $k(k - 1)$ cells are involved in the computation of L^2, but since one complete side of the table (e.g., the upper right) can be constructed from knowledge of the other side, only one-half of these cells (i.e., 6) were free to vary. Hence, in general, $v = k(k - 1)/2$. In particular, our result was $L^2(6) = 3.56$, $p <$ .74. The hypothesis of symmetrical change cannot be rejected.

We are most interested, however, in testing for symmetrical change using log-linear models, because even though the direct and the log-linear approach will yield the same results, for this and related problems the log-linear is more general and generative. A log-linear approach involves (1) expanding a two-dimensional $k \times k$ table into a three-dimensional $(k - 1) \times (k - 1) \times 2$ situation; (2) specifying a model that, if acceptable, describes symmetry; (3) fitting the F_{ijk}'s given by the model to observed f_{ijk}'s, many of which turn out to be *structural zeros*; and (4) comparing the fit of the specified model to another model or models to judge its acceptability. Again, the data provided by Holton and Nott (1980) will be used to demonstrate the approach just outlined.

Expanding to Three Dimensions. For the tables shown in Table 8.3, it has been established that the row variable is Variable A and the column variable is Variable B. We desire to introduce into this situation a new dichotomous variable, Variable C, where C_1 consists of off-diagonal entries in the lower-left "triangle" of a two-dimensional table and C_2 consists of the frequencies in the upper-right triangle of a two-dimensional table. Variable C, therefore, partitions the two-dimensional tables shown earlier into two triangular tables that, subsequent to reorganization, can be compared. It is hoped that the contents of Table 8.4 convey the reorganization and possibility for a tabular comparison.

Consider first the observed frequencies shown in the upper portion of Table 8.4. Specifically, notice how the *reduced* table of observed frequencies (i.e., the table of observed frequencies without entries in the principal diagonal) has been partitioned into a lower and upper triangular matrix. Then, to make the tables commensurate, the upper table is turned about to bring it into juxtaposition with the lower triangular matrix. To complete each matrix, *structural zeros* (to be discussed in a later section) are inserted in the void cells. In sum, for observed frequencies we now see a $3 \times 3 \times 2$ contingency table where Variable A is

Table 8.4
A Reorganization of Observed Frequencies and Those Expected Under the Hypothesis of Symmetrical Change

Observed Frequencies

Pre-test	Posttest				Posttest				Posttest			
	a	e	d	i	a	e	d	i	a	e	d	i
a						2	1	4				
e	6						2	5	2			
d	1	2						1	1	2		
i	8	4	1						4	5	1	
	(1) Lower Triangle				(2) Upper Triangle				(3) Transposed Triangle			

Expected Frequencies

Pre-test	a	e	d	i	a	e	d	i
a								
e	4				4			
d	1	2			1	2		
i	6	4.5	1		6	4.5	1	
	(1) Lower Triangle				(3) Transposed Triangle			

Note: In the log-linear analysis of those $3 \times 3 \times 2$ tables, structural zeros are entered in cells that are shown to be empty.

the new three-level row variable, B is the three-level column variable, and C is the two-level partitioning variable.

Consider next the frequencies in the lower portion of Table 8.4. We recognize these to be the frequencies under the hypothesis of symmetry. Using parallel procedures, the two-dimensional table of expected frequencies can be partitioned so as to yield a $3 \times 3 \times 2$ contingency table. The idea, of course, is to compare the observed and expected frequencies within the three-dimensional context; if it should be found that the expected frequencies approach the observed, symmetrical change is indicated.

The Model for Symmetry. Our present task is to deduce the factors (or terms) that will appear in a log-linear model that will produce the expected cell frequencies seen in Table 8.4. Clearly, differences among the F_i^a's and the F_j^b's are to be expected; therefore, τ_i^a and τ_j^b belong in the model for symmetry. But since $F_1^c = F_2^c$ by our construction of symmetry, τ_k^c will not be found in the model. Then if we collapse over levels of C to view expected frequencies in $[AB]$, it will become clear that the F_{ij}^{ab}'s cannot be generated by using only information in $[A]$ and $[B]$. Thus, it follows that interaction between A and B also must be included in the model. If, however, first-order interaction is present between Variables A and C, which would mean that effects for A are not the same at both C_1 and C_2, symmetry is obviated. Also, for the same reason, to have symmetry there cannot be interaction between Variables B and C. Finally, should τ^{abc} be needed in the model, suggesting a differential pattern of interaction between Variables A and B over levels of C, change cannot be symmetric. We conclude, therefore, that the model representing symmetrical change is,

$$F_{ijk} = \tau \, \tau_i^a \, \tau_j^b \, \tau_{ij}^{ab} \tag{8.3}$$

Fitting Expected Frequencies. The four-parameter model above will generate the F_{ijk}'s shown in Table 8.4. To do this, our hand calculations or our computer's iterative fitting algorithm must be constrained so that nonzero estimates are not given for the cells in which we inserted zeros. As it happens, BMDP/4F will permit these designated cells to be excluded from the iterative fitting process.

Assessing Goodness-of-Fit. A residual L^2 may be used to determine how well the F_{ijk}'s produced by Equation 8.3 fit the observed data. Keep in mind, however, that structural zeros are to be found in the three-dimensional tables of observed expected frequencies. When doing the analysis by hand, these cells are simply excluded from the consideration, for ultimately we would be asked to divide a zero by a zero, and division by zero is not a legitimate arithmetic operation. Strictly speaking, we are arbitrarily defining $0/0 = 0$. Also, when determining the number of degrees of freedom, we must subtract from the total a degree of freedom for every structural zero. Moreover, remember that half the nonzero cells have F_{ijk}'s that are determined by the other half. If you are given one triangular table, you can generate the F_{ijk}'s in the other table. Thus, in general, $v = k(k - 1)/2$. For our example, $v = (4 \times 3)/2 = 6$.

Finally, be reminded that we know how well Equation 8.3 fits the observed data, for we have computed the L^2 earlier in connection with the two-dimensional approach to the problem. Recall that $L^2(6) = 3.56, p < .74$. At this point we tentatively conclude that the symmetrical model constitutes a good fit, and that therefore it is doubtful whether those who changed from pretest to posttest did so in the direction of being more analytical.

Proportional Symmetry. Envision a situation where there are more tabulations in one triangular table than in another, that is, $f_1^c \neq f_2^c$. Even though symmetry, as previously defined, cannot come about in this situation—for one thing, we would have heterogeneity of the distributions in $[A]$ and $[B]$—nevertheless, the pattern of frequencies in the upper and lower triangles could be symmetric to a proportionality constant. For example, if there were twice as many frequencies in the lower triangle as in the upper triangle, and if symmetry could be produced by dividing each cell frequency in the lower triangle by two, a modified form of symmetry, *proportional symmetry*, is evidenced. Notice in the Holton-Nott data that tabulations in the lower triangular table exceed those in the upper table. Specifically, $f_1^c = 22$ while $f_2^c = 15$. Proportional symmetry would exist in the off-diagonal cells of the original two-dimensional table if

$$f_{ij} = (f_2^c/f_1^c) \, f_{ji} \tag{8.4}$$

Thus, accepting that there are differences in [C], cell frequencies to be expected in the $3 \times 3 \times 2$ table under the hypothesis of proportional symmetry are obtainable by fitting [C] in addition to [AB]. Therefore, the model that describes this modified form of symmetry is

$$F_{ijk} = \tau \, \tau^a \, \tau^b \, \tau^c \, \tau^{ab} \tag{8.5}$$

To the nearest tenth of a decimal place, the model yields the following cell entries:

4.8			3.2		
1.2	2.4		0.8	1.6	
7.1	5.4	1.2	4.9	3.7	0.8
Lower Triangle			Upper Triangle		

It can be seen that the relations given by Equation 8.4 do, in fact, apply to these data. Consider, for example, the expected frequency for the second row and second column of the original two-dimensional table. We have

$$
\begin{aligned}
F_{21} &= (f_2^c/f_1^c) \, F_{12} \\
&= (22/15)(3.2) \\
&= 4.7
\end{aligned}
$$

where a slight discrepancy due to rounding error is seen between the result (4.7) and F_{21} in the table above (i.e., 4.8).

What implications are associated with the acceptance of the model for proportional symmetry? First, acceptance indicates symmetry to a proportionality constant, as has been illustrated. Second, since more people fall in one of the triangular tables, there is more change flowing in one direction than in the other. To aid in the explanation of this point, assume for the moment that the principal variable in Holton-Nott was a true ordered polytomy. The lower end of the ordinal scale underlying the variable was occupied by analytical statements while the upper end was defined by indeterminate statements. If that were so, acceptance of Equation 8.5 would mean that of the 37 subjects who changed from pretest to posttest, more of them changed toward the lower end of the variable scale toward the analytic—than changed in direction toward the indeterminate class at the upper end of the scale. In fact, 22 subjects were judged to have a "lower" classification on the posttest, whereas only 15 were placed in a higher category on the posttest. Acceptance of the proportional change model, with the directionality of change just discussed, would speak in favor of the investigators' substantive hypothesis that reflective teaching can promote change toward higher level response, particularly analytical response. Acceptance, of course, would be most meaningful if the principal variable were, in fact, ordered—not partially ordered, as was the case. Even so, as we shall soon learn, one should accept and hence interpret this model only if done so with knowledge of the performance of other models, for example, symmetry and quasi-symmetry.

Before pointing out some limitations of this model, let us record how well it fits the data gathered by Holton and Nott. The resultant chi-square will be found to be $L^2(5) = 2.32$, $p < .80$. Hence, the fit is slightly better than that provided by Equation 8.3, the model for symmetry. Note that the number of degrees of freedom is one less than for symmetry. To be more specific, $v = [k(k-1)/2] - 1$, because the model for proportional symmetry contains τ^c and, as a result, there will be one less expected cell frequency that can vary.

As mentioned, despite its appeal, the model in question can be misleading if interpreted in isolation, for it makes no adjustment for differences among levels of the initial variable, the pretest variable. For example, by consulting the two-dimensional table of observed frequencies in Table 8.3, and then summing frequencies in cells off the principal diagonal, the number of subjects in each pretest category who changed categories during the experiment can be identified. When these subjects are so classified, the distribution is not uniform. Using $\bar{f}_i^a$ to denote the number of subjects in the ith level of pretest *who changed*, we find that $\bar{f}_1^a = 7$, $\bar{f}_2^a = 13$, $\bar{f}_3^a = 4$, and $\bar{f}_4^a = 13$. Moreover, because there are observed inequalities in levels of pretest, we can expect to see inequalities by level of pretest in the *expected* frequencies given by both the model for symmetry and the model for proportional symmetry. It is with the latter model, though, that this is a concern, for acceptance of proportional symmetry can lead, as we have learned, to the conclusion that a greater number of subjects changed toward a particular end of an ordered scale. The problem is that such a conclusion may be due to the simple fact that there were more subjects at some levels of the pretest than others, thus permitting more change to occur in a given direction.

Consider an extreme example where we will suppose that about half the subjects were put into A_4 during pretest and, as one would normally expect, the number of subjects in this pretest group who changed far exceeded that in any other pretest group. In what direction can these subjects change? Since change can only take place toward the lower end of the scale, and since there are so many subjects exhibiting this manner of change, the stage is set for a possible acceptance of proportional symmetry and an advancement of the finding that change flows toward the lower end of the scale. Granted, more subjects may be changing toward the lower end; but if pretest standing is taken into account, are *proportionately* more subjects at A_4 moving toward the lower end than subjects at, say, A_1 who are moving toward the higher end of the scale?

For a less extreme example, consider the expected frequencies under proportional symmetry for the Holton-Nott data and compare the number of subjects manifesting change at respective levels of the pretest. These expected frequencies are $\bar{F}_1^a = 8.9$, $\bar{F}_2^a = 10.0$, $\bar{F}_3^a = 4.4$, and $\bar{F}_4^a = 13.9$. There are more expected subjects at A_4 who will move lower on the variable scale than expected subjects at A_1 who will distribute themselves over higher levels on the posttest scale. Again, if adjustments are made for the differences in pretest standing, would change be symmetrical or, instead, would it flow in a particular direction or toward a particular level of the posttest variable? To answer this and the question of the preceding paragraph, a model for quasi-symmetry needs to be built and tested.

Quasi-Symmetry. A model for quasi-symmetry, in addition to all prior adjustments made for symmetry and proportional symmetry, must fit the observed marginals for the pretest variable in the three-dimensional situation, a $3 \times 3 \times 2$ situation at present. However, since the pretest is the row variable for the lower triangular table at C_1 and the column variable for the upper table at C_2, to fit pretest marginals we need to fit the observed configurations for both $[AC]$ and $[BC]$. By fitting both, however, adjustments will be made also for inequalities in the number of subjects who change when classified by level of posttest performance. Quasi-symmetry, therefore, is represented by expected frequencies from the full first-order model, namely

$$F_{ijk} = \tau\, \tau^a\, \tau^b\, \tau^c\, \tau^{ab}\, \tau^{ac}\, \tau^{bc} \tag{8.6}$$

If Equation 8.6 gives a good fit, it means that change is symmetrical following adjustments for unequal marginals. For Holton and Nott, a good fit would mean that change is *not* flowing primarily toward the lower end of the scale where analytic response resides. Should the model for quasi-symmetry not fit well, the saturated model would be adopted and change would be described either as a shift toward one end of the scale, if the scale is ordered, or as effects whose nature will be revealed through a study of the τ^{abc}'s.

Expected frequencies given by the quasi-symmetrical model for the working data are shown below.

```
5.7              2.3
1.3   1.7        0.7   2.3
8.0   4.0   1.0  4.0   5.0   1.0

Lower Triangle   Upper Triangle
```

Comparing the above to observed frequencies in Table 8.3 gives $L^2(3) = .33$, $p < .95$, where $v = [(k - 1)(k - 2)]/2$. The model appears to fit data well. Should we accept it, our conclusion will be that change is symmetric, not directed toward the analytic, if differences in main marginals (e.g., differences in pretest tabulations) are taken into account.[2]

Table 8.5
Summary of Analyses of Change of Treated Subjects in the Holton-Nott Study

Model No.	Model	Residual L^2	df	p	Component L^2	df	p
(8.3)	Symmetry	3.56	6	.74			
(8.5)	Proportional Symmetry	2.32	5	.80	1.24	1	.27
(8.6)	Quasi-Symmetry	.33	3	.95	1.99	2	.37
(Sat.)	Saturated	0.00	0		.33	3	.95

There is still another view of quasi-symmetry. Consider the two-dimensional table in Table 8.3. By fitting Equation 8.6, the observed main marginals of the two-dimensional tables are also fitted. Recall that to achieve symmetry, the marginals of the two-dimensional table first have to be homogeneous (i.e., $f_i^a = f_j^b$). If they are not, the capacity to achieve symmetry is accordingly reduced, and the L^2 for the simple symmetry model becomes large. By fitting [A] and [B] in the two-dimensional configuration, the model for quasi-symmetry in effect acknowledges the possibility of the heterogeneity of marginal proportions and, within the limits of this acknowledged constraint, proceeds to generate expected cell frequencies that are as symmetric as they can be under the circumstances. Hence, the acceptance of Equation 8.6 can be taken to mean that symmetrical change has taken place given the fact that pre-/posttest marginals were not homogeneous for the two-dimensional table, or were not equal in the three-dimensional situation.

Concluding Remarks. Before we summarize our investigation of change (or lack of change) for the 55 treated subjects in the Holton-Nott study, several points should be made. The first is that the questions that we have asked of data in this chapter were not the same as those asked by Holton and Nott in their analysis described in Chapter 5. Second, recall that even the findings in support of change advanced in Chapter 5 were somewhat tentative due to the fact that the composite logit-model test failed to achieve significance at a traditional level (see Table 5.8). With these points in mind, let us examine a summary of our work, as given in Table 8.5.

Adhering to past practice, an examination of residual chi-squares indicates that none of the models in Table 8.5 can initially be excluded due to gross poorness-of-fit. Next, an examination of component chi-squares reveals that the saturated model can be passed over in favor of an unsaturated model. In so doing, the hypothesis that pre-posttest change would be in the direction of analytic statements will not find support in this analysis. In short, most analysts would select Model 8.3, the symmetry model, since it is the most parsimonious while remaining consistent with observed data. Thus, there was some degree of change in classifications, but whereas some subjects moved toward the analytic, others moved away from the analytic. As so often happens in research, one type of question pursued by its logical method will produce from data one result while another question, pursued by its method, will yield a different, sometimes contradictory, result.

CAUSAL MODEL ANALOGUES

Conducting research from which one is able to infer causality is the ultimate goal of science. Conditions necessary and sufficient to advance causal inferences, however, are understandably complex and are best left to other sources for their exposition (e.g., Cook & Campbell, 1979; Heise, 1975). Suffice it to say that the requisites for serious causal thinking in the study of social behavior are rarely approached in the absence of well-controlled experimentation or a program of descriptive research based on extremely strong theory. With this caveat in mind, it is with circumspection that we devote the next few pages to a brief introduction to the use of log-linear models in path analysis and its application to causal thinking.

Modern path analysis subsumes a number of techniques that, when used appropriately, are useful for the study of the direct and indirect effects exerted by some variables on other variables. The earliest principles were formulated in the 1920s by Sewall Wright, a biologist (Heise, 1975, 112). The last two decades have seen extensive refinement and use of path techniques, particularly in fields like sociology, economics, and political science, where experiments, the classical vehicle for the study of causality, are difficult, if not impossible, to conduct. Recent developments have led to path analytical techniques being extended, integrated, and, in a sense, even superseded by a more comprehensive approach to modeling called *linear structural equations* or the *analysis of covariance structures* (Jöreskog, 1978; Bentler, 1980; Jöreskog & Sörbom, 1988). Unlike log-linear models, structural equation modeling is done with either observed or latent variables (constructs inferred from observable variables) where observed variables or indicators are measured on interval or, more recently, ordinal scales. Linear structural equations do not lend themselves to the analysis of qualitative/categorical data, however. Nevertheless, structural equations and log-linear models have much in common. They share a common basic approach: specification of a series of plausible models to explain relations or effects, estimation of parameters in these competing models, testing the goodness-of-fit of competing models through the use of the chi-square, and, finally, the selection of a model that represents the simplest explanation of observed data.

Figure 8.1
**Path Diagram Showing Four Main Variables and an Interactive Variable to Be
Used in Conjunction with the McLean Study**

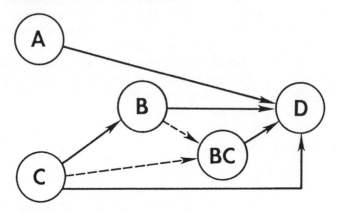

Developing a Causal Scheme

Returning to older forms, and assuming of the reader an elementary background in conventional path analysis, we will now illustrate how a number of
path analytical procedures can be applied in a qualitative setting. To fix ideas,
let us review several basic features that are common to path analyses irrespective
of setting. First and foremost, a sound system of a priori hypotheses (i.e., theory)
is central. Causal path analysis is used best as a rifle where careful aim is taken
to test a theory; it can be abused when used as a shotgun to scavenge for models
that simply appear interesting. Second, the sampling plan must support each
causal prediction that becomes part of the model. Shortly we will use again the
data gathered by McLean (1980) to test a model that we will develop, but to do
so, we will find it necessary to take liberties and assume sampling procedures
that, in fact, were not executed by McLean.

From the theory, one or more *path diagrams* are created which depict how
important variables are interrelated. For our purposes, we will consider only the
case where models depicted in diagrams are understood to be *recursive*, that is,
all causal influences flow in one direction, from left to right, across the diagram.
As is standard, arrows will be used to connect variables that are related. The
absence of an arrow between two variables indicates that the variables are believed not to be related. If a pair of variables is connected by a two-headed
arrow (↔), a bilateral association is indicated. If the arrow has one head, coming
from one variable and pointing toward another, a causal linkage in the suggested
direction is posited. The kind of diagram described here is shown in Figure 8.1.

For a concrete example, let us return to the study conducted by McLean and
modify it as need be to suit our pedagogical purposes. Turning to the hypothetical

scenario in Figure 8.1, note that it begins on the left with two *exogeneous* variables: Variable *A* (high vs. low ability) and Variable *C* (black vs. white students). Exogenous variables have "causes" outside the diagrammed system and are easily identified because they have no arrows pointing at them. If our theory held that exogenous Variables *A* and *C* were related, they would be connected by a curved line with arrowheads at each end. To test for the hypothesized relationship, a sample representative of the population of inference would need to be obtained and then jointly classified by Variables *A* and *C*. This cannot be said to have happened in the McLean study, but for a preliminary stage of our analysis, we will assume momentarily that it has. Notice, too, that exogenous Variable *A* has only one *direct* arrow or path from it to *endogenous* Variable *D*. Variable *D* (graduation vs. nongraduation) is the ultimate response variable in the diagram and can be called endogenous because it is affected by other variables in the system; in other words it has one or more arrows pointing at it. Variable *D* is also receiving the pointed end of a direct arrow from Variable *C*. Variable *C* is said to have a *direct* effect on students' choice of university, penultimate endogenous Variable *B*. Again, to legitimately subject this predicted effect to formal test, at the very least we would need to obtain representative samples of black and white students prior to determining whether they chose to attend a historically white or black university.

That aside, Variable *C* is also shown to affect Variable *D*, but *indirectly* through a mediating variable, namely, Variable *B*. Additionally, Variable *D* is believed to be influenced directly by an interactive variable, Variable *BC*, representing the simple first-order interaction at respective levels of *D*. Variables *B* and *C* are sending dotted arrows to interactive Variable *BC* to denote the fact that, in theory, and in many log-linear models, the first-order interaction is independent and, hence, not affected by its lower order relatives. However, some connection, such as the use of dotted arrows, seems appropriate to remind us that Variables *B* and *C* need to be crossed and present prior to the realization of the interaction in question. Interactive variables are not commonly seen in either conventional or log-linear causal diagrams, but since this particular interaction happens to reflect McLean's principal research hypothesis—that black students would show a higher rate of on-time graduation at the black university, we accept it as a challenge, and hence incorporate it into our model.

Having diagrammed the linkages between and among important variables, two methodological steps remain: (1) verification or rejection of each effect in the model and (2) an overall assessment of the adequacy of the model, or a revised version of the model, to fit the observed data. Before implementing these steps, notice that an important procedure in conventional path analysis was not mentioned. Specifically, the systematic decomposition of correlations into direct, indirect, and spurious effects—as described by Asher (1976, 35–44) or Kerlinger and Pedhazur (1973, 314–17), among others—cannot be done in the present circumstances because qualitative variables generally do not lend themselves to product-moment correlations. Nevertheless, there remains a number of working parallelisms to render the log-linear version of path analysis of value for testing theory.

The path diagram in Figure 8.1 presents a number of hypothesized causal links or paths that should be tested in addition to a number of engaging restrictions (relations or effects that have been hypothesized to be nil) that should be examined also. Substantively important paths that have been set to zero are just as important to the integrity of the theory as are the effects explicitly posited in the model. In fact, models become increasingly of interest as they become more restricted (as they omit paths) because the more restrictions, the greater the number of opportunities to reject statistically, and hence, the more valuable the model becomes to science in the long run.

Establishing Paths and Path Coefficients

Putting philosophy aside, it may be recalled from study elsewhere that the basic approach taken in a recursive path analysis is to formulate a predictive equation (or a series of equations in the log-linear) for each endogenous variable. The equation or equations that predict the endogenous variable contain all antecedent variables that are said to be having a direct effect on the predicted variable. Solutions are found for each equation in a series of stages moving from left to right in the recursive system. At each stage, coefficients that measure *partial associations* between antecedent variables and the endogenous response variable are calculated and tested for either statistical or practical significance, or both. For each partial association that is deemed significant, a path from the antecedent variable to the response variable is established and the coefficient is placed on the path to indicate the strength and direction of the causal inference. A similar approach is followed in log-linear path analysis.

The Two-Dimensional Stage. With respect to Figure 8.1, we commence in the standard manner by proceeding from left to right. On the left we find exogenous Variables A and C with no explicit linkage between them. This is appropriate under two sets of circumstances. First, a representative sample in which only n was arbitrarily fixed by the investigator was obtained, and the investigator's theory held that Variables A and C were *not* associated. Alternately, sampling was conducted in such a way that the frequencies in $[AC]$ were fixed or determined by the investigator. The latter would rule out any attempt to assess a relationship between these variables, or, in a logit-model analysis, to determine whether one variable affects another. McLean fixed the f_{ik}^{ac}'s in the two-way tables, which precludes a serious analysis of Variables A and C. However, as an exercise, suppose that McLean had obtained a representative sample of college students and that subsequently he had jointly classified them by ability and race. This would support a general log-linear analysis on the fourfold table. Thus, using the methodology described in Chapter 4, the model for independence and the saturated model could be fitted to $[AC]$. If the latter were accepted, the model would be revised by connecting A and C with a curved, double-headed arrow. To indicate the strength of the association, since we are dealing with a fourfold table, Yule's Q defined by Equation 4.26 would be an appropriate indicator.

Suppose instead that McLean arbitrarily fixed only the levels of one of the variables, say Variable A. Here, Variable A would be considered to be exogenous and explanatory while Variable C would be endogenous and response. The null logit model (i.e., the independence model in the symmetrical case) and the model representing main effects for Variable A would be fitted and, in turn, evaluated. If the main-effects model were to be accepted, a straight arrow would be drawn from explanatory A to response C. To suggest the strength and direction of effects, the numerical value of λ_{11}^{ac} from the saturated model is placed on the arrow and serves a function analogous to that of a path coefficient in an analysis done by regression. In addition, it is suggested that the probability value (p-value) associated with the z test on λ_{11}^{ac} also be placed on the path.

The results of an analysis performed on $[AC]$ are summarized in the top portion of Table 8.6. The L^2 from the fit of the independence model was $L_1^2(1) = 86.04$, $p < .00$. This would cause us to adopt the saturated model. Again, this analysis was performed simply as an exercise, for McLean's sampling procedures do not support either a general or a logit-model analysis.

The Three-Dimensional Stage. Moving to the right, Variable B is the first endogenous variable to be encountered. Recall that B_1 contained students who attended the historically white university while B_2 contained students who attended the historically black university. Assume that McLean did not fix the levels of this variable during sampling. Now, the object is to write and solve equations in which Variable B is the response variable and Variables A and C are predictor variables. That is, we desire to fit a series of logit models for endogenous Variable B so that we can determine whether (1) Variable A is having a direct effect on Variable B, subsequent to partialing from A effects shared with Variable C; (2) Variable C is exerting a direct effect on B, holding Variable A constant; or (3) independent of the above, interaction exists between A and C that in turn functions as a variable affecting B. Even though our model does not hypothesize that an interactive AC variable precipitates change in B, sound analysis would have us search for its possible presence.

Models fitted to the three-way $[ABC]$ table that are needed to implement our work at stage 2 are shown in Table 8.6. Decision making begins with Model 7, where we examine its component chi-square, which is the difference in residuals between the seven-parameter full first-order model ($L_4^2 = L_6^2 = 1.27$) and the eight-parameter saturated model ($L_7^2 = 0.00$). These models are being compared to determine if λ^{abc} is needed to achieve a reasonable fit. If it is, then our model will be revised to accommodate this interactive variable. But since the component does not approach significance ($p < .26$), we accept the absence of an interactive AC variable affecting Variable B.

The tests of direct effects from Variables A and C are tests of partial, not marginal, associations. As a case in point, to determine whether there is evidence

Table 8.6

Component L^2's for Model Fitted to the McLean Data in the Performance of a Causal Analysis

Model No.	Marginals Fitted		Residual Comparison	L^2	df	p
Preliminary Stage: The fit of models to the [AB] table						
(1)	A, B	(independence)				
(2)	AB	(saturated)	(2)-(1)	86.04	1	.00
Stage 1: The fit of logit models to the [ABC] configuration						
(3)	AC, B̄C					
(4)	AC, B̄C, ĀB		(3)-(4)	30.83	1	.00
(5)	AC, ĀB					
(6)	AC, ĀB, B̄C		(5)-(6)	591.05	1	.00
(7)	ĀB̄C		(6)-(7)	1.27	1	.26
Stage 2: The fit of logit models to the [ABCD̄] table						
(8)	ABC, BD̄, CD̄					
(9)	ABC, BD̄, CD̄, AD̄		(8)-(9)	9.37	1	.00
(10)	ABC, AD̄, CD̄					
(11)	ABC, AD̄, CD̄, BD̄		(10)-(11)	.12	1	.72
(12)	ABC, AD̄, BD̄					
(13)	ABC, AD̄, BD̄, CD̄		(12)-(13)	2.40	1	.12
(14)	ABC, ABD̄, ACD̄		(13)-(14)	3.37	2	.17
(15)	ABC, ABD̄, ACD̄, BCD̄		(14)-(15)	2.90	1	.09
(16)	ABCD̄		(15)-(16)	2.53	1	.11

for a direct path from C to endogenous B, we determine whether there is an association between these two variables after partialing from this association the contribution, if any, of Variable A. From our work in Chapter 5, we know that to test for a partial association, $\lambda^{\bar{b}c}$ is entered as the seventh or last term in the full first-order model, and the fit of this full model is compared to the fit given by a "comparable" six-parameter model, which is comparable in all respects except for the presence of $\lambda^{\bar{b}c}$. The comparison under discussion is made when the residual for Model 6 in the table, $L_6^2(1) = 1.27$, is subtracted from the residual fit of Model 5, $L_5^2(2) = 592.32$. The component that results, and that is used to test the partial association between C and B, is obviously large, $L^2_{5-6}(1) = 591.05$. A direct connection between C and B has been established.

A suitable coefficient for the path would be the value of λ^{bc}_{11} taken from the full first-order model. Its value is $\lambda^{bc}_{11} = -1.12$. Also on the same path, consider putting the ratio of lambda to its standard error, found to be $z = -18.44$, for the effect in question. If McLean's sampling permitted such an analysis, at this point we would conclude that a student's race affects his or her choice of university. Black students (C_1) tend to go to historically black universities (B_2) and vice versa.

Let us see if we can also substantiate a path from Variable A to response B. The strength of the partial association between these variables is reflective in the size of the component resulting from a comparison of Models 3 and 4. It turned out that $L^2_3(2) = 32.10$ and $L^2_4(1) = 1.27$. Thus, $L^2_{4-3}(1) = 30.83$, $p < .00$. If sampling were proper, a path between A and B could be established. Ability level would be said to influence choice of university. Here, λ^{ab}_{11} from full Model 4, or equivalent Model 6, would serve as the path coefficient, and the concurrent presentation of its associated z statistic would enhance our appreciation of the effect.

A few comments about path coefficients are in order. To start with, we concede that the synonymity between lambdas as path coefficients and partial regression coefficients (betas) in least-squares is less than perfect. To a degree, however, lambda path coefficients are amenable to similar interpretation. Goodman (1972a, 1979), for example, interprets lambda path coefficients as partials in terms of conditional odds. Consider in the example the effect of Race (Variable C) on Type of University (Variable B). Since the variables are both dichotomies, and since we have ruled out an interaction between A and C operating on B, by multiplying the lambda path coefficient by 2 (by converting a binomial logit to a full logit) we can obtain the log of the odds of being black and attending the predominantly white university, holding ability level constant. For the example, the logged odds are $2(-1.12) = -2.24$. Obtaining the antilog of -2.24, we can say that the odds of being black and being enrolled in the white university are about .11 to 1, holding levels of A constant. From the opposite perspective, since $2(\lambda^{ab}_{12}) = 2.24$, the odds of being white and being found in the predominantly white university are about 9.39 to 1. To the extent to which Variables A and C interact, however, the interpretation of effects in terms of the conditional can be misleading. Also realize that this manner of interpretation is appropriate only when both the antecedent and the response variables are dichotomous.

The direct interpretation of lambdas as logged ANOVA-like effects, however, remains our preference. To many, especially those trained to conduct experiments, the direct interpretation of lambdas presents few if any conceptual difficulties. At the very least, the magnitude of lambda path coefficients can be used as relative indicators within a given stage, to compare the strength of effects leading to the endogenous variable. Moreover, the direct approach can be extended more easily to paths between polytomous variables.

Irrespective of interpretation, when a path is drawn between variables that are not exclusively dichotomous, because multiple lambda coefficients arise, so do complications. This is yet another problem to be added to our growing list of log-linear applications that need further study. Until more satisfactory path measures become commonly known, it is suggested that the numerical values of component chi-squares be placed on the paths and, accompanying this analogue, the *p*-values of corresponding component chi-squares. Together, they, at the very least, provide good relative measures of the strength of paths that lead to the same endogenous variable.

The Four-Dimensional Stage. Finally, the ultimate response variable, Variable *D*, is encountered. Main Variables *A*, *C*, and *B* have direct paths leading to *D*. Also, it has been hypothesized that there is a path between interactive Variable *BC* and *D*, a variable that comes into being because of main Variables *B* and *C* but is considered to be independent of them. To assess these many effects of *D*, logit models in which *D* is the logit variable need to be constructed, fitted to the observed [*ABCD*], and subsequently evaluated. The models needed to do the work at this stage are presented, along with their components, at the bottom of Table 8.6.

We look at Table 8.6 first for evidence of an effect on *D* from the interaction of *A*, *B*, and *C*—a second-order-logit interaction that was, in effect, restricted to zero in the model. When the 16-parameter saturated model was compared to the full second-order model containing 15 parameters—Model 16 vs. Model 15—the resultant component was found to be $L^2_{15-16}(1) = 2.53$, $p < .11$. Evidence does not appear to be sufficient to contradict the restriction that $\lambda^{abcd} = 0$.

To assess the credibility of the most interesting path in Figure 8.1, that from *BC* to *D*, we compare the 15-parameter model, with λ^{bcd}, to the 14-parameter model without λ^{bcd}. The component for the former was $L^2_{14-15}(1) = 2.90$, $p < .09$. Because from the start we regarded this effect to be of greatest interest, and since it does approach traditional criteria for statistical significance, we argue strongly for its continued presence in the model.

The remaining interactive variables that were not explicitly cited in the model are examined collectively through the comparison of Model 14, which contains both λ^{abd} and λ^{acd}, with Model 13, which contains all the terms in Model 14 with the exception of these two. Although it is not the most rigorous test of the combined influence of these terms, $L^2_{13-14}(2) = 3.37$, $p < .17$. The component is not large enough to reject the restriction that interactive Variables *AB* and *AC* have little or no effect on *D*.

Main variable paths are each tested by model comparisons presented in pairs in the table. As a final example, consider whether there is sufficient support for rejecting the null hypothesis that Variable *C* has no effect on *D*, holding Variables *A* and *B* constant. As we have done repeatedly, the full first-order-logit model, Model 13, is compared to Model 12, a model with all relevant terms except λ^{cd}. The component observed for Model 13 was not significant ($p < .12$). Unless there are convincing arguments to the contrary, this path will be trimmed from

Figure 8.2
Revised Path Diagram for the McLean Study with Path Coefficients (Lambda Parameter Estimates) and z Tests (in Parentheses) Performed on the Coefficients

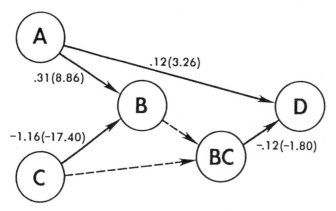

the model when it is revised. Moreover, the revised model will unquestionably not show a path from B to D ($p < .72$), but the path from A to D ($p < .00$) will be retained.

Before the results of our theory trimming are displayed, consider again the coefficients that might appear on the remaining paths. A most conservative approach would be to, where appropriate, use lambdas found from the fitting of the saturated model. However, if we have confidence in our efforts to trim the model, lambdas from the most acceptable logit model can be used. Using the definition for acceptability exercised so often in this text, we choose to take respective stage 2 coefficients from a model obtained by fitting observed marginals [ABD], [BCD], and [AD]. Our revised path diagram is seen in Figure 8.2.

Testing Models for Goodness-of-Fit

Before a serious investment is made in a path model, the model's ability to reproduce observed cell frequencies should be evaluated. Admittedly, specific judgments about the significance of specific links have been made at every stage, but restrictions that were also accepted at each stage can, when taken together, reduce greatly the model's ability to generate expected frequencies that reasonably approximate those that have been observed. Obviously, substantive investments in poor-fitting models are to be discouraged. Therefore, subsequent to model trimming, we try to judge how well the path model fits the observed data by constructing a log-linear model and assessing that model for overall goodness-of-fit.

Assume that we are reasonably satisfied with the path model displayed in Figure 8.2. As mentioned, the task then becomes that of evaluating the congruence between it and the observed data. To do this, we will build a log-linear model that tries to incorporate all sampling features, relations, and effects that are part of the path model. The path and log-linear models are not coincidental, for in the log-linear model it will not be possible to capture the temporal sequencing and network intricacies of the path model. Moreover, the log-linear model, if structured hierarchically, may contain surplus effects. Suppose, for example, that higher order effects like a *BC* interaction are posited in a hierarchical path model; then, by construction, its lower order relatives, which may not have been cited in the path model, will nevertheless appear in the log-linear representation.

To begin building the model, one first determines what has been fixed as part of the sampling procedure. Differences in a main marginal or among tabular cells that are due to sampling decisions must be taken into account; they must be built into the log-linear model. Let us continue to operate on the assumption, albeit a false one, that McLean fixed [*AC*] during sampling. As a consequence, the model under construction will fit [*AC*] and contain λ^{ac}.

Next, move to the work at the first stage, ignore the fact that logit models were fitted here, and pick up all relations and effects that have been judged to be significant. In our work, paths were established between Variables *A* and *B* and *C* and *B*. Hence, the emerging model will accommodate the fitting of [*AB*] and [*BC*].

Finally, move to the last stage. Again, ignoring the fact that logit models were used to detect effects, we simply identify established paths. In our example, it is evident that the model should fit [*BCD*] and [*AD*].

Putting everything together, the model that represents the path diagram shown in Figure 8.2 will be one that is produced by the fitting of the observed marginals [*AB*], [*AC*], [*AD*], and [*BCD*]. When the F_{ijkm}'s generated by this 12-parameter model were compared to f_{ijkm}'s, the residual chi-square was $L^2(4) = 6.60$, $p < .16$. Further, an examination of standard residuals revealed that they were not pronounced; they ranged from -1.1 to $.9$. The fit is indeed satisfactory.

Incidently, if it can be said that there is a best or ideal fit here, it would be one in which the residual chi-square was equal to 4, the number of degrees of freedom, since from Chapter 3 we know that $E(\chi^2) = v$. There is a prevailing belief that as a computed residual chi-square becomes less than v in magnitude, an increasingly better fit is indicated. This is a spurious belief. Models fit less well as the computed chi-square deviates from v in any direction.

In any event, just because McLean's data happened to be consistent with our log-linear model, this fact alone does not mean that we have substantiated the network of relations and effects in the path model. After all, the same set of variable relations could be rearranged so as to depict a different causal scenario, yet the same log-linear model, and hence the same fit, would result. Finally, if we had been serious in our efforts to trim and test the model of this section, the outcome would have been encouraging. If we had not been engaged in a heuristic exercise, we would possess a model with ample opportunities for rejection and refinement in future work, and during the interim, we would possess a tentative set of relations to help us better understand the nature of the problem.

ADDITIONAL CONCERNS

Though log-linear methodology has matured during the last two decades, a number of stubborn problems remain. There are two in particular that merit special recognition. They are the occurrence of "too many" empty cells, and the heavy reliance that many of us place on tests of statistical significance during decision making. In this section, brief discussions of these problems are offered more for edification than for the attainment of solutions.

Small and Zero Cell Frequencies

Problems with zero cell frequencies should not be confused with those associated with *sparse* contingency tables, in which many cells have small cell frequencies. Concern for the latter is historic and centers about the ability of the chi-square distribution to approximate satisfactorily the multinomial (or product multinomial) when *expected* cell frequencies are small. What is small? Unfortunately, authorities differ on the expected cell size that can be used comfortably, although the so-called rule of five, mentioned in earlier chapters, can be taken as a reasonable average for sparse tables. Authorities also differ on the merits of the well-known correction offered by Yates (1934) to improve the correspondence between the distribution of chi-square statistics and the continuous chi-square probability distribution. Some maintain that Yates's correction for continuity should be used routinely in small sample situations (Everitt, 1977), and others state that the resulting chi-square statistics are too conservative (Camilli & Hopkins, 1978; Grizzle, 1967), while one study has shown that Yates's correction is too conservative down to a certain sample size (the size depends on population proportions that were permitted to vary in the study), but as sample sizes become smaller, the correction resulted in an excess of Type I errors (Wenig, 1979). Most agree, however, that small expected cell sizes promote the same concerns for log-linear analysis as they do for the more traditional forms of chi-square analyses, and that problems are mitigated as the number of cells in sparse tables increase.

Remember, however, that small expected cell frequencies adversely affect only one component of a typical log-linear analysis—the accuracy of the residual and component chi-square statistics associated with the various competing models. Since as models become more restrictive, on average fewer small expected cell frequencies will be generated, so it would seem reasonable to assume, at least for the time being, that the chi-squares of parsimonious models will be less biased than those given by fuller models. In conclusion, although a legitimate concern, there is more to decision making in a log-linear analysis than acceptance or rejection of a hypothesis based on a single test statistic; therefore, in the larger arena of log-linear analysis, the problematic effects of small cell frequencies are not preeminent.

Void cells or zero cell frequencies in contingency tables can be a major concern, however. A discussion of the problems cannot begin without first making the distinction between *structural zeros* (sometimes called fixed or a priori zeros) and *sampling zeros* (sometimes called random zeros). A structural zero appears in a cell of a table because in the population no such subjects exist. If a table contained a cell for pregnant males, excluding the possibility of clerical error, at the moment at least that cross-classification would contain a structural zero. Sampling zeros, on the other hand, are not inherent. They appear only because the overall sample was not large enough to have drawn into it a representative of a particular cross-classification, a cross-classification that likely contains a small relative proportion of the population. Thus, sampling zeros decrease in occurrence as overall sample size increases. Recall that we saw a sampling zero in the data reported by Holton and Nott (Table 5.6).

The distinction between sampling and structural zeros carries with it important implications for analysis. Sampling zeros, unless numerous, constitute more of an annoyance than a defect. Structural zeros, in contrast, beget tables that are *incomplete* and that require analysis by methods beyond the pale of this introductory book.

Sampling Zeros. Fienberg (1977, 108) has pointed out that one of the most powerful properties of log-linear models is that in the presence of sampling zeros, provided that they are not excessive in number, cells with zero observed entries can be given nonzero maximum-likelihood expectancies. Thus, putting aside complications such as too many zeros or zeros that are inherently structural yet treated as sampling, the operational consequences are largely arithmetic and easily handled. As a case in point, consider the calculation of likelihood-ratio chi-squares, using Equation 3.11, and the fact that an observed frequency of zero can be divided by a nonzero expected frequency with the result being a zero; however, the log of zero is $-\infty$, which is unmanageable in practice. To overcome this and other related problems, rather widespread acceptance has been given to Goodman's suggestion that a small, innocuous quantity such as 0.5 be added to all elementary cells frequencies in the observed table.[3] On both the SPSSX LOG-LINEAR and BMDP/4F computer programs, for example, by requesting the option DELTA, 0.5 can be added to observed cell frequencies. However, the routine practice of adding 0.5 to all cells prior to the analysis of a table with sampling zeros has been questioned by Clogg and Eliason (1987), and most recently by Agresti, who maintains that this practice results in chi-square tests for highly restricted models that are far too conservative (1990, 249). Rather than adding 0.5 as a constant, Agresti suggests the use of a constant only when zeros presents computational problems, and even in these situations, the constant to be added to all frequencies should be extremely small (e.g., 10^{-8}). In sum, the addition of a small "delta quantity" does much to overcome difficulties with the chi-square. Problems with the estimation of effect parameters will only occur if sampling zeros are so numerous that one or more expected cell frequencies converge to zero during iterative fitting.

When sampling zeros are so numerous, one is apt to confront problems of (1) not having sufficient information on which to support an inference, (2) not having sufficient statistical power to drive the test of significance, and (3) not having sufficiently satisfied the assumptions that underlie the proper use of the chi-square which places great strain on the ability of the chi-square to approximate the multinomial. If that were not enough, zeros can be so distributed as to cause, in theory, expected cell frequencies to be negative. In practice, iterative fitting will result in values that converge to zero for these anomalous cells. Finally, in smaller tables, particularly, the presence of zeros in common levels of a table can result in a zero entry for the margin of table. When this occurs, modifications need to be made in both the fitting algorithms and the rule for determining the proper number of degrees of freedom. These latter modifications are discussed by Fienberg (1977, ch. 8) and Clogg and Eliason (1987).

Structural Zeros. As mentioned, zeros are considered to be structural if the cross-classification does not exist or if we intentionally force cells to have a zero frequency during iterative fitting and residual testing, as we did when working with models for symmetrical change. It is the former type of zero entry that causes difficulties because it makes the contingency tables incomplete. When incomplete tables are encountered, they are more likely to be seen in medicine and biology than in the social sciences. Undoubtedly, this difference reflects, in part, the general nature of the subject matter and, possibly, the greater ease with which social scientists can combine or eliminate classes to avoid missing cells. In any event, as the reader has surely surmised, incomplete tables are to be avoided if possible, but not at the expense of treating a structural zero as if it were a sampling zero or altering seriously the nature of the problem by collapsing over categories until zeros vanish.

One course of action that might work for a large incomplete table is to break it up into smaller complete configurations that make contextual sense and then to subject the smaller tables to separate log-linear analyses. If this cannot be done meaningfully, the table must be considered incomplete, and, therefore, as only amenable to analysis by *quasi-log-linear models*. Quasi-log-linear models are analogous to the models that we have been using on complete tables. For example, it is possible to structure and fit a model for *quasi-independence*, a model that generates expected cell frequencies for independence in the usual way except that columns (rows) that contain one or more zeros are not considered. Understandably, with more constraints imposed upon the data, it takes longer to determine whether the table can be analyzed and there is less assurance that it can be. Brief discussions of incomplete tables and quasi-log-linear models are offered by Fienberg (1977) and Upton (1978), though an early paper by Fienberg (1972) still merits the highest recommendation.

Chi-Square Values and Sample Size

Perhaps the greatest limitation of the approach that we have taken to log-linear analysis has been our heavy reliance on the statistical significance of chi-square values when faced with decisions about model appropriateness. At issue, of course, is the fact that the magnitude of a chi-square statistic, and thus its p-value, is a function of sample size. If a sample can be made large enough, any model, except the saturated model, can be rejected on the basis of a statistical criterion, because ultimately an n will be attained whereby the residual chi-square will be statistically significant. On the other hand, the probability of accepting a model increases as n decreases. Fortunately, subject matter researchers are becoming increasingly aware of the relationship between statistical significance and sample size, and are, formally or informally, adjusting their inferences accordingly. In some areas of analysis, statistical power tables and/ or measures of association that are independent of n are available. Unfortunately, in our area, as soon as we move beyond two-way tables, there are no widely accepted measures of association to help with the assessment of model fit.

Consider the problem as it applies to symmetrical inquiry where we search for the most restricted model that represents a plausible explanation of relations in data. Here, *acceptance* of restrictions (i.e., acceptance of null hypotheses) plays a major role, yet we know that in statistical decision theory, acceptance of a restriction is a weak form of decision. It is so weak that many would prefer that we do not even speak of "acceptance" but would instead say that we are "unable at the moment to reject." In any event, recall that in earlier chapters we retained for further examination only those models that did *not* yield large and significant L^2's. While implementing the strategy, we were aware that as samples become small, the likelihood will increase that all models, even the null model, will be retained as candidates for further study. Of course, as samples become large, the reverse is true; in the extreme, only the saturated model will be retained. Granted, the skillful analyst will not rely exclusively on residual chi-squares during the initial step. He or she will be constantly monitoring the distance between chi-square values and their numbers of degrees of freedom for $E(L^2) = v$ and respective AIC statistics. In addition, analyzing standardized or Freeman-Tukey deviates can be insightful.

Goodman (1971b, 1972b) has proposed a relatively straightforward coefficient that merits consideration by researchers who frequently find themselves working in the symmetrical mode. It is analogous to a semi-partial correlation in the framework of a forward-solution multiple regression, it is independent of sample size, and some (Zahn & Fein, 1979) have found it to be of value in their attempts to judge the goodness-of-fit of general models. The idea is to identify a baseline model, determine the residuum about that model, and then determine how much of that residuum can be explained by more saturated models of interest. It is most common to choose the model of mutual independence, say Model 0, as the baseline model, although this need not always be so. Then, for a less restricted model of interest, say Model i, Goodman's coefficient for the ith model is

$$\Lambda_i = \frac{(L_o^2 - L_i^2)}{L_o^2} \tag{8.7}$$

The coefficient denoted by uppercase Greek lambda ranges from 0.0 to 1.0, and for Model i it can be interpreted as the proportion of total variation in the residuum about the baseline model that can be explained by all nonbaseline terms in Model i. Thus, irrespective of statistical significance, as models become less restrictive and begin to account for between 80 and 90 percent of meaningfully defined residuum variation, goodness-of-fit is suggested. Unfortunately, minimum specific criteria for selecting models by this means have yet to be formulated.

Finally, when inquiry is asymmetrical, our strategy for decision making strikes a different emphasis, that of rejection—specifically, the rejection of component chi-squares if they are justifiably large. Unlike the statistical decision to accept, rejection is a strong, albeit conditional, decision. The size of samples affects the size of components, and hence their p values, but in a less beguiling way. Small samples promote Type II errors; large samples promote the ascription of statistical significance to effects that may not be practically significant. Nevertheless, we find ourselves on more comfortable ground because rejection of a null is the requisite for advancing a finding, and the burden for rejection, as a statistical tradition would have it, is on the shoulders of the researcher.

THE NEED FOR LOG-LINEAR METHODS

If a table's dimensionality exceeds two (i.e., $k > 2$) and inquiry is symmetrical, it is advantageous to analyze resultant data with log-linear methodology. The older methods of symmetrical analysis surveyed in Chapter 4 lack the comprehensiveness of log-linear analysis. They do not accommodate the simultaneous analysis of more than two categorical variables and therefore are not able to address important concepts such as conditional independence or partial association. Simply put, for inquiry that is symmetrical, there does not appear to be a contemporary or emerging system of analysis for qualitative data with advantages superior to those of log-linear models.

The eminence of log-linear analysis has been questioned, however, when the mode of inquiry is asymmetrical. Many have asked: Why bother with log-linear theory and technique when alternative techniques *appear* to exist, techniques such as multiple regression and linear discriminant analysis, which can be modified to accommodate categorial response? In short, when there is an obvious response variable, and that variable is dichotomous or polytomous, do we really need log-linear analysis?

Before we respond to this question, techniques that might appear to be serious competitors to logit-model analysis merit, at least, acknowledgment. While reading accounts of the studies conducted by McLean (1980) and Peters (1981), it may have crossed the reader's mind that instead of logit-model analysis, McLean conceivably could have used ordinary least-squares multiple regression or the related technique of two-group discriminant analysis. Moreover, Peters conceivably could have structured a canonical variate analysis (CVA) to perform the analysis on the polytomous response variable—or so it would seem. These established parametric procedures also happen to be described well in a number of texts on multivariate analyses (e.g., Stevens, 1986; Tatsuoka, 1988).

To partially illustrate these parametric possibilities, consider again the McLean study, where the dichotomous response variable (Variable D) consisted of students who either graduated or did not graduate from college during a specified period of time. Now McLean could have assigned the number 1 to all students who graduated "on time" and 0 to those who did not. By doing so, the original dichotomy would have been transformed to a univariate response that could serve, in effect, as the dependent variable in an ordinary least-squares regression, a regression in which the three independent variables, and the resulting four interaction variables, would be coded (e.g., by dummy coding, effect coding, orthogonal coding, etc.) to accommodate the analysis. Actually, the analysis being described can also be thought of as a three-way ANOVA on a dichotomous dependent variable. In any case, under ordinary circumstances, least-squares, not maximum likelihood, is the basis for estimation, and proportions, not logits, are the functional forms of the dependent variable.

A related alternative approach would be to treat the dichotomous response variable (Variable D) as a group variable and the coded variables (Variables A, B, and C) as "outcome" variables, and to perform a two-group linear discriminant analysis. Given that both ordinary least-squares regression and discriminant analysis are at present highly developed and their computer computations are most manageable, is there really anything to be gained by employing the log-linear methods of this book?

The answer to the question above is *yes*. Some of the reasons in support of the simple answer are, in turn, simple, while others are not; some are rooted in statistical theory, while others are rooted in application; and one argument even approaches the philosophical. We will entertain them in the order just suggested.

Arguments Based on Statistical Theory

Since the alternative analyses proposed above are parametric, by definition, certain assumptions are made about the distribution of variables in the population prior to mathematical development. Moreover, in practice, violations of these assumptions can lead to biased tests of statistical significance. Recall that *normality* and *homogeneity of variance* are two of the assumptions that are basic to univariate parametric testing, and multivariate normality and compound symmetry (equal variance-covariance matrices) are assumed to ensure the integrity of multivariate tests of significance. When the response variable is truly quali- tative, analysis of this response with either ordinary least-squares regression or discriminant analysis will likely contradict both of these basic assumptions.

For expository simplicity, consider a dichotomous response variable such as "pass" (coded as a 1) and "fail" (coded as a 0), and an explanatory variable such as Gender that also can be dummy coded readily. Mentally place these coded variables in a regression equation, or perceive the situation to be one where a t test will be performed on the dichotomous Pass-Fail variable. Both approaches are equivalent, and both assume that the dependent variable is dis- tributed normally in the population of females and males, and that the variances of the dependent variable for females and males are equal in these populations. Remember, however, in a logit-model analysis we want to know whether the profiles of *proportional* response are similar or different by gender. Therefore, in the current context, the basic assumptions are (1) that the proportion of 1's (passes) and 0's (failures) are normally distributed in each gender group, and (2) that the variance of proportional response to the Pass–Fail variable is equiv- alent over sex groups. The first assumption can be tenable only when the dis- tribution of 1's and 0's is about even, say a "50–50 split," within both the group of females and the group of males. The second assumption concerns within- group variance, which is a direct function of the distribution. If P stands for the proportion of 1's within a gender group, then the group's variance is equal to the product $P(1 - P)$. Therefore, only under a limited set of conditions will the assumption of equal variance be tenable.

If these were not enough, consider the related misapplication of discriminant analysis to the McLean study. The Graduation–Nongraduation variable (Variable D) would assume the status of the group or independent variable—yet in reality, it is a response variable. Accordingly, coded Variables A, B, and C, assume the status of response or dependent variables—yet in reality, they are explanatory variables. Moreover, to validly test for differences between the graduation and the nongraduation groups, the response measures (Variables A through C and their respective interactions) should be distributed as a multivariate normal dis- tribution within each group with equal dispersion (variance-covariance) matrices. This would be a tenable set of assumptions if Variables A through C were metric, but for reasons cited above, these assumptions are not tenable when the dependent variables in discriminant functions are distinctly qualitative.

In sum, to the extent to which response to the dichotomy deviates from an even distribution within groups, and to the extent to which response patterns are not similar within groups, both assumptions will be violated. To compound matters, in the presence of violations it is often difficult to determine the mag- nitude and direction of resultant bias in test statistics. As one would expect, the problem is magnified with an increase in the number of explanatory variables. Fortunately, a logit-model approach to the analysis is not dependent on the distributional assumptions of normality and homogeneity of variance.

There is still another fundamental problem that not only applies to ordinary least-squares but to weighted least-squares regression as well. As noted in Chapter 1, when regression procedures are used to solve for regression weights, which in turn are used in the equation to generate predicted values, the predicted values are proportions, but their range is unrestricted. It is theoretically possible, therefore, for the regression to fit cell proportions that are greater than unity or even proportions that are negative. Of course, there is nothing comparable in the reality of our subject matter, a reality where proportions find limits between zero and unity. Needless to say, unrestricted proportional estimates constitute a disturbing and unnecessary technical liability in the present context.

Arguments Based on Practice

Turning to points that are slightly more relevant to application, in comparison to its competitors, a logit-model analysis tends to fit observed data better, can be more powerful, is much easier to interpret when response is polytomous, and is relatively self-contained in that it possesses built-in follow-up devices. For readers of the preceding four chapters, few words need be written about the latter advantage, for repeatedly we have seen how estimates of effect parameters and focused comparisons can be used to assist in the explication of an omnibus result.

Closely tied to follow-up is the matter of substantive interpretability. The fact of the matter is that some statistical techniques are more readily understood, interpreted, and communicated in the language of the subject than are others. In general, it is fair to say that multivariate techniques have earned reputations for being difficult to interpret substantively, although strict mathematical interpretations are not difficult to make. Most prominent among multivariate procedures that are difficult to interpret is CVA. Granted, the significance of a canonical correlation coefficient is an indication that one or more effects is also significant, but remaining statistical outputs (e.g., canonical weights, structure coefficients, etc.) are more suited to the study of complex *relationships*, not effects. In short, a CVA is difficult to interpret in its own right, but even greater difficulties are encountered when an attempt is made to use this vehicle to study group difference.

Before matters of interpretability become a concern, effects must first be found to be significant, either statistically or practically. It may be remembered that in our discussion of maximum-likelihood (ML) estimation, it was mentioned that estimates obtained by ML procedures have somewhat smaller variances than comparable least-squares estimates (see Rao, 1965, Goodman, 1972b, Haber, 1985). Consequently, on average, ML procedures, and thus logit models, will be more efficient; they will give, on the average, smaller standard errors about effects. In the past it has been said that the loss of efficiency resulting from the use of least-squares regression was more than offset by the ease and availability of computational routines for regression (Grizzle, Starmer, and Koch, 1969), but the credibility of this argument has diminished as log-linear software became increasingly available during the last decade.

Another important advantage of logit models is that they tend to fit observed data better than their least-squares counterparts. That is, the differences between observed frequencies and the expected frequencies given by logit models tend to be relatively small. It should be conceded, however, that when observed proportions are all in the midrange, say between .25 and .75, differences in the numerical values of model parameters, and thus fit, are small. But as observed proportions in a table deviate from midrange values, the fit, and even the conclusions, can differ between types of models. Magidson (1978) compared several relevant unsaturated least-squares regression models with corresponding logit models within the context of a 2 × 2 × 2 table, and although there were no discrepancies in omnibus conclusions between model offerings, the logit models consistently were shown to fit data substantially better than the regression models. In short, logit models were more accurate representations of observed data. Magidson also illustrated several extreme situations in which the two approaches yielded different omnibus conclusions.

The Fundamental Argument

The strongest and best justification for the use of log-linear models in the general case and logit models in the asymmetrical case, however, is that these models are inherently compatible with the data at hand and the concepts that we use to understand those data. In the work described in this book, we have been primarily interested in proportional response. In both symmetrical and asymmetrical situations, ultimately, the question has been whether observed elementary cell proportions are similar to expected cell proportions given by a model that represents a hypothesis. Moreover, from Chapter 3 we know that proportional response and ML estimation go hand in hand, that ML estimates are both most efficient and sufficient estimators of population proportions. It follows, therefore, that ML estimation—not weighted or unweighted least-squares—is to be preferred when working with proportions in contingency tables.

There is more, however. Consider that throughout most of this book we have been dealing with formulations, and thinking with concepts, that are in their very nature multiplicative. Take, for example, a most basic concept such as *independence*. Independence, when used within the context of a contingency table, is a multiplicative formulation as evidenced by its definition in Equation 3.6 for two-way tables and Equation 5.5 for three-way tables. (Even the notion of a significant effect in the asymmetrical is multiplicative, for it represents a significant departure from proportions under the independence hypothesis.) Thus, it can be said that the majority of concepts with which we have been struggling are essentially multiplicative in origin, and we have been attempting to represent these concepts with models that are also essentially multiplicative: log-linear models. Granted, log-linear models are not multiplicative per se. But remember how we began our study of qualitative data. Because concepts were multiplicative, we initially couched our representations in multiplicative "terms" (so to speak). However, we found it easier to compute in the linear, and thus multiplicative factors were transformed to additive terms by taking the logs of the former. The point is this: Despite their appearance, log-linear models are fundamentally multiplicative and are true to the tables, data, and ideas that have occupied our attention over these many pages.

NOTES

1. Should the null-logit model be accepted, and should it also be found that for all practical purposes $\tau^{cd} = 0$, then not only can it be said that there are no differences in proportional response within $[CD]$ over levels of A, B, and so forth, but differences do not even exist if frequencies are inserted in the cells of the response table.

2. Since the L_s^2 produced by the fit of the symmetry model represents residual deviation from both symmetry and homogeneity of marginal distributions but the L_{qs}^2 produced by the model for quasi-symmetry represents only deviation from symmetry, a test on the hypothesis of homogeneity of marginal distributions is provided by $L_{hm}^2 = L_s^2 - L_{qs}^2$, where v for L_{hm}^2 is obtained by parallel subtraction. In the present example, $L_{hm}^2(3) = 3.56 - .33 = 3.32$, which falls short of significance at traditional levels. The marginals cannot be said to differ from pretest to posttest.

3. Goodman (1970) has even suggested that when fitting a saturated model to a table that does not present sampling zeros, it is still desirable to add 0.5 to observed frequencies, for this minor correction tends to reduce both the asymptotic bias and standard errors of lambda parameters in this particular model.

9

An Introduction to Configural
Frequency Analysis

Configural frequency analysis (CFA) is a taxonomical technique, introduced and developed by Krauth and Lienert (1973), that attempts to identify significant *configurations* (types and antitypes) in cross-classified data. For now, a configuration may be understood to be a variable description, namely a description of a group of subjects who respond in the same manner to two or more categorical variables. A configuration is identified by fitting a log-linear model and then performing a formal analysis of residuals about the expected cell frequencies given by that model. Subjects associated with an elementary cell that obviously is not well fit by a model comprise a configuration. Since typically not all subjects in a contingency table will belong to a configuration, CFA is a nonexhaustive clustering or taxonomical technique. CFA is basically a descriptive technique, but it possesses an inferential component in that significance testing is used to identify configurations.

As can be inferred, the objectives of CFA are different from those pursued in log-linear analyses. Whereas the objective in log-linear analyses is to identify *global relations* that explain observed data, in CFA the objective is to identify *local relations*—variable descriptions—peculiar to discernable groups.

To date, CFA has been described primarily in the psychological literature written in German, where it has largely been used to identify clinical syndromes and psychological types. A comprehensive treatment of CFA written in English, however, has recently been offered by von Eye (1990).[1] Since faithful readers of this text currently possess a knowledge of log-linear and residual analysis sufficient to appreciate CFA, devoting the final pages of this book to a brief description of this technique which, until recently, has not been disseminated widely, seems both timely and appropriate.

BASIC CONCEPTS AND NOMENCLATURE

We begin with an understanding that we are dealing exclusively with quali-tative data, that subjects have been cross-classified on the three or more cate-gorical variables. An underlying hypothesis will then be adopted, and a log-linear model representing the underlying hypothesis will be fitted to elementary cells of the contingency table.[2] Historically, underlying models were limited for the most part to models containing only terms for the main marginals (i.e., independence models), but modern analysts, as we shall see, are afforded greater flexibility in the choice of base models.

To keep things simple, let f denote the frequency observed in an elementary cell of a multidimensional table, and let F denote the frequency in that cell given by a log-linear model. The essential idea is to identify cells where the difference between an observed f is significantly different from its corresponding expected F. Thus, for all cells in an exploratory analysis, null hypotheses of the following nature:

$$H_0: F = f$$

are tested for statistical significance. Cells that are associated with significance constitute the basis for configurations. CFA is simply the identification and subsequent interpretation of configurations. Further, it should not come as a surprise that a major distinction is made between configurations where testing indicates that $F < f$, and configurations where $F > f$. The former, a configuration where the observed frequency exceeds the expected, is termed a *configural type*; the latter is termed a *configural antitype*. For reasons to be presented, we shall refer to these statistically discernable configurations as *statistical types* and *statistical antitypes*, respectively.

Statistical Types and Antitypes

Statistical Types (ST). In years past when the independence model was used almost exclusively to generate Fs, the conceptual definition of a configural type was "a multivariate class of qualities that occur more often together than may be expected by chance from the proportions of the respective qualities under the assumption of their independence" (Lienert & Krauth, 1975, 231). Today, we need not restrict our definition of type to occurrences beyond the assumption of independence. A type may be described more broadly as a group of subjects that share a common variable profile, or variable state, where members of this variable state are observed in greater numbers than would be expected under an assumption embodied by a log-linear model.

By way of example, suppose that several hundred patients in a psychiatric hospital were cross-classified on the basis of three dichotomous variables: Hys-teria (yes/no), Depression (yes/no), and Assertiveness (yes/no). Suppose further that Model 4, the independence model, was fit, and an elementary cell characterized by Hysteria-No, Depression-Yes, and Assertiveness-No (i.e., NYN) was found to contain significantly more patients than would be expected under the hypothesis of mutual independence. Since these patients share the same pattern of symptoms and the occurrence of this pattern exceeds chance expectation, a configural type has been identified.

Though the definition of a configural type in the CFA literature is statistically pleasing, notice that it embodies two conditions, and that one of these conditions need not be a requisite of the type construct as it is used in many areas in the social sciences. Granted, the notion that a type is indicative of individuals who share a common descriptive profile or pattern of response with respect to multiple variables is consistent with most conceptions of "type." But the second defining condition, the quantitative dimension whereby a type also is defined as a variable state in which there are more members than would be expected under some specified expectation, is not a necessary condition of type in all usage contexts. Personality theorists in psychology, for example, frequently employ a notion of type that is independent of the relative number of individuals who may be described as such. Hence, to communicate more clearly to readers of this text that a type in CFA also implies marked frequency of membership in excess of expectation, the qualifying adjective *statistical* will be used in conjunction with the type construct (and the term *antitype*), along with the suggestion that this adjective (or a similar one) be used in discussions of CFA beyond the pale of this manuscript. Finally, for reasons of economy, *statistical type* will be abbreviated ST on the pages that follow.

Statistical Antitypes (SATs). A statistical antitype is a variable state where there are fewer cases than would be expected under some assumption or hypothesis. Suppose in the psychiatric hospital of the previous example that it was found that the configuration Hysteria-Yes, Depression-Yes, and Assertiveness-Yes (i.e., *YYY*) contained fewer patients than would be expected by chance. The label *antitype* would be applied to this uncommon variable profile. For the reasons cited, we will call such a variable state a *statistical antitype*, abbreviated SAT.

Identifying Staistical Types and Antitypes

Numerous procedures have been advanced to determine whether cellular differences between Fs and fs are statistically different. If cell frequencies are small, for example, the exact binomial test, discussed in Chapter 2 (Equation 2.5), can be performed on all cells. Though exact, the binomial test is relatively conservative, and because it involves the calculation of $n!$ (n factorial), as cell frequencies become large, hand calculations become exceedingly tedious and many computer calculations become inexact. A computational alternative to the exact binomial that is purported to be useful in small sample situations uses Lehmacher's asymptotic hypergeometric test (Lehmacher, 1981), but unfortunately its use is limited to expected frequencies produced by the model of mutual independence.

For applications where the size of the sample is sufficiently large to ensure that expected cell frequencies are greater than five, two testing procedures are prominently mentioned. The first is the standard-normal approximation to the one-sample binomial. For a given cell in a table of total size n, with observed frequency f (hence, $p_1 = f/n$) and expected frequency F (hence, $P_1 = F/n$), the hypotheses are

$H_0: P_1 = F/n$

$H_a: P_1 \neq F/n$

Recalling our earlier discussions of the z test approximation to the binomial, we can extend previously cited Equation 2.6 as shown.

$$z = \frac{p_1 - P_1}{(P_1 P_2/n)^{1/2}} = \frac{np_1 - nP_1}{(n^2 P_1 P_2/n)^{1/2}} = \frac{f - F}{(F P_2)^{1/2}} \tag{9.1}$$

where, as before, $P_2 = 1 - P_1$. The z statistic can be used to assess the probability that a cell, with observed frequency f (or observed proportion $p_1 = f/n$), emanated from a binomial population with parameter $P_1 = F/n$.

The z score approximation of Equation 9.1 is most appropriate in large sample situations, where the *rule of five*, mentioned in Chapter 2, is satisfied. Because this rule is often not satisfied in CFA, serious consideration is given to z that is *corrected for continuity*, much like the correction for continuity suggested by Yates (1934), which is often applied to the ordinary chi-square statistic when it is computed on fourfold tables (Hays, 1988, 774). Here, the correction is affected by subtracting 0.5 from positive residuals and adding 0.5 to negative residuals. That is, corrected residuals are:

$CR = f - F - 0.5 \quad \text{if } f > F$

$CR = f - F + 0.5 \quad \text{if } f < F$

Whereas there is disagreement as to the utility of correcting for continuity when the purpose is to improve approximations to the exact chi-square distribution, the present correction does improve approximations to the exact binomial distribution, which is our reference distribution. The corrected z statistic is

$$z_c = \frac{CR}{(F P_2)^{1/2}} \tag{9.2}$$

Note that the two-tailed version of either Equation 9.1 or Equation 9.2 may be expressed as a single-*df* chi-square. The latter, for example, may be expressed as

$$\chi^2 = z^2 = \frac{CR^2}{F\,P_2} \tag{9.3}$$

The *z* statistics of Equations 9.1 or 9.2 are somewhat more useful than the chi-squares of Equation 9.3 simply because *z* tables generally present a wider range of critical *p* values than do chi-square tables. In any event, rejection of the null hypothesis with either the *z* or corrected *z* statistic, or their respective chi-square equivalents, is indicative of an ST if $f > F$, or an SAT if $f < F$.

An alternative to the one-sample binomial approximation, termed "the chi-square approximation," also has been proposed (Lienert & Krauth, 1975; von Eye, 1990, 24). This single-*df* alternative is

$$\chi^2 = \frac{(f - F)^2}{F} \tag{9.4}$$

We recognize Equation 9.4 as the contribution made by an individual cell to the Pearsonian chi-square for the entire table. Additionally, we know that the square root of Equation 9.4 defines a *standardized residual* (SR), discussed in connection with Equation 3.12, which, under optimal conditions, is distributed roughly as a *z* statistic.

Equation 9.4 is appealing because it is easy to compute and its counterpart, the SR, is provided by most computer programs. Despite their appeal, several factors militate against exclusive reliance on chi-square approximations or SRs in CFA. The χ^2's given by Equation 9.4 do not approximate directly the exact one-sample binomial—nor, for that matter, the two-sample binomial—and, when compared to the chi-square given by Equation 9.3, an examination of respective denominators reveals that when numerators are constant, the approximate χ^2's of Equation 9.4 are always less powerful than those associated with Equation 9.3. In fact, the χ^2's of Equation 9.3 become increasingly more powerful as F becomes large. More problematic in theory, however, is that the approximate chi-squares of Equation 9.4 are not equally sensitive, in a symmetrical sense, to given effects about the quantity: $F = n/2$. Moreover, for a given numeric value of $(f - F)^2$, the magnitude of χ^2 decreases monotonically as F increases. In sum, other than its use as a conservative screening procedure on cells where the F is not large—say $F < (n/5)$—the use of Equation 9.4 to identify STs and SATs in CFA should be discouraged. Obviously, this reproach applies equally to standardized residuals when put to similar use.

On the other hand, when requisite conditions are satisfied, there is much to recommend the use of approximations to the exact binomial, particularly the use of the corrected approximation given by Equation 9.2 or its chi-square equivalent. If, however, many cells are encountered where $F < 5$, two suggestions are offered. First, if the suspect cells are not substantively important, simply exclude them as viable candidates for an ST or SAT. Alternately, if they are deemed important, subject these cells to an exact binomial test as directed by Equation 2.5. Because of the limited number of times that the exact binomial will need to be computed, and because the small F will limit the number of specific probabilities that will need to be computed, this task is not as formidable as it might first appear.

Problems Associated with Simultaneous Testing

Having selected the corrected z of Equation 9.2 as our test of choice, and realizing that in an exploratory CFA it will be performed as many times as there are cells, the issue of Type I error inflation must be addressed. Consider the simple example of a $2 \times 2 \times 2$ table where, if eight tests are performed *independently* at the .05 level, the experimentwise error rate would be

$$\alpha_{EW} = 1 - (1 - \alpha)^8$$
$$= 1 - .95^8$$
$$= .337$$

The problem is twofold. First, the resultant experimentwise error rate is disturbing, particularly if the CFA is exploratory. Second, the contention that each test is independently determined is not tenable in CFA because a large positive effect $(f - F)$ in one cell implies smaller, or negative, effects in other cells. Though the related problems of alpha inflation and mutual dependencies are frequently overlooked when repeated omnibus tests are conducted in the ANOVA and in log-linear work, due to the potential severity of the problem and the finality of ST/SAT testing, these problems should not be ignored in CFA. Admittedly, these concerns are not as pronounced when a CFA is conducted to confirm STs or SATs that have been predicted in advance by strong theory, but to the extent to which the CFA departs from a confirmatory analysis, acknowledgment of, and compensation for, "runaway alpha" is required. In addition to intelligent data preparation and variable selection, additional measures must be taken to exercise control over the commission of excessive Type I errors during two phases of an exploratory investigation.

We will conduct a CFA in three distinct phases, the first two of which afford opportunities to exercise control over runaway alpha. Phase one will consist of assessing the fit of all relevant kth-order log-linear models, much as was done earlier as a screening procedure prior to the selection of a general log-linear model. One of the functions served by the kth-order analysis in CFA will be to minimize the possibilities of committing Type I errors. Suppose that an intended *global-model CFA* (to be discussed) involved three variables. At the outset, at least two kth-order log-linear models will be fit and evaluated: Model 4, the independence model, and Model 7, the full two-variable model. Should, for example, the fit of the independence model prove to be reasonably good such that its residual chi-square is *not* statistically significant, then the residuum about this model's expectancies is not sufficiently substantial to warrant further investigation and the increased risk of committing Type I errors.

Should the results of the kth-order analysis suggest that variable relations are present, then the CFA proper will be performed. In this second phase, the problem of alpha control can treated directly by employing the well-established Bonferroni procedure, or, better, the modified Bonferroni procedure proposed by Holm (1979) which was illustrated in Chapter 6 in connection with assessing multiple focused comparisons.

Recall that if there are eight elementary cells, and hence, eight z tests to be performed, and the desired experimentwise alpha has been established at .05, then the most prominent test statistic would need to achieve an outcome p value of .05/8 (or less) to be deemed statistically significant; the next most prominent statistic would need a p value of .05/7 to achieve significance, and so on. But then it is recognized that adjustments resulting from the use of the Bonferroni or Holm's procedure often prove to be too conservative in actual practice. To evoke an analogy, the situation is similar to that encountered in the ANOVA when significance, at, say, the .05 level, is observed at the omnibus level, but the execution of specific comparisons using extremely conservative Scheffé tests fails to document significant effects at the .05 level. In such situations, many investigators will follow the advice offered by Scheffé and employ the .10 level as the criterion to be achieved for significance (Scheffé, 1959, 71). This suggestion merits serious consideration with respect to the application of the Bonferroni or Holm procedures in CFA.

Types of CFA

The reader is asked to bear with our prefatory discussions a bit longer so that a number of the distinct applications of CFA can be surveyed.[3] The outline that follows cites the more salient CFA approaches, and it will suffice for our purposes. It reveals that there are two distinct classes of CFA: CFAs based on a *global* underlying log-linear models, and CFAs based on what are termed *regional* log-linear models.

Selected Types of Configural Frequency Analyses Based On:

Global Models	Regional Models
Zero-order CFA	Interaction Structure Analysis (ISA)
First-order CFA	Predictive CFA (PCFA)
Second-order CFA	Logit-Model CFA (LMCFA)
Third-order CFA, etc.	

Global-Model CFA. Global models are general log-linear models applied to all variables with no attempt to group variables into functional sets, such as a grouping of variables into a set designated as predictors and a set designated as criterion. All variables, therefore, are undifferentiated response variables, as is the case when log-linear inquiry is symmetrical. Incidentally, there is a penchant in CFA to fit global models that are amenable to clear-cut interpretations. For a three-dimensional table, for example, preferred models are *k*th-order models. As defined in Chapter 4, these models are (1) Model 1, the completely null model; (2) Model 4, the independence model; and (3) Model 7, the full bivariate interaction model.

The adoption of a preferred underlying log-linear model further designates a hierarchy of global-model analyses. Adoption of Model 1 specifies a *zero-order CFA*, an omnibus analysis in which identified configurations can be attributed to either main effects or interactions. Adoption of Model 4 lends itself to a *first-order CFA*, the "classical" version of CFA, in which significant configurations can be attributed to variable interactions. Fitting Model 7 is indicative of a *second-order CFA*, in which identified configurations are due to second-order variable interactions. If the contingency table were of four dimensions, in addition to zero, first-, and second-order analyses, it would be possible to conduct a *third-order analysis*, thus presenting the possibility of observing configurations described uniquely in terms of four variables. Our first concrete example will be a classical first-order CFA.

Regional-Model CFA. If variables are differentiated, then underlying log-linear models are called regional models. In a sense, regional models are not new. The asymmetrical log-linear models examined in previous chapters may be called regional models because variables were clearly designated as being either explanatory or response. However, in CFA, regional modeling conveys a more general understanding: the application of models to variables that have been divided into two sets. Variable differentiation gives rise to a number of specific variants of CFA, principal among them being *interaction structure analysis* (ISA) and *predictive CFA* (PCFA).

The former, ISA, is essentially a symmetrical analysis. In general, variables are grouped into two variable sets, say Set 1 and Set 2. Consider momentarily four variables labeled *A, B, C,* and *D*. Now organize these variables into sets as is suggested next:

Set 1
Variables *A* and *B*

Set 2
Variables *C* and *D*

The objective of an ISA is the identification of configurations based on symmetrical relations *between* sets, excluding relations *within* sets. To accomplish this objective, an underlying regional model is specified, containing within-set interactions (e.g., *AB*) but excludes between-set interactions (e.g., *AC*). The model that would be fit in the example above would be

$$\ln F_{ijk} = \lambda + \lambda_i^a + \lambda_j^b + \lambda_{ij}^{ab} + \lambda_k^c + \lambda_m^d + \lambda_{km}^{cd}$$

If Set 1 contained personality variables while Set 2 contained demographic variables, then statistically, discernable configuration would be elementary cells whose observed membership was greater than, or less then, that expected under the underlying model. Resultant STs or SATs would be comprised of subjects who share the same response configuration with respect to at least one personality variable and one demographic variable. All things considered, ISA would appear to be of interest primarily to investigators of social theory.

Predictive CFA (PCFA), though similar, differs from ISA in that relations between sets are perceived to be directional. One variable set is explicitly deemed the predictor set, and the other set is viewed as a criterion or response set. The objective is to determine whether predictor variable states can explain, and hence predict, criterion variable states. The regional model is the same as that presented above for ISA; therefore, if strong relations exist between predictor and criterion variables, STs or SATs predicated on response similarity to at least one predictor and one criterion variable are likely to materialize.

There is a variant of PCFA that deserves particular attention. It is used where there are multiple variables in the predictor or explanatory set but only one variable in the response set. In a four-variable context, for example, we could have

Set 1: Explanatory
Variables *A* and *B* and *C*

Set 2: Response
Variable *D*

Unlike either ISA or PCFA, however, the most appropriate underlying model, at least initially, will likely be

$$\ln F_{ijk} = \lambda + \lambda_i^a + \lambda_j^b + \lambda_k^c + \lambda_m^d + \lambda_{ij}^{ab} + \lambda_{ik}^{ac} + \lambda_{jk}^{bc} + \lambda_{ijk}^{abc}$$

which we recognize as the null-logit model for four-dimensional tables (see Chapter 7). Because of its linkage to logit-model analyses, we have taken the liberty to call this variant *logit-model CFA*, or LMCFA for short.

LMCFA would appear to be especially useful in marketing research and related fields where categorical variables abound and the identification of consumer profiles or target audiences is often of interest. Cells that deviate significantly from the expectancies of a logit-model contain subjects who have provided a common response to the outcome variable (e.g., satisfied, not satisfied, or undecided) and share a common explanatory variable profile (e.g., similar demographics). An example of an LMCFA also will be presented in this chapter.

A GLOBAL MODEL EXAMPLE

A reanalysis of psychopathology data offered by Lienert and Krauth (1975) has been chosen as our first illustration. Data were obtained from 65 volunteer subjects who were under the influence of lysergic acid diethylamide (LSD) and who were evaluated with respect to the following symptoms:

H:	hallucinations	(Y = yes/N = no)
B:	blackouts	(Y = yes/N = no)
T:	thinking disturbances	(Y = yes/N = no)
A:	affective reactions	(Y = yes/N = no)

Observed elementary cell frequencies may be viewed by skipping ahead to Table 9.2, where they are displayed in the "f" column.

Lienert and Krauth's psychopathology data are of interest in a number of respects. To start, the analysis of these data constitute the earliest account of a CFA described in the English language. Also, the tabular n ($n = 65$) was relatively small, and the table contained three zero cell frequencies, assumed to be due to the small sample. The sparse table will challenge the methodology of CFA. Finally, the CFA of these data (in phase 2 of our analysis) is typical of many of the published reports of global-model CFAs to date.

Our analysis will be more extensive than that which is typically reported. As mentioned, it will be performed in three phases:

Phase 1. A kth-order log-linear analysis similar to that applied to McLean's data (see Table 7.2) will be performed first.

Phase 2. The CFA proper that will attempt to identify STs and SATs by testing intracell discrepancies will be performed next.

Phase 3. Finally, the evaluation of selected log-linear models for the purpose of identifying variable relations that give rise to identified STs or SATs will complete the analysis.

Justification for performing exploratory CFAs along these lines will be offered during the three-phase analysis.

The Initial kth-Order Analysis

Five hierarchical models were fit to observed data. They were: Model 1, the completely null model which used only the tabular n to generate expected cell frequencies; Model 5, the independence model which used the four main mar-

Table 9.1
Fit of Global kth-Order Models to the Lienert-Krauth Psychopathology Data

kth-Order Model*	Residual			Component		
	L^2	df	p	L^2	df	p
(1)	49.878	15	.000			
(5)	41.312	11	.000	8.566	4	.073
(11)	37.288	5	.000	4.024	6	.673
(15)	0.065	1	.799	37.223	4	.000
(16)	0.000	0	1.000	0.065	1	.799

*Models are defined by number in Table 7.1.
Note: A delta value of 0.5 was added to observed frequencies to accommodate zero cell frequencies.

ginals; Model 11, which used the six two-variable marginals; Model 15, which used the four three-variable marginals; and Model 16, the saturated model. To accommodate the zero cell frequencies, a delta value of 0.5 was added to all cell frequencies prior to model fitting. The kth-order analysis is summarized in Table 9.1.

Although not yet a common practice, there are at least three reasons to support the performance of a kth-order analysis prior to an exploratory CFA. First, the fitting of kth-order models provides the analyst with the expected cell frequencies that are needed to conduct first-, second-, and third-order CFAs, and so forth. Second, as noted, a kth-order analysis yields comprehensive tests of classes of effects (e.g., all second-order effects) that can be used as a means of protection against the excessive commission of Type I errors. Finally, the analysis can be used to identify tentatively the order of variable relations that underlie STs and SATs, and thereby the number of *structural* variables that characterize them.

With respect to the latter, the number of underlying structural variables, consider that whereas subjects belonging to ST manifest a common response profile over all examined variables, often it is a response to a subset of examined variables that caused them to deviate as a group from the expectancies of an underlying model. The "causal" variables in such a subset will be termed *structural variables*. By way of illustration, suppose in addition to the residual fit of $L^2(11) = 41.31$ for Model 5 in Table 9.1, it happened that the fit of Model 11 was found to be $L^2(5) = 40.00$. With this information it can be said that the residuum about the independence model can be explained by either global third-order (three-variable) or fourth-order relations. But suppose that further examination revealed that the chi-square for Model 15 was $L^2(1) = 1.31$, $p < .252$, a revelation that would permit us to deduce that the residuum about the independence model is due to global third-order relations. Finally, assume that as a result of the third phase of our CFA (to be described) that we are able to attribute the residuum solely to third-order relations among Variables B, T, and A, and that during the *CFA* proper, we identified the following four STs.

H B T A	H B T A
- - - -	- - - -
Y Y Y Y	Y N Y Y
N Y Y Y	N N Y Y

The two STs on the left are distinctly different from the two STs on the right with respect to three underlying structural variables (*BTA*). If we collapse the table over the first variable (Variable *H*), which can be done here without a loss of data explanation, and proceeded to fit the full two-variable model to data in the collapsed $B \times T \times A$ table, we still would expect to be able to define the *YYY* and *NYY* configurations as STs. On the other hand, whereas the two STs within each set appear to manifest different response profiles (e.g., *YYYY* vs. *NYYY* on the left, *YNYY* vs. *NNYY* on the right), they do so because they have been identified as discrepant from the underlying model, because of their response to Variables B, T, and A. They have not been identified because of their response to Variable H. If, in a marketing study where the intent is to identify audiences with positive affective reactions (A = Yes), response patterns to Variables B and T are important, but the response of subjects to Variable H need not be considered as important.

Returning to Table 9.1 and the kth-order analysis of the Lienert-Krauth data, the conduct of a first-order CFA is justified due to the inability of the independence model to explain observed data well, $L^2(5) = 41.31$, $p < .000$. Moreover, the relatively substantial component chi-square associated with Model 15, $L^2(4) = 37.22$, $p < .000$, suggests that in the third phase of our analysis, one or more third-order relations will be identified that will explain most of the residuum about Model 5. Finally, note that significance was achieved for the residual chi-square produced by Model 11, $L^2(5) = 37.29$, an outcome that also will prompt us to conduct a second-order CFA.

The First-Order CFA

Here, respective cell residuals are tested for statistical significance. For the reader's consideration, three testing procedures are displayed in Table 9.2: exact binomials, nominal z-score approximations to the binomial from Equation 9.2, and corrected z-score approximations from Equation 9.3.[4] Since at this writing computer programs dedicated to the performance of CFAs were not readily available, the calculation of statistics shown in Table 9.2 was performed on an ad hoc SAS program which is offered for general use and which appears in Appendix A. It can be seen that even for this sparse table, the z statistic, particularly the corrected z statistic, provided a good approximation to the exact binomial.

Locate in Table 9.2 the first configuration, the YYYY configuration. Note

Table 9.2
Global First-Order CFA of Lienert-Krauth Psychopathology Data

Cell H B T A	Frequencies f	F	Exact Binomial*	Normal Approx. z	p	Corrected Approx. z_c	p
Y Y Y Y	12	5.00	.00369	3.258	.00056	3.026	.00124
Y Y Y N	0	2.74	.06085	-1.691	.04539	-1.383	.08338
Y Y N Y	1	4.56	.05222	-1.729	.04192	-1.486	.06863
Y Y N N	4	2.50	.24028	0.968	.16665	0.645	.25947
Y N Y Y	1	3.79	.10120	-1.477	.06986	-1.212	.11273
Y N Y N	3	2.07	.34255	0.657	.25561	0.304	.38066
Y N N Y	5	3.45	.26225	0.858	.19557	0.581	.28064
Y N N N	0	1.89	.14690	-1.395	.08148	-1.026	.15242
N Y Y Y	8	7.50	.47981	0.194	.42304	0.000	.50000
N Y Y N	1	4.11	.07718	-1.585	.05649	-1.332	.09173
N Y N Y	3	6.84	.07880	-1.552	.06031	-1.350	.08849
N Y N N	8	3.75	.03301	2.261	.01188	1.995	.02303
N N Y Y	2	5.68	.06896	-1.616	.05301	-1.397	.08125
N N Y N	7	3.11	.03544	2.261	.01189	1.970	.02442
N N N Y	10	5.18	.03242	2.208	.01364	1.979	.02393
N N N N	0	2.84	.05481	-1.723	.04242	-1.420	.07782

*Critical centile values are upper-tail values when $f > F$ and lower-tail when $f < F$.

that after determining P_2, which for this cell is $P_2 = 1 - P_1 = 1 - (5/65) = .9231$, the corrected z was computed as

$$
\begin{aligned}
z_c &= \frac{CR}{(F \, P_2)^{1/2}} \\
&= \frac{12 - 5 - 0.5}{[(5)(.9231)]^{1/2}} \\
&= \frac{6.5}{(4.6154)^{1/2}} \\
&= 3.026, \; p < .00124
\end{aligned}
$$

Recall that the comprehensive test performed in Phase 1 was manifestly significant, i.e., $L^2(11) = 41.31, p < .000$. This outcome prompts us to execute the Holm's procedure at the experimentwise .10 level of significance. And since the z statistic for configuration YYYY was most prominent, $p < .00124$, statistical significance can be claimed using the criterion p value of $.10/16 = .00625$. In sum, the YYYY configuration constitutes an ST. Incidentally, the next most prominent configuration, NNNY, did not produce a statistic whose p value was less than $.10/15 = .00667$. If a conservative posture is assumed, NNNY will not be advanced as an ST.

Returning to YYYY, the detected ST, the interpretation offered by Lienert and Krauth was, "The syndrome defined by hallucinations, blackouts, thinking disturbances and affective reactions may be fairly interpreted as the 'psychotoxic basis syndrome' described . . . as [and is] characteristic for LSD reaction in normal Ss [subjects] and neurotic patients" (1975, 235).

The Second-Order CFA

The poorness-of-fit exhibited by the full two-variable model, Model 11, prompted a second-order analysis of the psychopathology data. Whereas the first-order CFA identified configurations based on structural relations between two or more variables, the second-order analysis has the potential of being able to identify configurations based on similarity of response to three or more variables. To perform the second-order analysis, expected cell frequencies provided by Model 11 served as parameters and respective expected-observed residuals were tested to determine whether observed frequencies were significantly discrepant from their expected frequencies. The results of the intracell testing are shown in Table 9.3.

At the nominal comparisonwise .05 level, two configurations were observed:

N N N N, $p < .00786$

N N Y N, $p < .02906$

Table 9.3
Global Second-Order CFA of Lienert-Krauth Psychopathology Data

Cell				Frequencies		Exact	Corrected z		Holm's
H	B	T	A	f	F	Binomial*	z	p	p (.10)
Y	Y	Y	Y	12	8.11	.10539	1.272	.10161	
Y	Y	Y	N	0	2.84	.05481	-1.420	.07782	
Y	Y	N	Y	1	4.24	.06902	-1.376	.08436	
Y	Y	N	N	4	1.81	.10758	1.274	.10133	
Y	N	Y	Y	1	3.82	.09869	-1.224	.11057	
Y	N	Y	N	3	1.23	.12544	1.156	.12382	
Y	N	N	Y	5	2.83	.15285	1.015	.15504	
Y	N	N	N	0	1.12	.32311	-1.591	.27727	
N	Y	Y	Y	8	6.10	.26343	0.596	.27576	
N	Y	Y	N	1	3.96	.08770	-1.794	.10104	
N	Y	N	Y	3	5.55	.18363	-0.910	.18144	
N	Y	N	N	8	4.40	.07149	1.531	.06294	
N	N	Y	Y	2	4.97	.11729	-1.153	.12448	
N	N	Y	N	7	2.98	.02906	2.088	.01842	.00667
N	N	N	Y	10	6.38	.10138	1.301	.09668	
N	N	N	N	0	4.67	.00786	-2.003	.02260	.00625

*Critical centile values are upper-tail values when $f > F$ and lower-tail values when $f < F$.

Configuration NNNN exemplifies an antitype, a variable state in which fewer subjects exhibited this particular pattern of symptom designation than would be expected by chance. When assessed against Holm's experimentwise criterion, however, this apparent antitype fell just short of satisfying the criterion of $p = .00625$. Apparent type NNYN clearly failed to achieve significance beyond the criterion of $p = .00667$. Therefore, even though discernable configurations unique to three variables are insinuated, the limited size of the table ($n = 65$) did not provide the CFA with power sufficient to document them with authority.

Before we leave Table 9.2, consider what happened to the YYYY configuration during the second-order CFA. Certified as an ST in the first-order CFA, it was not found to be an ST ($p < .10539$) in the sequel. In the absence of knowledge concerning the structural relations that underlie first- and second-order results,

Table 9.4
Fit of Selected Log-Linear Models Applied to Assess the Underlying Structure of Second-Order Configurations

Model	Residual*			Component		
No.	L^2	df	p	L^2	df	p
(5)	41.312	11	.000			
(11)	37.288	5	.000	4.024	6	.673
(12)	36.175	4	.000	1.113	1	.291
(13)	35.667	3	.000	.508	1	.476
(14)	34.532	2	.000	1.135	1	.287
(15)	0.065	1	.799	34.467	1	.000
(16)	0.000	0	1.000	0.065	1	.799

Note: Models are defined by number in Table 7.1.
*A delta value of 0.5 was employed to accommodate a zero frequency in the reduced $B \times T \times A$ table.

knowledge that will be provided in phase 3, at this point it appears that the YYYY type identified in the classical CFA was due to the aggregate influences of first- and second-order relationships, but when first-order relations were removed, it was no longer evident that subjects who were judged to have manifested all four symptoms were distinctly different from subjects in any one of the remaining 15 configurations with respect to more than two symptom designations.

Following Up the CFA

The third phase is designed to uncover the structural relationships that explain the residuum about the underlying model so that a more complete understanding of STs and SATs might be gained. Since the kth-order analysis revealed that the residuum about the independence model most likely was attributable to one or more second-order relations, let us focus attention on the second-order CFA through which we will attempt to illuminate these results. To begin, in addition to the independence and the full two-variable models, all three-variable models (specified in Table 7.1) were fit and assessed. Results are found in Table 9.4, where it is observed that the residuum about underlying models can be attributed almost solely to second-order relations among Variables B, T, and A.

Upon examination of residuals and lambda estimates (not shown) associated with Model 15, the second-order BTA association is amenable to a number of verbal interpretations. It can be said, for example, that subjects who experienced blackouts also tended either to experience thinking or affective disorders, or to experience neither thinking or affective disorders. In contrast, subjects who did not experience blackouts tended to experience only one of the remaining two

Table 9.5
Global Second-Order CFA of Lienert-Krauth Psychopathology Data on Reduced $B \times T \times A$ Table

Cell	Frequencies		Corrected z		Holm's	ST /
B T A	f	F	z	p	p (.10)	SAT
Y Y Y	20	14.2	1.591	.05581		
Y Y N	1	6.8	-2.148	.01586	.02000	SAT
Y N Y	4	9.8	-1.837	.03309		
Y N N	12	6.2	2.238	.01261	.01667	ST
N Y Y	3	8.8	-1.921	.02734	.02500	
N Y N	10	4.2	2.674	.00375	.01250	ST
N N Y	15	9.2	1.886	.02965		
N N N	0	5.8	-2.306	.01056	.01429	SAT

Note: Expected frequencies were given by the full two-variable model subsequent to employing a delta value of 0.01.

symptoms—either they showed thinking disturbances but not affective reactions or they showed affective reactions but not thinking disturbances.

In any event, it is clear that the *BTA* association was the genesis of the STs and SATs that have been identified or suggested in the first- and second-order CFAs, respectively. It is also clear that the types and antitypes suggested by the second-order analysis possess a three-variable structure; they are determined by specific response patterns to Variables *B*, *T*, and *A*, whereas a specific response to Variable *H* is of minor consequence. Therefore, we can collapse the table over Variable *H* without prejudice and perform a second-order CFA on the reduced $B \times T \times A$ table. This reduced CFA can be expected to clarify still further the structure in these data.

To this end, the full two-variable model (*BT, BA, TA*) was fit to the $2 \times 2 \times 2$ table and, as expected, it did not fit the tabular data well, $L^2(1) = 39.284$, $p < .000.$[5] Expectancies from this underlying model were used in the reduced second-order CFA, reported in Table 9.5, where four statistically discernable configurations emerged. Two of the configurations were STs: NYN ($p < .00375$) and YNN ($p < .01261$). Apparently, a significant number of subjects who take LSD either exhibit only thinking disturbances or only blackouts. Strong evidence of types who concurrently exhibit more than one symptom has not been provided by this analysis. The remaining two configurations were SATs: YYY ($p < .01056$) and YYN ($p < .01586$). For all practical purposes, subjects under the influence of LSD who fail to manifest at least one symptom are nonexistent, and subjects who both have blackouts and show disturbed thinking but do not manifest adverse affective reactions are rare. Before leaving this example, be reminded that our intent here was not to offer a substantive revision of Lienert and Krauth's analysis, but rather to demonstrate the potential of CFA when combined with log-linear methods to affect relatively exhaustive analyses of contingency table data.

AN ASYMMETRICAL EXAMPLE

When one of the variables is a response variable, selected features of logit-model analyses may be employed to produce a variant of CFA that we called logit-model CFA (LMCFA).

An LMCFA could be useful, for example, in a marketing survey where, in addition to demographic information, subjects indicated whether they plan in the near future to purchase a certain product, say a personal computer. Assume that indicated response is trichotomous: "yes," "no," or "not sure." Assume further that demographic variables of interest are categories of family income, family composition, and whether the family currently possesses a personal computer. Granted, a logit-model analysis could be performed to identify specific descriptive variables that discriminate between the three types of respondents, but in this situation it might be just as important to generate descriptive profiles of families that will likely purchase a computer and families that likely will not. That is, to mount a successful marketing campaign, it would be advantageous to be able to generate a description of family types in terms of income, composition, and current ownership, *where response constitutes a structurally critical variable in the description.*

LMCFA is designed to provide such a description. Logit-model log-linear analysis, on the other hand, is designed to identify descriptive variables that separate or discriminate among the three types of respondents. Arguments pertaining to the relative merits of LMCFA and logit-model analysis would be pedantic here, for, as will be shown, the orchestrated use of both techniques will achieve optimum results.

Chosen for illustration was a study (Kaye, Sears & Kennedy, 1990) of 4,483 freshman and sophomore students at a large Midwestern university who indicated serious interest in entering teaching as a career as evidenced by their participation in an early experience program designed to acquaint incipient teachers with "the realities of the teaching profession." Students in this program were administered the Myers Briggs Type Indicator (MBTI), an established personality instrument described earlier in connection with the analysis of five-dimensional tables. Recall from Chapter 7 that the MBTI permits dichotomous classification on the following four personality variables:

A: *Extroversion (E) or Introversion (I)*
A_1 = classified as an E (f_1^a = 3,002)
A_2 = classified as an I (f_2^a = 1,481)

B: *Intuition (N) or Sensing (S)*
B_1 = classified as an N (f_1^b = 1,703)
B_2 = classified as an S (f_2^b = 2,780)

C: *Thinking (T) or Feeling (F)*
C_1 = classified as an T (f_1^c = 979)
C_2 = classified as an F (f_2^c = 3,504)

D: *Judging (J) or Perceiving (P)*
D_1 = classified as a J (f_1^d = 2,622)
D_2 = classified as a P (f_2^d = 1,861)

Upon participation in the introductory program, students elect to continue their preparation to teach by eventually obtaining a degree in education, or they elect to pursue other interests.

The intent of the study was to determine whether students who maintained their interest in teaching, as evidenced by the completion of an educational degree, and whether students who did not maintain this interest, as suggested by their failure to obtain such a degree, could be identified in terms of distinctive MBTI personality types. Accordingly, at least five years subsequent to participating in the early experience program, students who completed a teaching degree and students who did not complete a degree that would certify them to teach were identified. The obvious response variable in this study was

E: *Completed (Y) or Did Not Complete (N) a Degree in Education*
E_1 = completed an educational degree (f_1^e = 1,281)
E_2 = did not complete an educational degree (f_2^e = 3,202)

Subjects were cross-classified on the basis of the four MBTI variables and a response variable (Variable E) to form a $2 \times 2 \times 2 \times 2 \times 2$ table. Observed frequencies will be presented later in Table 9.7.

The analysis again will be conducted in three phases. First, a screening analysis similar in intent to the kth-order analysis that precedes a global-model CFA will be conducted. Second, the LMCFA proper will be performed. As we shall see, the LMCFA will differ from a global-model CFA in that resultant types and antitypes can be attributed to relations that directly involve the response variable. The third phase, if needed, will consist of fitting selected log-linear models for the purpose of detecting specific relations that underlie documented STs and SATs.

The Initial Screening Analysis

This analysis will help us determine whether a CFA can be conducted without incurring excessive Type I errors, and it may help us gain insight into the order of relations (i.e., first-order, second-order, etc.) that underlie STs and SATs, should they be found. The log-linear screening analysis that follows is different from the kth-order analysis that prefaced the global model CFA in that the null-logit model for five-dimensional tables will serve as the base model, not the independence model. Recall that the residuum about the expected cell frequencies given by the null-logit model, which, for five-variable problems, is defined by Model 0 in Table 7.11, is due to variable relations that directly involve Variable E, the response variable. Hence, should STs or SATs be discovered, they will be predicated on relations in which Variable E is a direct participant. The use of the independence model, in contrast, would not serve our present objectives well because types and antitypes from the independence model could be due to variable relations in which Variable E is inconsequential.

It follows that should an LMCFA be desired that parallels a second-order global model CFA, the base model should contain all possible terms with the exception of second-, third-, and fourth-order terms that involve Variable E. Model 4 in Table 7.11 is such a model. If an LMCFA that parallels a third-order global analysis is desired, Model 10 in Table 7.11 is the appropriate base model. Finally, if a fourth-order LMCFA is desired, where detected types and antitypes are determined by fourth-order $ABCDE$ relations, Model 14 should be fit.

The results of fitting the models mentioned above are summarized in Table 9.6. The first thing to note in this table is that the residual fit of the null-logit model, Model 0, is $L^2(15) = 33.114, p < .005$. The significant residuum about this model suggests that relations involving Variable E are likely present and that a further search for STs and SATs is warranted. A second observation based on resultant component chi-squares is that over half of the residuum appears to be due to first-order relations since the composite chi-square for all first-order relations comprising Variable E was $L^2(4) = 19.759, p < .001$. Finally, the significant component associated with the $ABCDE$ term, $L^2(1) = 5.226, p < .022$, alerts us to the possibility that the structure of potential STs and SATs may be determined by fourth-order relations.

The LMCFA Proper

The 32 observed elementary cell frequencies were compared to corresponding cell frequencies given by Model 0, the null-logit model, through the use of the SAS program reproduced in Appendix B. Table 9.7 presents observed and expected cell frequencies along with the results of corrected z tests from Equation 9.2. If an experimentwise error rate of .10 is adopted, statistical significance can be claimed only for the ESFJY configuration ($p < .002623$). A greater

Table 9.6
Prefatory Screening Analysis of Incipient Teacher Data

Model No.[*]	Marginals Fitted	Residual L^2	df	p	Component L^2	df	p
(0)	ABCD, E	33.114	15	.005			
(4)	ABCD, AE, BE, CE, DE	13.355	11	.271	19.759	4	.001
(10)	ABCD, ABE, ACE, ADE, BCE, BDE, CDE	6.914	5	.227	6.441	6	.376
(14)	ABCD, ABCE, ABDE, ACDE, BCDE	5.226	1	.022	1.688	4	.793
(15)	ABCDE	0.000	0	1.000	5.226	1	.022

Note: Variable E is the completion/noncompletion response variable.
*Model numbers and definitions correspond to those presented earlier in Table 7.11.

number of students than would be expected by chance may be described as Extroverted-Sensing-Feeling-Judging-Educational Degree Holders. And because of the CFA methodology employed, it can be said that the response variable designation, completion of an educational degree, is an integral component of the type description.

Prompted by the significant component associated with the *ABCDE* ($p < .022$) appearing in Table 9.6, additional efforts were made to compare observed cell frequencies to those produced by the full four-variable model, Model 14, a comparison that is analogous to a fourth-order CFA in the global modal case. STs and SATs detected by such an analysis would be structurally unique. That is, they would be statistically distinct from one another with respect to response over all five variables. In this instance, however, the performance of the analysis in question failed to identify an ST or SAT that approached significance.

In sum, whereas a global model analysis would have detected numerous STs and SATs, the more restrictive LMCFA pointed to only one significant configuration, the ESFJY type.[6] We will resist the temptation of exploring the implications of this finding for the teaching profession in favor of exploring in the next section the variable structure that underlies this ST.

The Follow-Up Log-Linear Analysis

Since the screening analysis in Table 9.6 pointed to associations of the first order as being most responsible for the residuum about the null-logit model, first-order models—namely, Models 1 through 4 as defined in Table 7.11—were

Table 9.7
LMCFA of Incipient Teacher Data

Cell	Frequencies		Corrected z tests		
A B C D E	f	F	z	p	
I N F J Y	45	44.567	.065	.47401	
I N F J N	111	111.424	-.041	.48378	
I N F P Y	62	72.294	-1.161	.12276	
I N F P N	191	180.706	.744	.22852	
I N T J Y	12	16.002	-.877	.19024	
I N T J N	44	39.998	.556	.28903	
I N T P Y	17	16.002	.250	.40132	
I N T P N	39	39.998	-.159	.43703	
I S F J Y	162	138.873	1.951	.02556	
I S F J N	324	347.128	-1.265	.10303	
I S F P Y	63	68.579	-.618	.26827	
I S F P N	177	171.421	.396	.34622	
I S T J Y	52	51.434	.079	.46837	
I S T J N	128	128.566	-.051	.47980	
I S T P Y	8	15.430	-1.767	.03859	
I S T P N	46	38.570	1.121	.13121	
E N F J Y	102	102.583	-.058	.47678	
E N F J N	257	256.417	.038	.48505	
E N F P Y	153	174.591	-1.628	.05174	
E N F P N	458	436.409	1.063	.14398	
E N T J Y	32	30.575	.168	.43335	
E N T J N	75	76.425	-.107	.45750	
E N T P Y	28	30.003	-.275	.39154	
E N T P N	77	74.997	.175	.43053	
E S F J Y	319	273.745	2.792	.00262	ST
E S F J N	639	684.256	-1.859	.03154	
E S F P Y	114	126.014	-1.040	.14907	
E S F P N	327	314.986	.673	.25053	
E S T J Y	81	91.439	-1.050	.14682	
E S T J N	239	228.561	.675	.24989	
E S T P Y	31	28.860	.306	.37970	
E S T P N	70	72.140	-.195	.42283	

fit to tabular data for the purpose of explicating the association or associations underlying the structure of the ESFJY type. Subsequent assessment of resultant component chi-squares revealed that two first-order relations were prominent; namely, the relationships between Variables B and E and Variables D and E. The marginal component for the former was $L^2(1)$ 5.925, $p < .015$, where, upon subsequent examination, it was found that proportionately more Sensing students ($P = .65$) continued in education than did Intuitive students ($P = .35$). The marginal component for the latter was $L^2(1) = 14.104$, $p < .000$, where it was found that proportionately more Judging students ($p = .63$) continued in education than did Perceiving students ($P = .37$).

As was anticipated from the results of the initial screening analysis, statistical significance was not observed for any of the six second-order terms (e.g., ABE, ACE, etc.) or for any of the four third-order terms (e.g., $ABCE$, $ABDE$, etc.) when all remaining models in Table 7.11 were fit and assessed. These negative findings, when combined with the earlier failure to detect significant configurations from the full four-variable model, indicate that the underlying structure of the ESFJY type is both diffuse and limited. The structure is diffuse in that it is based largely on two distinct first-order associations (BE and DE), and it is limited in the sense that the absence of a significance second-order BDE association does not permit us to conclude with authority that the BE response pattern in question (i.e., Sensing-Judging) is uniquely characteristic of students who obtain educational degrees.

CONCLUDING REMARKS

With our introduction to CFA behind us, we will now try to make more explicit the similarities and differences between log-linear analysis and CFA. Both approaches share a common methodological core. Each is applied to cross-classified frequencies and each involves the fitting of log-linear models. Yet as we have seen, log-linear analysis and CFA differ. They differ, however, not so much in method as in intent.

Simply put, the intent of a symmetrical log-linear analysis is to identify variable relationships that serve to explain cross-tabular data, and the intent of an asymmetrical analysis is to document variable effects relative to a categorical variable that has been deemed an outcome variable. Each log-linear orientation is decidedly inferential in that the concept of statistical significance guides the search for variable relationships and effects. In contrast to symmetrical log-linear analysis, global-model CFA seeks to identify a pattern of variable characteristics that describe a group of subjects that can be shown to be more or less numerous than would be expected by chance. The description of patterns of variable characteristics is also the intent of LMCFA, but here we impose conditions so that a specific variable, the designated response variable, becomes a structurally integral feature of the description. Statistical description, not inference, is primary in CFA, though statistical inference (e.g., z tests) is employed to determine whether groups to be described are sufficiently numerous or non-numerous.

Consider again the matter of intention and the Kaye, Sears, and Kennedy (1990) study of MBTI variables obtained on students who either completed or did not complete degrees in education. If the prime purpose happened to be the identification of MBTI variables that could be used as indicators or predictors of educational degree completion or noncompletion, then an asymmetrical log-linear analysis would constitute the principal method of choice. On the other hand, if a primary purpose was to posit an MBTI description of a type or types of students who pursued an educational degree through completion, or to posit a descriptive MBTI profile that was noticeably absent among students who completed educational degrees, then the variant of CFA that we have termed LMCFA would be appropriate.

At issue, therefore, is the appropriate matching of method and substantive intent. It is hoped that as a result of reading this chapter, the issue will not be couched in "either/or" terms, but rather—subsequent to exercising both log-linear modeling and *CFA* to their fullest—which of these complimentary approaches will receive greatest emphasis in the reporting of results.

A few final words pertaining to the generalizability of CFA are in order. The first comments pertain to the nature of categorical variables that are amenable to CFA. It is hoped that readers have not inferred mistakenly that variables must be exclusively dichotomous. Admittedly, the two concrete examples that were analyzed in this chapter presented only dichotomous variables, but there are no impediments other than increasing complexity of interpretation that prevent one from generalizing CFA principles and operations to cross-tables where some or all variables are polytomies. Moreover, the presented examples illustrated only two applications: (1) the use of global-model CFA in situations where all variables are perceived as response variables, and (2) LMCFA for situations where one variable is decided response while remaining variables are explanatory. Additional applications of CFA to situations where subjects have been measured on ordinal-level variables at different points in time have been developed and are discussed by von Eye (1990, ch. 6). Awaiting development at this writing are applications to settings in which response is dichotomous and the explanatory variable set consists of a mix of categorical and metric variables, an anticipated development that will likely be accomplished through the use of underlying logistic regression models. It is safe to conclude that whereas we can expect continued refinements of log-linear methods during the decade of the 1990s, we can expect in this decade to witness major refinements and entirely new applications of CFA as the knowledge of this technique, and the software to perform it, become more widely available.

In conclusion, I would like to compliment those who knew little about log-linear analysis at the outset, who have persisted through this book, and who, through their persistence, have obtained at least a working knowledge of log-linear models and configural frequency analysis. Granted, the journey has been long and at times difficult, but if this book has contributed in part to the acquisition of knowledge sufficient to pursue more advanced expositions and to the conduct of more sophisticated data analysis, then both the journey and the preparation of this second edition have been worthwhile.

NOTES

1. I was fortunate to have received an advance copy of von Eye (1990), and must acknowledge that much of the contents of this chapter is based directly or indirectly on this work. This chapter constitutes an introduction to CFA and should not be construed as a substitute for this more comprehensive and authoritative work.

2. During the decade of the 1970s, prior to ready access to log-linear software, ordinary least-squares (OLS) regression models were often used in lieu of, or in addition to, log-linear models in the early description of CFA. For the many reasons advanced in this text, the use of OLS models should be discouraged in favor of the use of log-linear models in contemporary applications of CFA.

3. A comprehensive discussion of the various types of CFA will be found in von Eye (1990).

4. Interested readers are encouraged to compare the results offered in Table 9.2 with those reported by Lienert and Krauth (1975, 234). Two major differences will be noted. First, whereas Lienert and Krauth gave cumulative p values for both the binomial and the corrected z approximation to the binomial, Table 9.2 gives relevant upper-tail or lower-tail critical rejection values, an expression of outcome that is more consistent with conventional hypothesis testing. Second, and more significant, are observable differences in the numeric values of z-score approximations. Lienert and Krauth subtracted 0.5 from residuals whenever $f < F$ (see Equation 9, p. 233), instead of adding 0.5 to such residuals as indicated by Equation 9.2 in this text. Consequently, their results for potential antitypes are markedly biased in a positive sense, in the sense that in the long run, an excessive number of Type I errors will be committed.

5. Since the NNN configuration presented a zero cell frequency, a delta value of 0.5 was employed prior to the application of the full two-variable model.

6. It can be verified that if the independence model is used as the base model, eight STs and nine SATs will be found (at .10 level, experimentwise). There is no assurance, however, that the STs and SATs identified by this first-order global model CFA are directly influenced by response variable designations. In fact, our knowledge of the outcome of the LMCFA permits us to conclude that all but the ESFJY type produced by the global model CFA are due to variable relations that exclude Variable E.

Appendix A: An SAS Program for Configural Frequency Analysis

As knowledge of configural frequency analysis becomes more widespread, it can be anticipated that computational routines specifically designed to accommodate the performance of this analysis will be incorporated into major statistical applications programs. Until this occurs, readers of this book who have access to SAS (Version 6) may find the programming statements that are given in this appendix of value. In its present form, the SAS program is written to accommodate the analysis of the psychopathology data discussed in Chapter 9.

For general use, subsequent to job control language (JCL) statements peculiar to the user's computer and desired optional introductory statements, the statements associated with reference lines 30 through 42 must be prepared and entered by the potential user *exactly as shown*. (Line numbers are for reference only; they should not be entered as part of the program per se.) Notice that the total frequency (N) for the user's table is entered in line 34. Then, beginning with reference line 43, cellular information pertaining to the user's data is entered. Each line or observation contains information pertaining to an elementary cell. For each cell, the user should specify (1) an identification label (e.g., NYNY), (2) the frequency *observed* in that cell (f_o), and (3) the frequency to be *expected* (F_e) under the hypothesis or model under consideration, information that is available from standard log-linear programs. These three items should be entered in the order specified above, and they should be separated by at least one blank space. Immediately following data entry, the programming statements given between reference lines 60 through 113 should be prepared exactly as shown.

For each elementary cell, the program is designed to produce as output the following:

1. The cell identification label, f_o, F_e, and the residual ($f_o - F_e$).

2. The observed proportion (p_o), the expected proportion (P_e), the probability of observing f_o given F_e, and the outcome p value associated with an exact binomial test.

3. The z statistic given by Equation 9.1 and its associated outcome p value, and the corrected z statistic given by Equation 9.2 and its associated p value.

4. The standardized residual given by Equation 3.13, the chi-square approximation given
   by Equation 9.4, and the outcome p value associated with these two related statistics.

   Comments and suggestions relative to the use and improvement of this program would
be greatly appreciated. Forward comments to me at Arps Hall, Ohio State University,
Columbus, Ohio, 43210.

```
 1.
 2.        Insert Institutional Job Language Control (JCL) Statements
 3.
 4.
 5.                        CONFIGURAL FREQUENCY ANALYSIS
 6.                        ----------------------------
 7.                        A SAS PROGRAM PREPARED BY
 8.                             JOHN J. KENNEDY
 9.                        ----------------------------
10.
11.        DIRECTIONS:
12.
13.        INPUT TOTAL TABLE N IN THE INPUT PARAGRAPH
14.
15.        CELL DATA ARE ENTERED IN THE DATA FILE.
16.        EACH CELL IS ENTERED ON A LINE AS AN OBSERVATION.
17.
18.        FOR EACH OBSERVATION (CELL) ENTER IN ORDER:
19.
20.            CELL - THE CELL LABEL OR CODE
21.            FO - THE OBSERVED CELL FREQUENCY IN INTEGER FORM
22.            FE - THE EXPECTED CELL FREQUENCY (MAY BE IN DECIMAL FORM)
23.
24.        DATA USED TO ILLUSTRATE AND TEST THIS PROGRAM ARE FROM
25.        LIENERT, G.A.,& KRAUTH, J. (1975). CONFIGURAL FREQUENCY
26.        ANALYSIS AS A TOOL FOR DEFINING TYPES. EDUCATIONAL AND
27.        PSYCHOLOGICAL MEASUREMENT, 35, 231-235.
28.
29.        *=================================================================*;
30.        TITLE 'ANALYSIS OF LIENERT AND KRAUTH (1975) PSYCHOPATHOLOGY DATA';
31.        DATA CELLS;
32.            INPUT CELL $ FO FE;
33.        COMMENT  ENTER THE TOTAL TABULAR N IMMEDIATELY BELOW;
34.            N = 65/*ENTER THE TABULAR SIZE*/;
35.            PO=FO/N;PE=FE/N;R=FO-FE;
36.            LABEL   FO=OBSERVED FREQUENCY
37.                    FE=EXPECTED FREQUENCY
38.                    R=RAW RESIDUAL
39.                    PO=OBSERVED PROPORTION
40.                    PE=EXPECTED PROPORTION;
41.        COMMENT  ENTER (1)CELL CODE, (2)FO, AND (3)FE FOR EACH CELL;
42.        CARDS;
43.        YYYY 12 5.00
44.        YYYN  0 2.74
45.        YYNY  1 4.56
46.        YYNN  4 2.50
47.        YNYY  1 3.79
48.        YNYN  3 2.07
49.        YNNY  5 3.45
50.        YNNN  0 1.89
51.        NYYY  8 7.50
52.        NYYN  1 4.11
53.        NYNY  3 6.84
54.        NYNN  8 3.75
55.        NNYY  2 5.68
56.        NNYN  7 3.11
57.        NNNY 10 5.18
58.        NNNN  0 2.84
59.        ;
```

```
60.        PROC PRINT DATA=CELLS LABEL;
61.            VAR CELL FO FE R;
62.            TITLE  'PRINTOUT OF BASIC CELLULAR INFORMATION';
63.        COMMENT   ROUTINE TO COMPUTE EXACT ONE-SAMPLE BINOMIAL TESTS;
64.        DATA BINOMIAL;SET CELLS;
65.            LABEL PFO=EXACT PROB. OF FO
66.                  A1=BINOMIAL ALPHA;
67.        LA1 = PROBBNML(PE,N,FO);
68.        FO1=FO - 1;
69.        IF FO1=-1 THEN FO1=0;
70.        LA2 = PROBBNML(PE,N,FO1);
71.        PFO=LA1 - LA2;
72.        IF PFO=.000000 THEN PFO=LA2;
73.        UP1=1.0 - LA2;
74.        IF LA1 <= UP1 THEN A1=LA1;ELSE A1=UP1;
75.        PROC PRINT DATA=BINOMIAL LABEL;
76.            VAR CELL PO PE PFO A1;
77.            TITLE 'EXACT ONE-SAMPLE BINOMIAL TESTS';
78.        COMMENT   ROUTINE TO COMPUTE APPROXIMATIONS TO BINOMIAL;
79.        DATA APPROX;SET BINOMIAL;
80.            LABEL Z=Z STATISTIC
81.                  CZ=CORRECTED Z
82.                  SR=STANDARDIZED RESIDUAL
83.                  CHI=CHI SQUARE COMPONENT
84.                  A2=P-VALUE Z-STATISTIC
85.                  A3=P-VALUE CORRECTED Z
86.                  A4=P-VALUE STAND. RESID.;
87.        R=FO-FE;
88.        QE = 1 - PE;
89.        Z = R / (FE * QE)**(.5);
90.        CRP=R-0.5;CRN=R+0.5;
91.        IF R >= 0.0 THEN CR=CRP;ELSE CR=CRN;
92.        IF CR <= 0.0 AND CR > -0.50 THEN CR=R;
93.        IF CR >= 0.0 AND CR < 0.50 THEN CR=R;
94.        CZ=CR/(FE*QE)**(.5);
95.        SR=R/FE**(.5);
96.        CHI=SR**2;
97.        PZ=PROBNORM(Z);
98.        PZU = PROBNORM(Z);PZL = 1 - PZU;
99.        PZC=PROBNORM(CZ);
100.       PZCU=PROBNORM(CZ);PZCL=1-PZCU;
101.       PSR=PROBNORM(SR);
102.       PSRUP=PROBNORM(SR);
103.       PSRLOW=1-PSRUP;
104.       IF PZU <= PZL THEN A2=PZU;ELSE A2=PZL;
105.       IF PZCU <= PZCL THEN A3=PZCU;ELSE A3=PZCL;
106.       IF PSRUP <= PSRLOW THEN A4=PSRUP;ELSE A4=PSRLOW;
107.       PROC PRINT DATA=APPROX LABEL;
108.           VAR CELL Z A2 CZ A3;
109.           TITLE 'Z SCORE APPROXIMATIONS TO THE BINOMIAL';
110.       PROC PRINT DATA=APPROX LABEL;
111.           VAR CELL SR A4 CHI;
112.           TITLE 'CHI-SQUARE APPROXIMATIONS TO THE BINOMIAL';
113.       //
```

Appendix B: Critical Values for Chi-Square Statistics

	Percentile						
	50	75	90	95	97.5	99	99.9
				p			
df	.50	.25	.10	.05	.025	.01	.001
1	.45	1.32	2.71	3.84	5.02	6.63	10.8
2	1.39	2.77	4.61	5.99	7.38	9.21	13.8
3	2.37	3.11	6.25	7.81	9.35	11.3	16.3
4	3.36	5.39	7.78	9.49	11.1	13.3	18.5
5	4.35	6.63	9.24	11.1	12.8	15.1	20.5
6	5.35	7.84	10.6	12.6	14.4	16.8	22.5
7	6.35	9.04	12.0	14.1	16.0	18.5	24.3
8	7.34	10.2	13.4	15.5	17.5	20.1	26.1
9	8.34	11.4	14.7	16.9	19.0	21.7	27.9
10	9.34	12.5	16.0	18.3	20.5	23.2	29.6
11	10.3	13.7	17.3	19.7	21.9	24.7	31.3
12	11.3	14.8	18.5	21.0	23.3	26.2	32.9
13	12.3	16.0	19.8	22.4	24.7	27.7	34.5
14	13.3	17.1	21.1	23.7	26.1	29.1	36.1
15	14.3	18.2	22.3	25.0	27.5	30.6	37.7
16	15.3	19.4	23.5	26.3	28.8	32.0	39.3
17	16.3	20.5	24.8	27.6	30.2	33.4	40.8
18	17.3	21.6	26.0	28.9	31.5	34.8	42.3
19	18.3	22.7	27.2	30.1	32.9	36.2	43.8

	Percentile						
	50	75	90	95	97.5	99	99.9
				p			
df	.50	.25	.10	.05	.025	.01	.001
20	19.3	23.8	28.4	31.4	34.2	37.6	45.3
21	20.3	24.9	29.6	32.7	35.5	38.9	46.8
22	21.3	26.0	30.8	33.9	36.8	40.3	48.3
23	22.3	27.1	32.0	35.2	38.1	41.6	49.7
24	23.3	28.2	33.2	36.4	39.4	43.0	51.2
25	24.3	29.3	34.4	37.7	40.6	44.3	52.6
26	25.3	30.4	35.6	38.9	41.9	45.6	54.1
27	26.3	31.5	36.7	40.1	43.2	47.0	55.5
28	27.3	32.6	37.9	41.3	44.5	48.3	56.9
29	28.3	33.7	39.1	42.6	45.7	49.6	58.3
30	29.3	34.8	40.3	43.8	47.0	50.9	59.7
40	39.3	45.6	51.8	55.8	59.3	63.7	73.4
50	49.3	56.3	63.2	67.5	71.4	76.2	86.7
60	59.3	67.0	74.4	79.1	83.3	88.4	99.6
100	99.3	109.1	118.5	124.3	129.6	135.8	149.5

Source: Adapted from table 8 in E. S. Pearson and H. O. Hartley (Eds.), *Biometrika Tables for Statisticians*, 3rd ed. (1966), by permission of the *Biometrika* Trustees.

References

Agresti, A. 1990. *Categorical data analysis*. New York: John Wiley.

Akaike, H. 1976. On entropy maximization principle. In P. R. Krishnaiah (Ed.), *Application of statistics* (pp. 27–41). Amsterdam: North-Holland.

Aldrich, J. H., and Nelson, F. D. 1984. *Linear probability, logit, and probit models*. Sage University Paper series on Quantitative Applications in the Social Sciences, no. 07–045. Beverly Hills: Sage Publications.

Asher, H. B. 1976. *Causal modeling*. Sage University Paper series on Quantitative Applications in the Social Sciences, no. 07–003. Beverly Hills: Sage Publications.

Bentler, P. M. 1980. Multivariate analysis with latent variables: Causal modeling. In M. R. Rosenzweig and L. W. Porter (Eds.), *Annual review of psychology, 31*. Palo Alto, CA: Annual Reviews.

Bishop, Y. M. M. 1969. Full contingency tables, logits, and split contingency tables. *Biometrics, 25*, 383–400.

Bishop, Y. M. M., Fienberg, S. E., and Holland, P. W. 1975. *Discrete multivariate analysis: Theory and practice*. Cambridge, MA: MIT Press.

Bock, R. D. 1975. *Multivariate statistical methods in behavioral research*. New York: McGraw-Hill.

Bock, R. D., and Yates, G. 1973. *MULTIQUAL: Log-linear analysis of nominal and ordinal data by the method of maximum likelihood*. Chicago: National Educational Resources.

Bresnahan, J. L., and Shapiro, M. M. 1966. A general equation and technique for the exact partitioning of chi-square contingency tables. *Psychological Bulletin, 66*, 252–56.

Brown, M. B. 1976. Screening effects in multidimensional contingency tables. *Applied Statistics, 25*, 37–46.

Bush, A. J. 1988. A perspective on applications of maximum likelihood and weighted least-squares procedures in the context of categorical data analysis. *Multiple Linear Regression Viewpoints, 16*, 1–35.

Camilli, G., and Hopkins, K. D. 1978. Applicability of chi-square to 2 × 2 contingency tables with small expected cell frequencies. *Psychological Bulletin, 85*, 163–67.

Castellan, N. J. 1965. On the partitioning of contingency tables. *Psychological Bulletin, 64*, 330–38.

Clogg, C. C., and Eliason, S. R. 1987. Some common problems in log-linear analysis. *Sociological Methods and Research, 16*, 8–44.

Cochran, W. G. 1954. Some methods for strengthening the common χ^2 tests. *Biometrics, 10*, 417–51.

Cohen, J., and Cohen, P. 1975. *Applied multiple regression/correlation analysis for the behavioral sciences.* Hillsdale, NJ: Erlbaum Publishers.

Cook, T. D., and Campbell, D. T. 1979. *Quasi-experimentation: Design and analysis issues for field settings.* Chicago: Rand McNally.

Cox, D. R. 1970. *The analysis of binary data.* London: Methuen.

Deming, W. E., and Stephan, F. F. 1940. On a least squares adjustment of a sampled frequency table when the expected marginal totals are known. *Annals of Mathematical Statistics, 11*, 427–44.

Dixon, W. J. (Ed.). 1983. *BMD P statistical software manual.* Berkeley: University of California Press.

Dixon, W. J., and Brown, M. B. 1979. *BMDP-79: Biomedical computer programs P-series.* Berkeley: University of California Press.

Everitt, B. S. 1977. *The analysis of contingency tables.* New York: Halsted Press.

Fay, R. E., and Goodman, L. A. 1975. *ECTA program: Description for users.* Chicago: University of Chicago.

Fienberg, S. E. 1970a. The analysis of multidimensional contingency tables. *Ecology, 51*, 419–33.

———. 1970b. An iterative procedure for estimation in contingency tables. *Annals of Mathematical Statistics, 41*, 907–17.

———. 1972. The analysis of incomplete multi-way contingency tables. *Biometrics, 28*, 177–202.

———. 1977. *The analysis of cross-classified categorical data.* Cambridge, MA: MIT Press.

Fisher, R. A. 1924. The conditions under which χ^2 measures the discrepancy between observed observations and hypothesis. *Journal of the Royal Statistical Society, 87*, 442–50.

Forthofer, R. N., and Lehnen, R. G. 1981. *Public program analysis: A new categorical data approach.* Belmont, CA: Lifetime Learning Publications.

Freeman, M. F., and Tukey, J. W. 1950. Transformation related to the angular and square root. *Annals of Mathematical Statistics, 21*, 607–11.

Goldsmid, C. A., Gruber, J. E., and Wilson, E. K. 1977. Perceived attributes of superior teachers (PAST): An inquiry into the giving of teacher awards. *American Educational Research Journal, 14*, 423–40.

Goodman, L. A. 1970. The multivariate analysis of qualitative data: Interactions among multiple classifications. *Journal of the American Statistical Association, 65*, 226–56.

———. 1971a. The analysis of multidimensional contingency tables: Stepwise procedures and direct estimation methods for building models for multiple classifications. *Technometrics, 13*, 33–61.

———. 1971b. Partitioning chi-square, analysis of marginal contingency tables, and estimation of expected frequencies in multidimensional contingency tables. *Journal of the American Statistical Association, 66*, 339–44.

———. 1972a. A general model for the analysis of surveys. *American Journal of Sociology, 77*, 1035–86.

———. 1972b. A modified multiple regression approach to the analysis of dichotomous variables. *American Sociological Review, 37*, 28–46.

———. 1973. Guided and unguided methods for the selection of models for a set of *T* multidimensional contingency tables. *Journal of the American Statistical Association, 68*, 165–75.

———. 1978. *Analyzing qualitative/categorical data.* Lanham, MD: University Press of America.

———. 1979. A brief guide to the causal analysis of data from surveys. *American Journal of Sociology, 84*, 1078–95.

Green, J. A. 1988. Loglinear analysis of cross-classified ordinal data: Applications in developmental research. *Child Development, 59*, 1–25.

Grizzle, J. E. 1967. Continuity correction in the χ^2 test for 2 × 2 tables. *American Statistician, 21*, 28–32.

Grizzle, J. E., Starmer, C. F., and Koch, G. G. 1969. Analysis of categorical data by linear models. *Biometrics, 25*, 489–504.

Grizzle, J. E., and Williams, O. D. 1972. Log-linear models and tests of independence for contingency tables. *Biometrics, 28*, 137–56.

Haber, M. 1985. Maximum likelihood methods for linear and log-linear models in categorical data. *Computational Statistics and Data Analysis, 3*, 1–10.

Haberman, S. J. 1972. Log-linear fit for contingency tables (Algorithm AS 51). *Applied Statistics, 21*, 218–25.

———. 1973. The analysis of residuals in cross-classified tables. *Biometrics, 29*, 205–20.

———. 1978. *Analysis of qualitative data: Introductory topics* (Vol. 1). New York: Academic Press.

Hays, W. L. 1988. *Statistics* (4th ed.). New York: Holt, Rinehart and Winston.

Heise, D. R. 1975. *Causal analysis.* New York: John Wiley.

Holland, B. S., and Copenhaver, M. D. 1988. Improved Bonferroni-type multiple testing procedures. *Psychological Bulletin, 104*, 145–49.

Holm, S. 1979. A simple sequential rejective multiple test procedure. *Scandinavian Journal of Statistics, 6*, 65–70.

Holton, J., and Nott, D. L. April 1980. *The experimental effects of reflective teaching upon preservice teachers' ability to think and talk critically about teaching.* Paper presented at the meeting of the American Educational Research Association, Boston, MA.

Hosmer, D. W., and Lemeshow, S. L. 1989. *Applied logistic regression.* New York: John Wiley.

Irwin, J. O. 1949. A note on the subdivision of χ^2 into components. *Biometrika, 36*, 130–34.

Jöreskog, K. G. 1978. Structural analysis of covariance and correlational matricies. *Psychometrika, 43*, 443–47.

Jöreskog, K. G., and Sörbom, D. 1988. *LISREL 7: A guide to the program and applications* (2nd ed.). Chicago: SPSS Inc.

Kastenbaum, M. A. A. 1960. A note on the additive partitioning of chi-square in contingency tables. *Biometrics, 16*, 416–22.

Kaye, G., Sears, S. J., and Kennedy, J. J. October 1990. *Personality types of students who complete and who do not complete degree programs in education.* Paper presented at the meeting of the Mid-Western Educational Research Association, Chicago.

Kennedy, J. J. 1982. Log-linear analysis. In H. Mitzel (Ed.), *Encyclopedia of educational research* (5th ed., pp. 1129–33). New York: Free Press.

———. 1983. *Analyzing qualitative data: Introductory log-linear analysis for behavioral research.* New York: Praeger.

———. 1988. Applying log-linear models in educational research. *Australian Journal of Education, 32*, 3–24.

Kennedy, J. J., and Bush, A. J. 1985. *An introduction to the design and analysis of experiments in behavioral research.* Lanham, MD: University Press of America.

———. April 1988. *Focused comparisons in logit-model contingency table analysis.* Paper presented at the meeting of the American Educational Research Association, New Orleans, LA.

Kerlinger, F. N., and Pedhauzer, E. J. 1973. *Multiple regression in behavioral research.* New York: Holt, Rinehart and Winston.

Kimball, A. W. 1954. Short-cut formulas for the exact partitioning of χ^2 in contingency tables. *Biometrics, 10*, 452–58.

Knoke, D., and Burke, P. J. 1980. *Log-linear models.* Sage University Paper series on Quantitative Applications in the Social Sciences, no. 07–020. Beverly Hills: Sage Publications.

Krauth, J., and Lienert, G. A. 1973. *KFA die konfigurationsfrequenzanalyse und ihre anwendung in psychologie und medizin.* Freiburg, W. Germany: Alber.

Lancaster, H. O. 1949. The division and partition of χ^2 in certain discrete distributions. *Biometrika, 36*, 117–29.

———. 1951. Complex contingency tables treated by the partition of chi-square. *Journal of the Royal Statistical Society, B13*, 242–49.

Lee, S. K. 1977. On the asymptotic variances of $\hat{\mu}$ terms in loglinear models of multidimensional contingency tables. *Journal of the American Statistical Association, 72*, 412–19.

Lehmacher, W. 1981. A more powerful simultaneous test procedure in configural frequency analysis. *Biometrical Journal, 23*, 429–36.

Lienert, G. A., and Krauth, J. 1975. Configural frequency analysis as a statistical tool for defining types. *Educational and Psychological Measurement, 35*, 231–38.

Lohnes, P. R., and Cooley, W. W. 1968. *Introduction to statistical procedures: With computer exercises.* New York: John Wiley.

Magidson, J. 1978. An illustrative comparison of Goodman's approach to logit analysis with dummy variable regression analysis. In L. A. Goodman (Ed.), *Analyzing qualitative/categorical data.* Lenham, MD: University Press of America.

Marks, E. 1975. Methods for analyzing multidimensional contingency tables. *Research in Higher Education, 3*, 217–31.

Maxwell, A. E. 1961. *Analyzing qualitative data.* London: Methuen and Co.

McLean, J. A. 1980. *Graduation and nongraduation rates of black and white freshman entering two state universities in Virginia.* Unpublished doctoral dissertation, Ohio State University, Columbus.

Mitroff, I. I., and Kilmann, R. H. 1978. *Methodological approaches to social sciences.* San Francisco: Jossey-Bass.

Myers, I. 1962. *Manual for the Myers-Briggs Type Indicator.* Princeton, NJ: Educational Testing Service.

Nunnally, J. C. 1978. *Psychometric theory* (2nd ed.). New York: McGraw-Hill.

O'Connor, G., and Sitkei, E. G. 1975. Study of a new frontier in community services: Residential facilities for the developmentally disabled. *Mental Retardation, 13,* 35–39.

Pearson, K. 1900. On a criterion that a given system of deviations from the probable in the case of a correlated system of variables is such that it can reasonably be supposed to have arisen from random sampling. *Philosophical Magazine, 50,* 157–75.

Peters, C. E. 1981. *An investigation of the relationship between Jungian psychological type and preferred styles of inquiry.* Unpublished doctoral dissertation, Ohio State University, Columbus.

Rao, C. R. 1963. Criteria of estimation in large samples. *Sankhya, 25,* 189–206.

Reynolds, H. T. 1984. *Analysis of nominal data* (2nd ed.). Sage University Paper series on Quantitative Applications in the Social Sciences, no. 07–007. Beverly Hills: Sage Publications.

Rice, J. C. Forthcoming. Logistic regression. In B. Thompson (Ed.), *Advances in social science methodology: A research annual* (Vol. 3). Greenwich, CT: JAI Press.

Rosenthal, R., and Rosnow, R. L. 1985. *Contrast analysis: Focused comparisons in the analysis of variance.* New York: Cambridge University Press.

Sakamoto, Y., and Akaike, H. 1978. Analysis of cross-classified data by AIC. *Annals of the Institute of Statistical Mathematics, 30* (Part B), 185–97.

SAS Institute. 1985. *SAS User's Guide: Statistics* (Version 5). Cary, NC: SAS Institute.

Scheffé, H. 1959. *The analysis of variance.* New York: John Wiley.

Shaffer, J. P. 1973. Defining and testing hypotheses in multidimensional contingency tables. *Psychological Bulletin, 79,* 127–41.

SPSS, Inc. 1983. *SPSS^x User's Guide.* New York: McGraw Hill.

Stevens, J. 1986. *Applied multivariate statistics for the social sciences.* Hillsdale, NJ: Erlbaum.

Stevens, S. S. 1946. On the theory of scales of measurement. *Science, 103,* 677–80.

Tatsuoka, M. M. 1988. *Multivariate analysis: Techniques for educational and psychological research* (2nd ed.). New York: Macmillan.

Theil, H. 1970. On the estimation of relationships involving qualitative variables. *American Journal of Sociology, 76,* 103–54.

Upton, G. J. G. 1978. *The analysis of cross-tabulated data.* New York: John Wiley.

von Eye, A. 1990. *Introduction to configural frequency analysis: The search for types and antitypes in cross-classifications.* New York: Cambridge University Press.

von Eye, A., and Bergman, L. R. 1987. A note on numerical approximations of the binomial test in configural frequency analysis. *EDP in Medicine and Biology, 17,* 108–11.

Wenig, R. G. 1979. *Tests of independence for 2 × 2 contingency tables when the sample size is small.* Unpublished masters thesis, University of Toledo.

Yates, F. 1934. Contingency tables involving small numbers and the χ^2 test. *Journal of the Royal Statistical Society Supplement, 1,* 217–35.

Yule, G. U. 1900. On the association of attributes in statistics. *Philosophical Transactions of the Royal Society, 194*, (Series A), 257–319.

Zahn, D. A., and Fein, S. B. 1979. Large contingency tables with large cell frequencies: A model search algorithm and alternative measures of fit. *Psychological Bulletin, 86*, 1189–1200.

Name Index

Subject Index

AIC (Akaike's Information Criterion) procedure/statistic, 124, 128–29, 130, 195, 250

ANOVA (analysis of variance): interaction in, 74, 88, 111–12, 120; models for, 73–76, 88, 106, 111

antilogarithms, 89, 243, 232

antitypes, in CFA, 257, 259. *See also* statistical antitypes (SATs)

approximate chi-square test, in CFA, 261

a priori (structural) zeros, 248

asymmetrical inquiry, defined, 7–8

basic parameters, in log-linear models, 89, 104, 106, 150

Bernoulli trials, 21–24

beta coefficients, in regression, 243

binomial law, 20, 24–29

binomial logits, 184, 205–8, 217, 243

binomial tests, 29, 259, 261–62

BMDP/4F (computer program), 112–13, 129, 151, 167, 188–89, 192, 211, 218, 224, 232

Bonferroni procedure, 163, 182, 263

canonical variate analysis (CVA), 232

categorical data, 1, 5

CATMOD (SAS computer program), 15–16, 129

cell mean graphs, 173

central limit theorem, 29, 48

CFA. *See* configural frequency analysis

chi-square, the sampling distribution of, 43–45

coding, 252

combining categories, 48

component chi-squares, 71, 93–93, 127–28, 155

conditional equiprobability, 79–82, 116–18

conditional odds, 100, 205

configural frequency analysis (CFA), 2, 6, 13–14, 17–18, 63, 65, 163, 257–81. *See also* logit-model CFA; predictive CFA

consistency, property of, 37

contingency tables, defined, 10

continuity correction, 247, 260

corrected z statistics, 260–61

covariance structure analysis, 237

Cramer's V statistic, 66

crossproduct ratio (CPR), 102

data, types of, 3–5

degrees of freedom, rule of thumb for, 92–93

delta method, for standard errors, 103–4

delta quantity, for zero frequencies, 145, 219, 248, 272–73

Deming-Stephan algorithm, 40–41, 72, 115